THE NEW AMERICAN COMMONWEALTH

THE NEW AMERICAN COMMONWEALTH

Louis Heren

WEIDENFELD AND NICOLSON
5 Winsley Street London W1

Acknowledgment is made for use of the material from two articles which appeared in *Harper's Magazine* in February and August of 1965 entitled "The King's Men: A British View of the White House" and "America the Middle-aged."

Acknowledgment is also gratefully made to Miss Margaret Bryce for permission to use quotations from Lord Bryce's *The American Commonwealth*.

SBN 297 76175 7

Printed in Great Britain by
Lowe & Brydone (Printers) Ltd., London

To the United States

Contents

Introduction   IX

PART I *Separate But Unequal*
1   THE PRESIDENCY   3
2   THE CONGRESS   36
3   THE SUPREME COURT   73

PART II *National Security*
4   THE DEPARTMENT OF STATE   105
5   THE DEPARTMENT OF DEFENSE   147
6   THE NATIONAL SECURITY COUNCIL   188

PART III *New World Symphony*
7   THE STATES AND CITIES   217
8   THE POLITICAL PARTIES AND ELECTIONS   255
9   THE PEOPLE   288

Appendices   325

Index   347

Introduction

The visitor to the United States is often surprised by the assertion of the natives that theirs is a young country. It is not. If the age of a nation is measured by the continuity of its political institutions, and I can think of no better yardstick, the United States is the second oldest country in the world. Only Britain is older. China, France, Germany, and India are all very much younger; indeed, they are mere adolescents with all the instability of extreme youth. In comparison, the United States is a mature, almost ancient land, made immensely stable by established tradition.

These bold statements may cause a certain restlessness, no less in New York and Washington than in Peking or Paris because the fetish of youth still receives exaggerated veneration from most Americans. But I cannot claim originality for this discovery. It was Gertrude Stein, I believe, who said that the United States was the oldest, not the second oldest, country because it was the first to enter the twentieth century. The facts are indisputable. Britain led the way into the nineteenth century with her crude industrialism, but the United States was clearly the first to understand, if not completely master, the mass production, distribution, and consumption techniques of this century.

The United States has other claims to antiquity. It has the oldest political party in the world, the Democratic Party. In the Civil War it acquired the first modern military establishment. Admiral Mahan, and not Lord Fisher, is the father of modern naval power, and the United States was the first nation to enter the nuclear age. It has gone on to think about the unthinkable, and to conceive a nuclear balance in strategy and diplomacy that makes peace a possibility for the first time since the assassination of Abel. This is maturity, indeed.

Presumably the United States is considered young and therefore immature because the two-hundredth anniversary of its political independence has yet to be celebrated, but the early English settlers, who arrived long before 1776, were not, as it were, newly delivered from the womb of time. They brought with them a political experience stretching back to de Montfort's first parliament, to Runnymede, and beyond. They had all the characteristics, good and bad, of their race. One was a happy facility to govern themselves, and for the most part they enjoyed internal self-government from the beginning. This historical fact may explode the simple mythology that passes for history in American schools. The men of 1776 were not an oppressed colonial people, but Anglo-Americans fighting for their English rights. I recall this not as a rebuke to the myth-makers, but to demonstrate that American self-government goes back beyond 1776.

The colonists were obviously a special breed, and the new environment quickly produced a distinctive American character, but it did not develop in intellectual isolation. The framers of the Constitution were fully conversant with the political philosophies then stirring the gentlemen of Europe. If the eighteenth century was the Age of Enlightenment, very few countries were more enlightened than colonial America. The Declaration of Independence could have been written by an Englishman who had no need to seek his fortune in America. I have always thought of Jefferson as the first American, although Cotton Mather used the label many decades before, but the Declaration was a true reflection of English political thought.

The United States Constitution, drafted in 1787, is a distillation of centuries of English experience applied to the American circumstance. It is also a direct descendant of the constitutions of some of the original thirteen states, which in turn descended from the royal charters under which the first English settlements were founded. Bryce traced this political pedigree to the old English guild. My own historical comparisons are also medieval, and will be later discussed. It is sufficient here to establish once and for all the great age of the United States with its blessings of continuity, stability, and political maturity. The American experience after independence is unequaled anywhere. Unity on a continental scale has been achieved and maintained, and with it the great American common market. To that extent, the United States is nearly two centuries older than Western Europe, including Britain.

I refer to the stumbling European movement toward unity. There, thirteen countries, as there were thirteen American states, are interested in varying degrees of unity, but only the six of the European Economic Community have made much progress. If I can switch historical periods for comparison, the seven countries of the European Free Trade Area are a sort of confederacy, which is not likely to have much more influence upon the future shape of a United States of Europe than the Southern Confederacy had upon the Union.

History rarely repeats itself, as those well-meaning Americans who tried after the Second World War to apply their national experience to Europe have discovered. I can recall no American parallel for President de Gaulle's rejection of Britain, but one can be fairly certain that behind the tariff wall of the Common Market, perhaps in Holland or Belgium, a second Calhoun is growing up. Nullification may eventually be translated into Dutch or Walloon. If complete European economic unity has yet to be achieved, political unity remains a dream. Britain, although renowned for its political sagacity, is still an offshore Massachusetts anxious for its mercantile trade and connections across the seas. Sweden is perhaps comparable to colonial Rhode Island, content with its rather special democracy and reluctant to consider union.

Beyond the Elbe, the future is more uncertain than it once was beyond the Mississippi, in spite of all the grand talk of a Europe reaching to the Urals. There are many pamphleteers, but not a single Hamilton or Jefferson. Churchill might have been a European Washington, but, alas, he was rejected by an electorate, ungrateful if you like, but perhaps disturbed by the thought that he might involve the country in another Indian war. He subsequently opposed the withdrawal of Britain from India. I am inclined to regard the United States not as the new world, but the old. I certainly know many Europeans who would like their continent to be as old as the United States, to have done with all the trials and tribulations of early union, and with a secure political future based on continuity, stability, maturity, and the habit of union.

The long history of the United States divides into three eras. The first began with independence, or more specifically with the ratification of the Constitution after the failure of Confederation. The Civil War ushered in the second, and the third and present era began in

1932 when the confident America described so well by Lord Bryce in *The American Commonwealth* seemed in danger of collapse.

His book, first published in 1888 and subsequently revised, is a classic. For decades it was a basic book for government classes at American universities, and American courtesy is not the only reason why a bust of the author stands in one of the corridors of Congress. He was superbly equipped for the task. An eminent Victorian of broad experience and profound scholarship, he was a politician and minister of the Crown as well as a historian. He was afterward British Ambassador to Washington.

Equally important, he was a Gladstonian Liberal who attached the greatest importance to political institutions, and in no other democracy is a knowledge of its political institutions more necessary for a proper understanding of its life than in the United States. The textual evidence is that he understood the Congress better than did President Woodrow Wilson. De Tocqueville was perhaps the better writer, but he had little experience of democratic government.

The institutions Bryce describes are still recognizable. This is not unexpected in a country with a written Constitution which has been amended only fifteen times since the Bill of Rights with its ten Amendments was ratified in 1791. Fundamental changes have been less numerous. The Twenty-first Amendment (ratified December 5, 1933), repealed the Eighteenth (January 29, 1919). The Fourteenth (July 28, 1868), Fifteenth (March 30, 1870), and Twenty-fourth (January 23, 1964) were largely new definitions of existing or assumed rights. The few fundamental changes have been the Thirteenth (December 18, 1865), which abolished slavery, the Nineteenth (August 26, 1920), which gave the vote to women, and perhaps the Sixteenth (February 25, 1913), which some Americans regard as unconstitutional because it introduced the income tax.

And yet almost everything has changed since 1787, and mostly since 1888. According to the census the population was 3,929,214 in 1790, 62,947,714 in 1890, and 179,323,175 in 1960. The land area was 888,811 square miles in 1790, 2,627,261 in 1890, and 3,615,-211 in 1960. The original thirteen states had grown to forty-four in 1890, and are now fifty. California, which was admitted to the Union in 1850, now has the largest population, and the balance of population, industry, and wealth continues to tilt more favorably in its direction.

The census for 1890 marked the end of the frontier period, and in 1920 established that the United States was no longer a predominantly rural country. By 1960 seven Americans in ten lived in cities. It ceased to be a predominantly Anglo-Saxon country at the turn of the century. About one citizen in nine is Negro, one in four Roman Catholic, and there are about six million Jews. If the melting pot had really worked, the modern American would be about 35 percent British, 14 percent German, 11 percent Negro, 9 percent Irish, 5 percent Italian, 3 percent Polish, and with sundry other strains such as Baltic, Lebanese, Red Indian, Spanish, Turkish, and Yugoslav.

He would speak a weird tongue. The Census Bureau counted ninety-nine different language groupings in 1960, and hundreds of dialects were reported. Among the more exotic were Bantu, Blackfoot, Calabrian, Concho, Coptic, Cossackian, Cree, Gypsy, Kickapoo, Kurdish, Kutzo-Vlach, Macedonian, Maori, Mon-Khmer, Nubian, Pashto, Salish, Tagalog, and Chimmesyan. Yiddish was the mother tongue of 503,000, and 581,000 spoke Polish.

In 1790 interest in foreign affairs was cautiously distant and defensive. The larger interest in 1890 can perhaps best be described as continentalism, occasionally disturbed by imperial dreams euphemistically known as Manifest Destiny. In 1940 the country was sternly isolationist come what may, including the threatened extermination of European Jews and the victory of Hitlerism. It is now the leader of what is known as the free world, and committed to the defense of more than forty countries. Hundreds of thousands of troops are permanently stationed overseas.

These paragraphs present but a caricature of the immense changes undergone since independence and the first publication of *The American Commonwealth*. But change, especially since 1888, has been more fundamental than the statistics suggest. Hence this book, which is not so much an attempt to bring Bryce up to date as a report on how American political institutions and the political process have adapted to the third and most challenging era that began in crisis.

The life and evolution of a country is never as tidy as some history books suggest, but the New Deal of President Franklin Roosevelt is an obvious turning point in American history. The first era ended with the Civil War, which once and for all time established the Union in the minds of Americans. Thereafter secession was never seriously threatened. The middle era witnessed the settlement of the American subcontinent, the astonishing industrial and agricultural development, and the tidal waves of immigrants. During this era the foundations of future greatness were laid, although the entire edifice seemed ready for collapse when the second Roosevelt was inaugurated.

Whether or not the New Deal saved the American economy is arguable. Certainly major improvement was not evident much before the preparations for war in Europe with their lucrative orders across the Atlantic. But it cannot be denied that the administrative machinery essential for a modern industrial democracy was assembled during the Roosevelt years. He was not the first to see the need for administrative change and Presidential initiative in the circumstance of the twentieth century. President Theodore Roosevelt established the theory of the President as Steward of the People, and President William Taft and President Woodrow Wilson made notable contributions. I must apologize if they and others receive less than fair mention in this book. Nevertheless it was the lot of the thirty-second President and his successors to deal with what I see as the modern triple revolution. The first is the technological revolution, the second the revolution of rising expectations, and the Negro revolution is the third. The interrelation between them is obvious, although the third did not erupt until well after the Second World War. They are the most potent forces in the shaping of the third American era.

The American technological revolution has gone farther than the Russian Communist Party in demonstrating the validity of the first Marxist doctrine that economic conditions determine history. Almost everything has become possible, from reaching for the moon and the stars to global nuclear destruction, from feeding much of the world's population to perhaps changing the nature of life. The old order is passing. Man can look forward to absolute freedom, to the domination of his environment, and a future fraught with difficulties as well as promise.

One consequence of the technological revolution has been the rising expectations of the American people, and if the first revolution has not devoured its children, it is largely because of the second. In some ways, the second has taken hold more quickly in the United States than elsewhere. Average personal incomes are the highest in the world, and a majority of Americans are accustomed to comforts and conveniences that still largely remain in the future for other peoples. With Oliver Twist, they ask for more, and with much more confidence in their expectations being realized. But there are always minorities, and the American minority, numbered in tens of millions, have yet to benefit much. Social services—I use the term in its widest possible sense—are still inadequate by most Western European standards. The appetite of the majority for the better life can be in conflict with the struggle of the minority, with obvious political repercussions.

The Negro revolution is peculiarly American, in that no other industrialized democracy has such a large racial minority. The revolution has found political expression only in recent years, and years of political conflict and physical violence must be expected. The Negro movement is not a revolution in itself. A minority cannot revolt against an overwhelming majority, but the basic objective of the movement, equality, can only be achieved by a social revolution of the majority. Legislation and equality before the law are not enough. If integration is too dangerous a word, there must be acceptance. For many white Americans this constitutes a problem larger than personal prejudice. It is one of the few they cannot physically escape from; the Negroes have also gone west.

The social and political consequences of the triple revolution are both forbidding and exciting, and apart from their interrelationship they have one thing in common. They demand Presidential leadership. These are the four most significant words in this book because the demand has transformed American politics. Since 1932 the American people have witnessed the aggrandizement of Presidential power, in relation not only to Congress but to the states.

Many Americans are apprehensive of this power, and they at least have cause to be watchful. Nevertheless, it was an American response to a situation stranger than anything that awaited the early pioneers on the other side of the Cumberland Gap. It was the political invention of a mature nation with all the security of great age. It is my hope that this book faithfully reports how the United States conducts its affairs in the third American era.

Washington, D.C.
April, 1967

"They know, and are content that all the world should know, the worst as well as the best in themselves. They have a boundless faith in free inquiry and full discussion. They admit the possibility of any temporary errors and delusions."

LORD BRYCE
The American Commonwealth

Part I

Separate But Unequal

"Every one who undertakes to describe the American system of government is obliged to follow the American division of it into three departments—Executive, Legislative, Judicial."

LORD BRYCE
The American Commonwealth

1 The Presidency

"Every four years there springs from the vote created by the whole people a President over that great nation. I think the whole world offers no finer spectacle than this; it offers no higher dignity; and there is no greater object of ambition on the political stage on which men are permitted to move. You may point, if you will, to hereditary rulers, to crowns coming down through successive generations of the same family, to thrones based on prescription or on conquest, to sceptres wielded over veteran legions and subject realms—but to my mind there is nothing more worthy of reverence and obedience, and nothing more sacred, than the authority of the freely chosen magistrate of a great and free people; and if there be on earth and amongst men any right divine to govern, surely it rests with a ruler so chosen and so appointed."

—JOHN BRIGHT, 1861

"It squints towards monarchy . . . your President may easily become King."

—PATRICK HENRY, 1787

Washington can be a confusing place for foreigners, and I dare say for most Americans, despite the constitutional blueprint for the separation of powers. The almost Germanic intensity of interest in what has become to be known as the power structure has yet to produce much clarity. Theories of monumental scholarship are expounded with meticulous care, and then are found not quite to fit after a Presidential election or a shift of power within Congress. A glance through one of the many inexpensive and excellent handbooks on the American system invariably shows that they do not fit the circumstances of the sixth, sixteenth, or twenty-sixth President, or the Twenty-fifty, Fiftieth, or Seventy-fifth Congress.

3

It is all the more surprising because, as every high school student of government knows, the United States is governed and administered at the federal level strictly according to the provisions of the Constitution. Despite the recent Amendments, the original document remains essentially unchanged; indeed, a few were ratified only to restate in more unequivocal language the intentions of the founders. Legislation is declared null and void by the Supreme Court when seen to offend the Constitution. The flexibility of the Constitution is of course one of its greatest glories, but that does not fully explain the confusion.

As a foreign correspondent in Washington, whose job for many years was largely to explain its goings-on, I read many of the scholarly works and handbooks. Officials within the three branches of government generously gave me much of their time in frequent attempts to clear a little of the fog. They must have found me a difficult, if eager, pupil. Part of the trouble was that as an Englishman I have a profound respect for political institutions. Politicians, Presidents, and Prime Ministers come and go, but in political democracies the institutions go on until they are changed by law or the slow attrition of practice. I was assured that there had been no basic change since 1787 except by constitutional amendment. I was aware that every department and agency maintained large staffs of lawyers, or general counsels, to ensure that they did not go beyond the letter and the spirit of the Constitution. But clearly change was continuous, with or without the blessing of the Supreme Court.

I was not alone with my confusion. It was matched by the downright anger of that minority of the American people who bear with pride the political label of Conservative Republican. The label, of course, had contributed to my confusion. Again as an Englishman, I did not have to be told that in the two-party system each party provides an umbrella for a variety of views, but I was unaccustomed to conservatives of one party invariably voting with conservatives of the other. The Conservative Republicans had it that the President was assuming dictatorial powers, and that the Supreme Court had usurped the legislative powers of Congress. It was an alarming view of the United States, which, however, the Presidential election of 1964 showed was not shared by the majority.

I am a political animal, with a good many years of experience of political reporting, east and west of the Iron Curtain, and north and south of the Equator, and eventually I decided to be guided by instinct, experience, and my own reading of history. Inevitably they led to a theory of my own. It is not suggested here that the Heren Theory makes nonsense of all preceding theories and the scholastic research and insight that produced them, but I do believe that the modern American Presidency makes sense as a political system only when it is seen to be a latter-day version of a British medieval monarchy, and I commend this approach to its loyal American subjects. Thus armed, they will be less bothered by the frustrations that usually attend the conventional method of measuring the incumbent against the constitutional yardstick. I am not denigrating the United States Constitution; as a foreign correspondent who has worked in too many countries, I am immensely respectful of it. Nevertheless, it is not always helpful when discussing the modern Presidency, and therefore the modern American system, and for a fuller understanding one must return to the medieval past of the British monarchy.

The theory is not so fanciful as the descendants of Patrick Henry and Thomas Jefferson may imagine. Then in London, as now in Washington, there existed a separation of powers. The triumvirate of Monarch, Barons, and Church was no less real than the President, Congress, and the Supreme Court. In fact, the Church was often more bothersome to the executive than the Court has become. There was, of course, the assertion of the Divine Right of Kings, but the modern President enjoys a similar supplementary source of authority. He derives it from the at times almost mystical connection between the Presidency and the people of the United States, who are the sole source of American power. In these agnostic times this is perhaps more useful than Divine Right. Certainly on occasions he seems to be haloed by a light of sacred quality the like of which has not illuminated an English king since Charles lost his head in Whitehall. John Bright, the English statesman, recognized that quality more than a hundred years ago despite his Quaker background.

The Presidential authority can be remarkably insecure, as it was with some of the old monarchs. Divine Right did not much help weak kings. The President's authority is strong, his writ runs, only when he can dominate or hold the balance in Congress and between the magnates. The power of modern political, industrial, agrarian, and labor magnates can in combination, and even separately, be as menacing as that of the territorial magnates of medieval times. He can rarely safely assume the loyalty of any group for long. There can be remarkably little unity in the United States. Even his political party is often divided. The question of his re-election can be in dispute almost from the moment of his triumphal entry into the White House.

A truly medieval example was provided by Senator Robert Kennedy of New York a few months after the assassination of his brother. Apparently believing the Presidency to be his right or destiny, he approached President Johnson with a request for the Vice Presidential nomination. He was refused, and there began a struggle that would have been instantly recognized by the magnates of old. It was not resolved at the time of writing, but it was not too fanciful to see Senator Kennedy as an American political prince. He was only the junior Senator from New York, but he wielded great power in his own right and was surrounded by a court or entourage. The Kennedy legend was not only an instrument in the struggle for power but proof of his legitimate claim. President Johnson, for all his electoral triumphs, was no less exposed than a medieval monarch who could not control his magnates.

If a President cannot take his authority for granted, its bounds have been extended beyond the most improbable dreams of any early monarch. His power of nuclear life and death over the entire world is well known. He can, and does, make war without a formal declaration by Congress. It is common to assume that he wears a number of hats, and they are certainly more numerous than medieval crowns. He is the Head of State, and, as such, represents the power and glory of the country. Some say that he is the embodiment of the people.

He is the First Executive; with those distant kings, he rules and reigns. The American administration is also an intensely personal business. No official, with the exception of those in the regulatory agencies, is answerable to any person but the President. He alone, with the advice and consent of the Senate, can appoint the several thousand senior officers of government, and he alone, without Senatorial consent, can dismiss them. He also has a large personal staff, similar to medieval royal households, that is an administration within the administration and all the more powerful because it acts directly for the President.

He is the First Diplomat. He alone can treat with Cousins England

and France, and confront Rival Russia. If Congress has a few constitutional prerogatives in foreign affairs, they are now often less important than they once were. As will be suggested in a later chapter, invariably the modern President has also been his own Secretary of State in times of trouble, and in recent years has been his own Secretary of State most of the time. He is of course Commander in Chief. The constitutional commission for the highest military rank is indisputable, and in recent years has become almost overpowerful and overpowering. He is the First Legislator. The State of the Union Message, or Speech from the Throne, is in effect the legislative calendar. He is Leader of the Party.

All this closely resembles the powers of the medieval monarch. In the Washington power structure even the parties are not entirely dissimilar from the baronial factions that swayed the fortunes of early England. Yet we have not finished with the resemblances. He is responsible for keeping the peace, the king's peace, and he is the last court of appeal for the citizenry. He alone represents all the people. He is the Great Benefactor. The United States is his constituency, and as the people offered up memorials in olden times so he is expected to be alert to their needs, expectations, and oppressions. If he does not, both he and the land will suffer. He can be impeached or deposed at the next election, as his medieval ancestors were deposed, and long before that his writ will cease to run.

The modern President is therefore not omnipotent, and neither were the earlier English kings, but they share one final power. Lincoln described it as the inherent powers of his office. It defies legal definition. It is nearly always disputed when exercised, but it is always available for a strong President. As in the Civil War, when the sixteenth President had to save the Union almost despite the Constitution, he can draw on a power that can only be described as the royal power of monarchs, the like of whom have not reigned in Britain for many a long century.

The Presidential establishment and trappings are no less royally medieval. His person is afforded infinitely more protection, although the casualty rate, alas, compares with the most violent periods of the Middle Ages. The Secret Servicemen are beefeaters with crewcuts and button-down shirts. The White House is as accessible as a medieval court. Old courtiers would immediately feel at home in the West Lobby with its somnolence and sudden bursts of activity as supplicants emerge from the Presidential presence. The White House moves with the President as the court moved with the king. The Cabinet, unelected and with no other authority than the Presidential pleasure, are the royal secretaries. It will be noted that apart from the Attorney General and the Postmaster General they are known as Secretaries and not Ministers. Occasionally they generate an authority of their own, and cannot be replaced without disturbing the essential balance. The President can be as lonely as a king, and his more sentimental subjects speak compassionately of his office as the loneliest job in the world. Yet he must have intimates upon whom he can depend, and his residence and offices are crowded with King's Men.

I am not a medieval scholar, but having gone so far I may as well go all the way and be more specific. The modern American Presidency can be compared with the British monarchy as it existed for a century or more after the signing of Magna Carta in 1215. Then there was no distinction between the king's interests and those of the state. Central government was no more than an extension of the king's household. By tradition he took advice from his companions, but it was advice to be accepted or rejected. Parliaments were called from time to time, but the routine business of the kingdom was conducted without them. The courts of the shire and hundred dispensed justice, but the king had an interest in the maintenance of peace. His justices were active throughout the country.

Under Magna Carta, the king was compelled to acknowledge his obligation to govern according to ancient customs of which public opinion approved. To control the king without recourse to rebellion was the first constitutional problem which the barons expected the Great Charter to resolve, but they were suspicious of promises and tried to foist their own counselors upon the king. They failed because the king could always use officers of his personal household for the government of the kingdom. The barons and burgesses who took part with the king in council in parliament could not control the administration, while the king was free to find new ways of action through his household when any one avenue was blocked. The king's independence of action remained more or less undiminished as long as he was strong and resourceful. Inevitably, of course, the complexity of government business led to the development of an impersonal administration more or less beyond the wrangles of kings and barons.

I would suggest with all seriousness that this period was not so very different in terms of executive power from the period that began with President Franklin Roosevelt. The President's interests are those of the country. No other American, in Congress, the Supreme Court or the states, can possibly match those interests. The federal government is an extension of his household. He and the Vice President are the only elected members of the executive branch, and as something less than a crown prince the Vice President does not count for much. The President is served with advice from his own personal staff, from the departments, the Cabinet, the National Security Council, and the Congressional leaders of his party, but he can accept or reject it. The routine business of administration is his responsibility alone, whether or not Congress is sitting. The federal and state courts dispense justice, but the President is ultimately responsible for law and order, and, as with Civil Rights disputes, his law officers are active throughout the country.

The President must govern under the provisions of the Constitution, but suspicion or jealousy of the executive branch has led to frequent attempts by Congress to interfere. They foisted the National Security Council upon him, but the President has more often preferred to use officers of his own household. An impersonal Civil Service has grown up, and must be a factor in any Presidential calculation, but the authority of his executive office has grown as the President's independence of action has progressively increased. Indeed, it can be said that the main difference between the modern American President and a medieval monarch is that there has been a steady increase rather than a diminution of his power. In comparative historical terms the United States has been moving steadily backward.

Despite all those renowned authorities on medieval history lurking in the great American universities, I am tempted to press my luck a little further. The Hundred Years' War was not unlike the unending wars and crises of the twentieth century. Edward the Third would have been regarded as a poor king if he had not gone to war with France, and his victories served him well. His parliaments always voted him money for war. Much the same can be said for the Presidents elected after the Second World War. There was dissent as in medieval times, but Congress has always voted more money for war than the President requested. In war, at least while victory was seen to be certain, the medieval king and modern President have always been supreme.

If the authorities on medieval history prove kind enough to maintain a polite silence on the Heren Theory, no doubt others will ask how I can explain away the democratic processes of the United States, which clearly did not exist in the thirteenth and fourteenth centuries. I cannot, simply because they are essential to the theory. It was the democratic processes, as they evolved over the years, that transformed the modern American Presidency into a latter-day version of a British medieval monarchy. The transformation is clear to anyone who has read American history without preconceived and mechanistic notions of a great country docilely living according to the Constitution.

In the first place, the founders labored long and hard at Philadelphia to establish a federal republic, and not a political democracy as now understood in the United States and Britain. Senator Goldwater had a point in the 1964 election, except that, typically, he was 177 years out of date. They were sensibly cautious about the House of Representatives, which they saw as the first legislative chamber, but far more apprehensive of the states, or territorial magnates. They had to concede much to win their loyalty, and thus in one brief summer these proud products of the Age of Enlightenment created with the federal form of government the political conditions of the Middle Ages. The Presidency they created was not half so weak as popular mythology would have it. Within four score years and ten an incumbent found it strong enough to suspend habeas corpus, the one sure defense of Anglo-Saxon liberties. But almost from the beginning the President was locked in conflict with states, and combinations of states, or Congress. The conflict was all the more painful when the territorial magnates were joined by those of trade, commerce, and the slave plantations. It was as if the medieval guilds had joined forces with Gloucester and Lancaster.

The greatness of President Jackson was that he had not forgotten the preamble to the Constitution: "We the People of the United States, in Order to form a more perfect Union, establish Justice, insure domestic Tranquillity, provide for the common defence, promote the general Welfare, and secure the Blessings of Liberty to ourselves and our Posterity . . ." Who or what were the People in 1787? Obviously they were not the slaves. Clearly Jefferson did not include the slum dwellers of the cities. There was no universal suffrage, and certainly the women were not thought of. All the evidence suggests that the founders were thinking only of the states, and were not certain how many would ratify the Constitution.

If the preamble was but a bit of rhetoric of which Americans have always been fond, it was seized upon by President Jackson, who recognized that the source of semidivine or sacred Presidential power was the people. After years of Congressional supremacy, or rule by magnates, he not so much revived the powers of Presidential office as remade them. His methods would not have surprised a medieval monarch. He regained control of the executive branch, forced Congress into retreat, if only temporarily, and revived the veto. He asserted his independence of the territorial magnates, until they screamed "tyrant" at him. It was Henry Clay who spoke for all Whigs when he said, "We are in the midst of a revolution, hitherto bloodless, but tending rapidly towards a total change of the pure republican character of the Government, and to the concentration of all power in the hands of one man."

There were indeed the beginnings of a revolution. The basis of government shifted protestingly from the landed gentry, the slave-owners, the merchants, and the bankers to the people, the white people, that is. Most reluctantly the United States was getting its first taste of democracy. The conditions of the Middle Ages, so surprisingly re-created in the New World by free and enlightened men, were demanding the monarchical leader they required. Only the President could speak for the People, and President Jackson knew it: "The President is the direct representative of the American people; he possesses original executive powers, and absorbs in himself all executive functions and responsibilities; and it is his special duty to protect the liberties and rights of the people and the integrity of the Constitution against the Senate or the House of Representatives, or both together."

There was a reaction of course. The American Presidential electoral system, no less than the hereditary system, has often failed to produce suitable successors for strong Presidents. The inner tensions of nineteenth-century America were even more powerful than those of thirteenth- and fourteenth-century England. President Buchanan even denied his authority to save the Union. It was saved by President Lincoln, but his assassination (so medieval) again left the Presidency enfeebled. The reaction of the magnates was extraordinarily savage, and President Andrew Johnson came within one vote of impeachment. Thereafter the United States was, for the most part, in the grip of the magnates until the election of the first modern President, Franklin Roosevelt. Historians can rightly argue that their grip was loosened by Theodore Roosevelt, Taft, and Wilson, but the aggrandizement of Presidential power accelerated under the second Roosevelt.

After the Civil War American conditions somewhat resembled those of the worst of the Middle Ages. The internecine struggles left a large part of the country, the South, depressed and oppressed, and for a period helpless against the plunderings of trained bands and camp followers. A kind of religious war swept the country as prophets such as Thaddeus Stevens sought retribution and rejected compromise as obscene. Then came the heyday of the new industrial magnates of the North, who built the largest industrial empire ever seen. They presented the People with an undreamed-of patrimony, but it seemed to be an overdraft by the early thirties and the magnates undischarged bankrupts. The land was laid to waste, figuratively speaking, but there was nothing figurative about the awful condition of tens of millions of people. They could only turn to President Roosevelt, and on his inauguration day the American Restoration began. The present happy position of the land is surely indisputable evidence that the American system flourishes under a King-President.

This is the Heren Theory. I do not expect an egalitarian people to accept it. Historians will surely question my haphazard reading of English and American history. Nevertheless, I respectfully offer it as the way to a true understanding of the American Presidency and the system that requires such a monarchical office. Before we regretfully turn to more mundane matters, I would like to emphasize that the theory is not a criticism. Nor am I the advance flak of some English Young Pretender to the Washington throne. I like the United States the way it is, or rather the way I think it is going to be. The Heren Theory at least indicates why American politics can be much more exciting than, if I may say so, the more advanced democracies such as Britain and Scandinavia. Its one deficiency is that it lacks a Shakespeare to write of the American Age of Kings.

There is no evidence that any of the founders were thinking specifically of English medieval monarchs when they met in Philadelphia that hot summer. Presumably they had George the Third very much on their minds, but if they had rebelled against him, they were not revolutionaries in the modern sense. There was no subsequent wholesale destruction of political institutions. Nor for that matter was there any revolutionary nonsense about abolishing slavery or canceling the debts of a hard-pressed yeomanry. Shays had been pursued as a seditionist. Despite the romanticism of the Englishman Tom Paine, British historians are closer to the truth in describing the troubles between 1775 and 1783 as the American War of Independence and not the Revolutionary War. The founders were concerned primarily with the transfer of power, as was Mr. Nehru when the second British Empire passed away.

The shadow of the Hanoverian King was there, but it does not explain the separation of powers. As already noted, they had long been separated in England. The founders were eighteenth-century English gentlemen who understood this. It must have been in their bones. Their forebears had fought the good fight for an independent parliament against the Tudor and Stuart kings, and the English Bill of Rights of 1689 was their witness.

Their Englishness explains the Constitution. They took as their examples the political institutions of the original colonies, which were modeled on the British system. The Presidency is the lineal descendant of the colonial office of governor, who represented the king. Twelve of the original thirteen were commanders in chief of local forces, nine had the power of pardon, and almost all had been required to take an executive oath of office. Nothing could have been more English or regal, and of course the governors, and the English kings from time out of mind, had gone to the legislature for revenue.

They were wary of a strong executive, but equally cautious about the legislature. They believed an executive veto was essential, although the English monarchy had long conceded that power. They looked not to the constitutions of Rhode Island or North Carolina with their provincial faith in truly democratic and powerful legislatures but to those of New York and Massachusetts, which recognized the need for a strong executive. Altogether it was a brilliant attempt to create a more perfect Union by improving and adapting the English model. If it was not a total success, the difficulty of finding a republican replacement for the monarchy was one obvious reason.

The Presidential electoral system was the only feature of the Constitution not suggested by English experience. There was no precedent. When the English had got rid or had run out of kings in the past, they had gone shopping around Europe for a replacement. The Electoral College was an obvious failure, but the idea of electing a king was most novel, if only because the system of electing the Holy Roman Emperor was more often nominal and hardly democratic.

The Presidency they evolved was perforce out of a royal die borrowed from eighteenth-century England. It had external and internal power. Very few new limits were placed on the external power. They realized that the direction of national security, as it is now called, must be the responsibility of the executive. The external power remains undiminished, and in fact has been extended. It is a power shared by very few modern prime ministers because the model was an eighteenth-century king.

Internal power, like that of the English king, was not so great, but was nevertheless considerable. It was rarely exercised or allowed to be exercised, however, and the consequence could be described as an aggrandizement of Congressional power. An imbalance in the relationship between the Presidency and Congress was created to the latter's advantage. Congressional government flourished, with occasional setbacks under strong Presidents, until the modern Presidency was firmly established in 1933. This, I believe, was not so much a questionable departure, as some critics would have it, as a return to the approximate balance the founders had groped for. It was hardly their fault that in returning to the past the Presidency overshot the eighteenth century and finished up in the thirteenth. The ills of the federal system, another American invention that has not worked too well, the circumstances of modern American life, and the long years of Congressional government made the excessive swing inevitable.

The nature of the intended balance between the Presidency and Congress is evident in the Constitution. Some of the relevant articles and sections are worth pondering again.

Article I, Section 7, Paragraphs 2 and 3: "Every Bill which shall have passed the House of Representatives and the Senate, shall, before it become a Law, be presented to the President of the United States; if he approve he shall sign it, but if not he shall return it, with his Objections . . ."

This is the veto power, and if the founders did not know that the royal veto in Britain had not been used for eighty years, this misunderstanding did not prevent Presidents from using their own.

President Franklin Roosevelt even tried to veto a revenue bill in 1944, something that a British king had never tried. As the first of the modern Presidents, he vetoed 505 bills in his first two terms. About half of them were so-called pocket vetoes. That is, he failed to return the bills before Congress adjourned and thus allowed them to die silently. The effectiveness of the veto as an instrument of Presidential power in relation to Congress is unquestioned, witness the frequent attempts to reduce it by constitutional amendment. Although the power of the veto is qualified, it has been effective nine times out of ten; moreover, it does not have to be exercised to influence legislation. The fact that it exists is a powerful deterrent to those legislators not certain of the two-thirds majority required to override it. The veto is, alas, a bludgeon. The President cannot veto an offensive part of a bill, but all of it. Hence the demand for a more discriminate instrument, generally known as an item veto. No action has been taken.

Article II, Section 1, Paragraph 1: "The executive Power shall be vested in a President of the United States of America. He shall hold his Office during the Term of four Years . . ."

The first sentence needs no explanation. The President's executive power is unqualified. The second, to my mind, provides a large measure of the basic strength of the Presidency. I do not want to be tedious with these apparent paradoxes. I have read most of the misleading comparisons with the British parliamentary system. If the Prime Minister requires only a simple majority to govern, only a simple minority vote is enough to bring him down. Not so with the President. He does not stand or fall on a vote in Congress. His party can be the minority in both houses, but it matters not. He is elected for a four-year term, and nothing can remove him except death, disability defined under the most rigid conditions, or the medieval instrument of impeachment. His term of office is measured and guaranteed not in years, months, or days but by the split second. The Twentieth Amendment (ratified February 6, 1933) is quite specific. "The terms of the President and Vice-President shall end at noon on the 20th day of January . . . and the terms of their successors shall then begin."

The President can be re-elected for a second term. Until the Twenty-second Amendment (ratified February 26, 1951), one of the last attacks of the Whigs against the royalist party, he could in theory serve for a lifetime. President Franklin Roosevelt was elected for a fourth term and died in office. He reigned as long as most kings, and might well have been re-elected again had he lived. The arbitrary termination of the Twenty-second Amendment is perhaps unnecessary and even dangerous. No matter how popular, effective, or good a President may be, he cannot serve more than two complete terms. No matter if the country is at war or in the depths of some awful crisis, the transfer of power must be made at the specified time. The dangers are obvious if not yet proved. But that is not the point at issue. Most Presidents can expect to serve eight years, which is longer than the average British Prime Minister spends in office. More American Presidents have held office for eight years than have British Prime Ministers since the younger Pitt, who only survived President Washington by a few years.

The importance of guaranteed tenure is evident. A British Prime Minister may be better served by his Cabinet, but this is of little consequence for him if he loses an election after two or three years. The scope it gives to a newly inaugurated President is immense. The world and domestic rivals must come to terms with him. He can plan his legislative program. If he knows what he is doing, and he could hardly hope to be a strong President if he did not, he can establish himself and achieve much even with weak Congressional support. Whether or not a majority of Congress shares his politics it must treat with him if only because of the veto power.

Article II, Section 3: "He shall from time to time give to the Congress Information of the State of the Union, and recommend to their Consideration such Measures as he shall judge necessary and expedient; he may, on extraordinary Occasions, convene both Houses, or either of them, and in Case of Disagreement between them with Respect to the Time of Adjournment, he may adjourn them to such Time as he shall think proper; he shall receive Ambassadors and other public Ministers; he shall take Care that the Laws be faithfully executed, and shall Commission all the Officers of the United States."

Here is a quiverful of power from patronage to a mandate for Presidential legislative leadership. The latter was recognized by President Theodore Roosevelt and President Wilson, who was the first to appear before a special session of Congress to request legislation. If they seized the initiative, President Franklin Roosevelt established it as a permanent prerogative beyond dispute. Important legislation is now invariably drafted by the White House or the departments. The legislative program of Congress is the President's legislative program. They are no longer masters in their own houses despite all the sergeants at arms and ancient traditions.

Here are the three constitutional mandates for the internal power of the modern Presidency, but there are other factors. The next is the acceptance of Presidential autonomy. President Jackson first asserted it. President Theodore Roosevelt restated it. He wrote in his *Autobiography*:

I declined to adopt the view that what was imperatively necessary for the Nation could not be done by the President unless he could find some specific authorization to do it. My belief was that it was not only his right but his duty to do anything that the needs of the Nation demanded unless such action was forbidden by the Constitution or by the laws. Under this interpretation of executive power I did and caused to be done many things not previously done by the President and the heads of the Departments. I did not usurp power, but I did greatly broaden the use of executive power. In other words, I acted for the public welfare, I acted for the common well-being of all our people, whenever and in whatever manner was necessary, unless prevented by direct constitutional or legislative prohibition.

This is the theory of the President as the Steward of the People. It was asserted by President Theodore Roosevelt, who also served before his time, because Congress had generally failed to represent the interests of the people. During the post–Civil War period of economic expansion especially, Congress largely represented industrial, commercial, and landed interests which dominated both political parties. The business of America, as a more recent and complacent President said, was business. Elihu Root spoke of the invisible government, and the English socialist, Professor Harold Laski, preferred his own despised aristocracy. Despite their limitations as a class, he said, they had a real sense of public service.

There were, of course, many popular protests. The American political animal was not always utterly supine, but only recent strong Presidents made protest effective. The New Freedom, the Square Deal, the New Deal, the Fair Deal, the New Frontier, and the Great Society were the Presidential slogans of the rising tide of protest, which became a flood that no Congressional Canute could stop.

B

The reason is obvious. A majority of Americans demanded a reforming government, to meet and satisfy, first, their wants and then their rising expectations. Only the President could respond.

The history of the modern internal Presidency is to a large extent the history of American social and economic reform. The new internal power flows not only from the Constitution but from a triple revolution. The technological and economic revolution has helped to bring about the second revolution of rising expectations. It is sustained in large measure by the solving of problems they combine to create. They call for programs that would have caused the Philadelphia Convention to break up in disorder if they had been merely suggested or whispered. They also call for what amounts to a continuing state of emergency, and this tends to make the President's internal power self-perpetuating.

A strong President can always choose to see an emergency requiring a display or extension of his power. An emergency does not have to be invented of course, but only seen to exist. There is a similarity between the modern President's internal and external power. For instance, there was little evidence to suggest that conditions in Santo Domingo prior to the most recent American intervention amounted to an American emergency. There was not much more when President Kennedy earlier decided that Negro freedom riders must be allowed to exercise their constitutional right to drink the rather dreadful coffee of the sleazy but segregated refreshment room of the interstate bus depot in Montgomery, Alabama. Nevertheless, he took command of the State's National Guard, which wore the old Confederate flag, to ensure that right. In so doing, he gave the third of the current American revolutions a sturdy shove forward.

To a large extent the modern Presidency has been assisted, if unwittingly, by the third branch of government, the Supreme Court. The government of the United States is said to be a government of laws, but the Court is nine men, and their awareness of social and political requirements has played havoc with the laws. In 1935 the Court declared unconstitutional much of the New Deal legislation, as in the previous century it had in effect come out in support of slavery in the Dred Scott case. But in recent years it has emerged as the oracle of national conscience. It is now first the protector of individual liberties rather than the defender of property. Inevitably it has strengthened the modern Presidency, especially in its relationship to the states.

The Court has in fact required Presidential activism. For instance, in 1954 when it handed down the historic decision on *Brown* v. *Board of Education,* which declared racial segregation in schools unconstitutional, the President had to act, although Mr. Eisenhower showed small personal enthusiasm. In upholding subsequent Civil Rights legislation, it maintained the momentum of the third revolution and extended Presidential power.

Indeed, the imperative of solving nationwide problems at the national level demands Presidential activism. It is the new kind of politics for the United States, and it is largely Presidential politics. Every problem seen, discovered, or rediscovered seems to require a further extension of Presidential power. It was no doubt historically inevitable because of the American political system. Only the comparatively sudden emergence of the King-President was a surprise, perhaps because of factors no less real because they are intangible.

One is the new respect for the Presidency. Another is the sense of national greatness, sharply enhanced since the assumption of world leadership. The new pride demands, no matter how inarticulately, a strong external President for national security and a strong internal President to remove the unnecessary blemishes of American society. The two demands have interacted and combined, and elevated the Presidency above the Congress.

If I have emphasized the recent extensions of Presidential power, it is not to suggest omnipotence. That, to say the least, would be misleading. What I do believe is that congressional government, as it flourished with occasional fluctuation from President Andrew Johnson to President Hoover, has had its day. The checks and balances remain, if the imbalance no longer favors Congress. The subordinate centers of power are more numerous. The modern magnates and barons can be as recalcitrant as their medieval forebears, even when they know where the power lies. But a strong President has the power to rule as long as he enjoys and can organize the support of the people.

After establishing the nature of the enormous power wielded by the modern Presidency it is now necessary to explain how it is wielded. The first instuments are the King's Men, or members of the Presidential staffs. There are hundreds of them, and they are indispensable. They are also unique in modern democracies. Only in Washington, and perhaps in equally exotic places such as Phnom Penh and Am-man, do such men still survive and wield so much undemocratic influence—that is, undemocratic to the extent that they are not elected. The imperious Dr. Adenauer brought West Germany up from the depths of national defeat and shame with only a State Secretary and some office help. President de Gaulle never needed anybody but President de Gaulle. Nobody remotely resembles them in Britain, where their lineal descendants are mere palace ciphers dancing a pavane to a convenient political institution known as the Constitutional Monarchy.

The Prime Minister requires and gets only the Secretary of the Cabinet, four personal private secretaries, and one or two press secretaries. Apart from the latter, they are career Civil Servants who serve masters of either political color with equal diligence and loyalty if not affection. For instance, the PPSs of Sir Alec Douglas-Home, the Conservative unbelted earl from Scotland, served Mr. Harold Wilson, the Labour economist from lower-middle-class Yorkshire. The switch was achieved without a pause. One moment Sir Alec was there, and the next he was gone, leaving his wife to pack while Mr. Wilson got down to work in the Cabinet Room below.

Why can 10 Downing Street be run by a few Civil Servants, and at a time when some political scientists, wrongheaded as usual, see Britain in the beginnings of a system similar to the American Presidency? Again I would suggest that the usual constitutional references be treated with my customary suspicion. The fact rather than the theory of the matter is that the United Kingdom, despite the monarch, is a modern republic with no place for a King-President and courtiers such as the King's Men.

The Prime Minister needs only a small personal staff because he can, and indeed must, depend upon his Cabinet, united under the principle of collective responsibility and accountable to Parliament on a day-to-day basis. He is directly responsible and responsive to the elected representatives of the people in a way that the President can never be. He stands or falls on their majority vote. If a democratic republic is a sovereign state ruled by representatives of an inclusive electorate, political Britain is a good deal closer to the Hellenic ideal than the United States, in spite of, or perhaps because of, the Queen, God Bless Her. It is certainly more democratic, and more in tune with the spirit of republicanism. There can be no question of a candidate for the highest office being selected in some smoke-filled room or Chicago motel, no room for a Colonel House, and no scope for a Mrs. Wilson—Mrs. Woodrow Wilson, that is, not Mrs. Harold Wilson, who was known to send out for food when guests were expected.

Equally important, the duties of the Prime Minister's small staff are narrowly defined and known to all. They are to ensure that the Prime Minister receives advice and information from the appropriate authority, and that his or the Cabinet's decisions are properly and clearly conveyed. The advice from the departments must nearly always have the authority of the departmental minister. Apart from helping to provide this last essential link between the Prime Minister and his Cabinet, and in turn Parliament and the people, they are responsible only for office routine, the keeping of the records, and the handling of secret and confidential business. That is all. If they aspire to more direct power and influence, they must seek elective office.

Britain achieved true political democracy by retaining the monarchy, and it is useless for Americans to object and refer to the founders. Those eighteenth-century English gentlemen were captives of their past, and failed to realize that the establishment of a republican form of government required something more than the limiting of its head to four-year periods. That is in passing. What is important to remember is that the American system, monarchical constitutionalism, presidential monarchy, or call it what you will, can only work with the assistance of the King's Men. There is no mention of them in the Constitution, but their leaders can wield immense influence and occasionally real power. I can well understand the local interest in them. If I were living in the Middle Ages, I would also want to know what was happening behind the arras. I, as a free-born Englishman, would not accept the admonition that there is more between heaven and earth than in my political philosophy or knowledge, as many Americans seem to do.

They are necessary because the President, who is as lonely as a medieval monarch, needs all the help he can get to maintain the essential balance of power at home and abroad. They are a comparatively recent innovation. In President Grant's day the White House staff cost $13,800 a year. President Hoover, who was a first-class administrator if a second-class President, had a staff of only forty-two. President Eisenhower, who thought that he was a modern constitutional monarch, finished up with staffs of more than two thousand officials. This did not, of course, include the thousands who work for the Central Intelligence Agency. Today, the White House costs some $100 million a year, and the staffs continue to grow. Such a sum would hardly be credited in Europe, except as yet another example of the built-in inefficiency of the American system.

The architecture of the 1600 block of Pennsylvania Avenue, NW, reflects much of this development. At one time the White House was not unlike the residence of a minor British colonial governor, a more or less modest mansion of classical pretentions in which the occupant lived, worked, and entertained. This changed with the realization that the President could not escape his monarchical lineage. The east and west wings, discreetly subdued by landscaping, were added for the billeting of the early King's Men. As their master's dominion over palm and pine spread, the old State, Army, Navy Building next door was taken over. This superb example of Victorian wedding cake, now known as the Executive Office Building, once housed, as the name suggests, the Departments of State, Army, and Navy, but today is not nearly big enough for the President's staffs, and annexes abound.

Known officially and collectively as the Executive Office of the President, his staffs man a number of offices. These are the White House Office, the Bureau of the Budget, the Council of Economic Advisers, the National Security Council, the Central Intelligence Agency, the National Aeronautics and Space Council, the Office of Economic Opportunity, the Office of Emergency Planning, the Office of Science and Technology, and the Office of the Special Representative for Trade Negotiations. Then there is a variety of Presidential committees, commissions, and councils, ranging from labor-management and consumer interests to aging and foreign intelligence. They can be temporary, but the total always seems to increase.

The present vast organization was officially launched by Executive Order 8248 of September 8, 1939. It has been described as a nearly unnoticed but nonetheless epoch-making event in the history of American institutions. No one, certainly not a member of Congress, would now regard this as an exaggeration. As so often happens, the Executive Order only belatedly recognized something that existed. President Franklin Roosevelt had assumed a burden of responsibilities, unprecedented and unconstitutional according to some, without being able to equip himself with adequate formal staffs. The Constitution and practice had yielded him the household of an eighteenth-century colonial governor and not that of a medieval monarch. He had accordingly organized a Brain Trust to respond to the demands of his time.

The purposes of the Executive Order were to tidy this up and to provide the President with adequate information, to anticipate issues and problems and plan for the future, to protect him from hasty and poor judgments, and to ensure compliance with policy and Executive Orders. It cannot be said that the last purpose has been altogether successfully achieved, but the results of the original order were much more than a tidier and more efficient Presidential Office. The Presidency is now an institution. The flow of business handled is now vastly beyond the capacity of one man, and indeed much of it is never seen or much heard about by the President. If it sounds impersonal, the institution nevertheless has maintained his interests, authority, and influence, and in so doing has helped perversely to create a personal rule the like of which earlier Americans never contemplated in their most disturbing nightmares of a dictatorial President. In meeting the responsibilities of a modern President, the institution has in fact expanded them.

The constitutional significance of this is immense. In the first place it saved the Presidency, and helped it survive in a guise that could be dimly recognized by the founders. Without it, even the most Whiggish of Republican Presidents would have been overwhelmed; proposals for a pluralistic executive could have been irresistible. But it did more than that. In making it possible for the President to maintain his corner of the triangular American government, it equipped him to meet rising popular expectations and make these United States, as Walt Whitman would have it, a better place to live in.

The importance of the Executive Office calls for an inspection of some of its components. An Englishman might assume the Bureau of the Budget to be the most powerful, and certainly it is indispensable. First created in 1921, and transferred to the Executive Office in 1939, its first function is, of course, to prepare the budget, the framework of any democratic administration. To some extent its staff is the American equivalent of the cream of the Treasury in London. It does not coordinate economic policy or manage the Civil Service, as do the Lord Commissioners in London, but it is the President's administrative general staff. It helps him to conduct government business efficiently and economically, and keeps him informed of the activities and progress of the departments and agencies. Its influence and control become particularly noticeable as the ambitions and pet projects of departmental secretaries wither or are chopped down to size as budget time approaches. Through the Bureau the President maintains control of the executive branch where it means most.

The Council of Economic Advisers was created by the Employment Act of 1946 to analyze the national economy, advise the President on economic developments, and recommend policies for economic growth and stability. It sounds all rather dreary, but some see the Council as the most exciting office in Washington. It has certainly proved to be a subtly, even surreptitiously, effective office. This may be surprising because, as everyone knows, the capitalist system made the United States rich if not great, and the American businessman knows best. It is equally well established that government interference in the market place, or rather the executive suite of the corporations, can lead only to Socialism and economic disaster. It is perhaps less well known that American business is regulated, supported, and subsidized by tax rebates and allowances and often direct government loans to an extent that would turn the supposedly coddled European businessman green with envy. This, however, is only the latest chapter of American economic history with its tariffs and giveaways to the railroads and more recent "Buy American" legislation.

The importance of the Council is both its scholarly and skillful use of modern economic theories and methods to help flatten out the awful waves of boom and bust without too much ideological warfare. All this has to be done of course without mention of John Maynard Keynes, whose marriage to a Russian ballet dancer warned all paid-up members of Chambers of Commerce of the color of his politics. Nevertheless, with this occasionally embarrassing impediment, his pupils on the Council have helped to save American business from its worst self.

With tax proposals, guidelines, and other examples of the economist's ingenuity, the Council has eased, if not eliminated, many of the inner contradictions of capitalistic society. President Roosevelt saved it in the thirties. The Council has helped to consolidate the rescue. It deserves the thanks of all non-Marxists, including those abroad whose exchanges catch cold when the tycoons of Wall Street sneeze. Much of this is now recognized by the giant corporations, if not by the small-town businessmen despite the paternal efforts of the Small Business Administration to protect their interests.

The functions of most of the other offices are obvious, and the National Security Council is discussed fully in another chapter, but another that causes excitement, derision, and apprehension is the Office of Economic Opportunity. It was established in 1964 soon after poverty was somewhat belatedly discovered, and its purpose is to eliminate the paradox of poverty in the midst of plenty. Its youth, conservation, work training, adult education, and employment incentive programs are unexceptional, but imagination is evident in the urban and rural community action programs.

These programs are certainly unusual, in that the law requires the poor to help in developing and applying the antipoverty measures. Expert opinion agreed that this was the only way to give them self-respect as well as something better than relief checks, but it was hotly resisted by most mayors and machine bosses of the big cities. They were not trying to save the poor from themselves, but their own power and influence, which rested to a large degree on the control of federal funds and patronage. Many saw the program as an attempt by the President of the United States to add control of political wards and precincts to his already tremendous power. They were perhaps only half wrong as to the possible consequence if not the intention of the program.

Thus it can be seen that through the institutionalized Presidency the incumbent can actually reach up to the moon and the stars and down to the gutters of the slums of New York and Chicago. He can defy the Presidium in Moscow and the political machines near home. He can personally command the most powerful military forces in history and be his own Secretary of State. He can prepare for Doomsday-plus-1, after 100 million Americans may have been incinerated in a nuclear attack, and negotiate the price of wheat with the European Economic Community. He can hope to create another million jobs, spy on friend and enemy alike, and engineer revolts in distant countries. He can influence the direction of scientific research and keep his departmental Secretaries in line.

All this power, inherent in his constitutional authority, and broadened and extended by new responsibilities and rising popular expectations, has been organized and made usable by the Executive Office. It is, or ought to be, awesome in the extreme, but of all the

B*

faceless men and women who work in the Executive Office Building and its annexes as the nerves, sinews, muscles, and perhaps fat of the institutionalized Presidency, few attract as much attention, innocent and otherwise, as do the members of the White House office—and with good reason, because they are the Lords of the Bedchamber and the Wardrobe of the King-President. Among the King's Men, they are the most intimate, and therefore often the most powerful. They also represent, to my mind, one of the intrinsic weaknesses as well as the basic strengths of the modern Presidency.

The weakness of the system must strike the new President as soon as he enters the White House. When he saunters under the collonade to his office, he finds, despite all his great powers and responsibilities and the unbroken continuity of the Presidency, that he has inherited empty offices. Apart from the executive clerk, the police and domestic staff, the place is deserted. Across the way, in the Executive Office Building, the minions, if not necessarily the Director of the Budget Bureau, are hard at work, but the staff of the White House office has departed with their lord and master. It must be very disconcerting, no matter how often he anticipated this great day.

He arrives, of course, with his own staff, or the beginning of it, but its members can be complete strangers to Washington. They also are always due for a surprise. The Presidency is a continuing office, and they must know the new incumbent has inherited drawers-full of problems. He may have been elected with a brave new program. He may have a New Deal, Fair Deal, New Frontier, or a Great Society in mind or on tattered campaign posters, but the past is likely to cast long shadows over the bright promise of the future. They can be cast from the most unlikely places, but the President's staff can be certain of only one thing. Nothing will be found in the White House files; all have been emptied to stock the Kennedy, Eisenhower, Truman, and Roosevelt libraries, the monarchical principle having long established that state papers are the personal property of the outgoing ruler.

One can argue, of course, that it is nice to start afresh, that at least there will be more room for the new President's papers. It is a charming idea, but it presents some problems for those concerned with continuity of government. Gestures are made at least at the pretense of handing-over. President-elect Kennedy had a couple of chats with President Eisenhower, although eight years earlier the good general ignored President Truman's helping hand. The Director of the Central Intelligence Agency is available for briefings, but the transfer of power cannot be anything but haphazard. The system, especially when the two men belong to different parties, prevents a more orderly or thorough transfer.

The first hazard, of course, is the newness of the new incumbent. There will be more on this later, but for the time being it is sufficient to remember that very few Presidents have had much more than the vaguest idea of how to do their new job. President Kennedy must have been painfully aware of this deficiency when during the 1960 election campaign he asked Professor Richard Neustadt of Columbia University to prepare some notes on staffing. He was presented with a sheaf of memoranda aboard the family aircraft *Caroline* mid-flight between Chicago and New York four days before the election.

It was a historic flight. The professor had not prepared notes for a lecture, or for the normal group of undergraduates, but for a candidate to the most powerful elective office in the world. A man who was to assume the leadership of the free world and the awful responsibility of the largest nuclear armory had no clear idea, from no fault of his own, of how to run his office. The situation is worth pondering. At a time when the world was agog with the vision of America moving again, neither the Presidential candidate nor his intimates knew how to move an interdepartmental memorandum. Relations with Cuba had not yet been severed, but plans were being secretly prepared for an invasion of that island. Nobody knew what Mr. Krushchev was up to over Berlin, Laos was falling apart again, and unemployment at home was reaching crisis proportions. Gold was leaving Fort Knox by the truckload, and only the increasing population was helping to expand the economy, and then at a miserable rate. By any standards the country was in a bit of a mess, and yet the candidate was forced to seek the advice of an outsider on the mechanics of power.

The Neustadt memoranda no doubt filled the void. They anticipated immediate problems such as the designation of personal and executive assistants, the nomination of Cabinet officers, innumerable other appointments, and the first message to Congress. The bureaucracy had to be reassured, and Congressional leadership consulted. There were pages referring to the writing of the Inaugural Address, an item described as organizing for reorganizing, the actual physical takeover, and the development of a program. Last and by no means least, the candidate was advised on the selection of the White House office staff.

As far as is known, its members do not wield real power, except in bureaucratic combat, although one can never be certain because they move in a sphere of the greatest intimacy. As President Truman wrote, "No one can know all the processes and stages of [a President's] thinking in making important decisions. Even those closest to him . . . never know all the reasons why he does certain things and why he comes to certain conclusions." Their roles are necessarily limited if only because they have no constitutional existence. Only the President can act. Nevertheless, without them there can be little action. They manage his daily chores, provide information for decision-making, and help to control their implementation. They project the will of the President in departments ruled by men supposedly appointed by the President for that purpose, and meet the needs of officials outside the White House for Presidential support, judgment, decision, or the borrowing of his prestige.

It must be assumed because of the intimate nature of their relationship with the President that they can influence policy. They are more readily available than other advisers. They help to write the speeches, but not as mere ghost writers. Although official information and advice are available to them, they are generally expected to seek out the unofficial and some of their own must stick to it. One or more of them is present at most of the President's confidential meetings to take notes, a task that can go far beyond that of a stenographer. The range of their activities is extensive. One special assistant is responsible for national security affairs, and another for Congressional. The remainder among them keep an eye on almost everything, and, of course, the Press Secretary ensures that the eyes of the nation are upon the President.

Britain, which has had its fill of courtiers in the past, and most other political democracies prefer the Cabinet system responsible to parliament. This is of course impossible in the United States, but there is a body known as the Cabinet. There is no mention of it in the Constitution. The founders were apparently unaware of the developments that led to the subsequent creation of the British Cabinet, but better information probably would have not much influenced their work. Article I, Section 6, states, "No Senator or Representative shall, during the Time for which he was elected, be appointed to any civil Office under the Authority of the United States." This constitutional edict has not been carried out to the letter, but it clearly prevents a serving member from joining the Cabinet.

The American Cabinet is a creation of custom and tradition, going back to President Washington, and it functions at the pleasure of the President. Significantly the *United States Government Organization Manual* refers to it as the Cabinet of the President. Article II, Section 2, of the Constitution states, "The President . . . may require the Opinion, in writing, of the principal Officer in each of the executive Departments, upon any Subject relating to the Duties of their respective Offices." This is not a provision for Cabinet responsibility. There have been Presidents who leaned toward the British model, the influence of Burke and Bagehot was considerable, but President Lincoln rejected collective responsibility, as did most other strong Presidents after they had learned their job. The process was apparently painful for President Wilson.

It should not be surprising, as it is for many people, that the King's Men, as members of the Presidential institution, can and do wield more influence than the Cabinet. But fundamentally this does not really matter. Not one member of either institution is elected, and in a lesser sense they are all King's Men.

At the time of writing, the Cabinet was quite small by British standards. It comprised the heads of the twelve executive departments, and the Permanent Representative to the United Nations. The Vice President also participated. The departments were State, Treasury, Defense, Justice, Post Office, Interior, Agriculture, Commerce, Labor, Health, Education and Welfare, Housing and Urban Development, and Transportation. The Secretaries of these departments can be considerable men, with an authority of their own if they represent some powerful political or regional faction. They can be subordinate centers of power with whom the President must treat.

Generally speaking, however, and with the possible exception of the Secretaries of State and Defense, they are what Germans know as *Fachministers,* or experts in their own fields. The assumption is that their expert knowledge, say of agriculture or commerce, does not entitle them to share in the process of Presidential decision-making. They also tend to become protagonists of the interests of those who deal with their departments. This is a second source of power, but it makes their advice suspect. Cabinet members can also be registered members of the opposition party, which does not normally make for a cozy relationship with the President. It must be recorded, however, that a nominal Republican Secretary of Defense, Robert McNamara, had the closest possible relationship with two Democratic Presidents, Kennedy and Johnson. Douglas Dillon, a more enthusiastic Republican, served Mr. Kennedy as Secretary of the Treasury.

Such executive institutions depend, of course, upon the requirements or fancy of the President. Mr. Eisenhower preferred the orderly approach to government which can be a by-product of a body such as the Cabinet. As the National Security Council became a powerful institution with its own bureaucracy in his reign, so did the Cabinet. It met regularly, and a secretariat organized the agenda, kept the necessary minutes, and tried to ensure that its decisions were acted upon. There were also a subcabinet and a number of Cabinet committees. Their effectiveness is arguable, but President Kennedy dismantled the apparatus and largely ignored the Cabinet without any obvious deleterious consequences. He was plainly bored by the whole thing. With other modern Presidents, he called Cabinets only because he felt that tradition required it, or as a demonstration of executive unity in times of crisis.

President Johnson was a little more formal, but not much. If he called more Cabinet meetings, he occasionally invited the press to attend. They then became joint press conferences, a little farcical and embarrassing for the Cabinet officers. It is true that in turn he invited them to his normal press conferences, which was revealing. Seated uncomfortably under the television lights and barely distinguishable from the reporters, they were seen, if at all, not as participants in the decision-making process, but onlookers of the process of communicating Presidential decisions to the people.

It is quite possible that this will change again, and in any event the personal power that individual Cabinet officers can wield must not be ignored. The Vice Presidency, however, is an office of even less consequence, although it is the only other elective office in the executive branch. John Garner, who was Vice President to Franklin Roosevelt, once said with Texan candor that it was not worth a bucket of warm spit. There have been no developments since the thirties to suggest anything but a change of metaphor to describe the power of the office.

Yet powerful and ambitious men have often sought or accepted the Vice Presidential nomination, including Kennedy in 1956 and Johnson in 1960. The subsequent elevation of Johnson presumably provides the reason. Four Presidents have been assassinated, and others have died in office. If the Presidential nomination is beyond the reach of the ambitious, the second place on the ticket is no bad place to be. Vice Presidents can also be future candidates if their lord and master survives assassination or retires in good health.

The Vice President is therefore a possible crown prince, and prudence at least should require that a suitable man be nominated. This has not always been the case, if only because the Presidential candidate does not take to the hustings with possible early death in mind. He has too much else to think about, such as winning the election, and the Vice Presidential candidate can be chosen to balance the ticket. That is, if the first candidate is an Eastern Catholic, political prudence requires him to select or accept, say, a Texan Protestant as the second. All this is understandable, and, if it is regrettable, the assumption is that a man thought fit to run as second on the ticket should in an emergency be capable of the Presidency. Theodore Roosevelt, Harry Truman, and Lyndon Johnson are sufficient proof of the validity of this theory.

Presidential death and assassination have persuaded people in recent years to pay more attention to the Vice Presidency, if not to the selection of a candidate. The incumbent attends Cabinet meetings, as noted, and is a statutory member of the National Security Council. He serves in a number of capacities for the President, as his representative at home and abroad and on a number of councils and committees. He is, of course, the President of the Senate, which is no sinecure and in certain circumstances can be a useful office. It remains that the Vice Presidency has no power of its own, is an uncomfortable office and often the target for sly fun. No President worth his salt is prepared to share real power, even if he could, and like the monarch of old he is apparently suspicious of the ambitions of the crown prince.

The Vice President, the Executive Office, and the Cabinet are usually seen as the components of the Presidential institution, but I would add two more, the Central Intelligence Agency and the Federal Bureau of Investigation. The CIA is indisputably one of the institutional components. It acts under the direction of the National Security Council, and Congress does not control supplies. Indeed, the Agency's budget is not published, and a special Congressional committee has only the vaguest idea of the purposes of the amounts appropriated which are buried in other departmental budgets.

The connection between the President and the FBI is more tenuous. It is a bureau of the Department of Justice, and a tradition of independence has been firmly established by J. Edgar Hoover, its first director.

It remains, because of its responsibility for investigating the violation of federal laws, including treason, espionage, and other subversive activities, that the Bureau is well placed to act for the President. An obvious example was its investigation of possible collusion between steel companies when President Kennedy felt himself to have been treated too contemptuously by one of the great steel magnates. The correctness of this investigation was questioned at the time; it included the arousing of some witnesses in the early hours, but not by the Bureau. In special circumstances, therefore, the FBI acts as the special agent for the President. It has more than fifty field divisions.

The CIA is part of the national security apparatus and is discussed elsewhere, but its function as a Presidential instrument cannot be overlooked. Apart from the collecting and evaluating of intelligence it performs such other functions and duties affecting the national security as the NSC may from time to time direct. In other words, the President can direct it to interfere in the internal affairs of foreign countries, overthrow governments, and even organize invasions. Presidents have exercised this power. They created no precedent; from the rise of nation-states such interference has been common enough, but among free countries no national leader has such a secret instrument as the CIA. They simply could not afford it.

There is a Washington myth that somehow the Agency is an invisible government, more or less free to do what it wants. Nothing could be farther from the truth. It is under the President. The ultimate responsibility is clear, and it is more than a constitutional principle. Control of its covert operations is tight at all stages, certainly a good deal tighter than elsewhere within the executive branch, where decisions are made every day without Presidential knowledge.

No large covert operation can be mounted without a NSC directive, which means a Presidential directive. A Cabinet committee reviews all sizable operations. There is close and continuing cooperation at all levels, at weekly meetings with representatives of the Secretaries of State and Defense, and often daily meetings for subordinates. The President's Foreign Intelligence Advisory Board is a constant watchdog.

There is naturally a reluctance to discuss the President's responsibility in this area. After all, he is supposed to subscribe to the theories of sovereignty and the right of all nations to be free from outside interference, but there is another reason. In 1967 it was revealed that the Agency had financed American student and labor organizations and other groups. The revelations caused considerable concern for a number of cogent reasons. One was that the President had the power to finance organizations divorced from intelligence work without Congressional approval.

This is the modern Presidential institution. It is vast, occasionally confusing, and full of contradictions, but with the exceptions of the Central Intelligence Agency and the Federal Bureau of Investigation it is represented to the American people as one man, the President. The official mainly responsible is the White House Press Secretary.

The importance of this function cannot be overestimated, although Washington correspondents occasionally overestimate the part they are required to play in it. Neither the President nor his Cabinet officers sits in Congress, and there is no question time on the Westminster model. The public dialogue between the President and Congress must for the most part be conducted through the press and other mass communications media because he only appears at joint sessions on special occasions.

Direct communication with the people is also obviously essential for maintaining the internal power of the modern Presidency. He must seek support for his programs or defend them, but he can have other purposes. He can deflect public attention from his critics and enemies simply by issuing a statement or holding a press conference at the time the attack is expected.

All this is generally done with considerable professional skill. Edition times are kept in mind, and the Presidential day can be so organized that the part which he wants televised will reach the largest audiences. Reporters and photographers are always in attendance at the White House. When the President travels, he is not so much pursued as accompanied by the press. They are members of his entourage, and their bags bear the proud label, "Trip of the President." Aircraft and other transport are arranged by the White House.

Press offices are established wherever he goes, even when he goes to the hospital.

There is never a pause. On holiday, on Christmas Day, in church or the theater, the reporters are there. They expect and generally receive two daily briefings from the Press Secretary, and frequent meetings with the President on or off the record. His formal press conferences are television spectaculars. The official verbatim reports are available generally within minutes. Copies of speeches and messages are invariably distributed before delivery, and quite often briefings are held to explain or draw attention to important passages. No wonder there are always more reporters in the west lobby of the White House than in the Senate or House press galleries.

It might also be added that the talk of image-building is not Madison Avenue jargon. The Presidential institution must be made personal. An image of the President must be created to inspire confidence and loyalty. Nothing can be overlooked. If he is President of all the people, he must be all things to all men. Dog lovers and teetotalers must be reassured even if he hates dogs and likes a couple of martinis after a hard day at the office. This helps to explain the many women reporters at the White House, and the columns of gushing inconsequence which are read so assiduously. The result can be rather synthetic. The casual reader can wonder if a real man actually exists, or if it is some elaborate personalized façade for a faceless institution.

Indeed, more attentive observers must wonder where the image stops and the real man begins, who is the President and what is the Presidential institution. The requirements of the modern office, constitutional, political, and personal, are so numerous that common sense says that they cannot be met by one man. Earlier I referred to the number of hats the President is supposed to wear. It is a convenient if hackneyed way of enumerating his many responsibilities, but it is misleading. There is little that he can do as First Executive without seeking the advice of the First Legislator and the Leader of the Party. The First Diplomat and the Commander in Chief must invariably act in unison. When he supports, for instance, the aspirations of the Negro, he is both the Great Benefactor and Keeper of the Peace, and the First Legislator and Leader of the Party are never absent from the office. And even in such domestic situations the

Commander in Chief is in the anteroom and the Chief Diplomat is not free from apprehension.

He is all these men. He is omnipresent, if not omnipotent. That is the theory and the fact. That is the reality behind the image. He wears only one hat, and that is the President's hat. There are no others. Only he has the right to reign and rule for four or eight years. Only he can act. The only task of the King's Men is to ensure that the vast resources of the executive branch help him to act sensibly. They are the synthesists of the modern Presidency.

2   The Congress

> "Here, Sir, the people govern."   —ALEXANDER HAMILTON

> "I am convinced that the office of the President is not such a very difficult one to fill, his duties being mainly to execute the laws of Congress."   —ADMIRAL GEORGE DEWEY

In Washington all roads lead to the Capitol. The gridiron pattern of minor streets begins its numerical and alphabetical progression from the small hill on which it stands, and thus the address of every house and government office is determined by its distance and direction from the Hill. The White House is 1600 Pennsylvania Avenue, NW, that is to say sixteen city blocks northwest of the Capitol. Rising above a platform of Senate and House office buildings, it is the exact center of the city which its dome was designed to dominate.

The building has enormous classical splendor. It looks down on the Mall to the Washington Monument and the Lincoln Memorial, and beyond to Arlington where lie the heroic dead of the Republic. One cannot but be impressed, that is if one looks determinedly toward the west.

The other prospects invite no comparison with Rome. Urban renewal has improved the southwest, but in other directions the half-empty railway station, the hotels past their prime, the shabby stores and crowding Negro slums are constant reminders that the citizens of the new imperial city have fled westward to where the power lies.

At times one cannot avoid the impression that the receding tide of power has left Congress stranded high and dry on its little hill, rather like an abandoned political Noah's Ark. Yet this is the Congress of the United States, in which the Constitution vests all federal legislative powers. It is also empowered to assess and collect taxes, historically the most potent power of a legislature, regulate interstate and foreign commerce, coin money, establish post offices and post roads, establish lower courts, declare war, and raise and maintain the armed forces.

The House of Representatives has the sole power of impeachment, and the Senate to try the impeached. The Senate must ratify all treaties and confirm all important Presidential appointments to office, including Cabinet members, federal judges, ambassadors, and military officers. Congress also authorizes administrative action under the Constitution, investigates government conduct, and holds the executive accountable.

Its members are directly elected by the people. Indeed, with the President they are the essential difference between Washington and Moscow or Peking. The administration below the President is appointed and not directly accountable to any electorate or to Congress. To that extent it is not so very different from the Soviet apparatus. Alexander Hamilton said of the House of Representatives at the New York Convention, "Here, Sir, the people govern." This proud defense may sound a little archaic nowadays, but the fact remains that members of both houses are directly accountable to the people.

Since the rise of the modern Presidency there has been no constitutional amendment to diminish the considerable powers of Congress, yet there is little honor for most of the 535 American descendants of de Montfort. It may well be argued that there is now little honor for legislators elsewhere, even in the parliamentary democracies. The reputations of French deputies have hardly recovered from the mess they made of the Fourth Republic. The latest stab at democratic government in West Germany has not enhanced the prestige of the *Abgeordneten*. The backbenchers in Britain have fared a little better, but executive authority requires the three-line whip and all the other instruments of party discipline.

The complexities of modern life clearly demand some subordination of the legislature to the executive, but this is small comfort for members of Congress who, unlike their colleagues in Westminster or the *Bundestag,* cannot hope to graduate to executive power as ministers. The aggrandizement of Presidential power has dealt hardly with Congress in more ways than one. Not only are its members shut off from executive power, unless they choose to run for President, but collectively they now wield little or no positive power. Congress has also been obliged to delegate authority to the executive despite the constitutional theory that this is impossible.

The extent of the change can perhaps best be indicated by the words of two Senators. Roger Sherman of Connecticut, the only member of the Continental Congress to sign the Declaration of 1774, the Declaration of Independence, the Articles of Confederation, and the Constitution, had this to say about the Presidency: "The Executive Magistracy [is] nothing more than an institution for carrying the will of the legislature into effect." Senator William Fulbright, the chairman of the Senate Foreign Relations Committee, said in 1965, "We are advised of what the administration is going to do. I often get a telephone call after 5 o'clock saying that there will be an announcement at 5:30 that such and such is going to take place. I don't complain about that. It isn't necessary for them to ask my advice unless they think my advice is worth something."

There were frequent assertions in the past that the "advice and consent" clause meant something more than the ratification of treaties and a late telephone call, but the fact of the matter is that Senator Fulbright's reading of the Constitution is now widely accepted. Even with domestic matters, where the constitutional position is clearer-cut than with foreign affairs, it is the President who drafts the legislative program. The President has in effect become the third house of Congress. To that extent the American Presidential system has moved closer to the British, despite the claims to the contrary.

Congress has not accepted its diminished stature with the weary grace of the Rhodes scholar from Arkansas. Apart from the breast-beating over executive usurpation of power, there have been sallies by Congressional forces into executive areas protected by the Constitution. For the most part the attackers have been beaten back, bloody if unbowed, as have most efforts to undermine executive positions by constitutional amendment. I do not automatically condemn such attempted trespass, as do many other observers. If there is need for Presidential aggrandizement, there is equally a case for redeployment of Congressional authority, but few American observers would seem to agree.

The *Sturm und Drang* up and down Pennsylvania Avenue engages many others, however, perhaps because they perceive through the smoke and clamor of battle the process of checks and balances at work. The separation of powers assumes inner conflict, of course, but Congressional reaction to the aggrandizement of the internal power of the modern Presidency is rather more than that.

Indeed, some Americans believe that the imbalance between the executive and Congress which has brought about the storm and stress is not entirely due to the extension of Presidential power. As they see it, unlike the Presidency the Congress has failed to adjust itself to the demands of the times. It is not a matter of snuffboxes and quill pens in the Senate, or archaic rules in the House. The rules can certainly hinder the advance into the mid-twentieth century, but they have been reformed too often in the past with little more than passing improvement. One argument is that Congress, as presently constituted, is incapable of adequately performing the functions now required of it.

All the fuss is said to be little more than the death throes of an ancient body that took the wrong turning in a Darwinian process of political development. What they seem to be saying is that the Constitution has failed in its prime purpose of establishing democratic government in the United States. It is a grave charge, and if Congress is not yet ready to be declared a permanent exhibit of the Smithsonian Institution, there is obviously something wrong with it.

The founders cannot escape some responsibility for the present dissatisfactions, even if they could not have been expected to free themselves entirely from the past. The House of Commons was their model, but Congress was not given a Prime Minister. The Speaker of the House of Representatives had to step into the breach, and whatever may be said of the tactics of Czar Reed and Speaker Cannon in the past, they were often necessary for effective action. The Speaker is now often a Presidential creature to the extent that the enactment of the official legislation is his first concern. He is a distinguished member of the leadership, or third house of Congress, but his leadership, to say the least, is not always effective.

The collapse of the party caucus, once for Republicans as stern as British party discipline, made indiscipline unavoidable. The passing of Congressional government completed the disarray. Its performance was less than ideal, and for reasons that still plague Congress, but what is politics without positive power? Congress still has to address itself to the question, but perhaps there are good reasons for avoiding it.

A likely one is that Congress has not well performed its vital representative function, because its members are delegates and not representatives. The charge is often echoed by English visitors, and is therefore suspect. Congress is an American institution functioning in the American environment for American purposes. Nevertheless, those who despair of Congress are fond of quoting an election address delivered by Edmund Burke in Bristol in 1774, and for that reason the relevant passages are given here.

Certainly, Gentlemen, it ought to be the happiness and glory of a representative to live in the strictest union, the closest correspondence, and the most unreserved communication with his constituents. Their wishes ought to have great weight with him; their opinions high respect; their business unremitted attention. It is his duty to sacrifice his repose, his pleasure, his satisfactions, to theirs, and above all, and in all cases, to prefer their interest to his own.

But his unbiased opinion, his mature judgment, his enlightened conscience, he ought not to sacrifice to you, to any man, or any set of men living. These he does not derive from your pleasure, no, nor from the law and the Constitution. They are a trust from Providence, for the abuse of which he is deeply answerable. Your representative owes you, not his industry only, but his judgment; and he betrays, instead of serving you, if he sacrifices it to your opinion. . . .

Parliament is not a congress of ambassadors from different and hostile interests, which interests each must maintain, as an agent and advocate, against other agents and advocates; but Parliament is a deliberative assembly of one nation, with one interest, that of the whole where not local purposes, not local prejudices, ought to guide, but the general good, resulting from the general reason of the whole. You choose a member, indeed; but when you have chosen him, he is not a member of Bristol, but he is a member of Parliament.

There are certainly very few members of Congress bold enough to address their constituents thus. They would not remain members very long. They do address their constituents on every possible occasion, and a typical American address was one given in 1965 by Representative Henry Reuss, Democrat from the Fifth District of Wisconsin. In reporting "the most productive session in the 177-year old history of Congress" he listed the following achievements:

(1) 2,032 residents of Milwaukee trained under the Manpower Development and Training Act; (2) $3,717,000 provided for the city's war on poverty; (3) a Small Business Development center in the city; (4) $36,500,000 for Wisconsin's schools and colleges; (5)

the Ice Age National Scientific Reserve near Milwaukee; (6) the felling of diseased elms by the Job Corps; (7) a Peace Corps training center at the University of Wisconsin; (8) a new post office and railway center; (9) the withdrawal of a federal objection to a harbor bridge; (10) the retention of a district customs office in Milwaukee.

Mr. Reuss, at the time, was a hard-working member of the House Committee on Banking and Currency, the House Government Operations Committee, and the Joint Economic Committee. He was more concerned with national and international questions than many of his colleagues, but an inordinate amount of his time had to be spent on running errands or taking care of the interests of his constituents. It is hardly likely that Burke would have had time to defend the American colonists by opposing Lord North's administration if he had been in Mr. Reuss's shoes.

Congressmen have long been required to act as delegates if they are to survive. It would be very wrong to read too much into large campaign contributions, but the recipients are expected to project the constituent's interests. The Capitol, in fact, houses a congress of ambassadors from different and often hostile interests. Congressmen must be agents and advocates. Mature judgment and enlightened conscience may be a trust from Providence, as Burke would have it, but if necessary they must be sacrificed for the benefit of the state or district.

Too much can be made of their delegate status. There were few Burkes from agricultural constituencies when Britain negotiated to enter the European Economic Community. Elected representatives everywhere ought to have a lively interest in the well-being of constituents. Who else is there? Perhaps Burke's sympathy for the American colonists would have been less had he not represented a seaport trading across the Atlantic.

It is a matter of degree, and if delegate status has been grossly enhanced in Congress, there are good historical reasons for it. Before the United States assumed superpower there were remarkably few occasions when the national interest in terms of foreign or defense policies was a lively issue. Isolationism was first continentalism, or an absorbing interest in the development of a subcontinent. There was no federal fiat. Members of Congress were elected by the developers. What better way could they represent their own states and districts than as delegates for those developing them? The system obviously worked well enough, if by the standards of the mid-twentieth century some activities were rather dubious.

Congress is a captive of its past no less than were the founders, but the new American circumstance is more demanding. Not only are members at the beck and call of business and other local interests, but they must share the concerns of the predominant ethnic group at home. These can range from some form of recognition for a national hero to federal jobs for their boys. They may be utterly irrelevant to the national interest, but not to the ethnic group seeking a national identity and the individual Congressman.

Federal patronage was one of the first prizes for Congressional agents and advocates. Bryce attributed considerable power to the Secretary of State because in his day the President was thought to be too preoccupied with patronage. President Lincoln was powerless without it when he pressed for the Thirteenth Amendment to abolish slavery. He decided that the only way to ensure ratification was to create a new state, Nevada, and he bought three House votes to guarantee the territory's admission to the Union.

The Presidential gift has declined considerably since President Jackson inaugurated the spoils system. Only about ten thousand appointments are still free of Civil Service regulation, and the competition has become intense. It can be a bore for President and Congressmen, but office seekers, if they no longer clutter the stairs of the White House, can no more be ignored than the local Chamber of Commerce or the Ancient Order of Hibernians.

Federal works projects soon became another prize, and the competition for defense contracts has been fierce in recent years. The stakes are high with defense spending running at some $50 billion a year, and as with salesmen the future of Congressmen can depend upon full order books. Many former members of the administration have campaigned for office with the claim that they intimately know the guardians of the federal cornucopia.

Much of the money goes to the industrial states, or those with acknowledged scientific facilities such as California or Massachusetts, but Congressmen will fight almost to the death for the retention of some obsolescent military post. In April 1966, when President Johnson could think of little else than the situation in Vietnam and its inflationary consequences at home, the New York Democratic delegation was up in arms against a proposed transfer of a military office from New York to Texas. When contracts are won, they are announced by the successful Congressman like so many battle honors.

Congressmen maintain staffs who do little else than take care of constituents, but they are also expected to intercede personally. This is but one aspect of what is known as the despotism of minorities and special interests. The term may be too harsh, and oblivious of American circumstance, but there can be no doubt that too much time is spent on appeasing mendicants from home at the cost of a proper consideration of larger issues. Some Congressmen act as if there is no larger issue, and are engaged most of the time in flagrant horse-trading.

Attempts have been made to hold the President to ransom even by members of the same party. The first bill of the Kennedy administration to reach the floor of the House was almost defeated by Democrats of Italian parentage because their community had been denied some patronage. Even with a determined Defense Secretary in command at the Pentagon military policies can be influenced by where the money is spent.

If Congressmen are rarely honored, they have their defenders who insist that the people still govern on the Hill. The shortcomings are admitted, but are seen to be the direct consequence of the realities of American political life. They do not argue about them; the realities are seen to be unarguable, but they see in the mire of the federal trough a strange alchemy that somehow brings forth a reasonable balance of interests. They concede the horse-trading, but suggest that it is not unlike diplomatic negotiation, perhaps rather more informal than the Congress of Vienna but nevertheless capable of satisfactory compromise.

They also suggest that the alchemy is understandable only to the initiated, and if the case for Congress is rarely heard, it is perhaps because there are very few initiates. The press and other communications media have gone where the power lies. The House and Senate press 'galleries are invariably more than half empty, and much that goes on in and out of the chambers is unreported. Great newspapers such as the *New York Times* have only three or four reporters permanently assigned to Congress.

It is, of course, immensely difficult to report. Maneuverings in the cloakrooms have for the most part replaced open debate, and there are few Congressmen who want to share cloakroom secrets. The committees, especially in the House, do much of the work, and only the spectacular hearings receive attention. Any number of inconsequential speeches were made in 1965 while 200,000 American troops were committed in Vietnam without a formal declaration of war, but there was no formal debate. There were a number of interesting exchanges in the Senate, but they were sparsely reported because reporters were not in the press gallery. The *Congressional Record* can be little more than a hodgepodge of speeches for local consumption, some of which are not actually delivered, and newspaper articles that caught the eye of some member. It might as well be published in Tibetan for all the public attention it gets.

I am not one of those initiated into the mysteries of Congress. Even members can still feel themselves to be outsiders after one or two terms. Nevertheless, I find it hard to disagree altogether with its defenders. The deficiencies of Congress are numerous, but it has succeeded in making democratic government work on a continental scale. I happen to believe that the liberties of the individual are better protected by the House of Commons, but it began with one great advantage. Fortunately Britain is a tight little island and not a subcontinental union of fifty states populated by peoples of diverse origin, and some of recent arrival.

The Westminster version of parliamentary democracy is not necessarily unworkable on a continental scale. India, the world's largest political democracy, is also a subcontinent and a union of states, each with its own governor and legislature. It has inherited almost unmanageable problems, the like of which have never confronted the United States, or any other political democracy for that matter. Nevertheless, it has remained remarkably stable largely because, I believe, the central government closely resembles the British model.

The President of India is in effect a constitutional monarch, and all executive power is vested in Parliament. The authority of the central government over the states is infinitely greater than in America. The President, on the advice of the Prime Minister, can depose a state government, and enforce Presidential or emergency rule until such time as it is considered appropriate to hold elections. The Indian state is merely an administrative unit. There is no suggestion of fictional sovereignty as with the American state.

Parliamentary democracy and this degree of centralism require national parties. They have their state organizations of course, but party discipline is generally observed in the Lok Sabah, or lower house. The platform of the ruling party is the government's program. Not so in the United States, where the Democratic and Republican parties are state parties first. There are not two but 102 parties, including those in the District of Columbia. The National Committees really come to life only at election time.

Their prime interest is the Presidential election, and the platforms are essentially accommodations to internal conflicts to help win the election. During the campaign the candidates are truly the party leaders. The successful candidate remains the titular head of the party after the election, but he cannot assume the loyalty of the Congressional party.

The reason is clear. Members, including those in close sympathy with the Presidential purpose, cannot always accept party discipline because it is essentially the discipline of the President, a national discipline that can be at odds with state or local requirements. Once again they must become ambassadors, agents, and advocates. It could not be otherwise for most of them because local pressures are too persistent and regional differences too great.

It was always so, and it is perhaps worth recalling the experience of John Adams at the Continental Congress of 1774, where he met Southern planters for the first time. He was horrified, and reported home how he dreaded the consequences of this dissimilitude of character. The wonder of it is that the Union survived the Civil War and Reconstruction, and the distempers of Congress are perhaps a small price to pay. They are the price exacted by American federalism and continental and ethnic differences. The future of India as a political democracy, it must be assumed, is still in doubt despite its parliamentary form of government and strong centralism.

I am almost persuaded that there exists in the United States a sinister conspiracy against democratic government, worthy of the attention of the House Un-American Activities Committee. The American circumstance requires the Congressman to be a delegate rather than a representative. In the House the Congressional system requires him to delegate much of his responsibility to standing committees which can meet in private and often appear unresponsive, if not downright disdainful, of what passes for the national interest.

In the House there is little debate of controversial legislation on the floor except under rules which can make it a mockery. Committee membership means remarkably little for a junior Congressman except as a promise of future power. The seniority system demands a discipline which enhances the authority of the ranking members, especially the chairman. Generally speaking, Congressional power in both houses is wielded not by members in Congress assembled, but by a handful of the more powerful chairmen. These elderly gentlemen are the final flowering, if that is the appropriate phrase, of the American delegate system.

The Constitution makes no mention of committees. It simply and unequivocably states: "All legislative Powers herein granted shall be vested in a Congress of the United States, which shall consist of a Senate and House of Representatives." Nevertheless, the committees have assumed positions of great and often crucial importance in the legislative process.

The chairmen, who can have power of life and death over legislation, are not an assembly of elders in whose collective experience is distilled the wisdom of Congress but independent Congressional chieftains. They are the archetype of another American political phenomenon, professional politicians who can yield rather less than nominal loyalty to the President and party. They are responsible only to their own state or district, which can be a captured one-party state or a rotten borough.

If the committee system has no constitutional authority, it has all the force of tradition, which dominates both houses of Congress. The system is almost as old as the Republic. In the beginning bills were first considered on the floor and then referred to a select committee, not unlike the practice of the House of Commons. It was dissolved as soon as the bill had been reported out, and during the Third Congress there were about three hundred such committees. To save time and introduce a little order, both houses turned to standing committees in the early nineteenth century.

Their numbers varied over the years; in 1913 there were 73 Senate standing committees, or almost one to a Senator. The Legislative Reorganization Act of 1946 reduced House committees from 48 to 19 and Senate committees from 33 to 15. This severe pruning in Washington's humid climate led to riotous vegetation, and in the sixties the grand total of standing committees, subcommittees, and joint subcommittees just exceeded three hundred. At the time of writing, the Senate committees and their numerical strengths were as follows. The number of subcommittees are given in parentheses.

Aeronautical and Space Sciences, 16	(none)
Agriculture and Forestry, 15	(5)
Appropriations, 27	(14)
Armed Services, 17	(5)
Banking and Currency, 14	(6)
Commerce, 18	(4)
District of Columbia, 7	(4)
Finance, 17	(none)
Foreign Relations, 19	(10)
Government Operations, 14	(6)
Interior and Insular Affairs, 16	(6)
Judiciary, 16	(15)
Labor and Public Welfare, 16	(7)
Post Office and Civil Service, 12	(5)
Public Works, 17	(4)
Rules and Administration, 9	(6)

There was also a Select Committee on Small Business, 17, and a Special Committee on Aging, 21. Each had 6 subcommittees.
The House committees were:

Agriculture, 36	(15)
Appropriations, 50	(12)
Armed Services, 38	(12)
Banking and Currency, 33	(7)
District of Columbia, 25	(6)
Education and Labor, 31	(9)
Foreign Affairs, 36	(10)
Government Operations, 34	(10)
House Administration, 25	(7)
Interior and Insular Affairs, 34	(6)
Interstate and Foreign Commerce, 33	(6)
Judiciary, 35	(7)
Merchant Marine and Fisheries, 31	(6)
Post Office and Civil Service, 25	(8)
Public Works, 34	(6)
Rules, 15	(none)
Science and Astronautics, 31	(6)
Un-American Activities, 9	(none)
Veterans' Affairs, 25	(5)
Ways and Means, 25	(none)

There was also a Select Committee on Small Business with 15 members and 6 subcommittees.

The joint committees were:

Atomic Energy, 18	(7)
Defense Production, 10	(none)
Economic, 16	(7)
Immigration and National Policy, 10	(none)
Internal Revenue Taxation, 10	(none)
Reduction of Nonessential Federal Expenditures, 15	(none)

There were more joint housekeeping committees and commissions such as the Battle of New Orleans Sesquicentennial Celebration Commission, but apart from these there was a total of 987 committee assignments. The Senate, being the smaller house, did best with about three assignments for each member. In the House the statistical average was about one and a half. The assignments tend to be permanent, although the occasional inadequate chairman has been persuaded to move elsewhere, and there is a scramble for membership on the more important committees as electoral defeat or death creates vacancies.

Party representation on the committees more or less reflects their strength in the Senate and House, and the chairman is always the senior committee member of the majority party. The senior of the minority party is known as the ranking minority member, and the crossing of party lines in Congress can begin in committee. After serving together for many years, senior members of both parties tend to generate a cooperative spirit. Their ages also help to blur party lines. If the Democratic Party tends to be the more liberal and adventurous party, the liberalism and adventurism can wear pretty thin in old age.

Not all the chairmen of the House, Senate, and joint standing committees are chieftains in the sense that they wield considerable power in vital areas of public life. Much obviously depends upon the jurisdiction of the committee, and the most powerful are the Appropriations and Armed Services committees in both chambers; Ways and Means, Rules, and Foreign Affairs committees in the House; and Finance and Foreign Relations committees in the Senate. But some of the subcommittees can be personal fiefdoms, especially in the Appropriations committees. The subcommittee's decisions are invariably accepted by the entire committee, and in turn by the parent body.

The system has been justified by the distinction made by John Stuart Mill "between the function of making laws, for which a numerous popular assembly is radically unfit, and that of getting good laws made, which is its proper duty." It is claimed to be the most logical organization available, without which Congress would be in a state of constant chaos. When more than twenty thousand bills can be introduced in a single Congress, it has obvious advantages.

The size of the House, 435 members, is also said to make useful debate impossible, although the House of Commons with 630 members manages nicely. A degree of specialization is clearly preferable if Congressional authority over the vast expenditures of modern government is to be meaningful. This requires something more than a nodding acquaintance with esoteric subjects such as nuclear energy and space science. Expert knowledge is assumed to be the fruit of years of specialization by members, who in turn are supported by their own personal assistants and committee staffs.

It is an assumption that cannot be easily dismissed, and some Englishmen are persuaded that the system could be profitably exported to Westminster. There, of course, authority is wielded only by the full assembly of the House of Commons. It does not delegate to committees the power of life and death over legislation and the conduct of investigation. The principle and theory of a bill, and its enacting clauses, are decided in open debate, with the social passions, party emotions, the flow of information, and the contending interests focused in the one body to the public view.

This is the theory, but there are Englishmen who claim that the Member of Parliament, without a personal staff or even office space, is ill-equipped to contribute much to debate. The kind of information produced by a good Congressional committee hearing is said not to be easily available. Despite the tradition of the Prime Minister informing the Leader of the Opposition on great national issues, the argument is that the latter can know remarkably little.

This can be described as the view of the new English Whigs, who look to Washington for ways and means of improving the Westminster system. There are many in Washington, especially the heads of departments, who agree that the committees could be exported to Britain. Indeed, they would like to see the entire apparatus exported, lock, stock, and barrel, across the Atlantic, or anywhere as long as it could be got rid of!

Certainly the work of reform has been troubled by a number of

c

problems, and the obvious one is jurisdiction or rather the overlapping of it. The most recent thorough reform, the 1946 Reorganization Act, tried not only to reduce the number of committees but also to divide responsibility among the three main groups. Request for spending authority was to be reviewed by the Appropriations Committees, the administering of appropriations by the Government Operations Committees, and policy by the legislative committees.

The organizational charts look very neat. Alas, some legislation unavoidably involves more than one committee. Or a chairman can insist that it does. Moreover, any bill involving the spending of money must go through the House mill twice. No appropriation can be approved unless it has been specifically authorized by a separate act of Congress. Thus all federal appropriations must be examined twice at the House committee level, first by the legislative committee with formal jurisdiction to authorize and then by the Appropriations Committee, or one of its subcommittees, and twice by the House itself. Then, of course, it also has to be approved by the Senate and signed by the President.

The unenthusiasm of the executive is at least understandable. As the *Congressional Quarterly* observed at the time:

Between January 30 and February 21, 1963, for example, Secretary of Defense Robert S. McNamara delivered 20 hours of testimony before the Senate Armed Services Committee during four days of appearances, 18 hours of testimony before the House Armed Services Committee during five days, and 27 hours of testimony before the House Defense Appropriations Subcommittee during six days—a total of 65 hours within a 3-week period.

This was not unusual, and hearings are only part of the budgetary process for the Defense Secretary. It can be a doubly wearing process. The committees have their experts capable and anxious to do their work well, but there are also members defending the interests of the individual armed services and manufacturers. Others simply do not like the Secretary's face. Many hours have to be spent in careful preparation, and the Secretary is not the only official of his department to testify.

Other departments have similar ordeals. The appropriation of the State Department is comparatively small, and the Foreign Relations and Foreign Affairs committees have always attracted men of high personal caliber. The Senate Foreign Relations Committee with its special responsibility for treaties enjoys considerable prestige, but it can never be sure of its jurisdiction. About half a dozen other committees invariably make their own claims, and about twice as many concern themselves with foreign economic matters. The House Appropriations Subcommittee on Foreign Operations has long had its own pet policies and phobias. The chairman for many years was opposed to foreign aid, and one member did not like diplomats.

Accountability, or the absence of it, is seen to be another drawback of the system. Committees are supposed to be responsible to the parent body, but the House, and to some extent the Senate, has largely abdicated to them responsibility over legislation. In the House it is seldom that anybody but members of the committee handling the bill is given the opportunity to speak in debate or to have an amendment accepted.

Committees, or their chairmen, can just sit on bills. Much important legislation never sees the light of day for years, and bills urgently wanted by the President can be subjected to inordinate delay. To discharge a bill from a reluctant House legislative committee requires a majority vote of the parent body on what is known as a discharge petition. The device has seldom been successful because members do not like to declare their positions or to record themselves in opposition to the chairman. At the time of writing, 349 petitions had been filed since 1923, but only 22 bills were actually discharged.

This is only one of the major legislative hurdles erected by the committee system. The chairman, after the bill has been reported out, must ask the Rules Committee to report a resolution, or rule, setting forth the terms of debate. A closed rule, normally given to complicated legislation such as a tax bill, permits no floor amendments. The House just has to accept the committee version. An open rule permits unlimited amendments, but the Rules Committee can specify the amendments that may be offered and place a time limit on debate. Or it can just sit on the bill.

The Rules Committee also has the very important power of deciding whether bills passed by the House and Senate in different form may be enacted. The unanimous consent of the House is required to send a bill to conference, where members of both houses compose their differences and perhaps rewrite much of the bill, or to consider Senate amendments to House bills. A single objection is sufficient to kill the bill, and it can only be revived if the Rules Committee reports, and the House agrees, to send it to conference.

The function of the Rules Committee is supposedly procedural, to schedule legislation for floor action. In fact it is a policy committee of supreme importance because the legislative timetable is one of the first concerns of the leadership. For that reason the majority party has long been overwhelmingly represented on it, no matter how small its majority may be in the House. Nevertheless the leadership has had its troubles because the chairman has simply assumed personal responsibility for the timetable. For many years he was a Southern conservative Democrat who just did not like modern liberal legislation and decided to delay or kill much of it.

He did not relent when a Democratic President was elected in 1960. Indeed, his opposition increased because President Kennedy proposed a program more liberal than that of his predecessor. The chairman could not be deposed by the House leadership, but a dramatic struggle ended with an increase of the committee's membership. The assumption was that the new and younger men would help to outvote the conservatives, but there is little reason to believe that the stratagem has brought permanent relief.

One device to overcome the Rules Committee is known as Calendar Wednesday. This permits chairmen to call up on Wednesday the bills reported by their committees, but it is used infrequently because of procedural delays. The Senate also has its troubles. To discharge a bill requires a majority vote on a motion made at least a day in advance, but Senators tend to be tolerant of their colleagues' intolerances and are generally loath to circumvent committees.

Of all the recognized weaknesses of the Congressional system the one that is said to be the most damaging is the seniority system. There are numerous arguments for and against it, but the main defense rests on the assumption that experience and age bring knowledge if not wisdom. It is also the easiest way of awarding assignments, and avoids favoritism and cloakroom plots. This is the argument that many find the most persuasive, but in 1963 there were complaints that liberals who had sought to reform Senate procedures were punished by being denied the committee assignments they were entitled to under the seniority system.

A member is rarely dropped from a committee unless he is thoroughly disliked by the chairman or party leadership, and as he rises from the bottom of the list his chances of being heard and managing major legislation increase. Most aspire to a subcommittee chairmanship and ultimately the chairmanship, but much depends upon the chairman. The pressure to conform is therefore considerable. Often they are on committees with jurisdiction over affairs that vitally affect their state or district. For instance, a member from an agricultural state tries hard to get on the Agricultural Committee. Once his ambition is realized it is more than his future is worth to antagonize the chairman.

The chairman's power to defy the leadership and the President depends largely upon the delegate system in all its infinite variations, his ability to do favors for others, and what the English used to call the old-boy net. Considerable as the interest of members may be in legislation designed to serve the national interest, political survival depends upon satisfying local demands. Much of this can take the form of pork-barrel legislation, a term derived from the old Southern habit of rewarding quiescent slaves with a barrel of pork. To get his pork, which may be some public works project, the member must secure the consent of those who control legislation, and in return he is expected to vote as he is told on other bills.

This is known as logrolling, another phrase from the American past when pioneers helped each other to clear the primeval forests and cut logs for building cabins or for burning. The pork barrel is supposedly in the hands of the leadership, whose loyalties are divided between the Presidency and Congress, but some chairmen have their hands in it. They also control appointments to the committee staff, and the disbursal of authorized travel funds. They are thus well equipped to reward the cooperative member and punish the independent, not only in their own committees but by logrolling with other chairmen.

At this level much depends upon the old-boy net, or the very human tendency to help one's own kind. The wrath of a chairman when a colleague does not play the game can be terrible, as Senator Wayne Morse (Democrat, Oregon) discovered in 1962 when he voted against an aquarium for Washington, D.C. The sponsor of this worthy educational project was Representative Mike Kirwan, chairman of the Appropriations Subcommittee on Public Works. Mr. Kirwan was not noted for a special devotion to piscatology, or to the disfranchised inhabitants of the District of Columbia. But he was, so the story goes, devoted to a legislative assistant, an enthusiastic fisherman, who when asked on his deathbed if he had a final wish mentioned a Washington aquarium.

An appropriation for $10 million was immediately requested, and the chairman was understandably incensed when the Senator said in debate that the money could be better spent on new textbooks for the District schools. He immediately caused the deletion of four Oregon projects from a pending public works bill. Senator Morse's pain was instant and articulate, but he showed no remorse and the squabble began to get in the way of other legislation. President Kennedy showed concern, and eventually the peacemakers reached an equitable arrangement. The Senator got his public works and the chairman his aquarium, but not before the thirty-fifth President was heard to use some strong language.

The ease with which most chairmen control their committees often astounds the outsider, but given the weapons and conditions mentioned here it generally amounts only to influencing a few members. For instance, of the fifteen members of the Rules Committee, five are from the minority party, who can often be assumed to oppose the President's legislative program. Most of those from the majority party, nine apart from the chairman, may be well disposed toward the President's program, but the chairman needs only two of them for an effective committee majority.

In other committees the party ratio reflects their strengths in the House. When the President's party is returned with an overwhelming majority, the chairmen's power is in theory and in fact often reduced. There are too many members of the majority party willing to vote for much of the President's program. But overwhelming victories are few and far between. The pendulum invariably swings, Presidents come and go, but not the chairmen or ranking minority members, at least generally not until death takes them to a more heavenly committee room.

The power of the committee chairmen was recognized at a very early stage. In 1816 a member from Kentucky said that the House had developed an "unconquerable indisposition to alter, change or modify anything reported by one of the standing committees." In his *Congressional Government,* Mr. Woodrow Wilson wrote: "The leaders of the House are the chairmen of the Standing Committees. Indeed, to be entirely accurate, the House has as many leaders as there are leading classes of legislation . . . each committee goes its own way at its own pace." The late Representative Clem Miller said in 1962, "The Committees with their chairmen are like a string of forts."

The modern Presidency has, of course, intruded upon the Congressional domain. It has been called the third house of Congress because it proposes major legislation, and maintains close liaison with the leadership. The President's special assistant for Congressional relations, and his staff, are lobbyists and extra whips. They also have their hand in the pork barrel. When one Western Senator criticized American involvement in Vietnam, President Johnson made it known that the Senator might have a little difficulty next time he wanted a dam for his state.

Yet Presidential power does not make many committee chairmen apprehensive. They are defended not so much by the separation of powers, a theory that is not so splendidly simple and effective as was once imagined, as by the Presidential inability to bring sufficient pressure to bear. Safe constituencies and the seniority system combine to bring about a power that the founders never dreamed of. If the power of the modern Presidency raises serious questions as to the validity of old constitutional theories, the chairmen do not so much reassert the constitutional authority of Congress as form a faction within it. They are political chieftains, enjoying an easy relationship with their peers but nevertheless as independent as was any medieval baron commanding the marches.

They are men who for the most part were from the beginning of their political careers consumed with a single ambition: to become a committee chairman. The so-called Potomac fever which infects many politicians when they see the White House rarely bothered them. They were immunized by their smaller ambition, and coming from safe constituencies they could afford to wait. Some are from one-party states where elections can be a mere formality, not unlike a Communist election except that the polls are desperately low. The primary can be the only democratic contest they need bother about, and it can be farcical if they have well served the machine or courthouses and other local interests.

These chieftains have helped to create the medieval environment of the modern Presidency. Their disdain of loyalty to the President and the national party, the modern equivalent of medieval fealty to the monarch, beyond a few conventional gestures is possible because of the strength of their local fiefdoms and the respect or caution their Congressional powers command. Obviously they prefer to have a man from their own party in the White House, but not if he challenges or tries to by-pass them.

Their primary interest is not to help select a President and support his program, but to defend their own position in Congress, in the state party, and at home. They are not, of course, indifferent to the national interest. They just do not feel constrained to accept the President's view of it. Some are not prepared to be persuaded, and are content if the balance of power permits them to retire to their committee keeps. There, with the drawbridge raised, they wait out the siege, the arrival of a royal messenger to negotiate, or the coronation of a new King-President.

A medieval monarch would surely recognize them, and the Presidential method of dealing with them. He must treat with them, and come to terms whenever necessary. He can never ignore them, even when returned with an overwhelming majority, as was President Johnson in 1964. Johnson had the country behind him, and could act like a medieval monarch reasonably certain of his subjects' fealty. Not so for President Kennedy. After the chairmen had taken their measure of him, much of his legislative program disappeared into the dungeons of committee castles, where it lurked until his successor effected a rescue. Nevertheless, Johnson was careful not to storm their battlements with his big battalions.

With all this, it is difficult for an Englishman to accept a common American view that Congress, as presently constituted, represents democratic government at its best. The delegate status of Congressmen appears to be less than ideal, and the further delegation of their national responsibilities to committees a grave dereliction of duty. This is not a criticism of committees as such. I think that the new English Whigs' admiration for the Congressional committee system, or what they take it to be, is understandable. A little more expertise would not be out of place in Westminster, although not by any means are all Congressional committeemen experts.

Rather am I criticizing the power yielded to the chairman, and the secrecy of the committee room. Patrick Henry, even though his preference for liberty over life was perhaps rather rhetorical, would have a hard time sounding off if he lived today and his personal modesty permitted him to represent Hanover County, Virginia, in Congress. It is unlikely that he would get a liberty-or-death bill into committee, but if he did, say, into the House Un-American Activities Committee, the chairman would surely sit on it in defense of property, commerce, and Americanism.

Americans have long been concerned about what has been described as the despotism of minorities in their political system, and the committee system seems so ordered as to ensure that it will long continue. Collectively the chairmen provide another form of despotism. In the Eighty-eighth Congress seventeen chairmen of House committees and fifteen of the ranking minority members came from rural areas. Most of the Democratic chairmen came from the South and the Republican ranking members from the Midwest. In the Senate twelve chairmen were from the South. These men from two unrepresentative areas wielded enormous influence in the affairs of modern urban America.

I have nothing against countrymen, or the South or Midwest. The politics of the latter seems to be as dreary as the landscape, perhaps because, as an American colleague once remarked, it is the politics of small-town businessmen who have just made their first million. The South, or rather the Southern politician, is much more sophisticated. Indeed, in many ways he provides a fine excuse for the existing system.

Perhaps it is the aristocratic flavor of their region, and the earlier devotion to the works of Sir Walter Scott. There may be a good deal of spuriousness behind the ante bellum houses and the courtly manners, there is obviously much sordidness, but the Southerner can take a larger view of life. Before the War between the States, it was said that the Southerner was interested in this world, and the Northerner in the next. Certainly the meanness of spirit of some Southern religious fundamentalist sects is not a trait of the politician. The first of the nation's great, Washington and Jefferson, were Southerners, and from Calhoun onward the names of Southern politicians read like a drumbeat of Congressional history.

Most of them have well served the Republic except—and it is an awful exception—in the matter of race. All their considerable parliamentary skill has been used to oppose Civil Rights legislation. Since 1917 when the cloture vote was introduced in the Senate, twelve have been taken to stop filibusters against Civil Rights bills, and only one

c*

was successful. The Southerners, although a minority, successfully thwarted attempts to introduce legislation against lynching, the poll tax, and literacy tests.

More than that, in their determination to maintain racial segregation they opposed much else of the Presidential legislative programs if only to repay the support received from other Senators in their racial struggle. Much of the recent malaise in Congress was due not only to the chieftains' defense of their fiefdoms against the modern Presidency but also to the Southern opposition to Civil Rights. It is possible that with passage of the Civil Rights Acts of 1964 and 1965 the worst has passed, for Congress if not for the country, but clearly there is something radically wrong with a system that allows two minority groups so much power to obstruct.

There has long been a good deal of talk about reform. The proposals have included joint hearings on appropriations bills, the transfer of committee authority from the chairman to the majority, the secret election of chairmen, and compulsory retirement at seventy. These and others may well be considered one of these decades, but there is little faith in reform as such. The House Rules Committee is one reason.

Before 1910 it functioned merely as an arm of the leadership in deciding which legislation should be brought to the floor, but was made independent after the revolt against the despotism of Speaker Cannon. It was supposed to have been a famous liberal victory for the Progressive movement, but over the years the committee became a bastion of conservatism, garrisoned by a coalition of elderly Democrats and Republicans. In many ways its despotism was not less than the Cannon variety until the battle of the superpowers of 1961. Then President Kennedy and the late Speaker, Sam Rayburn, a Congressional giant, had to do battle with the chairman, Representative Howard Smith of Virginia, just to add a couple of more Congressmen to the committee. As already suggested, there is little reason to assume that the victory will be a lasting one.

Much of this has made for dreary reading, but it must be admitted that the dreariness quickly disappears when one visits Congress. For a start, it does itself rather well. In 1965, according to a Budget Bureau estimate, Congress spent $179 million on itself, compared with $22 million in 1946 when the United States accepted the responsibilities of superpower. The Capitol has been given a new face lift, and more palatial offices have been built. The House Rayburn Building is said to be the most expensive office block in the world. But it is not the affluence that attracts—some of the new building is, in fact, rather ghastly—but rather the admixture of great age and politics.

Nowhere in Washington is the age of political America more obvious. The corridors are crowded with statues, there is even one of Lord Bryce, and great murals and paintings recall old glories. The civilized courtesy is as pervasive as the smell of furniture wax. Even the chairman of the Rules Committee for many years blocked legislation with the diffident grace of an old Virginia gentleman. The Negro waiters in the restaurants serve with the respectful familiarity of old family retainers. Wonderful monstrosities of overstuffed Victorian chairs fill the offices of the majority and minority leaders, and the cuspidors are polished every day.

One has to be remarkably insensitive to atmosphere not to be aware of the roots reaching back into the distant past. Englishmen are invariably first attracted to the House of Representatives, which was modeled on the House of Commons. Nevertheless it has its surprises for the pilgrim from Westminster. The Speaker is not an impartial chairman, but a party politician who can descend from the chair to participate in debate. The case-hardened rules and the outside demands upon its 435 members allow little or no time for deliberation. Bryce compared the noise and turmoil of the floor to the sound of short sharp waves in a Highland loch, fretting under a squall against a rocky shore. It is an apt description for conflict under rules as confining as any landlocked area. Nevertheless, there lies the mace, and if it is ornamented with the fasces of Rome and not the crown of colonial America, it suggests a classicism that influenced the other house at Westminster.

Its defenders also claim for it a legislative initiative proving the enlightened concern for the condition of the people it is supposed to represent. Rural electrification, aid for education, the Tennessee Valley Authority, and, indeed, most of the component bills of President Johnson's Great Society program are said to have first originated in the House. If they did not get very far without Presidential assistance, then the frustration is only a consequence of the fiercely competitive balance of interests within the nation that required, and in fact brought forth, the modern Presidency to resolve.

The Senate is a very different place with its hundred members, its fewer rules, and tradition of almost unlimited debate. It is safe to say that there is not another elective assembly quite like it anywhere in the world. It is not an upper house in the British sense. It does not necessarily provide a reflective balance to the hasty decisions of the other place as the House of Lords was supposed to do until it was stripped of almost everything but its coronets and ermine. Indeed, both houses of Congress are supposed to be co-equal as are other components of the federal government. The Senate initiates legislation, and has even disputed the exclusive right of the House on money matters.

Article I, Section 7, of the Constitution states: "All bills for raising Revenue shall originate in the House of Representatives; but the Senate may propose or concur with Amendments as on other Bills." The qualification concedes some authority to the Senate, but in 1962 Senator Carl Hayden, chairman of the Senate Appropriations Committee, held that the Senate could initiate its own appropriations bills as well as amend those passed by the House. Representative Clarence Cannon, the chairman of the House Appropriations Committee, took exception to this of course, and for some months the dispute denied the administration the funds it urgently required. At one time it degenerated into a wrangle over where the two committees could meet to resolve their differences, and there was talk of calling in surveyors to establish the middle point between the two chambers. A series of compromises rescued the government from bankruptcy, but a permanent solution is not anticipated.

Nevertheless, the Senate has the air of a superior chamber, and in their heart of hearts most members of the other house would probably concede that this is not altogether misleading. Senators are after all ambassadors of states, and their period of office, six years compared with two in the House, enhances their sense of tolerant dignity.

It is also a continuing body of equals who, in Webster's words, know no master and accept no dictation. There is in fact an inner establishment, as in almost every group or assembly, but there is no Speaker to exert authority. The Vice President of the United States sits as President of the Senate, but with a vote only in case of a tie. He is relieved as required by the President Pro Tempore and other

Senators, generally very junior ones, but in any case his authority in questions of order is very limited.

Here, tradition has it, is a chamber in which to debate the great issues and where great thoughts can shine through the rhetoric. They occasionally do. Many great debates have been recorded, but very many more distracting and delaying speeches. The filibuster has become the great defensive weapon for liberals as well as conservatives, and there are respectable men who regard it as the best defense against what is known as the transitory majority. Nevertheless, the Senate is less exposed than the House to steamroller tactics, and freedom of debate also gives it a whip hand over legislation.

The chamber has not always resounded with the rolling periods of Clays, Calhouns, and Websters. After the Senate wrested power from the Presidency in the post–Civil War period, many of its members were party bosses, spoilsmen, and creatures of the industrial barons. The main reason was that Article I, Section 3, of the Constitution provided for the appointment of Senators by state legislatures and in effect created a number of rotten boroughs. Many of the legislatures were bought, and with them Senate seats. In buying the power to decide which railroads to build and industries to protect with tariffs, the industrial barons legally wielded a power that would have shamed the robber barons of old.

They went too far, of course. Even some of the state legislature worms turned, and in 1911 reformers such as Senator Robert La Follette of Wisconsin and Senator William Borah of Idaho secured the passage of the Seventeenth Amendment (ratified May 31, 1913) providing for direct election to the Senate. Its subsequent members, with a few exceptions, have been generally regarded as pillars of propriety. In recent years they have collectively become more liberal, except on Civil Rights. Their delegate function is still considerable, but on the whole they have come closer than members of the House to Burke's ideal of an elected representative.

Age and continuity are not the only attractions of Congress. The executive branch is swollen with brigades of well-educated men led by industrial titans on leave from great corporations, ornaments of the American Establishment, and experts of acknowledged distinction, yet in government there is nothing like a politician. Very few who have not run for public office can intimately know the separate political components of political America, its ambitions and venality as well as its higher aspirations and common sense. Fewer have the instinct for compromise, even between venality and morality when necessary. This is no place to eulogize politicians of any nationality, although heaven knows they could do with a little sympathy, but perhaps it is as well to quote Einstein. When once asked why politicians had failed to keep pace with the scientists, he said that politics was much harder than physics.

It is a conclusion I would no more dispute than the Einstein general theory of relativity or for that matter his development of Planck's quantum theory, and to my mind American politics is the hardest and most sophisticated in the world. Not every Congressman is a sophisticated politician, but the American political system demands more from its participants than others do. In comparison the life of the British Member of Parliament is undemanding, simple, and well ordered.

In modern Britain there is no separation of powers as there was in medieval times or in the modern United States. It is a union of kingdoms, but government is unitary not federal. The judiciary is of course independent, but supreme legislative authority is vested in the Queen in Parliament, that is to say, the House of Lords and the elected House of Commons. Within practical limits there is nothing that it cannot legally do. In law, its supremacy is absolute, and in fact this means the Commons. The upper chamber, the House of Lords, passes all financial and appropriations bills without amendment. It cannot delay other bills for long, or require the Commons to accept its amendments. The Lords is now only a useful deliberative body providing time for further reflection, and it has little power in the accepted political sense.

Thus for a beginning the British legislative system is structurally simpler than the American in that there is one house which is supreme. The simplicity could make for a dangerous instability, but this has been avoided because the House of Commons is not absolutist in practice. The theory is that Members bear in mind the common law, which has grown up for a thousand years or more, and act as far as possible in accordance with precedent and tradition. This is the textbook answer, and it is another way of saying that the British have an enhanced sense of country and national unity. Given absolute power, Parliament tends to use it with great caution. The proof, I think, is that the liberties of the individual are better protected than under the American system with its defined powers. The checks and balances are, as it were, built in and not imposed.

There are also no set terms of office. The statutory life of Parliament is five years in time of peace, but it is more often less. The Commons is therefore necessarily more responsive to the electorate, and the executive stands or falls on what amount to votes of confidence. The degree of responsiveness is influenced by the size of the majority, but in any case party discipline is essential. Whatever may be said about the three-line whip, a device so called because notices of important votes are thrice underlined, it again simplifies life for the backbencher or ordinary Members. Some do bolt the party whip from time to time, but rarely the government whip when majorities are small.

Majority rule, if nothing else, is absolute. Everything is decided by a straightforward 51 percent majority vote of those present, or less. (The Commons has 630 members, and a bare majority can be fractionally less than 51 percent.) There is no question of a two-thirds majority to amend the Constitution, because there is no such document. There can be no filibusters, because there is no cloture rule requiring a two-thirds majority vote. There are no committee chairmen who can obstruct, or unofficial coalitions of liberals or conservatives from both parties. Party discipline also protects the Member from the importunities of constituents. The strict control of electoral expenses ensures that he does not become obligated to those who might have been canvassed to meet them had they been higher. Traditionally he is a representative and not a delegate. Party rivalry and strife can be more intense than in Congress, but the minority party generally agrees that the majority must govern, which in turn sets aside time for minority criticism to be heard. The detailed arrangements of government business are settled, under the direction of the Prime Minister and the Leader of the House, by the government chief whip in consultation with the opposition chief whip.

This is a brief and incomplete account of the British system. It is not put forward here as a model for all other countries, but to suggest how much easier life is for the Member of Parliament than for the Congressman. It is a prelude to an anthem of praise to Congressmen and the manner in which they shoulder their heavier burden.

The introductory passages have been played already—the delegate status of Congressmen, the duplication of legislation, the committees, the chairmen, the rules, and the seniority system. Much of this could make insupportable demands on a Congressman's time. For instance, the 1951 report of the Senate Government Operations Committee on Congress said that constituency work consumes about 80 percent of a Congressman's working day. It is not all trivial. Nor does it always serve special interests. One estimate has it that 30 percent of a Congressman's time is spent seeking redress for ordinary constituents. There is in fact a direct relationship with the growth of federal power.

The country is big, the federal system complicated, and its bureaucracy cumbersome. The average supplicant feels that he can only find his way through the distant labyrinth with the guiding hand of his Congressman. Much of this work is therefore similar to that done in Scandinavia by the Ombudsmen. The appointment of such an official has been proposed to share with the Congressman responsibility for Social Security and veterans' problems, complaints against the armed services, claims of discrimination in defense contracts, and immigration disputes. It is unlikely to be pursued.

The Congressman is, of course, helped by a personal staff. A member of the House can have from seven to ten in Washington, and one or two in his district; a Senator from fifteen to more than thirty, of whom several might be in his state. Their offices would also make foreign politicians envious, but the problem remains fundamentally undiminished. There is now much more to do than in the past and only about the same number of Congressmen to do it. The dimensions of the problem were well described by Vice President Humphrey.

As a Senator in 1949 he had an office with four rooms and two telephones, and he received about fifty letters and thirty calls a day. An out-of-town visitor was an event. In 1962 he had eight office rooms and twelve telephones, answered five hundred letters and a similar number of telephone calls a day, and received an average of 120 visitors. By that time Mr. Humphrey was an important member of four committees, the Senate Majority Whip, and a member of the chamber's inner club. Nevertheless, about half of the visitors were constituents, and his state of Minnesota is a thousand miles and more from Washington.

This extralegislative work perhaps provides another reason for the committee system, and the same Senate committee reported in 1957 that about 90 percent of legislative business was transacted in committee. It added, however, that Senators had insufficient time to give to committee work. The situation would be desperate, no doubt, if it were not for the Congressman's personal staff. Its members also spend most of their time on constituency work, but collectively they and the Congressman can be assumed to have more time to give to legislative matters than the backbencher in Westminster, who is not provided even with a personal secretary.

If I may digress briefly, this would seem to suggest that the United States has moved toward political collectivism. I have described the Presidential institution with its component staffs of at least two thousand officials. Now it can be seen that the good people of the United States vote into power not so much 535 Congressmen as so many Congressional institutions. The Hamiltonian theory of a people's government has been further diminished. The people now govern to a large extent through the Presidential institution. They elect the President, but have no control over the appointment of the thousands who are the muscle, sinew, and nerve center of the Presidential institution, and individually these can be very much more powerful in their own field than elected representatives.

Inevitably because of the press of work, the Congressman has also acquired his own staff. It can be said to be one of the few Congressional adjustments to the conditions of modern America, but a Congressman can be terribly dependent upon his staff. Any well-informed reporter at the Capitol can identify the staff source of legislative proposals as well as some of the rhetoric. Some committee staffs have assumed a life of their own, and issue reports on a number of subjects and problems.

There is nothing unusual in this further delegation of political authority and labor, except again in degree. Joseph Schumpeter, the Austrian political economist, has defined elective government as government by competing elites. The vote is still fundamental, but it does not decide the policies a government follows. Rather does it determine who is to choose them. The United States should perhaps be congratulated for devising means of governing itself in the second half of the twentieth century without doing too much damage to its eighteenth-century Constitution.

The land of the ghost writer has invented what could almost be called the ghost President and Congressman. Indeed, almost every responsible official in Washington, elected or appointed, seems to lack substance as he moves about accompanied by counsels, special assistants, and speech writers. It is all very necessary, but one can wonder if the Declaration of Independence and the Gettysburg Address would have inspired the nation and much of the world if they had been written by a ghost Jefferson and Lincoln. One cannot imagine an institutionalized Churchill leading Britain in her finest hour. But I digress.

Times have changed, and if the essential nature of Congress is still what the Constitution says it is, its power is less than was earlier assumed for it. It now rarely initiates important legislation, but rather processes the President's program. It exercises some surveillance over the executive, but knows it to be incomplete. Despite its investigating authority, it is still largely dependent on information provided by the executive, which is unlikely to produce any that might cast doubt on its own wisdom.

The fiscal role of Congress, the authority to provide government agencies with money to perform their functions, is said to be its principal source of power over the executive. The authority is indisputable. Article I, Section 9, Paragraph 7, of the Constitution says: "No money shall be drawn from the Treasury, but in Consequence of Appropriations made by Law. . . ." Since 1837 the House has also required that appropriations must be previously authorized by law, that is, authorization as well as appropriations bills must be enacted.

This double grip on the nation's purse strings is supposed to strengthen Congressional control over the executive. The theory is that the President goes up the Hill cap in hand and offers his program for approval. Congress magisterially signifies its pleasure or displeasure by granting or withholding funds. As much else in this age of Presidential power and federal budgets in excess of $100 billion, the reality is not so simple.

For a start, Congressional control is relatively limited. There is little control over departments and agencies with normally consistent expenses. Certain fixed expenses also recur annually, such as veterans' benefits and interest on the public debt ($5,100 million and $11,100 million respectively in 1965), which circumscribe the power to vote appropriations. Then departments with long-range procurement programs can require authorization years before payment is required. This is especially true of the Defense Department, which accounts for half of the federal budget. Thus proposed expenditures for any given year may have been authorized by previous Congresses, and be beyond the control of the Congress to which the budget is submitted. In the budget proposed for 1965 about $40 billion of the $97.9 billion requested had already been authorized.

"Backdoor spending" is a term for numerous devices used by executive agencies to escape Congressional control, and there are contingency funds enabling the President to intervene in foreign crises without a Congressional consent. In any case, the budget is so large, the purposes it is to finance so varied and numerous, and the budgetary process so complicated, that Congressional control, as normally assumed, cannot exist. Only the Bureau of the Budget, which is part of the Presidential institution, can control it, and this was hardly the intention of the founders.

Congress can oppose, it can raid agencies it does not much like and make life generally burdensome for the executive. It can wallow in pork barrels, but it cannot control. At best it can delay, but it cannot dictate. When it authorizes and appropriates for programs that the President does not want, he can simply refuse to carry them out. The constitutional power of Congress has diminished, but not that of the President.

Collisions between the President and Congress are rarer than the rhetoric would suggest. A $100 billion budget is a very sophisticated business, and there can be a close working relationship between the experts of the agencies and the Congressional committees. Congress also has a great deal to contribute. The Presidential institution has no monopoly of wisdom or knowledge. Bills and budgets can be, and are, improved by Congress. Its investigations often bring about a new and better understanding of complicated situations. If this is considerably less than the power of Congressional government as exercised in the second half of the nineteenth century, it remains immensely important.

Nevertheless, this is not its prime collective function, nor the most sophisticated. The United States, one must constantly remind oneself in these days of Presidential and federal power, is a union. The quasi sovereignty of the states is to some extent a legal fiction, but singly or in groups their territorial boundaries do encompass, and their politics defend, vastly different regions and interests. In internal affairs—and most Congressmen normally see them to be the most important—the prime function is to reconcile the internal differences of the Union.

For the Congressman, it is rather like a game of three-dimensional chess under the most severe rules. He must try to satisfy the demands of his constituents, which is the first dimension. The second is to serve the national interest, and the third to strike a balance with state or regional interests. It is a difficult game that no British politician is called upon to perform. The variation of compromise is infinite. The horse-trading, the logrolling, and the pork barrel are part of it, and if they appear to be questionable instruments, they can nevertheless amount to a very delicate process.

The chess game explains to a large extent the failure of Congress to reform itself according to the dictates of political scientists into an efficient legislating machine such as the House of Commons. Reforms tend to mean more discipline, and there can be no party discipline in the British sense when the constituency and regional interests of Congressmen belonging to the same party are in conflict. It may be regretted by the purists, but the crossing of party lines to form loose coalitions to defend common interests is inevitable. It is no doubt doubly regrettable when lines are crossed to defend questionable interests, but is equally inevitable given the state of human development anywhere in the world.

The confusion and frustration can be great, but one majority leader in the House said that it was the lesser of two evils. The larger was splinter parties, and perhaps the eventual Balkanization of the United States.

The internal conflicts are further increased, of course, by the separation of powers. It creates an intense competitiveness, which in Congress often tends to break through what for an Englishman are the unnatural limits placed upon an elected legislature denied executive authority and liable to judicial review. It explains, I think, forays against executive power such as the Bricker Amendment and the innumerable bills introduced to reduce the authority of the Supreme Court. It encourages intemperate demands while the absolutism of the House of Commons requires caution. Competitiveness, which in any case is a national characteristic, is further enhanced by constituency and regional pressures.

The national interests, the primary concern of the President, although of course he is not the only patriot, could be trampled in the rough and tumble of competitive politics were it not for what appears to be the instinctive distrust of simple majority rule. The distrust is more prevalent among the established classes and older ethnic groups, but it still pervades the system. It is here where the political processes of the United States and Britain are sharply different, and of course there are historical as well as other reasons for it. Without a written Constitution, the aristocratic factions of eighteenth-century Britain could develop over the decades into modern political parties. It was not accomplished without a struggle, of which the Reform Bills are the legislative monuments. Nevertheless, there was an acceptance even then of the inevitability of the consequences of popular representation, although few could have anticipated that a Socialist party would emerge and replace the descendant of the old Whig oligarchs in the two-party system.

In the United States, however, the counterparts of the Tory and Whig parties did not see independence as a transfer of power from a king to the people. George Washington feared that a sovereign people, like its royal predecessors, would be subject to what he described as the various passions which are the concomitants of fallibility. The suspicion of the smaller states of the more populous, the first political demonstration of regional interests, led to the creation of the Senate, the first unequal political institution. Suspicion of majority rule was thus enshrined in the Constitution. Subsequent suspicion, fed largely by immigration, allowed what Englishmen would regard as the growth of unequal practices.

Much of what is said to be wrong with Congress continues because of this suspicion of simple majority rule. The ultimate authority is of course the American people, but there is a general refusal to see it in the opinions of 51 percent of the people at any particular election. Simple majorities decide most elections, as they do most of the legislation enacted by Congress, but there is a readiness to accept much that impedes Congressional business, to escape simple majority decisions. This is true of the filibuster and of the power of committee chairmen to block legislation.

Rationalization is often sought in the Constitution. It requires a two-thirds majority for constitutional amendment and the ratification of treaties. Therefore, the argument goes, almost anything that makes a simple majority decision harder to reach has the blessing, once removed as it were, of the founders. I am not so certain that those gentlemen would have accepted the Southern obstructionism to Civil Rights, although they did dodge the question of slavery. A close reading of the Constitution has not persuaded me that an overwhelming public demand is required to prevent lunatics from buying high-powered rifles from a mail-order house to shoot Presidents and lesser citizens.

The argument cannot be defended on constitutional grounds. Nevertheless, it is difficult to refute as a practical argument because of the American circumstance. Despite all the political theories, and a great deal of high-sounding nonsense, in a union of vastly different regions and peoples the welfare of one ought not be improved at the expense, or what is seen to be the expense, of others. Therefore when a Congressman plays his three-dimensional chess, he cannot always treat a bill on its merits. Even when he favors it, and is a member of the President's party, the other considerations cannot be ignored.

Three-dimensional politics leads to indecisiveness. It perhaps also helps to explain what Europeans see as the innate conservatism of America. With controversial legislation, especially when it does not benefit his constituents directly, a Congressman tends to sit on the fence. A little dissatisfaction expressed at home can quickly persuade him to straddle it. The opinion of his committee chairman can make him lift a tentative foot, or hook it more securely under the rail. The only thing that can really move him, and a majority of his colleagues when they are not vitally concerned, is a strong national consensus.

Consensus has become the magic word in American politics. With a consensus, it is said, almost anything can be achieved, and little or nothing without it. One must also add that what progress is achieved can be abysmally slow because a working consensus is generally believed to be a measure of popular support for action equal to about two-thirds of the electorate. It is impossible to be precise; much depends upon the issue at stake and the strength of the President's party in both houses of Congress, but fortunately, if gratuitously for the constitutionalists, most American politicians act on the assumption that controversial legislation, especially that effecting social reform, requires a measure of popular support fractionally not much less than the number of votes for the amendment of the Constitution.

The significance for the President is clear. Electoral victory is in more ways than one only the first step toward the realization of his program. Every controversial bill must be submitted to what amounts to a haphazard referendum, a fact that can make life very difficult for him in that it requires a more vigorous leadership than that expected of most other heads of government. In many cases, the consensus may exist but is disorganized or not very articulate. The President must make it be seen to exist. He must campaign for it, with the assistance of citizens' groups that are invariably created for the purpose. The interest of the press and television must be aroused, speeches delivered, and personal appearances made.

It is no less significant for Congress. In encouraging popular interest, consensus politics can help individual Congressmen to resolve their three-dimensional chess problem. Special interests can successfully persuade them to ignore a simple majority opinion, but the interests can be disarmed by a large consensus. A recent example was the public outcry over the lack of safety measures in the construction of automobiles which caused the country's largest industry and its powerful Congressional lobby to retreat. Extraconstitutional checks within Congress, such as interparty coalitions, the committee chairmen, and exploitation of the rules, can generally be overcome when it is demonstrably proved that an overwhelming majority of the electorate will not be gainsaid.

It is possible that these checks are part of an ordained and grand design to maintain the Union and keep the Republic free and brave. As reported earlier, I have failed to find the evidence in the tablets handed down by the founders. If the size of the consensus is part of the price exacted from the President by the Congressional chieftains, the reason why their power remains seriously unquestioned is largely because of the widespread suspicion of simple majority rule.

On the whole, the power of the chieftains works against Congress. Consensus politics requires energetic Presidential leadership, but in meeting or creating wide popular demand the Presidency is strengthened. Consensus politics, when successful, brings political unity to a union of diverse regions and peoples, to a subcontinental industrial society caught up in the triple revolution, and it unites them under the President.

There are Congressmen who believe that their power has been largely reduced to a sort of veto power. They exaggerate, but given all the essentials of consensus politics, the issue, Presidential leadership, and wide popular support, that veto or blocking power can be overridden. Consensus politics is for the President what party discipline is for the British Prime Minister. It demands a good deal more from him, but simplicity has never been the hallmark of American politics. If politics is harder than physics, the American variety is the hardest, for the individual Congressman as well as for the President.

3 The Supreme Court

"This Court neither approves nor condemns any legislative policy. Its delicate and difficult office is to ascertain and declare whether the legislation is in accordance with, or in contravention of, the provisions of the Constitution; and having done that its duty ends."
                                    —JUSTICE OWEN J. ROBERTS

"Preoccupation by our people with the constitutionality, instead of with the wisdom, of legislation or executive action is preoccupation with a false whim."   —JUSTICE FELIX FRANKFURTER

"But law is again coming alive as a living process responsive to changing human needs. The shift is to justice and away from fine-spun technicalities and abstract rules."
                              —JUSTICE WILLIAM J. BRENNAN, JR.

The United States Supreme Court sits in a marble Corinthian temple dwarfed by the massive splendor of the Capitol and the Congressional office blocks. It is appropriately withdrawn, and essentially as modest as the White House. Not even the rather grand sweep of steps suggests that it is the repository of great restraining power or, as its critics would have it, unrestrained power. Despite the marble and the ordered solemnity of the chamber, it has in fact been for many years a fount of revolutionary power requiring and obtaining radical change in American society. If, as at 1600 Pennsylvania Avenue, NW, the monumental architecture of official Washington has failed to announce where the power lies, the Court has succeeded wonderfully in demonstrating the vitality of the renewing processes of American democracy.

Juridical success has been achieved in reinterpreting the Constitution, an eighteenth-century document written for thirteen primitive seaboard states, to meet the demands of the largest industrial superpower of the nuclear age. Its political success—and let there be no doubt whatsoever that the Court is capable and willing to act as a political institution—has been in formulating answers for fundamental problems that the executive and legislative branches failed or refused to solve. This is a proud record, but perhaps the greatest success, the third one achieved by the Court, has been in asserting and defending the freedom and rights of all citizens.

Since the *Brown* v. *Board of Education* decision of 1954, which declared racial segregation in schools to be unconstitutional, it has once again become the storm center of controversy. The creative period of the fifties and sixties was preceded by years of enlightened precedent, and there is small reason to believe that it will not continue for some time to come. History suggests that enlightenment and power are cyclical, propelled by forces that are not always apparent. The Court may again move into a period of quiet and caution, but new traditions have been established and one can assume that they will surely long guide the Court whenever necessary.

This triple crown of success has been fashioned from the forces of the same triple revolution that helped to establish the modern Presidency, but unlike that large institution it is worn by a court of limited jurisdiction, narrow processes, and small capacity for handling mass litigation. Its independence is unquestioned, but in vital respects it is a dependent body. The justices enjoy life tenure, but they are nominated and confirmed by the political branches. Their number may be changed at any time. The only condition is agreement between the two other branches. At present they are nine, but the Constitution fixes no limit. The executive's power to increase or reduce membership in order to influence the course of decision was used before it was proposed by President Franklin Roosevelt in the famous but ill-fated attempt to pack the Court in 1937.

Its jurisdiction is appellate and original, and the latter, although irrevocable, is limited. Article III, Section 2, of the Constitution states:

The judicial Power shall extend to all Cases in Law and Equity, arising under this Constitution, the Laws of the United States, and Treaties made, or which shall be made, under their authority . . . to all Cases of admiralty and maritime Jurisdiction . . . to Controversies between two or more states; between a State and Citizens of another State; —between Citizens of different States; —between Citizens of the same State claiming Lands under Grants of different States, and between a State, or Citizens thereof, and foreign States, Citizens or Subjects.

In all cases affecting Ambassadors, other public Ministers and Consuls, and those in which State shall be Party, the supreme Court shall have original Jurisdiction. In all the Cases before mentioned, the supreme Court shall have appellate Jurisdiction, both as to Law and Fact, with such Exceptions, and under such Regulations as the Congress shall make.

The radical Congress of the immediate post–Civil War period voted that the Court had no jurisdiction over the first Reconstruction Act, and the Court submitted. The Court is also dependent upon the political branches for the enforcement of its mandates, and President Andrew Jackson once withheld enforcement. He said of the then Chief Justice, "John Marshall has made his decision—now let him enforce it." But the most significant and perhaps least comprehended limitation is that judicial power extends only to cases and controversies. There is no question of advisory opinions. The Court can only decide lawsuits, it acts for the most part on the record of inferior courts, and its decisions generally bind only the parties concerned. A Court decision therefore can often be merely a weather vane showing which way the judicial wind is blowing—a precedent that the Court is likely to follow in similar cases.

It also seems to be overworked. In an average term, from October to June, the Court passes upon about fifteen thousand cases, and writes perhaps a hundred opinions. When a case is argued, the maximum time allowed to each side is about one hour, and is often less. The Court then meets in conference, never in small committees, and the nine justices act on every petition expressly or by acquiescence. Statistically, only about three or four minutes can be given to each case, an inadequate time in which to initiate a social revolution, declare unconstitutional an act of Congress, or right a wrong against an individual. A great many petitions, some frivolous, are of course disposed of without discussion, and it must be assumed that others are not taken up because the time may not be ripe for demolishing or establishing legal precedents influencing government and society.

As already mentioned, appointment to the Court is a political gift, and the justices are supposed to reflect the political color of the

Presidents who appointed them. They have been known to divide along party lines in the past. Appointment can also be a political reward or pay-off, but the record suggests that on the whole Presidents have dispensed this form of patronage with great care or that the Court creates justices in its own image.

Experience on the bench is not required, and members of the Court come from very different backgrounds. At the time of writing, the Chief Justice was Earl Warren, who had been Governor and Attorney General of California and earlier a district attorney. Justice Abe Fortas was an old friend of President Johnson, who appointed him. Justice Hugo Black, subsequently honored for his liberalism, was a member of the Ku Klux Klan in his youth, and Justice Byron White an All-American football player. All were men of distinction, but only Justice Black had previously sat on a bench, and that was in a police court.

There is much for the critics to complain about, but criticism and attacks have been of little or no avail. The Court is indispensable to government under a written constitution. It is also a unit of a complex, interdependent scheme of government from which it cannot be severed, and the supremacy it enjoys is sustained by public veneration. Despite the bills frequently introduced in Congress to reduce its jurisdiction, it is generally seen to be the most detached, dispassionate, and trustworthy custodian of the Constitution. Given this veneration and support, it is free to exercise its supremacy, which rests on the power to hold unconstitutional and judicially unenforceable an act of the President, the Congress, or a state.

This power is not expressly granted by the Constitution, but rather rests on logical implication. The logic was first seen and established by Chief Justice John Marshall (1755–1835), who saw the Constitution as an instrument of national unity and federal power. It might be added that there is no direct reference in the Constitution to the separation of power and checks and balances, or any of the other fine theories that rationalized the process of its remarkable transformation from a precise and rather prosaic document to a living instrument of government. The process was of course influenced by many forces, but in having the last legal word the role of the Court was considerable.

We return here to that area where democratic government defies the explanations of the political scientists and borders on the semi-mystical. And again some comprehension may be found in comparing the American and British systems, if only because they stem from the same ancient sources. Britain, although it is a unitary state, does not have a single body of law, and certainly no written constitution. Separate systems are in force in England, Wales, Northern Ireland, and Scotland. Their one common feature is that there is no complete code. Their sources of law include statutes and unwritten or common law. The common law of England originated in the customs of the realm and was added to by court decisions. A supplementary system, known as equity, came into being during the Middle Ages to provide and enforce more effective protection for existing rights. It was administered by a separate court until 1873, when the two courts became one and the law of equity prevailed.

Statute law includes Acts of Parliament and delegated or subordinate legislation made under powers conferred by Parliament. It is absolutely binding on all courts of the United Kingdom, taking precedence over any other source of law. The British judiciary is of course independent, in reality more independent than the American bench, but there is no judicial review. The absolute power of Parliament is again evident. Nor does the authority of British statutes differ. All are made by Parliament, and all can be changed by Parliament. What are called constitutional statutes—Magna Carta, the Bill of Rights, the Act of Settlement, and the Act of Union with Scotland—are ordinary laws. They can be repealed by Parliament at any moment in exactly the same way as it can repeal the nationalization of the steel industry or increase the duty on beer or tobacco.

The American system is utterly different. The Constitution designates a particular instrument which is the foundation of national government. It was ratified and made binding, not by Congress, which then did not exist, but by the people acting through thirteen state conventions. It created a legislature of two houses, but the Congress has no power to alter the Constitution without reference to the states. That which the people have enacted, only the people can alter or repeal.

Here, Bryce observed, were the capital differences between the two great English-speaking democracies. Britain has left the outlines as well as the details of her system of government to be gathered from a multitude of statutes and cases. The United States has drawn them together in one comprehensive fundamental enactment. Britain has

placed the so-called constitutional laws at the mercy of the legislature, which can abolish whenever it pleases any institution of the
country, the Crown, the Established Church, and, indeed, Parliament
itself. The United States has placed the Constitution altogether out of
the reach of Congress, providing a method of amendment whose
difficulty is shown by the fact that it has been sparingly used.

Parliament is omnipotent, Congress is doubly restricted. It can
make laws only for certain purposes specified in the Constitution, and
in legislating for these purposes it must not transgress any constitutional provision. The stream cannot rise above its source. The dam,
as it were, is the Supreme Court. It is not supreme as the Parliament
at Westminster is supreme. The people, the qualified voters, are the
supreme lawmaking power in the United States.

Realists can argue, of course, that this is a bit of mystical fiction
common in all republics with a constitution serving for a monarch.
Their citizens may well be more emotionally patriotic perhaps because they are actually revering themselves, but the preamble of the
United States Constitution begins: "We, the People of the United
States . . ." only because the founders did not know whether their
work would be ratified by all the states. There is no mention in that
document of the supremacy of the people. In fact, Englishmen are no
less supreme in their realm than are Americans in their Republic.

The founders, of course, were in a unique situation. For their
descendants, the Constitution is what the Ten Commandants were to
the children of Israel, but they could not claim that they were handed
down on some American Sinai. Subsequent interpretations of the
First Amendment would have declared such a claim unconstitutional.
In breaking with their English past, they perforce had to codify much
of that past into supreme law. The monarch personified Britain. In
law, she remains today the head of the executive, an integral part of
the legislature, the head of the judiciary, the commander in chief, and
the temporal head of the established Church of England. In practice,
she is none of these things. All power has passed to the people acting
through their elected representatives.

In the United States the assumption of the power of the people had
to precede the reality. There was no other alternative except to elect
George Washington king, and he was a modest man who eschewed
the fancy titles thrust upon him. Norway established such a precedent
when it declared its independence from Sweden in 1905 and elected a

Danish prince king, and I cannot think of a more democratic country. But by that time the United States was an old established country. In 1787 the supreme law had to stem from the people.

Under the Constitution, laws that conform are vested with all its authority. Those that go beyond it are invalid. Thus the principle of the power of the people has dealt hardly with its elected representatives in Congress. The President, as I have already demonstrated, now has similar authority to that of a medieval monarch. The Court, from its own implied logic, has assumed, as the final court of appeal, the authority to determine the validity or invalidity of the acts of Congress.

According to Bryce, such determination is effected by setting the law side by side with the Constitution, and considering where there is any discrepancy between them. This is a rather simplistic version of what really happens, as will be seen. The Constitution is not immutable, at least not in the eyes of the Court. The Library of Congress established in 1963 that the Court had reversed 109 of its earlier decisions, the first time in 1810. It has gone through many cycles of interpretation, from the great days of Marshall, who strengthened federal power, to 1935, when the Court held that Congress could not act to meet the social and economic crises of the Great Depression.

In the intervening period, the Court was primarily the defender of private property. Before Abolition, even property in human beings was held sacred. Long after slavery had been abolished by Britain and most other countries, the Court decided in the Dred Scott case of 1857 that Congress could not deprive persons of any kind of property anywhere in the United States. In so doing, the Missouri Compromise, which had set territorial boundaries to slavery, was declared unconstitutional, and the stage was set for the Civil War.

During the post–Civil War period of immense economic growth, the American social and political system was based on industrial property rights to a greater degree than was ever the case in European countries. In the Old World there had always been some opposition between government and the industrial classes. In the United States no such tradition existed. Instead, industrial freeholding was the foundation of the social system.

The industrialists, robber barons, or call them what you will, also took advantage of constitutional legalities. The Fifth and Fourteenth Amendments are for lawyers significantly different from Magna

Carta, suggesting that the barons and magnates of the thirteenth century were more adept at reading fine print. The Charter secures the rights of all free men, the amendments the rights of all persons, and in law persons may be real or fictitious, an unemployed laborer or a gigantic corporation.

The tide turned against rampant individualism at the end of the nineteenth century, and toward the establishment of public equities. Nevertheless, the American historian Charles Beard long afterward regretted the disparity, or basic inequality, between individuals and corporate persons of wealth, economic power, and political influence.

If corporations cannot provide employment for the millions of the American proletariat—for such we have, in spite of all claptrap to the contrary—can corporate persons expect to protect themselves forever, through Constitutional and judicial processes, against the distresses and distempers of natural persons twisting and turning in their search for the rights of life, liberty and property declared in the American creed?*

They did for many years. If the people, then as now, were the supreme lawmaking power, they were either misrepresented or the Court heard only the property owners. The tide slowly turned, and reached the flood under Chief Justice Warren. Since then the Court has been attacked by its critics as liberal, activist, centralist, and power-hungry. It may be many of these things; certainly the old ideas of separation of powers are not strictly relevant. I happen to believe that, fortunately for the United States, with the President it has responded to the modern triple revolution. With Marshall, the Court views the Constitution as a living instrument of government to be interpreted and, whenever necessary, to expand the power of the Presidency, which can be said to represent the people.

In its relationship to the modern Presidency, the Court is what the church was to a medieval monarch. It necessarily has a federal approach, as does the President, and it is concerned with the general welfare as the medieval church was concerned with souls and relieved the distress of the people. It can also come in conflict with the President and prevail, at least for a time.

Before inspecting more closely the Court's triple crown of success, it is perhaps better to describe, if only briefly, the federal and states'

* Charles Beard, "Corporations and Natural Rights," *Virginia Quarterly Review*, Volume 12, July 1936.

judiciaries. The federal system, which administers the laws of the United States, comprises the Supreme Court, the United States Courts of Appeals, the United States District Courts, and the Courts of the District of Columbia. There are also special courts, such as the United States Court of Claims, the Territorial Courts in overseas territories, and the United States Court of Military Appeals.

The Courts of Appeals are intermediate appellate courts created in 1891 to relieve the Supreme Court of considering all appeals in cases originally decided by the federal trial courts. These courts dispose of most appeals, and can contribute a great deal to doctrine. They are empowered to review and enforce orders of many federal administrative bodies, and their decisions are final except when they are subject to discretionary review or appeal in the Supreme Court. There are eleven judicial circuits, with a Court of Appeal for each, and each of the fifty states and the territories is assigned to one of them. At the time of writing there were seventy-eight judges.

The eighty-eight District Courts are the trial courts with general federal jurisdiction. Each state has at least one District Court, while the more populous have as many as four. There are 301 district judges, and two in Puerto Rico. The staff of each District Court, which has from one to twenty-four judges, includes a United States attorney, a United States marshal, one or more United States commissioners, referees in bankruptcy, and probation officers. Most cases from the district courts can be referred to the Courts of Appeals. The exceptions are injunction orders of special District Courts, decisions holding acts of Congress unconstitutional, and those criminal decisions that may be appealed directly to the Supreme Court.

The great mass of law cases is handled exclusively by state and local courts, although the state courts can have a concurrent jurisdiction with the federal courts and a litigant a choice of tribunals. They administer state constitutional and statutory law, and in the more advanced states many statutes have been codified. The English systems of common law and equity arrived with the first colonists, and after independence some of the state constitutions provided for their continuance. Courts of most other states view them as binding, except as modified by local statute.

The lesser state courts range from justices of the peace, county courts, urban police and municipal civil courts possessing limited

D

jurisdiction to circuit or district courts with broad original and appellate jurisdiction. There are often special courts, such as administrative, chancery, children's, claims, and probate courts. At the apex of the judicial system of each state is the court of last appeal, known as the supreme court, the court of appeals, or the supreme judicial courts. Their decisions are final in purely state controversies. State judges are either elected by popular vote or appointed by the legislature or governor.

The jurisdiction of state courts is as wide as that of any independent country, with the exception, of course, of the Constitutional reservations. The Supreme Court of the United States can pass on the validity of state and local government legislation and appeals from the decisions of state courts when the appellant believes that his Constitutional rights are involved. This has considerably increased the work of the Court in recent years, especially in the area of civil and individual rights, but the Supreme Court chose to intervene in the states from an early period.

In deciding against the validity of a state statute, the Court, as with federal statutes, does not officially abrogate it. Instead, in declaring it void it refuses enforcement in the case under review. This could, in theory, cause considerable confusion when the statute has been on the books for many years, but in specific cases the Court will uphold substantial rights established under the authority of a law which, strictly speaking, was invalid from the day of enactment.

This appellate system has all the clumsiness which is the price of federalism and bigness, and state courts can resist the supremacy of the Court. Their resistance has a long history, going back to Calhoun's doctrine of nullification, and is still maintained under the banner of states' rights by white supremacists and others who expect greater acquiescence from state courts. Not all of this resistance is questionable. A perfect balance between the federal government and the states has yet to be struck, but while free men continue to seek redress they will appeal to the highest court in the land.

The Court therefore stands at the apex of the federal and fifty state judicial systems. To that extent it is similar to the Judicial Committee of the Privy Council in London, which is the final court of appeal for British overseas dependencies and certain states of the Commonwealth, but there the comparison ends. The Court can also wield an authority ultimately superior to that of the President as well as of

Congress. For instance, President Truman seized the steel mills during an industrial dispute, and the Court ordered him to return them forthwith to their lawful owners. He did.

The case bears re-examination because Presidential power was involved. President Truman ordered the seizure of the steel industry when the Secretary of Defense certified that a prolonged strike would cripple the Korean War effort. A very real state of emergency existed, but not a formal state of war, and President Truman did not enjoy the war powers granted to President Franklin Roosevelt. The companies went to the courts, and the Supreme Court rendered judgment. It was split six to three, but in ordering the mills to be returned it was careful not to circumscribe Presidential power.

Justice Douglas said in a separate opinion:

The emergency did not create power; it merely marked an occasion when power should be exercised. And the fact that it was necessary that measures be taken to keep steel in production does not mean that the President, rather than the Congress, has the constitutional authority to act. The Congress, as well as the President, is trustee of the national welfare. . . . If we sanctioned the present exercise of power by the President, we would be expanding Article II of the Constitution and rewriting it to suit the political convenience of the present emergency. . . . Today a kindly President uses the seizure power to effect a wage increase and to keep the steel furnaces in production. Yet tomorrow another President might use the same power to prevent a wage increase, to curb trade unions, to regiment labor as oppressively as industry thinks it has been regimented by this seizure.

Justice Black also tried to circumscribe Presidential power, but the majority did not. The steel case was of historical interest because it raised once again the question posed by President Jefferson when in retirement he discussed the principles at stake in the Louisiana Purchase. A strict observance of the written laws, he said, was doubtless one of the highest duties of a good citizen, but not the highest. The higher law was the law of necessity, of self-preservation. "To lose our country by a scrupulous adherence to the written law, would be to lose the law itself, with life, liberty, property and all those who are enjoying them with us; thus absurdly sacrificing the end to the means."

The Court evidently did not believe that the steel dispute gravely threatened the national interest. The mills were returned to the owners by a six-to-three majority, but seven justices in effect joined in refusing to dictate Presidential action in future national emergencies. They preferred, instead, to allow events to decide the merits of any further cases which might arise. In refusing a fresh interpretation of the Constitution, the Court wisely left unanswered the question posed by President Jefferson. There was no assertion of supremacy. Instead, the President's inherent powers were left untouched.

Not all cases reaching the Court are so dramatic, but the vast majority, dramatic or otherwise, rise through the strata of inferior courts until it decides to pass, or not pass, on them. The process is enveloped by a certain contrived mystery, but it has been dispelled from time to time by justices in memoirs and lectures and something is known of what happens when the justices in their black robes disappear from the Court behind its red velour curtain.

They meet alone, rather like a jury, in the oak-paneled conference room under the portrait of Chief Justice Marshall. There are no clerks, stenographers, or page boys. Many decades ago two pages waited on them, but an assumed leak of an opinion led to their exclusion. It was subsequently discovered that the youngsters were guiltless, that no leak had occurred, but since then the justices have always met alone in conference. Their conduct observes a pleasing and archaic correctness. They address each other as "Brother," and shake hands all around. These politenesses completed, they attend to their business in a manner also regulated by tradition.

Appeals are always dealt with first, then petitions for certiorari, *in forma pauperis* cases, and finally the cases argued previously in the courtroom. These are acted upon during the same week in which they are argued. They can involve questions concerning the Constitution, statutory construction, individual and state rights, unions, Indians, executive power, taxation, subversion, application for bar membership, and a hundred other subjects.

The Chief Justice begins by calling the first case on the list, and then discussing it. He yields to the senior associate justice and on around the table until each justice who wishes to speak has been heard. There is no time limit, and there are supposed to be no interruptions. A vote is taken, and the result is entered into large docket books, which are fitted with locks. The junior justices vote first in order to ensure that they are not influenced by their elders. Five votes are required to decide a case, but only four to grant a writ of certiorari, the writ required to remove a case from an inferior court. Thus the Court tries to make certain that any case deserving argument is heard. If the rejection of the vast majority of writs seems arbitrary, it is perhaps inevitable.

The late Chief Justice Vinson once said that the Court had never been primarily concerned with correcting the errors of lower courts. The certiorari was not to see that justice was done; every appellate had already had at least one trial and one appeal. Another Chief Justice, the late John Rutledge, said that the Court's purpose was to secure the national rights and uniformity of judgments. When certiorari was denied, it meant that the case did not come within the rule, not that the result was right.

Each justice present passes on every piece of business, unless he disqualifies himself in the event of a conflict of interest, because judicial power is vested in only one Supreme Court. There can be no delegation of justice, no committees or panels. The task of writing the opinion is assigned by the Chief Justice or the senior justice voting with the majority. This is a firm rule, and helps to explain the power of the Chief Justice.

The writing calls for painstaking research as well as an expert knowledge of the law, and it is to be assumed that the justices are assisted by their law clerks. The late Justice Benjamin Cardozo said that a justice must be a historian and prophet. We have it from Justice Tom Clark that an opinion can require three weeks of preparatory work. It is then printed in the Supreme Court Building, and circulated to the justices. In controversial cases, the process of reaching an acceptable version can take weeks or months. The final form is agreed upon at one of the Friday conferences, and of course any justice may dissent and write his own opinion.

A divided decision is common enough—unlike jurymen the justices do not have to seek unanimity—but the publication of dissenting opinion bothers some people. The arithmetic of division can be weighed by the political branches and the bar, and if a five-to-four decision has all the legal force of unanimity, it is sometimes said to undermine the Court's authority. Certainly it is at odds with the practice of most continental European courts, where anonymity is also generally observed.

Some justices have believed that a dissenting opinion strove to discredit the Court's reasoning, and was irresponsible. Not so Justice

William Douglas, who in a notable defense of dissent, agreed with Oliver Wendell Holmes that the lawyer's search for certainty was illusory. Law is not what has been or is. Law in the lawyer's sense is the prediction of things to come, the prediction of what decree will be written by designated judges on specified facts.

Proof and credibility, Mr. Douglas continued, were often in doubt, and uncertainty increased with new and difficult problems under ambiguous statutes. Difficulties increased when constitutional questions emerged, because the Constitution was not a code but a rule of action, a statement of philosophy and a point of view, a summation of general principles, a delineation of the broad outlines of a regime designed by the founders.

Certainty and unanimity in the law were only possible under Fascist and Communist systems, where they were indispensable because complete subservience to the political regime was a *sine qua non* to judicial survival under either regime. Disagreement among judges was as true to the character of democracy as freedom of speech itself. The dissenting opinion was as genuinely American as Otis' denunciation of the general warrants, as Thomas Paine's, Thomas Jefferson's, or James Madison's briefs for civil liberties.

Unanimous or divided, the written opinion is the end product of the Supreme Court. It is the instrument that resolves, if only temporarily, the problems that beset American society. It is the reference for future protagonists and antagonists, and often the starting point for another great struggle. The text is all-important. The precedents referred to and the line of argument pursued are minutely examined by the administration and the bar. For the laymen, it reveals the final process of the work of the Court.

There is no better way of illustrating this than by quoting the text of an opinion. I have selected the *Brown* v. *Board of Education* for two reasons. It demonstrates the reasoning of the Court; the orderly examination of legal precedent, the relating, in this case, of constitutional amendment to the circumstances of the present and the time of its ratification; and then, when precedent and circumstance may be inconclusive, of simply deciding what is right or wrong.

The second reason is that this decision on school desegration initiated a social revolution the like of which had never occurred before in the United States or elsewhere. It was not the last desegregation decision, and indeed the revolution has yet to be completed.

Nevertheless, it is all the more remarkable because the revolution was not launched at the barricades but argued before nine men in black robes sitting in an air-conditioned marble chamber.

The opinion, delivered by Chief Justice Earl Warren on May 17, 1954, is as follows:

These cases come to us from the States of Kansas, South Carolina, Virginia and Delaware. They are premised on different facts and different local conditions, but a common legal question justifies their consideration together in this consolidated opinion.

In each of the cases, minors of the Negro race, through their legal representatives, seek the aid of the courts in obtaining admission to the public schools of their community on a nonsegregated basis. In each instance, they had been denied admission to the public schools of their community on a nonsegregated basis. In each instance, they had been denied admission to schools attended by white children under laws requiring or permitting segregation according to race. This segregation was alleged to deprive the plaintiffs of the equal protection of the laws under the Fourteenth Amendment. In each of the cases other than the Delaware case, a three-judge federal district court denied relief to the plaintiffs on the so-called "separate but equal" doctrine announced by this Court in *Plessy* v. *Ferguson*. Under that doctrine, equality of treatment is accorded when the races are provided substantially equal facilities, even though these facilities be separate. In the Delaware case, the Supreme Court of Delaware adhered to that doctrine, but ordered that the plaintiffs be admitted to the white schools because of their superiority to the Negro schools.

The plaintiffs contend that segregated schools are not "equal" and cannot be made "equal" and that hence they are deprived of the equal protection of the laws. Because of the obvious importance of the question presented, the Court took jurisdiction. Argument was heard in the 1952 Term, and reargument was heard this Term on certain questions propounded by the Court.

Reargument was largely devoted to the circumstances surrounding the adoption of the Fourteenth Amendment in 1868. It covered exhaustively consideration of the Amendment in Congress, ratification by the states, then existing practices in racial segregation, and the views of proponents and opponents of the Amendment. This discussion and our own investigation convince us that, although these sources cast some light, it is not enough to resolve the problem with which we are faced. At best, they are inconclusive. The most avid proponents of the post-War Amendments undoubtedly intended them to remove all legal distinctions among "all persons born or naturalized in the United States." Their opponents, just as certainly, were antagonistic to both the letter and the spirit of the Amendments and wished them to have the most limited effect. What others in Congress and the state legislatures had in mind cannot be determined with any degree of certainty.

An additional reason for the inconclusive nature of the Amendment's history, with respect to segregated schools, is the status of public education at that time. In the South, the movement toward free common schools, supported by general taxation, had not yet taken hold. Education of white children was largely in the hands of private groups. Education of Negroes was almost non-existent, and practically all of the race were illiterate. In fact, any education of Negroes was forbidden by law in some states. Today, in contrast, many Negroes have achieved outstanding success in the arts and sciences as well as in the business and professional worlds. It is true that public school education at the time of the Amendment had advanced further in the North, but the effect of the Amendment on Northern States was generally ignored in the congressional debates. Even in the North, the conditions of public education did not approximate those existing today. The curriculum was usually rudimentary; ungraded schools were common in rural areas; the school term was but three months a year in many states; and compulsory school attendance was virtually unknown. As a consequence, it is not surprising that there should be so little in the history of the Fourteenth Amendment relating to its intended effect on public education.

In the first cases in this Court construing the Fourteenth Amendment, decided shortly after its adoption, the Court interpreted it as proscribing all state-imposed discriminations against the Negro race. The doctrine of "separate but equal" did not make its appearance in this Court until 1896 in the case of *Plessy* v. *Ferguson* involving not education but transportation. American courts have since labored with the doctrine for over half a century. In this Court, there have been six cases involving the "separate but equal" doctrine in the field of public education. In *Cumming* v. *County Board of Education* and *Gong Lum* v. *Rice* the validity of the doctrine itself was not challenged. In more recent cases, all on the graduate school level, inequality was found in that specific benefits enjoyed by white students were denied to Negro students of the same educational qualifications. In none of these cases was it necessary to re-examine the doctrine to grant relief to the Negro plaintiff. And in *Sweatt* v. *Painter* the Court expressly reserved decision on the question whether *Plessy* v. *Ferguson* should be held inapplicable to public education.

In the instant cases, that question is directly presented. Here, unlike *Sweatt* v. *Painter,* there are findings below that the Negro and white schools involved have been equalized, or are being equalized, with respect to buildings, curricula, qualifications and salaries of teachers, and other "tangible" factors. Our decision, therefore, cannot turn on merely a comparison of these tangible factors in the Negro and white schools involved in each of the cases. We must look instead to the effect of segregation itself on public education.

In approaching this problem, we cannot turn the clock back to 1868 when the Amendment was adopted, or even to 1896 when *Plessy* v. *Ferguson* was written. We must consider public education in the light of its full development and its present place in American life throughout the Nation. Only in this way can it be determined if segregation in public schools deprives these plaintiffs of the equal protection of the laws.

Today, education is perhaps the most important function of state and local governments. Compulsory school attendance laws and the great expenditures for education both demonstrate our recognition of the importance of education to our democratic society. It is required in the performance of our most basic public responsibilities, even service in the armed forces. It is the very foundation of good citizenship. Today it is a principal instrument in awakening the child to cultural values, in preparing him for later professional training, and in helping him to adjust normally to his environment. In these days, it is doubtful that any child may reasonably be expected to succeed in life if he is denied the opportunity of an education. Such an opportunity, where the state has undertaken to provide it, is a right which must be made available to all on equal terms.

We come then to the question presented: Does segregation of children in public schools solely on the basis of race, even though the physical facilities and other "tangible" factors may be equal, deprive the children of the minority group of equal educational opportunities? We believe that it does.

In *Sweatt* v. *Painter* in finding that a segregated law school for Negroes could not provide them equal educational opportunities, this Court relied in large part on "those qualities which are incapable of objective measurement but which make for greatness in a law school." In *McLaurin* v. *Oklahoma State Regents* the Court, in requiring that a Negro admitted to a white graduate school be treated like all other students, again resorted to intangible considerations; ". . . his ability to study, to engage in discussions and exchange of views with other students, and, in general, to learn his profession." Such considerations apply with added force to children in grade and high schools. To separate them from others of similar age and qualifications solely because of their race generates a feeling of inferiority as to their status in the community that may affect their hearts and minds in a way unlikely ever to be undone. The effect of this separa-

D*

tion on their educational opportunities was well stated by a finding in the Kansas case by a court which nevertheless felt compelled to rule against the Negro plaintiffs:

"Segregation of white and colored children in public schools has a detrimental effect upon the colored children. The impact is greater when it has the sanction of the law; for the policy of separating the races is usually interpreted as denoting the inferiority of the negro group. A sense of inferiority affects the motivation of a child to learn. Segregation with the sanction of law, therefore, has a tendency to (retard) the education and mental development of negro children and to deprive them of some of the benefits they would receive in a racial(ly) integrated school system."

Whatever may have been the extent of psychological knowledge at the time of *Plessy* v. *Ferguson*, this finding is amply supported by modern authority. Any language in *Plessy* v. *Ferguson* contrary to this finding is rejected.

We conclude that in the field of public education the doctrine of "separate but equal" has no place. Separate educational facilities are inherently unequal. Therefore, we hold that the plaintiffs and others similarly situated for whom the actions have been brought are, by reason of the segregation complained of, deprived of the equal protection of the laws guaranteed by the Fourteenth Amendment.

Because these are class actions, because of the wide applicability of this decision, and because of the great variety of local conditions, the formulation of decrees in these cases presents problems of considerable complexity. On reargument, the consideration of appropriate relief was necessarily subordinated to the primary question—the constitutionality of segregation in public education. We have now announced that such segregation is a denial of the equal protection of the laws. In order that we may have the full assistance of the parties in formulating decrees, the cases will be restored to the docket, and the parties are requested to present further argument on Questions 4 and 5 previously propounded by the Court for the reargument this Term. The Attorney General of the United States is again invited to participate. The Attorneys General of the states requiring or permitting segregation in public education will also be permitted to appear as *amici curiae* upon request to do so by September 15, 1954, and submission of briefs by October 1, 1954.

The influence of the Brown decision was profound, and went far beyond the Negro question. Justice William Brennan said that the law had come alive again. A decade later, the American Bar Association had this to say in its annual report:

The new trend is not back to an exaggerated individualism, which has been corrected in part by the notion of a sociological jurisprudence.

Neither is it a re-affirmation of the "jurisprudence of interests," which was a positivistic effort to spell out in jurisprudential terms the property and power priorities of society.

The new jurisprudence constitutes, rather, a recognition of human beings, as the most distinctive and important feature of the universe which confronts our senses, and of the function of law as the historic means of guaranteeing that pre-eminence. . . . In a scientific age it asks, in effect, what is the nature of man, and what is the nature of the universe with which he is confronted . . . ? Why is a human being important; what gives him dignity; what limits his freedom to do whatever he likes; what are his essential needs; whence comes his sense of injustice?

This august body, it may be noted, was asking much the same questions as the New Left, the group of undergraduate organizations which about the same time was launching its offensive against middle-aged middle-class American society. The Port Huron statement of the Students for a Democratic Society, the most vocal component of the New Left, said:

We are people of this generation, bred in at least modest comfort, housed in universities, looking uncomfortably to the world we inherit. . . .
The first effort, then, should be to state a vision: what is the perimeter of human possibility in this epoch? The second effort, if we are to be politically responsible, is to evaluate the prospects for obtaining at least a substantial part of that vision in our epoch: what are the social forces that exist, or that must exist, if we are to be successful? And what role have we ourselves to play as a social force?

If the ABA and the New Left were in some kind of improbable agreement, the nine quiet men, self-effacing to a point where they could almost disappear in a society dedicated to self-expression and self-assertion, were to a large extent responsible for releasing the new forces and avoiding a violent social upheaval. It was all the more impressive because the Constitution which the Court must interpret did not expressly mention equality prior to the Fourteenth Amendment. There is, I know, a widespread belief that equality is an American invention, but the amendment was not ratified until about 650 years after the signing of Magna Carta. The fortieth clause of the Charter was unequivocal: "To no one will we sell, to no one will we deny or delay the right to justice." The Constitution ratified by the state conventions was silent.

The idea of equality pervades the document of course, and the founders must have assumed it to be inseparable from the concept of liberty. They were also Englishmen. Equality was certainly guaranteed in many of the state constitutions, which were assumed to afford adequate protection. This assumption explained the original omission of a Bill of Rights. Looking back over the ages to Philadelphia, one cannot but make or invent excuses, but it remains that equality was not guaranteed under the Constitution because of the political difficulty of achieving union without foundering on the hard reality of slavery.

The unavoidable inconsistency, said Arthur Goldberg during his brief membership on the Court, reflected a fundamental departure from the American creed, a departure which it took a civil war to set right. It took rather more than that. The adoption of the Thirteenth, Fourteenth, and Fifteenth Amendments did not clear the way for "a new kind of society—fresh, equal, just, open, free, and forever respectful of conscience." The Supreme Court denied that shining purpose with *Plessy* v. *Ferguson* and other decisions. In 1954 the Court returned to the real meaning of the equal-protection clause and broadened it, but in the long intervening period there was what the ABA described as exaggerated individualism and the jurisprudence of interests.

Outside the Court, but with its sufferance, indifference to the rights of others in many cases hardened into positive hostility, and not only toward American Indians, Negroes, and Orientals. Almost every successive wave of immigrants felt it, but especially the Irish, Slavs, and Southern Europeans. With some degree of assimilation, they in turn became indifferent to the rights of later arrivals. The immigrant generally accepted an inferior status, occasionally because he knew no better, but more often as the price for his children's future. As an assimilation process it worked rather well, but the result was untrammeled individualism or indifference to the rights of others. It is still a powerful motivation in American life, politics, culture, and mythology, but is gradually being tempered with the help of the Court.

This it has managed to do because unanimity has been achieved within its conference room on two counts, although of course the Court continues to disagree when delivering opinions. First, it holds that except within the terms of the commerce clause it has no constitutional power to review economic or social legislation. Second, it has assumed final responsibility for the protection of the fundamental rights of the citizen.

The assumption of this responsibility was to have a profound effect upon the relations between the federal government and the states which had grown up during the previous years of complacency. In effect the Court extended the Bill of Rights to the states under the Fourteenth Amendment. Paragraph 1 of the Amendment reads: "All persons born or naturalized in the United States, and subject to the jurisdiction thereof, are citizens of the United States and of the State wherein they reside. No State shall make or enforce any law which shall abridge the privileges or immunities of citizens of the United States; nor shall any State deprive any person of life, liberty, or property, without due process of law."

The reason seemed to be clear enough. There was little point in making obeisances to the United States Constitution if it was not to apply in state courts which handle most litigation. Nevertheless, the extension of the Fourteenth Amendment shocked many good citizens as well as white supremacists, primitive anti-Communists, and those who felt that the protection of life and property was more important than the constitutional rights of alleged criminals. Their concern was generally explained by fear of federal supremacy, but it did in fact reveal once again that federal-state relationship is another of the great unresolved problems. Nevertheless the Court acted only because many of the states had failed in providing due process and equal protection. The Bill of Rights was intended as protection against the federal government, but the Court had to extend it to the states under the Fourteenth Amendment to afford protection to the individual against the states.

In the first two postwar decades, rather more than a hundred important decisions were handed down under this extension, ranging from freedom of association to political rights. Certainly protection of rights was not confined to the Negro. The Court hastened the return to sanity after McCarthyism by invalidating sedition acts in forty-two states. In 1956 it held that the summary dismissal of government employees as security risks applied only to those in sensitive jobs. The following year, in a contempt-of-Congress case, it required that questions put to witnesses by committees be shown to be pertinent to the inquiry.

In 1958 it held that the State Department had no authority to withhold passports because of the beliefs and political associations of applicants, and in the following year overturned a ban against *Lady*

Chatterley's Lover. The reading of prayers in public schools was held to violate the First Amendment in 1962, an assertion of disestablishmentarianism that caused great anguish even among those who had never bothered with the religious education of their children. In 1964 it struck down unfair deportation, search without warrant, and loyalty oaths.

Some of its notable decisions vitally affected the proceedings of state courts. *Mapp* v. *Ohio* in 1961 prohibited admission into state courts of evidence obtained in violation of the Fourth Amendment. The Eighth Amendment's prohibition of cruel and unusual punishment (*Robinson* v. *California* 1962), the Sixth Amendment's provision of counsel in criminal cases (*Gideon* v. *Wainwright* 1963), and the Fifth Amendment's protection against compulsory self-incrimination (*Malloy* v. *Hogan* and *Escobedo* v. *Illinois* 1964) were all held applicable in the states.

A second departure for the Court with consequences for the states was the development of the doctrine of pre-emption by implication, under which state laws in direct conflict with federal law are invalidated. The doctrine has a firm constitutional basis. Article VI, Section 2, reads:

> This Constitution and the Laws of the United States which shall be made in Pursuance thereof; and all Treaties made, or which shall be made, under the Authority of the United States, shall be the supreme Law of the Land; and the Judges in every State shall be bound thereby, any Thing in the Constitution or Laws of any State to the Contrary notwithstanding.

The doctrine was seen, however, to go beyond Article VI. Apart from direct conflict, the doctrine applies when Congress has stated an intention to pre-empt a given field of legislation, or when its intention was not stated but could be inferred. Hence pre-emption by implication.

Critics have not contested the supremacy of federal law in cases of direct conflict. As early as 1824 *Gibbons* v. *Ogden* defined the constitutional power of Congress to regulate interstate commerce. The necessity of federal regulation to maintain the American common market was subsequently never seriously questioned, although of course there were some necessary modifications over the years. But the supremacy doctrine came under fire with the disputed decision handed down in 1956 in *Pennsylvania* v. *Nelson*. In striking down portions of that state's sedition law on the grounds that it was pre-empted by the Smith Act, the Court's decision rested on a number of criteria. One was that the scheme of federal regulation was so pervasive as to make reasonable the inference that Congress left no room for the states to supplement it.

This was established despite the fact that the Smith Act appeared in Title 18 of the United States Code, which stated that nothing in the title should be held to take away or impair the jurisdiction of state courts. The Court was seen not to pre-empt by implication but in spite of the intention of Congress specifically to reserve jurisdiction for the states.

Much of the political friction caused by the pre-emption doctrine and the extension of the Bill of Rights under the Fourteenth Amendment could be avoided if uniform standards of justice applied in the states. The Court would appear to be determined to establish such uniformity in defense of the rights of the individual, but the opposition has been intense and bitter. It has been fought under the rallying cry of "Impeach Chief Justice Warren."

Southerners angered by desegregation decisions have charged that the Court has upset established precedents, and acted under sociological rather than legal principles. Conservative Republicans have held that it violated the constitutional relationship between the federal government and the states. There was a measure of truth in their arguments as far as the tradition of federal-state relationship is concerned, but they missed the point. The Court presumably had read the Constitution from time to time, including the Tenth Amendment, which is always quoted in defense of states' rights.

It reads: "The powers not delegated to the United States by the Constitution, nor prohibited by it to the States, are reserved to the States respectively, or to the people." The Amendment is said to be unequivocal, but no more than the first Eight Amendments, the Fourteenth, and Article VI. The Court had to decide between states' rights and individual rights, and emphatically came down in defense of the latter.

Congressional critics nevertheless stocked a cornucopia of bills over the years to curb its powers. The Eighty-fourth Congress (1955–56) produced a bumper crop of seventy. Nothing came of this, and a group of state legislators, known as the General Assembly of the States, proposed three constitutional amendments. Among them was one to establish a Court of the Union, comprising the chief justices of the fifty states, to review and reverse Supreme Court decisions involving the rights reserved to the states and the people. At the time of writing about one-third of the states had approved one or more of the proposals, but they threaten the very foundations of the Supreme Court and are unlikely to get very far because they could be the first steps toward the dissolution of the Union.

In surviving these attacks, the Court has truly led the country safely into a new era of jurisprudence. It might be said that the Supreme Court has made the United States a free country, but for the admiring Englishman the record had its surprises. Apart from the oppression of the Negroes, which was bad enough, how was it possible that so many wrongs were not righted before? The former Justice Robert Jackson suggested one possible reason in 1955:

I have been repeatedly impressed with the speed and certainty with which the slightest invasion of British individual freedom or minority rights by officials of the government is picked up in Parliament, not merely by the opposition but by the party in power, and made the subject of persistent questioning, criticism, and sometimes rebuke. There is no waiting on the theory that the judges will take care of it. In this country, on the contrary, we rarely have a political issue made of any kind of invasion of civil liberty. . . .

In Great Britain, to observe civil liberties is good politics and to transgress the rights of the individual or the minority is bad politics. In the United States, I cannot say that this is so. Whether the political conscience is relieved because the responsibility here is made largely a legal one, I cannot say, but of this I am sure: any court which undertakes by its legal processes to enforce civil liberties needs the support of an enlightened and vigorous public opinion which will be intelligent and discriminating as to what cases really are civil liberties cases and what questions really are involved in those cases. I do not think the American public is enlightened on this subject.*

I happen to believe that subsequent events proved the justice to be too pessimistic. In any event, there have always been many Americans with a lively sense of righteous indignation, and the American Civil Liberties Union has long been active. The United States is less homogeneous than Britain and its federal system of government

* *The Supreme Court in the American System of Government,* Cambridge, Harvard University Press, 1955, pp. 52, 83.

necessarily more cumbersome, but denial or invasion of civil liberty can be made a political issue. It takes time, and this as with other defects of the system is largely the price of bigness, but in defending the rights of the individual, all 190 million of them, the Court cannot be said to have served federal supremacy at the expense of the states. Charges of judicial activism, usurpation of political power, and worse are beneath contempt.

Members of the Court have in their quiet way tried to answer some of the charges. Some justices feel that the Court tends to strengthen decentralization. They are prepared to permit the states to conduct political, social, and economic experiments as long as they do not impair the commerce clause of the Constitution or impinge upon the fundamental rights of the individual. Their main defense, however, is that the Court has returned to the Constitution. Justice Goldberg said that in discarding the technicalities and abstract rules of the past the Court had returned to the original intentions of the founders.

A judge when writing an opinion today, he continued, naturally studied the Constitution and referred to legal precedent, but his clerks also quarried deeply into the writings of the founders and the commentaries of their times. They studied the speeches of the great Presidents, and the reports and investigations of Congressional committees. Modern constitutionalists have also argued that many of the justices of the eighties and thirties were creatures of their times, victims of aberration and ill-equipped to administer justice in a changing world. The recent changes were not only a matter of popular attitude, but the result of experience and better legal research.

This has not necessarily persuaded the critics of the Court, whose anger knows no bounds when it enters the political field. Many of its decisions have political or sociopolitical consequences, but the most audacious political act of the Court was a series of opinions requiring the reapportionment of the United States House of Representatives and many state legislatures. It began in 1962 with the acceptance of jurisdiction over such cases, previously held by the late Justice Felix Frankfurter not to be "justiciable" and too political, and Congress in its anger was brought almost to a standstill. In retrospect one can only wonder what all the fuss was about. The Court only held to the principle of one man, one vote, which is surely fundamental to representative democracy. One can only assume that the United

States, ever suspicious of democracy, was as reluctant as those who founded it to face up to the logical consequences.

In fact, the triple revolution was still at work. The new urban United States with its half-digested immigrant population had been not so much ignored as controlled politically by the rural areas with their not so simple or bucolic connections with the leaders of an older America. This was perpetrated by flagrant malapportionment of seats, especially in the state legislatures. In 1960 the disparity in all state legislatures in the representation of the most densely populated urban districts and the emptiest rural areas was at least two to one. Similarly, the imbalance between Congressional districts in some states was also unequal and unrepresentative.

The Supreme Court approached this political mine field with great caution, and in the first case, *Baker* v. *Carr,* only held that lower federal courts had jurisdiction. It did, however, state the constitutional position. Justice Brennan said, "The mere fact that a suit seeks protection of a political right does not mean it presents a political question. . . . The question here is the consistency of state action with the Federal Constitution."

The following year, in *Gray* v. *Sanders,* the Court went further. The Georgia county-unit vote system was held to be unconstitutional because "Within a given constituency, there can be room for but a single Constitutional rule—one voter, one vote." Justice Douglas said that the concept of political equality from the Declaration of Independence to Lincoln's Gettysburg Address, to the Fifteenth, Seventeenth, and Nineteenth Amendments could mean only one thing: one person, one vote.

The very American idea that political representation should not be confined to people but encompass special interests persisted until the Court heard appeals against the electoral systems of Alabama and Colorado. Chief Justice Warren then said that legislators represented people, not trees or acres, and they were elected by voters, not by farms, cities, or economic interests. He also struck down the idea that a state may have a little federal system, that is, one chamber of a bicameral legislature based on area as is the United States Senate.

The federal analogy was inapposite because the system of representation in the Senate was the price of federalism. It was a compromise between the larger and smaller states, formerly independent, that averted a deadlock in the Constitutional Convention. Political subdivisions in states, such as counties and cities, had never been considered as sovereign entities. The equal-protection clause required that both houses of a state legislature be apportioned on a population basis. The Chief Justice also rejected the idea that a state had the right to choose its own electoral system. The right of an individual to cast an equal vote could not be denied even by a majority of a state's electorate.

Equality at the polling booth was also established at the federal level in *Wesberry* v. *Sanders*. Here the constitutionality of the Court's decision was plain to see in Article I, Section 2, but the degree of inequality that had existed for so long was evident in the dissenting opinion of Justice Harlan. Assuming that a disparity of more than 100,000 voters between a state's largest and smallest districts violated the Constitution, he said that 398 members of the House of Representatives from 37 states had been unconstitutionally elected. That left a constitutional House of 37 members.

The political consequences of the decisions over the years will be considerable. An urbanized America will eventually be represented at the federal and state levels by legislators largely from urban and not rural areas. The problems of the urban majority will presumably be given proper consideration because more representatives will be directly accountable. It is quite possible that the internal power of the Presidency will diminish somewhat as Americans learn to look more to a responsive Congress. It is equally possible that the Court may not have to intervene in political situations quite so often. The assumption must be that it does so reluctantly, and only when the political branches fail in their constitutional tasks. Certainly it is undeniable that Congress and the state legislatures have prime responsibility, and the accountability forced upon them by the Court may well do much to redress the balance between the three branches of government and between Washington and the states.

The Supreme Court will, however, remain a political institution as long as democratic government as practiced in the United States remains a confused struggle fought under the Queensbury rules of the Constitution. The confusion, as suggested in this book, arises because the political parties are exposed to internal division. Regional, ideological, and special-interest groups within each party can have different objectives, and do not always submit to central command. The legislative process, always one of compromise, is qualified still further with often impossible adjustments.

When differences are too great, and the legislative process rendered impotent, the Court must intervene when requested, as it did in the racial issue. Even when they are not too great, the final Congressional compromise may be contradictory. The bill becomes law, is found wanting, and is referred to the Court for interpretation. In other words, the battle that raged in Congress is transferred to the Court, and the conflict breaks out again. Its interpretation is juridical of course, but it can have important political implications. The justices may be accused of taking sides, and of usurping the role of Congress, but they cannot do otherwise when contradictions have to be resolved. There is only the Court or the streets.

There is, of course, more uncertainty when constitutional questions have to be answered. The justices cannot ignore precedent, but they have sworn to defend the Constitution, and not the interpretations of their predecessors. The narrow legalistic notions of earlier generations cannot enthrall the future. Dealing with constitutional problems calls for courage as well as wisdom, and disagreement must be expected. When the Court disagrees, Justice Douglas has said, it is because society is divided. To that extent the law is uncertain, but it remains the highest form of compromise between competing interests. It is the product of attempted reconciliation between the many diverse groups of a society in which the Court as well as Congress is inescapably involved.

The political function of the Court will continue to increase while it remains deeply concerned about the rights of the individual. My Englishness may be too apparent here, but in a society with so many citizens whose American origins are recent this function is fundamental. It must not only interpret and reinterpret the Constitution but also be fully aware of the long struggle for human liberty of which the Constitution is but one landmark, if a notable one.

It is a document that wisely left a great deal unsaid. The founders evidently thought it safe to assume much, but as this short review of the Court's recent work suggests, the assumption was not altogether well founded. Violations of the spirit of the Constitution were no doubt inevitable when short cuts had to be taken in building a new nation. Because of constant reference, the letter rather than the spirit perhaps naturally assumed greater importance. Probably it could not have been otherwise.

Nevertheless, one American institution has to be aware of the spirit and the verities of the past. To that extent the Court is the American equivalent of the medieval church. Its business, of course, is not revealed religion but remembrance of things past, of the long struggle for human liberty. This, rather than a mastery of legal precedent, helps to explain the present greatness of the Court. Magna Carta, common law, and the English Bill of Rights of 1689 are part of that living past which the Court helps to keep alive. Modern America has many origins and its sources of inspiration are certainly not only English, but the Constitution was written by Englishmen and in interpreting it the Court more often than not returns to the English past.

The early American suspicion of government power, indeed, had its intellectual roots in the writings of an Englishman, John Locke, the seventeenth-century philosopher known as the founder of English empiricism. His writings justified the English Revolution of 1689, and he helped to draw up a constitution, not a very good one, for the proprietary colony that afterward became the Carolinas. He was a strong advocate of individual liberty, and argued in his *Two Treatises of Government* for democracy based on natural law. He was perhaps the first to say that sovereignty resides in the people, who have the moral obligation to withdraw by revolution their support of a government that does not reflect the popular will.

Of government power, he wrote: "Their power in the utmost bounds of it is limited to the public good of the society. It is a power that hath no other end but preservation and therefore can never have a right to destroy, enslave, or designedly to impoverish the subjects." The American Bill of Rights curbs all branches of government, but by applying it more rigorously to the states, as we have seen, the Court has required state governors as well as the President, state legislatures and Congress, local and federal courts, and government agencies to respect the rights of the people.

In keeping the past alive, the Court has helped to resolve some of the problems of federalism, but it represents the future as well as the past. The triple revolution will create its own problems and dangers to the rights of the individual. There is no reason to assume that an urban majority properly represented will be any more respectful of the rights of others than a rural political majority, or that freedom will be more secure in a materially affluent society. The Supreme Court will be a political institution for as long as politicians and the people they represent are human.

Part II

National Security

"It has fallen to America's lot to organize and lead that portion of the world which adheres to the principle of consent in the ordering of human affairs. It is an assignment we undertook not by choice but by necessity and without prior experience. The burden is without historical parallel and so is the danger, and so is our response. The first phrase is ending. The outward thrust of aggression in Europe has been arrested. Now we shall have to address ourselves to Asia, to perpetual siege and to the unending tasks of greatness. For the quest for peace and security is not a day's or a decade's work. For us it may be everlasting."

ADLAI STEVENSON
Harvard, 1954

4   The Department of State

"The most dignified place in the cabinet is that of the Secretary of State. It is the great prize often bestowed on the man to whom the President is chiefly indebted for his election, or at any rate on one of the leaders of the party. In the early days, it was regarded as the stepping-stone to the presidency. Jefferson, Madison, Monroe, J. Q. Adams, and Van Buren, had all served as secretaries to preceding presidents. The conduct of foreign affairs is the chief duty of the State Department: its head has therefore a larger stage to play on than any other minister, and more chances of fame. His personal importance is all the greater because the President is usually so much absorbed by questions of patronage as to be forced to leave the secretary to his own devices. Hence the foreign policy of the administration is practically that of the secretary, except so far as the latter is controlled by the Senate."

—JAMES BRYCE
The American Commonwealth

A foreigner in Washington cannot but be impressed by the Open Door policy of the Department of State. I do not refer to the China policy of John Hay, a former Secretary of State, but its open front door on C Street in Washington. It gives onto a rather splendid lobby, angular in the modern manner, and draped with flags of many nations with which the United States maintains diplomatic relations. Until the American Legion complained of the lack of security and a rape was attempted on a staircase in 1965, anybody could step in and admire them. Today some form of identification is required, but the visitor can still ask the genial lady at the information desk for the quickest way through the steel and concrete labyrinth to the Secretary's office, and disappear unattended in one of the many automatic elevators.

An Assistant Secretary of State once boasted before a Congressional committee that copies of the department's telephone directory, which lists the private numbers as well as office extensions of all officials, are pressed upon newspaper reporters. Thus the front doors of hundreds of Foreign Service officers are figuratively left on the latch. Office space is made available in the department for diplomatic correspondents, and their country cousins on small-town newspapers, radio and television stations are regularly flown in to be briefed by senior officials.

Apart from regular press conferences and briefings, on and off the record, the Secretary and other senior officials frequently receive correspondents, both domestic and foreign, singly and in small groups. The department also conducts briefings for the public. Any perspiring tourist can step in, and for an hour or so rest in air-conditioned comfort in one of the many auditoriums while an earnest diplomat brings him up to date on national goals and aspirations or some confused situation abroad. Regional foreign policy conferences are conducted in various parts of the country.

Much of this, of course, is standard practice in Washington. The right of the public to know is accepted, although officials occasionally offend against this splendid principle when neither security nor discretion is involved. The processes of American government also demand a public or semipublic traffic in ideas and information. The executive has no direct representation in Congress. There are few formal channels, and those that exist are liable to sudden change. The Secretary of State, or an assistant, can brief the appropriate Congressional committee. He does not address Congress on the floor of either chamber, although it is constitutionally admissible. The American system demands an open door. The American ego possibly demands public satisfaction; officials want to be heard.

That said, the open door remains very impressive. I cannot think of another foreign ministry which pursues a similar policy. The Foreign Office in London is as closed as the Communist Party's Central Committee Building in East Berlin. Correspondents rarely get beyond information officers, and when they do must be accompanied by guards. The parliamentary system requires official information to be made known first to the House of Commons, but this hardly explains the lack of normal communication between the press and the Foreign Office. The Quai d'Orsai in Paris is equally withdrawn and aloof. Business with other countries must of course be conducted with discretion, but in the free world there cannot be a capital more conscious of security than Washington. One can only conclude that the blank façades of European ministries were erected on the assumption that diplomacy with its aristocratic origins is not the concern of the ordinary man or is above his comprehension.

No American diplomat could safely act on that assumption. The United States is an open society, with a healthy suspicion of official secrecy, especially in foreign affairs. Open agreements more or less openly arrived at is an article of faith that bothers the State Department at times but is nevertheless sound. Moreover, no mystery is seen in diplomacy. Rather is it accepted as a perfectly understandable process evolved to secure the national interest, to help defend the Republic from its enemies, and to maintain civilized relations with other countries. If the complexity of the process confuses, if problems do not lend themselves to obvious solutions, then the public has the right to know.

Foreign governments are no doubt discomfited by the drafts through the open door, but this is the American way. The State Department, despite the international nature of its purpose and the protocols governing much of its business, is essentially a national product as are few other foreign ministries, and largely of the post-second war period. To that extent past diplomatic experience is seen to be of little help. It can be argued that the department has small experience to fall back upon. This is not strictly true, but for about eighty years, from the declaration of the Monroe Doctrine to the war with Spain, no need was seen for an active foreign policy. Some Americans believe that the very nature of foreign policy, of what it consists and how it is formed, was largely forgotten in those eight decades, and a few Europeans would agree with them. The failure to form a policy in the subsequent half-century, according to Walter Lippmann, was due to the fact that the country no longer knew what was needed. Mr. Lippmann was perhaps unduly harsh, but much had to be learned, and in the nuclear age much had to be devised. American diplomacy is the new diplomacy.

Once through the open door on C Street, the foreigner is impressed by the sheer size of the building. It occupies four city blocks, and rises to eight floors, the eighth being a large penthouse, with a decor reminiscent of Hitler's Chancellory, where official entertaining is done.

The Pentagon is bigger, but the Defense Department commands and administers vast armies, fleets, and air forces, and in recent years has spent more than $50 billion a year. Apart from foreign aid, the annual appropriation of the State Department is generally less than $400 million, or about the cost of a single aircraft carrier.

Other government departments have larger staffs, but by the standards of the old diplomacy the State Department is enormous. At the time of writing, rather more than forty thousand were employed, including members of the Agency for International Development and the Peace Corps. About fourteen thousand Americans were in the Foreign Service and its affiliated civil services, half in Washington and the remainder with overseas posts, which number more than three hundred. The latter were assisted by ten thousand foreign nationals. Another 25,000 more Americans were also attached to the diplomatic missions abroad, representing most of the federal government's departments and agencies, and the armed services. Even the Coast Guard was represented. It was not always so. The department is fond of wryly recalling that the first Secretary of State, Thomas Jefferson, had a staff of five clerks, a part-time translator of French, and two messengers. As late as the 1930s the department was comfortably accommodated in a building shared with the old War Department. At the outbreak of the Second World War the staff numbered only eight hundred.

The telephone directory pressed upon every reporter provides an institutionalized version of the responsibilities accepted by the United States since those cozy days. The Secretary is immediately assisted by two Under Secretaries, for political and economic affairs, although these labels only approximately indicate their areas of responsibility. The senior Under Secretary generally drops the ancillary label. Then there are ambassadors at large, often known as troubleshooters, the chairman of the Policy Planning Council, and the Director of Intelligence and Research. Special assistants abound, as do legal and scientific advisers and experts in fields such as fisheries and wildlife and Soviet affairs.

Beneath the heavily supported triumvirate on the seventh floor are Assistant Secretaries of State for Public, Congressional, Educational, and Cultural Affairs, and five more in charge of the regional bureaus. These deal with Africa, the American Hemisphere, Europe, the Far East, and the Near East and South Asia. There is also an Assistant

Secretary of State for International Organization Affairs. He is primarily concerned with the United Nations and its agencies, and there is a permanent UN representative of Cabinet rank. Below this second layer in the department is a phalanx of Deputy Assistant Secretaries, in charge of offices within the bureaus. For instance, within the Bureau of European Affairs there are offices dealing with political areas such as Northern and Eastern Europe, and specialized offices concerned with Atlantic political and military and political-economic affairs. All these posts are political appointments, although some are always occupied by members of the Foreign Service, especially at the lower levels.

The specialized offices are the bureaucratic answer to the many responsibilities and preoccupations of superpower. They are clearly necessary, and an improvement on past organization. The regional bureaus also multiplied over the years. For instance, there was no Far Eastern Bureau when Mr. Hay wrote his Open Door notes, which perhaps explains why his policy was borrowed from a visiting Englishman, Mr. Hippisley. Traditional diplomacy also depends upon bilateral relations requiring a great deal of humdrum work such as dealing with alleged trade discrimination in the button industry or rescuing drunken sailors from foreign jails. But the organization does not meet all the requirements of the Secretary of State. He is concerned primarily with alliances and not countries, with multilateral ventures and not bilateral relations, with entire regions where political boundaries may be meaningless. This can perhaps be described as the layering of responsibility inevitable for a superpower. In dozens of foreign ministries the first concern is relations with the United States. In Washington the state of these relations is important, but often only to the extent that they affect alliances. Loyalty from allies is expected, but direct reciprocity is rejected. The United States has too many interests and allies, often in conflict, to permit such a simple relationship.

The sheer complexity of these world-wide relationships requires a continual process of adjustment and compromise, and there can be occasions when other countries feel that their interests have been compromised or adjusted out of existence. The regional bureaus deal with such complexities, but they can also contribute to them. There are pro-German and pro-French movements within the department fiercely defending the ally of their choice. There is an assumption that as a whole the department leans toward Britain, which is not necessarily correct at all times. A dilemma can emerge from the confusion; for instance, the nuclear-test-ban treaty was alleged to discriminate against West Germany. Caught between the traditional horns, the Secretary of State must have a realistic conception of the totality of the American national interest. To meet this need the Policy Planning Council was established after the Second World War. Ideally, it is a group of men lifted above the humdrum and inter-bureau conflict, and indeed it does sit on the seventh floor, and is paid to think. On the whole, it has served this purpose well, although its members incline to become fierce protagonists of their Great Thoughts. In the early attempt to launch a multilateral nuclear force there was no fiercer protagonist than those who conceived it, and the stresses within the alliance were such that the totality of national interest was overlooked, and President Johnson had to scuttle the project.

But the Secretary of State cannot remain long preoccupied with great thoughts in the stratosphere of higher diplomacy. The United States can hope to influence events abroad; it cannot control many. Crises suddenly erupt, often in unimportant places but compete for the highest attention if they are seen to endanger the global balance of political, ideological, or territorial power. At first, the vast organization at Foggy Bottom was more often than not found wanting. Nowadays *ad hoc* committees, known as task forces since the Kennedy administration, proliferate overnight, and command posts are set up at a moment's notice. There are also special ambassadorial and intergovernmental committees to take care of particularly sensitive problems requiring joint Allied action such as Berlin.

Apart from these temporary arrangements, which have a habit of perpetuating themselves, there are four agencies associated with the department. Two are described as semiautonomous, and two are separate but receive over-all policy guidance from the department. The first are the Agency for International Development (AID), which spent some $100 billion in foreign aid in the first two decades of its existence, and the Peace Corps, which recruits skilled or eager volunteers for service in underdeveloped countries. The others are the Arms Control and Disarmament Agency (ACDA) and the United States Information Agency (USIA), which also runs the Voice of America, a world-wide radio network broadcasting in more than thirty languages for some eight hundred hours a week.

One can wonder what a Metternich would have thought of a diplomatic service concerned with teaching Indian peasants how to grow more rice, providing young teachers and craftsmen to work with missionary zeal all over the world, and broadcasting jazz and news of the latest race riot in Alabama to Africa. He would certainly have been confounded by the political appointments in the department, which more often than not are filled by members of what can be called the American Establishment. If the term should be resented in an egalitarian society, it remains that in the United States there is a rather special breed who look remarkably similar to Establishment men in Britain. Perhaps it is easier first to describe the British prototype, which is neither sinisterly secret nor exclusive, as is often imagined on this side of the Atlantic.

The term—it is nothing more—was borrowed from the Established Church to describe those men capable and available to run the country in the way most Englishmen expect it to be run. They can be Members of Parliament, civil servants, lawyers, newspaper editors, senior officers of the armed services, or scientists, active or retired, in office or out of office. Birth, education, and wealth cannot guarantee membership, although because of the aristocratic or genteel origins of British society and its stratified education system many are well connected or went to fashionable schools. A poor boy of talent can, and does, win acceptance. What they all share is experience, some ability, and a willingness to serve in almost any capacity. Clearly they have not been members of some secret society or cabal. If they do not inspire universal respect and affection, it is because of the suspicion that they prevent a wider and more equitable distribution of appointments, power, and influence. The suspicion is not unfounded, but even rebels can, and are, absorbed. The radical Labour politician of yesteryear is likely to be a pillar of the Establishment tomorrow.

In political America, and especially in the conduct of foreign policy, a similar alliance became evident in the early decades of this century when political liberals such as Theodore Roosevelt and Woodrow Wilson established connections with scholars, lawyers, and businessmen concerned about the beginnings of an active American responsibility in the world. Each group no doubt had its special interest, such as the maintenance of open world markets or a world environment hospitable to the basic freedoms. Basically it was an alliance against the extremism of the left and the right, with conservative ends but more or less liberal means. The vast majority were

Anglo-American or had Northern European origins, and they tended to come from the better Eastern universities or from the great law firms in New York and Washington. They did not share the common contempt for Europe.

They came into their own with the final emergence of the United States as a superpower. The new burden of global responsibility required many shoulders, and they belonged to men who were ready and willing and concerned—the American Establishment. The base was broadened to include rather more academics from the universities, especially from the more recently established centers of specialized study, and the private foundations such as the Ford and Rockefeller Foundations. The majority of Ivy League Wasps was diminished, but it remained dominant. When President Kennedy formed his administration, he looked almost exclusively to them. A member of his staff told me when the somewhat haphazard recruitment was completed that most of the new men found that they knew each other, often intimately. Some were related or connected by marriage. The New Frontiersmen turned out to be Establishment men.

The interlocking of law firms, universities, and foundations is the core of the American Establishment, whereas in Britain it is largely politics and the Civil Service. The reason explains a good deal about the American system. Congress does not easily provide the avenues to power and influence over foreign policy. The chairman of the Senate Foreign Relations Committee can exert great influence, but he is one among a hundred, and in recent years has been burdened with the unenviable chore of securing legislative passage for the controversial foreign aid program. The formal occasions when he can shine, as with the ratification of treaties, are few. The right of advice and consent remains a constitutional prerogative, but in the informal exchanges that precede all important Presidential decisions his voice can be only one among many.

Nor does the Foreign Service offer a more certain path to power. The important ambassadorial posts are generally political rewards, and are often beyond the ambition of the career officer. Loyal service and talent are rewarded a little more generously than in the past, but an experienced diplomat can still be denied advancement by a political appointee. In the fifties one of them did not know the name of the prime minister of the country in which he was to serve. It would be foolish of the career officer to aspire to the secretaryship.

Bryce has it that the Secretary comes from the party leadership, and that the President regards the appointment as a payment of a political debt. Times have changed. President Kennedy had not met Dean Rusk before appointing him in 1961. He was afterward confirmed in office by President Johnson.

For the Establishment man, the power which the State Department represents is a citadel to be stormed. Not for them the long and occasionally grubby years in Congress representing the interests of constituents. Not for them a dreary apprenticeship in the consulate in Liverpool or Oslo. Or for that matter, not for them a lifetime of toil in government service. They come and go, often with changes in administrations but not always. Political affiliation does not appear to be important; Republicans serve in Democratic administrations, and Democrats in Republican administrations, although the latter is not so common. Quite often they go simply because the bureaucracy becomes too tiresome, or they return to the law practice to replenish the family fortune. If this sounds like diplomacy by dilettantism, I have given the wrong impression. The dilettanti are present, but the majority are serious and capable men who over the years gain wide experience of world affairs, diplomacy, and government procedures.

The young man fresh from university, or from law clerking for a Supreme Court justice, can begin by working for a Presidential candidate and work his way up the ladder if the candidate proves to be both successful and grateful. Many years later, and perhaps after some interruption in government service, he is established well enough to be called upon to fill a senior appointment in the State Department or for special duty. This is the well-beaten path to advancement, influence, and power, but it is not only one. Some well-placed men merely pull family strings; others begin in political journalism. A few have come from the armed services. Dean Rusk, who made it to the top, took a more circuitous route. There was the Rhodes scholarship, which is always a great help, a university appointment, and then military service in the Second World War. It is perhaps little known that the quiet Secretary enjoyed army life and considered a career in uniform, but he attracted attention and when the late General Marshall went to the State Department he took Mr. Rusk along. Then came an assistant secretaryship, the chairmanship of the Rockefeller Foundation, and finally the office on the seventh floor.

E

Presumably the State Department could function well enough without the Establishment men, but I doubt it. The American system concentrates enormous power upon the President, and then fails to support him with anything comparable to the British Cabinet. He needs not only competent men for his own personal staff, but also his own men in the great departments, especially the State Department. They do not have to be known personally to him. It is sufficient if they belong to the same party, or that they share his ambitions for the country, or are known to his Cabinet officers. The Establishment is a corps of talented men to whom he or his advisers can turn.

The deficiencies of the system, as is often the case, can prove to be blessings. The Establishment men bring a fresh view and experience always invaluable in the leavening of official thinking. They are available. Equally important, their influence can be beneficial even when they are out of office. The late fifties provide a fairly recent example, when after the launching of the Soviet Sputnik a number came together to write the Rockefeller reports. The crisis that drew them together was seen to be grave in the extreme. Sputnik demonstrated a potential Soviet capability to launch a missile attack against the United States, a capability that could irrevocably upset the balance of superpower. Nelson Rockefeller, who had earlier resigned from President Eisenhower's staff, apparently after differences over defense and foreign aid expenditures, organized a general review of American problems and policies, domestic and foreign. The members of the panels included some typical Establishment men, who because of their government experience were well informed on military and foreign policy matters. Many had enjoyed past access to secret information. They came from both parties, but were united in what they considered to be the defense of the Republic. The reports not only had a quick if somewhat limited effect upon President Eisenhower's policies; they provided a firm foundation upon which President Kennedy and President Johnson could build.

As in Britain, the Establishment is not widely loved. The professional diplomat perhaps eyes its members warily, although service together presumably wears down some of the sharp corners of professional pride and jealousy. But whatever reservations the professionals may have, many admit that they are as essential to the department as they are to the President. Their political connections can be all-important when a new policy is being promoted below the top level of the administration. As in the medieval monarchies, anybody who can approach the President or his personal staff is a powerful ally. They tend also to provide a continuity of political thought. The young man who served, no matter how modestly, in the early postwar years when the Marshall Plan and NATO were conceived is likely to strengthen the forces of internationalism when he returns for another stint in government service in later years.

Metternich would have been no less confounded by the strange language American diplomacy began to use in the sixties. Earlier the emergence of the United States as a superpower willing to accept the responsibilities of superpower had changed the language of diplomacy from French to English. This was momentous enough, but the strange language of the sixties was as far removed from diplomatic French as the Houston Space Center was from the Congress of Vienna. "Input," "output," "matrix," and "feedback" were but a few examples, and they suggested that American diplomacy was about to be automated. The State Department was not prepared to go that far, the Secretary was not quite ready to exchange his handsome mahogany desk for a computer console. But the restless American research for efficiency had led to the adoption of program review and analysis, management planning, program control, and systems analysis as management tools of foreign affairs. A new age of diplomacy had begun.

Not all American diplomats took kindly to the idea of describing a United States Embassy as a Component Field Organization (CFO) or the Ambassador as the Chief Foreign Affairs Field Manager. There were some rather old-fashioned objections to assessing their ancient craft in terms of man-hours and cost and performance effectiveness. Wry jokes were reported from CFOs as far afield as Bogotá and Cairo about punching time clocks and meeting the weekly quota. Variations on such themes must have kept diplomatic dinners going from the soup to the nuts, but programming for foreign affairs, as the new diplomacy was called, was in fact an imaginative and very serious attempt to master the growing complexity of foreign affairs.

The complexity arose partly from the world-wide system of defensive alliances and the proliferation of sovereign states. Through the years policy-planning had produced a number of policy and strategy positions or statements. For one country in 1962 there existed seven separate policy positions. The first step taken toward a coordination of foreign affairs was the development of National Policy Papers. These were developed by the Policy Planning Council, and were comprehensive and authoritative statements of American policy toward particular countries. But there were also causes for complexity in Washington. It was estimated at the time that the United States spent more than $5 billion a year in foreign operations. The budget of the State Department was less than one-tenth of this enormous sum. The bulk went in financing foreign aid, the United States Information Services, Food for Peace, and the Peace Corps. The objectives of these programs were identical, to serve the national interest abroad, but before the new diplomatic age there was no effective central control. There were no means of controlling the procedures that caused agencies to carry out plans or commit budgets for the attainment of the goals suggested in the National Policy Papers.

The problem had been long weighed and nibbled at. President Kennedy had ordered that the ambassador must be responsible for all official operations in the country to which he was accredited. The Herter Committee had proposed a system of programming for the State Department. Eventually, the department's Office of Management Planning was requested to devise means to give the Secretary of State control over all foreign operations similar to that exercised by the Secretary of Defense over the armed forces and national security.

For the management experts, the task was not much different from, say, improving the productivity of a biscuit factory. The first task was to devise an information system which when fully operational could be used for a variety of programming purposes. In foreign affairs, as they saw it, the input was the resources available, money, materials, and men such as ambassadors, military attachés, CIA agents, agricultural advisers, and the like. Output was the specific activities in which the resources were used in any given country, such as diplomatic reporting and representing and furthering the American interest. The matrix was the country, situation, or crisis in which resources were translated into activities. Feedback was the information continually fed back into the system to keep it up to date. The purpose was to reflect at any given time the state of operations in a country or crisis.

American thoroughness was evident in the early investigations that were carried out in some thirty countries, in which computers were

eventually used. A *Comprehensive Country Program Book* was produced for each country, with output categories such as Management,
International Relations, Internal Development, Standard Services,
and Administration. The intention was not so much to standardize
operations or reduce costs, although both were seen to be important,
as to inform the Chief Foreign Affairs Field Manager, or Ambassador, of all the capabilities of his Component Field Organization, or
Embassy, and give him the means to control them. Simulation tests
were conducted, rather like the exercises without troops military
commanders had done for years. CFOs were asked to assume, for
instance, that a party or movement inimical to the American interest
might come into power. What could be done to help the friendly
government to survive? Who could possibly influence the course of
events? Which member of the CFO, or Country Team to use the
accepted label, knew whom? Were outside resources required to
maintain the balance? And so on.

Perhaps some readers may be shocked by the suggestion of American interference in the internal affairs of other countries. Metternich
would not have been shocked, nor President Theodore Roosevelt for
that matter. Great powers have always accepted the necessity to
intervene. Diplomacy has made discreet intervention possible when
gunboats were inappropriate or dangerous. What the United States
did in the sixties was to apply modern management tools to situations
infinitely more complex than any which Metternich had to deal with.
And the use of these management tools improved and to some extent
changed the nature of American diplomacy. In putting its own
inimitable stamp upon it the United States has created a new diplomacy.

At the apex of the sprawling and somewhat chaotic organization at
Foggy Bottom, but not above the turmoil, stands the Secretary of
State. His is a position of great dignity and responsibility. He is the
principal adviser to the President in the determination and execution
of foreign policy. As the first Cabinet officer, he is in line of
succession to the Presidency. He is the custodian of the Great Seal of
the United States. He is a member of the National Security Council,
the National Aeronautics and Space Council, the Civil and Defense
Mobilization Board, the Export Control Review Board, the Establishment of the Smithsonian Institution, and the Board of Trustees of

the National Gallery of Art. Only the President, the Vice President, and the Speaker of the House of Representatives take precedence over him on occasions of state. He travels abroad like a medieval magnate, complete with personal standard.

If the President has over-all responsibility for the direction of foreign policy, the Secretary of State has primary responsibility for initiating and implementing foreign policies. He is charged with studying the bearing of domestic conditions on foreign policy and must correlate the activities of other government agencies that affect foreign relations. He must propose measures for promoting solidarity with friendly countries and the advancement of American ideals. He develops policies for American participation in the United Nations and other international organizations. He corresponds with American diplomatic and consular representatives abroad, in a never-ending exchange of five thousand communications a day, and maintains relations with foreign ambassadors in Washington. He must expect to travel extensively, participate in negotiations of immense complexity, and personally know the foreign ministers of many countries.

The power and the glory are indisputable, but neither can be taken for granted. His responsibilities have increased with American responsibilities, but they have also been reduced and redefined. If he must now be alert to any mutation in the balance of power anywhere in the world, the prerogative of Presidential intervention is more often exercised. There can be no easy assumption that the White House does not have to be informed. It is informed, and by an agency over which the Secretary of State has no control. He is now essentially a staff officer, a very superior staff officer, and one who, if he does his duty, must deny himself any reasonable hope of being a future candidate for the Presidency. The days when a Jefferson or a Madison could use the State Department as a steppingstone to the White House are over. It is now extremely doubtful whether a Presidential candidate would want to be a Secretary of State, or whether he would grace the office.

The unpopular character of much that the Secretary is required to do when popular emotion is aroused could destroy his political availability. The responsibilities are too demanding to allow time for politicking. The talents and qualities demanded of a competent Secretary are so highly specialized that they are almost certainly a disqualification for the Presidency. He must be independent, but cannot be detached. He must cooperate with Congress, but not be subservient to it. Superior ability must not be an affront, as it was, alas, with Dean Acheson. A commanding general would no doubt recognize in this list the shape of a good chief of staff.

For the Secretary, the commanding general is of course the President. He bears the ultimate responsibility, nobody else can, and he must make the decisions. This is the constitutional position, and in times of crisis the President has traditionally become his own Secretary of State. The tradition was established, or the necessity was first recognized, by Washington in 1793 at the time of the Citizen Genêt affair. There have been occasions, however, and they have become increasingly more common in this century, when the President exercised his powers with scant regard for the Secretary of State.

When the United States entered the First World War, and assumed a major share of the responsibility for the making of the peace, President Wilson looked outside the State Department for his staff work. A special group was formed in 1917 under Colonel House to prepare for the peace conference, and in acquiescing, the Secretary of State, Robert Lansing, divorced the department from the peacemaking process. Whether or not this contributed to President Wilson's subsequent failure, it remains that the Secretary and the department were not closely associated with one of the greatest settlements diplomacy has been called upon to make.

It was an error, if the loyal but disgruntled submission to the President can be so described, that profoundly affected the status and influence of the department when its hour struck again more than two decades later. In 1940, despite widespread opposition and reluctance, President Roosevelt anticipated the eventual American entry into the Second World War, and began military and economic negotiations with Britain. The negotiations were far more fundamental than they then appeared to be. American military, economic, and political strength was about to be committed on a global scale for the first time. The balance of world power was to be irrevocably changed. Yet this momentous departure, which ended at the pinnacle of superpower and free world leadership, took place with the State Department more or less stranded on the platform waving good-bye.

The President was thereafter firmly at the controls, but the crew was a motley assortment of activists from the White House staff, the Treasury, the Lend-Lease Administration, and the Board of Economic Warfare. The State Department was greatly expanded, but the effect at the time was to dilute and weaken the professional Foreign Service. The Secretary of State, Cordell Hull, found himself mainly explaining the President's policies to Congress, and with his responsibilities for foreign policy severely limited. The department lost out not only to the activists, but to the military, which was more important because it could perpetuate itself. Admiral Leahy, President Roosevelt's military representative, was to say afterward that the Joint Chiefs of Staff were under no civilian control whatever.

President Kennedy was equally cavalier in his dealings with the department, of which he is said to have had less than a low opinion. He regarded it mainly as a pool of technicians upon whose individual services he could call upon at will. A kind of Hertz Rent A Diplomat. Many a simple desk officer was surprised to be telephoned by the President, and the considerable confusion did not add to the stature of the Secretary. According to a memoir by one of his personal advisers, Professor Arthur Schlesinger, Jr., President Kennedy apparently dreamed of a secret office of thirty people or so to run foreign policy. The failure of the attempted Cuban invasion of 1961, which was planned by such a small secret group, did not convince him that the department might be more helpful in the future. Instead, task forces and executive committees proliferated, and the State Department failed to dominate most of them. President Kennedy took the Rooseveltian method as his model, and modernized it.

The postwar pattern was of course broken by President Eisenhower, who served to support the observation of Bryce that a President is run by his Secretary of State only when the Secretary is the stronger man. President Eisenhower confused the Presidential office with that of a modern constitutional monarch. He failed to realize that an American President is a medieval monarch. His quietism allowed the activism of his Secretary of State free play. During the Eisenhower administration American foreign policy was practically the policy of John Foster Dulles.

The thirty-fourth President's administration was hardly typical of the postwar era, in which the Presidential prerogative was progressively extended. Wilson and Roosevelt intervened during two great wars. All postwar Presidents, with the exception of President Eisenhower, have felt obliged to intervene at early stages in disputes that need not directly concern the United States. It is no longer a matter of Presidential intervention in the conduct of foreign policy in time of crisis. Intervention can be, and often is, required even when a crisis does not threaten. The President must now be prepared to direct and coordinate policies as well as determine and execute. He is his own Secretary of State at all times.

The main reasons are obvious enough in the nuclear age. He cannot afford to ignore a minor conflict in some distant jungle or desert with an unpronounceable name because of the possibility that it may bring the two superpowers into direct confrontation. A famine in Asia, a tribal clash in Africa, or a *coup d'état* in Central America could change the ideological or power balance between the two superpowers. The clandestine activities of guerrilla bands are as potentially dangerous as the deployment of large conventional forces. The halting of convoys on the road to West Berlin could be an ultimatum. When fuses are seen to be leading from all over the world to the underground missile silos, precautionary or corrective action must be taken as early as possible.

The President is not only the American Chief Executive and Commander in Chief; he is also the leader of the free world and of regional alliances commanding millions of troops. His control of nuclear weapons gives him the power of life and death over the nation's allies and enemies alike. Relations with allied countries can be intimate when their existence depends upon the United States. They can also be very complicated and sensitive. In either case they cannot be always conducted at the level of the Secretary of State. The President must be heard personally and frequently.

There is also the pressure upon him to meet his enemies at so-called summit conferences. They can be profitless, but the pressure is there because of the knowledge that only the President can act. These meetings with heads of state or government, either friendly, neutral, or belligerent, bear little resemblance to the great state visits of the past. If the pomp and circumstance are maintained, they are more often than not solemn exchanges with the Asian guerrilla, the Berlin road, and the missile silos in mind. The missiles are underground and capped by huge concrete and steel slabs, but they cast a constant shadow over the White House. To avoid a confrontation that might raise those slabs, to maintain alliances considered essential for American security, and a dialogue with the enemy to make them one day unnecessary, are the basic goals of American foreign policy. The

E*

United States no longer pursues foreign and defense policies as normally understood, but a national security policy.

This is not a bureaucratic play on words, and it does not ignore the traditional connections between diplomacy and defense, or between the State Department and the Defense Department. It does mean that the old division of responsibility between the two departments is largely irrelevant, that a degree of cooperation and coordination is required that was rarely if ever attempted before. Only the President can achieve it, and in the process the Secretary of State becomes no more than a senior staff officer.

Much of the criticism by uncomprehending commentators of Dean Rusk in the early years of his office as Secretary of State was that he had reduced his ancient office to that level. The criticism appeared valid to some because of the personalities involved. He served strong Presidents, and was a self-effacing but by no means weak man. Nevertheless, in the new situation he could not be anything but a very senior staff officer.

The nature of the new situation was perceived soon after the Second World War when, with the passage of the National Security Act in 1947, the National Security Council was established. Its function is to advise the President with respect to the integration of domestic, foreign, and military policies relating to national security. Its duties are to assess and appraise the objectives, commitments, and risks of the United States in relation to its actual and potential military power. It also considers policies on matters of common interest to the departments and agencies of the government concerned with national security.

The official definition is hardly elegant, but its clumsiness is explained to some extent by multitudinous efforts now seen to be required by national security. The NSC has its own staff directed by the Special Assistant to the President for National Security Affairs. Under the direction of the Council is the Central Intelligence Agency, which was also established by the 1947 act. In its comparatively short existence, the NSC has not suited every President. President Kennedy found very little use for it. As with the State Department, he frequently met or telephoned individual members, but the Council was rarely used as a corporate body. The collective wisdom, experience, and expertise such bodies are assumed to acquire, which is supposed to be greater than the sum of its parts, was dissipated and never established in his lifetime. For those who put their faith in political institutions, there was perhaps cause for regret, but that is the American way. What was an irksome necessity for President Truman, who nevertheless distrusted the Council, and suited the military staff training of President Eisenhower, plainly bored President Kennedy. President Johnson's respect for established institutions was greater, but he became a free-wheeling activist.

To a large extent the work of the Council is now done by the staff. The director, the Special Assistant to the President for National Security Affairs, has become a considerable power within the administration, despite his modest title. He is, as it were, the President's Secretary of State when the President is acting as Secretary of State. If this sounds rather confusing—and it can be most confusing for the Secretary of State, the one who sits on the seventh floor of the State Department—the process that led to it is quite understandable. The NSC was created to advise the President, a function that required a new organizational pyramid based on the Departments of State and Defense and the Central Intelligence Agency. If the Council did not meet with unanimous Presidential approval, the problems it was created to deal with and the organizational pyramid remained. At the top stood the Special Assistant to the President for National Security Affairs.

The loftiness of his position is further elevated by the simple fact that he works in the basement of the White House, below the President's office. He is immediately available. Across his desk come all the communications from the great departments. He is more intimately aware of defense questions than is the Secretary of State, and of diplomatic questions than is the Secretary of Defense. He maintains an operations room which in times of crisis becomes the nerve center of all the vast apparatus for controlling the American armed forces. Across the river, in the Pentagon, there is a more elaborate control room where general officers are in constant touch with far-flung armies, fleets, air flotillas, the lonely crews manning the intercontinental ballistic missiles underground and Polaris missile submarines under the sea. Somewhere in a nearby mountain range there is a deep control center ready for the President, his family, staff, Cabinet officers, and other senior officials, should a nuclear attack on Washington appear imminent. Fortunately, the President has not had to retire to this Wagnerian cave, although such a move was contemplated during the 1962 Cuban crisis, and the basement room in the White House has remained the vital communications center.

It does not have to be emphasized that the man who controls such an apparatus, who can emerge as soon as the President beckons or calls, is in a remarkable position to bring influence to bear. His personal staff, whose members singly or in pairs specialize in the affairs of geographical regions or specific long-standing problems, is a stripped-down State Department, depending for much of their information upon the department down at Foggy Bottom but also seeking it from outside sources. The Special Assistant sees all the national security papers sent to the President, and to some extent decides what should be forwarded to him. In times of emergency, those who want the President's urgent attention call the Special Assistant. Any secret information from the CIA invariably passes through his hands. He is also the man who decides whether the President should be awakened when a crisis breaks in the small hours.

During the Johnson administration he became the third member of the triumvirate who advise the President on national security affairs, the others being the Secretaries of State and Defense. Their regular weekly luncheons at the Presidential table provided the informal acknowledgment, not uncommon in Washington, of where the power rested. The presence of the Secretary of Defense indicated the final stage in the erosion of the pre-eminence of the office of the Secretary of State. He was there, of course, because foreign policy could no longer be separated from defense. Robert McNamara, the first Defense Secretary to join the triumvirate, had also shown extraordinary energy and organizational ability since President Kennedy plucked him from the chairman's office of the Ford Motor Company. His status was further enhanced by the reassertion of civil authority over the military, and once again one must look to the past to understand the present.

During the Second World War there was an extraordinary revolution in the relationship between the civil and military authorities. Generals and admirals moved from political isolation into seats of power, and played a more important role in the conduct of the war than the military in any other country with the exception of Japan. The Secretary of State, and indeed the Navy and War Secretaries, played only marginal roles, and were not always present when the great politico-military decisions were made. The Second World War marked an unprecedented spring tide of military influence in the

American government, and military requirements to a large extent dictated foreign policy for many years afterward.

There was good reason for much of this, once it had been decided that Soviet imperialism must be contained. Few will argue that a position of strength was first required before diplomacy could be effective. This is not the place to assess the wisdom of the policy, or pass judgment. For the immediate purpose, it is sufficient to note how the power of the military remained more or less undiminished after the end of the Second World War. In this atmosphere every other general appeared to have his own foreign policy, and was allowed to state it publicly even when it conflicted with official policy. Much of this may have been harmless, if ill-advised, but the military attempt to influence public opinion would have appalled George Washington. It continued until President Kennedy put a stop to it when he "muzzled the military," as their publicists had it.

The so-called muzzling reasserted civil authority in the person of the Defense Secretary. He emerged as a co-equal with the Secretary of State, except in the official order of precedence, and a member of the triumvirate. In his annual presentation of the military budget to Congress, he now prefaces his requests for half of the federal budget with a long foreign policy review. The Defense Department has a Bureau for International Security Affairs, which is its own State Department. Thus when the Secretary of State ponders the possible development of some policy or the launching of a new initiative, he must bear in mind those two other State Departments in the White House and the Pentagon. And that is not all. At times he must look rather uneasily in the direction of a nearby suburb in Virginia where the Central Intelligence Agency has its vast headquarters.

The first statutory purpose of the CIA is the coordination of intelligence, but it has also encroached upon the areas of responsibility traditionally reserved for the State Department. The first is in the reporting and evaluation of conditions and events abroad. All American embassies, and most consulates, have CIA agents on their staffs, whose more overt activities place them in competition with the State Department. This is not altogether unusual in the postwar world. Britain has intelligence agents in her embassies, as no doubt do other countries, but their reporting functions are normally limited to areas that do not usually concern diplomats. The wider responsibilities of the CIA are perhaps an inevitable consequence of Washington's conception of national security, and the establishment of the

National Security Council, but again things have worked out differently than was intended. The agency's Director enjoys direct access to the President, to whom he presents, or has presented, each morning a comprehensive report on major events and developments abroad. This alone compromises a traditional function of the Secretary of State.

In the pursuit of its more clandestine objectives, the agency can and does influence policy and events abroad. It has helped to overthrow governments. Its most dramatic operation, as far as is known, was the attempted invasion of Cuba in 1961. This ill-fated expedition has been variously explained, but the CIA was clearly responsible for its conception, organization, and execution.

The Secretary of State has thus seen his office diminished in a period when for the first time in its history the United States has played a predominant role in world affairs. The President has become his own Secretary of State, and foreign policy has been largely subordinated to national security policy. It can be assumed that this will continue while the world remains dominated by two great power blocs, although a future President may make changes in the policy-making process.

It can be argued that this is what the authors of the Constitution intended him to be, no more and no less. If earlier Presidents allowed their Secretaries more freedom, it was largely because foreign affairs were of little consequence to them. History shows that when foreign affairs intruded, Presidents were quick to assert themselves. It can also be said that after the nadir of two world wars the status of the Secretary has been retrieved, that he can no longer be largely ignored in times of extreme crisis. If a small conflict in some distant country can threaten to bring about a superpower confrontation, military requirements can in turn create political instability no less dangerous. A stable deterrent is not the only requirement for peace. Nuclear stability generates its own problems, for which the only known answer is arms control and disarmament. The Secretary of State now helps to bear the burden of heavy responsibilities, and because the ultimate responsibility must rest with the President it seems at best unkind to condemn him for being a staff officer.

When foreign policy is discussed in the United States, a great deal is said about American aspirations, beliefs, and goals. Much of this talk can make Europeans impatient, not because they do not have aspirations, beliefs, and goals, but because the harsh realities of power have too often dominated their national experience. When Jefferson proclaimed his self-evident truths about the unalienable rights of men to life, liberty, and the pursuit of happiness, Frederick the Great was completing the transformation of Prussia into a militarist state. His was an achievement that was to influence the course of European history for about 170 years and eventually bring the continent to utter ruination and the United States to the pinnacle of power. The fundamental reason for this diversion of national objectives was not because the Prussians then were necessarily more militaristic than the Americans, who were certainly militant and also showed a taste for military adventure. The reason was that the United States was sheltered by two of the world's largest oceans and Prussia had no natural boundary, not even a decent-size river. This, of course, does not detract from the intrinsic value of American aspirations, but it does mean that the United States emerged on the world scene with a greater attachment to them, perhaps too great.

The aspirations and beliefs, including Jefferson's immortal truths, are expressed in the Declaration of Independence and the Constitution. They are a belief in God, conscience, and moral values, "a decent respect to the opinions of mankind," and the conviction that government derives its just powers from the consent of the governed. Then comes the right of the people to representation in the legislature, the independence of the judiciary, and the pre-eminence of civil power over the military. There is also the assertion in the Declaration of Independence "that whenever any Form of Government becomes destructive of these ends, it is the Right of the People to alter or to abolish it, and to institute new Government, laying its foundation on such principles and organizing its powers in such form, as to them shall seem most likely to effect their Safety and Happiness." This belief now hardly enjoys the authority and popularity it did when the colonists abolished the form of government imposed by King George the Third. Nevertheless, Americans have remained true to their birthright, despite occasional backsliding, hypocrisy, and plain wrongheadedness.

The goal was to ensure that the birthright could be enjoyed. President Wilson, when requesting Congress to declare war on Germany on April 2, 1917, said, "The World must be made safe for

democracy." Two months earlier, he had said, "I am proposing
. . . that no nation should seek to extend its polity over any other
nation or people, but that every people should be left free to
determine its own polity, its own way of development, unhindered,
unthreatened, unafraid, the little along with the great." Forty-five
years later, on January 11, 1962, President Kennedy said in his State
of the Union message:

> Yet our basic goal remains the same: a peaceful world community of
> free and independent states, free to choose their own future and their
> own system, so long as it does not threaten the freedom of others. Some
> may choose forms and ways that we would not choose for ourselves, but
> it is not for us that they are choosing. We can welcome diversity; the
> Communists cannot. For we offer a world of choice; they offer the world
> of coercion.

That same month, Dean Rusk, the Secretary of State, was more
specific, and spoke of five major elements of American foreign
policy.

One, to deter or defeat aggression at any level, whether of nuclear
attack or limited war or subversion and guerrilla tactics.

Two, to bring about a closer association of the more industrialized
democracies of Western Europe, North America, and Asia (specifically
Japan) in promoting the prosperity and security of the entire free world.

Three, to help the less developed areas of the world carry through
their revolution of modernization without sacrificing their independence or
their pursuit of democracy.

Four, to assist in the gradual emergence of a genuine world community,
based on cooperation and law, through the establishment and development
of such organs as the United Nations, the World Court, the World Bank
and Monetary Fund, and other global and regional institutions.

Five, to strive tirelessly to end the arms race and reduce the risk of
war, to narrow the areas of conflict with the Communist bloc, and to
continue to spin the infinity of threads that bind peace together.

The realization of American aspirations had thus for obvious
reasons become a most complex task. It required the will and means
to fight war of every kind everywhere, alliances and combinations for
prosperous peace and victorious war, foreign assistance, the acceptance of some measure of supranational authority, disarmament, and
efforts to bring about what the Communists call peaceful coexistence.
The enormity of the task explains the size of the diplomatic factory in

Washington's Foggy Bottom, and the intricate web of relations and alliances encompassing the world. The United States maintains diplomatic relations with more than 115 foreign countries. It is a member of more than fifty international organizations, including of course the United Nations and its specialized agencies, and is represented at others such as the European Economic Community.

The number of international agreements it is party to runs into thousands. At the time of writing, apart from the obligations under the United Nations Charter, it was committed under eight collective defense treaties to the defense of forty-two countries: the Rio Treaty (September 2, 1947), the North Atlantic Treaty (April 4, 1949), the Philippines Treaty (August 30, 1951), the Australia–New Zealand–United States Treaty (September 1, 1951), the Korea Treaty (October 1, 1953), the Southeast Asia Treaty (September 8, 1954), the Formosa Treaty (December 2, 1954), and the Japanese Treaty (January 19, 1960). It was also associated with the Central Treaty Organization, comprising Iran, Pakistan, Turkey, and Britain.

These are the structural bones of American foreign policy as it has developed since the Second World War. Membership in the United Nations is a reversal of the position after the First World War when Congress rejected the League of Nations. The collective defense treaties represent an even more momentous departure. Neutrality had long been the basis of American foreign policy. A Proclamation of Neutrality was issued as early as April 22, 1793, and Washington's Farewell Address laid the groundwork for isolationism. Hamilton, who helped to draft the address, saw an alliance with countries outside the hemisphere as unnatural. America was so distant from Europe that it did not belong naturally to the European system. The general principle of foreign policy propounded by Washington and Hamilton could accept a temporary alliance in a time of emergency, but not a permanent alliance.

The departure was brought about, of course, by the postwar exhaustion of Britain and a devastated Western Europe confronted by Soviet imperialism. The Stalinist challenge was seen as a threat to the very basis of civilization and to the safety of the free world, the only kind of world in which that civilization could exist. The situation was stated in unequivocal language by Dean Acheson, the Secretary of State: "The main obstacle to peace is easy to identify, and there should be no mistake in anyone's mind about it. The obstacle has been created by the policies of the Soviet government." The Soviet challenge did not directly threaten the security of the United States at that time. Intercontinental ballistic missiles had yet to be developed, and the only missiles then in existence, the German V-1 and V-2 rockets, were of limited range and doubtful accuracy. Bombers could cross the Atlantic but were not certain of return. The United States still enjoyed a nuclear monopoly.

It was, however, in the American interest to maintain a balance of power, or a world environment which would permit the continuing development of American society in circumstances not antagonistic to its humanistic traditions. The old balance of power in Europe no longer existed, and a friendly or neutral environment was seen to be threatened mainly because of a geopolitical conception of the world. There was no question of an anti-Communist crusade, at least not among those responsible for foreign policy, or a return to the Manifest Destiny of the last century. The United States had been willing enough to accept a Soviet sphere of influence in Eastern Europe. This was made evident at Yalta. President Roosevelt did not suppose that American troops would remain in Western Europe after the war for more than two years. Only when Soviet imperialism threatened Western Europe, when it was likely that one power might dominate the Eurasian land mass, did the departure from neutrality or isolationism become inevitable.

This could not be countenanced because of the geopolitical conception that the United States is a continental island off the greater land mass of Eurasia, with its larger resources and superior military potential. This simple fact had long been ignored, except by the few founding members of the Establishment. They had been aware that the security of the United States depended to a large degree upon the position of Britain, which depended in turn upon the maintenance of a balance of power in continental Europe. It had been as essential for the United States as it had been for Britain that no continental power, or combination of powers, dominated the Eurasian land mass. The American interest had rested on a balance that could prevent one country or combination of countries from becoming a great sea and land power, subjecting or reducing Britain, and embarking upon overseas expansion. The United States therefore had a special stake in the prosperity and independence of the coastal European and Asian countries.

Much of this was generally forgotten in the long years of isolation. Americans became so accustomed to their security that they forgot that it depended upon Eurasia. British continental diplomacy, which was vital for the American interest, was rejected as unwarranted interference in the affairs of others, Machiavellian, and even immoral. American security was seen to be the reward of superior wisdom in standing aloof from the sordid differences of the Old World. Nevertheless, the realities were never really lost sight of, and today a grasp of this conception is fundamental to an understanding of postwar American foreign policy.

It is a realistic and unsentimental view, as recent history proves. The excesses of Nazi Germany and Fascist Italy angered many Americans, but they did not persuade the country to align itself with the Western democracies because it was assumed that Britain and France would continue to maintain the power balance in Europe. The Jewish vote may have been responsible for the haste with which President Truman later recognized Israel in 1948, but Congress remained opposed to a revision of the Neutrality Act after the sufferings of European Jews had already begun. In the autumn of 1939, when the final solution of the so-called Jewish problem was being pondered in Berlin, when German Jews were already wearing their yellow stars, a national poll indicated that 96.5 percent of the American people felt that the United States should stay out of the war. French appeals for help went unanswered, and as the appeals went, so did France. The Battle of Britain was desperately fought without American aircraft, and in September 1940 President Roosevelt strained legality when he transferred fifty ancient destroyers to Britain in exchange for bases in British possessions in the Western Hemisphere. During his third election campaign the President felt required to say in Boston on October 30, "Your boys are not going to be sent into any foreign war." The issue was decided by the Japanese fleet at Pearl Harbor and the subsequent German declaration of war against the United States.

One might wish that this sequence of events had been different, but these are the facts of history. President Roosevelt was of course very much concerned, as were some other Americans, but Lend-Lease became possible only after the continued survival of Britain was in doubt. The passage of the Lend-Lease legislation with sizable majorities in Congress demonstrated that the lesson of geopolitics had been learned. If it was only partially learned, as was indicated by General

Eisenhower's refusal to take Berlin and the dismissal of Churchill's apprehension over Russian intentions in Eastern Europe, it was finally taken after the war. Some Congressional dissension remained. There was the Taft-Hoover Doctrine, with its advocacy of what was known as continentalism or Fortress America. But the realities, especially the exhaustion of Britain, could not be avoided, and the North Atlantic Treaty was ratified by a vote of 82–13.

The turning point had come in 1947 with the Truman Doctrine, declaring that the security of the United States was involved wherever direct or indirect aggression threatened the peace. This momentous pronouncement was quickly followed by the Marshall Plan, which showed that the American conception of geopolitics was not confined to geography, resources, and military potential. It was seen that more had to be done than deny Western Europe physically to the Soviet Union. The world environment in which the United States could continue to develop also depended upon the survival or revival of other democratic societies. It could not flourish as an island in a totalitarian sea. The Marshall Plan was an unprecedented act of generosity, but it was also evidence of a very deep and clear understanding of what the American future required. American fortunes as well as lives and sacred honor were pledged to maintain the ideological as well as geopolitical balance.

It is possibly rather ironic to quote from the Declaration of Independence to illustrate the degree of the American commitment to Western Europe, and therefore a large measure of dependence. The situation would not perhaps have offended Washington, although one cannot be so certain of Jefferson. Certainly Washington and Hamilton understood geopolitics when the power situation was reversed, and the young and weak Republic was unable to defend itself against a European combination. The geopolitics of the eighteenth century demanded isolation, and the circumstances of the time called for a diplomacy that 170 years later was dismissed by Mr. Dulles as immoral. Indeed, American independence was achieved by exploiting British and French differences, and in the nineteenth century the United States expanded and consolidated its power on the North American continent by taking advantage of the power conflicts of Eurasia. To this extent, American history denied the idea of a United States safely isolated by geography. Its relationship to Eurasia had always been the first factor in its security. In the early postwar years the freedom and friendship of Western Europe were seen to be as essential to American security as the continued independence of the Latin-American states.

The North Atlantic Treaty and the Rio Treaty were solemn, far-reaching commitments. It was agreed that an attack against one member of either alliance would be considered as an attack against all its members. In other words, the United States committed itself to respond instantly to aggression against twenty Latin-American countries and thirteen Western European countries and Canada. The Rio Treaty provided legal justification for applying the Monroe Doctrine, a declaration which earlier had little more force than could be given it by an unspoken British commitment. The North Atlantic Treaty in effect extended the Monroe Doctrine to the River Elbe. In a way it annexed Western Europe and attached it to the American continental island.

The acceptance of Article 5 of the North Atlantic Treaty, which declared that an attack against one member of the alliance would be considered as an attack against all, achieved more. In theory it offended against the constitutional prerogative of Congress to declare war, but Congressional hearings on the treaty showed an awareness of the absurdity of waiting upon Congress to declare war while missiles might be falling upon New York or Washington. While all the appropriate genuflections were made to the constitutional division of power, it was realized and accepted that there could be circumstances when only the President could act, and that he must be free to act. Thus the treaty increased the Presidential authority beyond the wildest fears of the founders and the latter-day constitutional fundamentalists. It raised the President to a seat of power above Congress as well as the elected governments and ancient monarchies of fourteen foreign countries. The treaty was an unprecedented act, approved by the Senate and freely accepted by Western Europe and Canada, that also became the cornerstone of American national security policy.

No other collective defense treaty entered into after the war went so far as the North Atlantic and Rio treaties. To some extent, the United States committed itself to defend vast areas of the world, from the North Cape to Tierra del Fuego, from Vietnam to Berlin. The commitments, however, varied. One or two can be regarded as so much diplomatic bric-a-brac picked up along the road to confident superpower, at a time during and after the Korean War when there appeared to be remarkably little public confidence. The other treaties also included a limited commitment. Each party to them recognized that an armed attack against any member would be dangerous to its own peace, but only declared that it would act to meet the common danger in accordance with its constitutional procedures. There was agreement to consult, but not a commitment of military action. These treaties were useful enough in providing some legal basis for possible future American intervention. One obvious instance was the deployment of troops in South Vietnam. This was done in the name of the Southeast Asia Treaty, although without the agreement of other members.

The limited commitment of these treaties was rather surprising on the face of it. The lesser treaty organizations that they established were for the defense of the Pacific. This second American ocean had in the past engaged American attention much more than the Atlantic. If the United States turned its back on Europe for many decades, the Asian shore of the Pacific had long been a powerful magnet. The war with Spain, which began over Cuba, led to the colonization of the Philippines and the annexation of Guam and Hawaii. There is no satisfactory explanation for this expansionism beyond the continental limits of North America, except perhaps that in the nineteenth century all Christian industrialized nations were prone to colonialism. It was an imperialist takeover, just as shameless as any European grab in Asia or Africa, and it led to the deployment of American military forces along the eastern rim of the Eurasian land mass, and the establishment of a naval base in Hawaii that eventually dominated the Pacific as far westward as the Formosan Straits.

No extension of American power across the Atlantic was even considered until half a century later. It can therefore be said that the United States long ago acquired the habit of authority in the Pacific, which was strengthened by the curious connection with China. The diplomatic history of this connection began with the Open Door notes of 1899 and 1900, one of which specifically stated that American policy was to seek the preservation of the territorial and administrative entity of China. The notes, like so much of American diplomacy at the time, were empty rhetoric, although many years later Washington chose to interpret them as a commitment to protect China. Diplomacy, inept or otherwise, was only half of it. There was also the extraordinary sentimental attachment to China, which was rather patronizing or paternal but developed into something very close to a moral responsibility. No doubt this was because the country had become the main missionary field for American churches. These connections and sentimental attachments were not all; in recent decades the United States has fought three wars in Asia.

The connections with the eastern end of the Eurasian land mass are clear, but the commitments assumed there between 1951 and 1960 were deliberately obscured. There was the readiness to act, as indeed the United States did subsequently act in South Vietnam, Laos, and Thailand, but only when it wanted to act. There was joint planning, but no merging of standing forces under an international command. These omissions amounted to a powerful reservation on the part of the United States, and the reasons were obvious enough. Even a John Foster Dulles, who negotiated so many of them, could have a surfeit of alliances. Even American power was seen not to be omnipotent. The American military, which had most assumed the habit of authority in Asia, was averse to committing troops there. With the exception of Japan, there was no Asian country with an economy that could appreciably strengthen an enemy. Apart from Australia and New Zealand, there was no Pacific nation with established democratic institutions. It can perhaps be assumed, *sotto voce,* that racial and cultural differences made more difficult the intimate relationship and sense of common identity upon which NATO ultimately depends.

Geopolitics did not altogether explain American policy as it developed in the postwar years. A return to isolationism was rejected, in the words of General Marshall, as "psychologically wrong, militarily wrong, and just wrong generally." But preventive and pre-emptive wars were also ruled out. The objectives were essentially cautious, limited, and peaceful. A position of strength was built at enormous cost only in order that an eventual peaceful settlement could be negotiated.

During the most trying periods, when Communism threatened to envelop much of Western Europe and Asia, when Berlin was blockaded and South Korea invaded, the administration never lost sight of its peaceful objective. It was not universally popular. There was unrest in the armed services, especially over the refusal to bomb Chinese airfields during the Korean War. Extremists denounced what was described as a "no-win" policy, and long afterward some residual popular impatience helped Barry Goldwater to win the Republican Presidential nomination in 1964. The ultimate objective of a peaceful solution required a discipline which prepared the United States for the nuclear age, but it evolved first from a basic understanding of what was required and from American ideals. In this the American people should take pride, but by the time the Soviet Union had also acquired the nuclear capability to destroy much of the world the discipline became a powerful influence in the continuing formulation of American foreign policy as well as military strategy. By the early sixties its influence had become overpowering, and the age of super-power diplomacy had begun.

A search through the archives of the State Department for an agreement providing the terms of reference for such diplomacy would be in vain. The partial nuclear-test-ban treaty of 1963 is only the birth certificate, as it were, of a new understanding conceived during the Cuban confrontation of the previous year. But no formal agreement was necessary. The irrefutable fact that either side had the means to destroy the other, even after a nuclear attack, required a degree of caution and discipline that had never before been imposed upon a great nation. The superdiscipline accepted by the superpowers could not bring about a *rapprochement* in the first instance. Their national interests, as defined at the time, were still in conflict, or were seen to be in conflict.

Nevertheless, a curious dialogue was begun, in private correspondence between the two heads of government, in continuing diplomatic traffic, and in a number of official and unofficial exchanges. The discipline was defined. There was talk of a coincidence of policy, of mutual example, and a parallel commonality. These phrases largely meant that cooperation was possible in areas where neither national interest was involved, that no formal agreement or arranged reciprocity was necessary, and that it was in the interest of both superpowers to avoid confrontations and, indeed, to cooperate if possible in preventing a foreign dispute from bringing them into confrontation. The most dramatic development was the so-called hot line between Washington and Moscow after the Cuban crisis of 1962. It is, in fact, a teleprinter circuit, and the need for it was explained at the time by the inordinate delay in transmitting messages between the two capitals during the crisis. It was, of course, more than that. The circuit was installed because both countries had realized their responsibility as superpowers to avoid a nuclear war.

The intercontinental ballistic missile did not destroy the geopolitical conception of the relationship of the American continental island to the European land mass. The conception, in fact, became more painfully indisputable. No longer was it a matter only of denying Western Europe to the Soviet Union and sustaining its democracies. With its own cities exposed to direct nuclear attack, the United States had also to ensure that the Soviet Union would not be provoked into a war in Western Europe that could lead to a nuclear exchange. The discipline accepted by the United States had to be applied to Western Europe. This development was first explained in military terms, in the need to concentrate the command and control of nuclear weapons in the hands of the President, but the political consequences were far-reaching. It was more than the logical extension of the Monroe Doctrine to the River Elbe; it was an assumption, even a demand, that Western Europe would and should be content to accept a dependent status for the foreseeable future. The closest comparison, which is not farfetched, is with the Government of India Act of 1935 under which Britain gave India independence except in the fields of defense, foreign affairs, and communications. The comparison has some validity to the extent that the Western European democracies were expected to yield to the United States in defense and foreign affairs where the national interests of the superpowers were seen to be vital.

The assumption of acquiescence was not so impertinent as the French Gaullists chose to see it. Western Europe had gratefully depended upon American arms for its security since the Second World War. The smaller countries were prepared to remain dependent, and in any event had no choice. West Germany had no nuclear weapons, and was bound by treaty not to develop them. Britain, which had a useful nuclear force of its own, was prepared to accept American leadership with a few unspoken reservations. The American assumption was further strengthened by the proliferation issue. The alternative to unified nuclear control was a scramble to assemble national nuclear forces that could make nuclear war more likely, and in Western Europe France alone refused to ratify the nuclear-test-ban treaty. The United States did not ignore European sensibilities. Arrangements were offered to associate the Allies with the American strategic nuclear force. Strong support for European union continued, which in turn produced more theories on nuclear control, but always it was made clear that the United States intended to retain direct control over nuclear weapons and therefore the destiny of Europe.

This was the superpower position in the Northern Hemisphere which emerged in the sixties, and American national security policy likely to be based upon it for the foreseeable future. It is a position that many people find hard to understand. Some Europeans see it as an attempt to impose an American hegemony, and others fear or pretend to fear a future superpower settlement paying small regard to their national interests. There are Americans who regard the Soviet-American understanding as treason. Others glory in superpower, and seem to believe that the mission of the United States is to defend the peace everywhere in the world, fairly but sternly whenever lesser peoples misbehave. They can perhaps be forgiven. The responsibilities of superpower are such that at times the American armed forces do appear to be a universal police force. The American reaction to Soviet support for what Moscow chose to describe as wars of liberation tended to confirm this view. In effect, the Soviet Union was limiting the new superpower understanding to the Northern Hemisphere, a limitation unacceptable to the United States. Special forces were raised to deal with subversion and guerrilla war, and the army was given increased mobility to fight the so-called wars of liberation. The United States was prepared to create confrontations almost anywhere, as it did in Vietnam, to persuade the Soviets to extend superpower responsibility around the globe.

It was a novel response. The United States threatened a confrontation to avoid Soviet involvement in a train of events that could ultimately make a superpower confrontation unavoidable. It was what earlier strategists would have described as a forward policy, perhaps dangerously provocative as well as novel. The United States did not take this view. The balance of ideology was seen to require intervention when threatened by Communist subversion or insurrection. This explained the commitment of American troops in Vietnam in 1965. It brought the Soviet-American dialogue to a standstill for a time, but the two countries remained in touch and subsequently went on with their *détente* diplomacy. Throughout the Vietnam war the American negotiating position in regard to the Soviet Union was a constant factor in official calculations.

These were the beginnings of superpower diplomacy, and if it required the United States to demand a discipline of its Western European allies, the Soviet Union quickly discovered that it could not discipline China. The term "Sino-Soviet bloc" became patently meaningless after the Soviet Union refused to continue to provide nuclear information and assistance to China. The one country, apart from the United States and the Soviet Union, with an obvious superpower capability rejected the discipline they considered necessary to avoid the possibility of a disastrous nuclear exchange. For the two established superpowers China had become to a large extent the major threat to the peace.

This short review in geopolitical and strategic terms of American foreign policy in its most creative period reveals, I think, many of the principles and hard realities that will surely continue to dictate or influence its future development. The application has been on the whole impressively successful. This conclusion may surprise those who recall the headlines of the yesteryears, the talk of agonizing reappraisal, McCarthyism, Goldwaterism, Congressional confusion, and military militancy. Nevertheless, the record shows, if memory does not always recall, that throughout the turbulent postwar period when the United States became a superpower the hard realities of the world were rarely ignored, and American ideals often remained unimpaired. There is adequate room for criticism, which is often concerned not so much with performance as with the entire American system.

Some eminent critics believe that the machinery for decision-making and for the implementation of policy suffers from a lack of privacy and deliberation, and a failure to think beyond the short terms. There are a few who believe that these difficulties cannot be disposed of within the present constitutional framework. They see little room for improvement without constitutional reform that would create a parliamentary system similar to that which exists in Britain. The advantages of the British system are said to be that the government falls when it loses the confidence of Parliament, that it provides opportunity to consult the people on the great issues and to adjust policies in accordance with the will of the people.

The most serious American fault is seen by many to lie in the legalistic-moralistic approach to international problems, as reflected in the past by the Hague conferences and the Kellogg Pact. Coupled with this is the belief that chaotic and dangerous aspirations of governments can be suppressed by the acceptance of some system of legal rules and restraints. There can be no doubt of the depth of this belief. It partly represents an attempt to transpose the Anglo-Saxon concept of individual law into the international field, and make it applicable to governments. It stems from the origins of the American political system, that the conflicts between the thirteen colonies could be resolved within a common institutional and juridical framework. This is said to explain the assumption that the ambitions of other peoples are for the most part neither creditable nor important, and must take second place behind the desirability of an orderly world untroubled by international violence.

American statesmanship, stemming as it does largely from the legal profession, persists in seeking an international institutional framework capable of fulfilling this function, and when the law is broken, its indignation knows no bounds short of unconditional surrender. The legalistic approach, rooted in the desire to do away with war and violence, makes violence more enduring, more terrible, and more destructive to political stability than did the older motives of national interest. War fought in the name of high moral principle finds no early end short of some form of total domination.

This criticism was best articulated by George Kennan, an eminent American diplomat and a chairman of the Policy Planning Council, and it has long been shared by many. Sir Harold Nicolson, the British diplomat and writer, once said, "The worst kind of diplomatists are missionaries, fanatics, and lawyers." There is no doubt that the United States has rather more than its fair share of lawyers and missionaries who have played, and continue to play, a prominent role in the formulation and implementation of foreign policy. It can be said that together they have been guilty of the anthropomorphic fallacy of seeing international relations in terms of strict analogy with human relations within an organized society. This fallacy of failing to recognize the differences between a society of nations, such as the League or the UN, and a society of men within a sovereign state, is admittedly common in the United States.

There are, of course, two vital differences. No sovereign power governs relations between nations, as the federal government governs and regulates relations between the states, and between nations the concepts of peace and justice are not inseparable as they are in Anglo-Saxon countries such as the United States and Britain. The fallacy is more widely held in the United States presumably because it has a written Constitution. Americans are more inclined than the British to attempt the resolution of the world's problems within the framework of a similar legal document such as the United Nations Charter, or to think of them in legalistic terms. This might well explain some of the extremes in American thinking. In a court of law there are two parties to a case, one of whom is right and the other wrong. The right must prevail absolutely, because compromise or prevarication will render the legal process impotent.

That said, and I think that the criticism is valid as far as it goes, there is no reason to condemn entirely this legalistic-moralistic approach to foreign affairs, especially in the nuclear age when the observance of some form of international rules and regulations may well be vital for survival. Indeed, there is a persuasive argument for the proposition that the successful application of American foreign policy is largely due to this approach. The Anglo-Saxon belief that peace and justice are inseparable (the oldest legal office in Britain is the justice of the peace) might be difficult to project into international affairs, but the League of Nations largely failed because it preferred peace to justice. On the occasions when the United Nations has preferred to enforce justice, even at the temporary expense of peace as in Korea, it was because the United States was determined that the cause of justice not be deferred to peace.

The United Nations would probably not have survived without this determination to see justice done, but the organization has suffered from the American anthropomorphic fallacy. When the United States insisted under Article 19 of the Charter that the Soviet Union pay for peace-keeping operations that it had opposed, it was assuming that a sovereignty governed international relations. Whatever the legal arguments, the United States was accepting as law the paradox that a country, even a superpower, that had voted against a proposed measure was expected to help carry it out. The American case was supposed to have been strengthened by a ruling of the International Court, whose jurisdiction the United States does not entirely accept, but the fallacy is also evident at The Hague. The Court is what its name implies, but unlike a national court countries theoretically subject to its decisions have the right to opt out of them. The price paid by the UN General Assembly was a year of potentially danger-ous inactivity. The United States afterward recognized the possibility of some future occasion when it, as a superpower, might also object to a similar majority decision. The basic problem of financing peace-keeping operations was more or less resolved in an empirical manner by Britain with the proposal for voluntary donations, and a down payment of $10 million. It was a small price to pay for Anglo-Saxon countries which now believe that peace and justice should be insepa-rable.

This concept is also reflected in the refusal of the United States to accept the notion that war is impossible in the nuclear age. The dictum of Clausewitz that war is an extension of politics by other means is held still to apply. Without it there could only be paralysis in the face of aggression, and eventual defeat. It must not be assumed that the United States is prepared to go up in a nuclear cloud with the President clutching the Constitution and the Old Testament. That, indeed, was the unlovely prospect when military strategy was summed up in the phrase "massive retaliation," but the United States quickly moved on to suggest a new set of rules. However, on the military side there was the refinement offered in the strategy of options, of which more will be said in the next chapter. On the political side the need was seen to avoid superpower confrontations by coming to some arrangement with the Soviet Union. Thus the legalistic approach, the search for some institutional framework, finds expression in superpower relations.

Clearly it is no bad idea to institutionalize, if possible, arrange-ments to prevent nuclear war, but the attempt to resolve the problems of the North Atlantic Alliance in terms of the American experience have not been altogether successful. It is natural enough for the American people to give the President the complete and undisputed command and control of nuclear weapons. There is no other way, although it does appear to offend the Constitution. Nevertheless, Western Europeans do not elect him. They have been asked in effect to accept the possibility of nuclear death without representation, which is rather more than the American colonists had to accept under the Stamp Acts. Much more is asked of the Prime Minister of Britain, the President of France, and the Chancellor of West Germany than of the Governor of Alabama or that other sovereign state, Mississippi. These gentlemen have ignored, or flagrantly broken, the law of the land with impunity. It can be argued that the comparison is unfair, and that there is no alternative to Presidential control. There are obvious difficulties, but there are perhaps alternatives outside the American experience.

The complaint that machinery for decision-making and the implementation of policy suffers from a lack of privacy and deliberation is one that can be expected from a Foreign Service officer, even one of Mr. Kennan's stature. I am not certain that it is true or, if there is some substance in it, that it is valid in the United States. It must also be assumed that the Constitution is not going to be amended to allow for the transplanting of the British parliamentary system, despite the hankering of the professional diplomat for the studied silence of the Foreign Office in London. The postwar record surely proves that the disorderly American way is not fundamentally unsound. If it is expensive in time and effort, then it is only characteristic of the entire system, but when working well it does ensure the maximum debate in and out of official circles, and an astonishing amount of information and a variety of opinion are made available. There are weaknesses, of course, as in other systems, and perhaps the most prominent is Presidential intervention for political purposes.

The President is his own Secretary of State for obvious reasons, but also because on his performance in this role depends to a large extent his political future and place in history. President Roosevelt is remembered for his war leadership as well as for the New Deal. The Great Society of President Johnson would not be sufficient to guarantee his place in history books. One must assume that Presidents will continue to attach considerable importance to their political and historical future, only second perhaps to national security and continued life on this planet. The connection between national security and Presidential prestige does not have to be labored, but it can be an unhappy one.

The President often feels compelled to initiate a new policy, even when one is not absolutely called for or when insufficient time has been given for consideration. An example is the bad mishandling of the Point Four program, largely because something was urgently required as an ornament for President Truman's Inaugural Address. If this is regrettable, it is a fact of American political life that a President has a set period in which to make his mark, theoretically four years, or eight years at the most, but it can be less if he loses majority support in Congress or public confidence. Moreover, he ascends to his awful throne of power with little or no intimate experience of foreign affairs. Unlike a British Prime Minister, he has not shared collective Cabinet responsibility and experience. He has rarely been party to decision-making. Professor Schlesinger claimed for President Kennedy a most varied and extensive international experience. As a young man, the professor solemnly reported, he had talked to Franklin D. Roosevelt, Neville Chamberlain, and Stanley Baldwin. Unimpressive as this early experience may strike readers, it was more than that of some other Presidents.

Thus a new President finds that he is to be tested in a field of which he has little or no experience, under the compulsions of public expectation and the personal desire to make his mark. In such circumstances he tends to attach too little importance to continuity, and indeed may resent it. I can recall another of President Kennedy's advisers complaining bitterly that the only foreign problems exercising the President were those inherited from his predecessor. He was quite angry about it. This adviser was also an academic, and presumably an intelligent, man, but apparently he had supposed that the world started afresh, that a new page was turned, whenever a new American President was elected. If this was naïveté, it was not uncommon. An adviser of President Johnson made the same complaint, and no doubt it will be echoed by the advisers of his successor. It is unfortunate, and occasionally dangerous, as in 1961 when President Kennedy allowed the invasion of Cuba to take place. His apologists have explained this disaster by largely placing the blame upon the Secretary of State and the Joint Chiefs of Staff for not opposing the venture. The fact of the matter, as admitted by one member of his staff who did not seek quick fame and fortune in memoir writing, was that President Kennedy, although new to office and with almost no experience, wanted to invade Cuba. When a President wants to do something badly, it is very difficult for a subordinate to oppose him.

Presidential initiatives, if rarely so dangerous, can be disruptive because diplomacy is a continuing process, with well-defined goals if you chose to define them, but with modest expectations of only approximate results and no dependable timetable. It is not unlike domestic politics in the United States, and one of the great American mysteries is that this experience stops at the water's edge. Internally, it is accepted that the legislative crop is rarely harvested by the President who sows it. An example is the Medicare Act, designed to provide medical care for the aged under Social Security. It was finally enacted during the Johnson administration in 1965, and was hailed as the fulfillment of the Kennedy program. President Johnson, with his fine sense of theatrical symbolism, and no doubt resenting constant comparison with his predecessor, flew to Independence, Missouri, to sign it into law in the presence of the former President Truman, who first introduced the bill many years before. This domestic time lag is accepted, but not in international affairs. Newly installed Presidents always seem to believe that they can achieve more, neatly and swiftly, abroad where generally the United States cannot control events. This is a recurring weakness that follows a Presidential inauguration as day follows night. Fortunately most Presidents learn and adjust themselves very quickly, as did President Kennedy.

The criticism, serious as much of it is, does not much diminish the conclusion that the rather disorderly American system of formulating foreign policy and making decisions has served the country well. It is at times difficult to remember that prior to the Second World War the foreign policy of the United States was almost nonexistent, unless inactivity, not always masterly, can be regarded as policy. The American diplomat of the prewar years was essentially un-American. Diplomacy offered small scope for moralistic articulation, and policy, or nonpolicy, denied activism. The skills of the diplomat's trade as developed in the nineteenth century were atypical of the American style, for they were patience, detached observation, reflection, restraint, and a degree of cosmopolitanism offensive to the largely provincial society he represented. He was estranged from American society, an unfortunate condition that survived the war for many years and also helps to explain the suspicion that made McCarthyism possible.

In rising to the challenge to national security, the United States came to terms with the world, dominated much of it, and made over diplomacy in its own image. It had immense advantages: the nuclear monopoly for some years, the dependence upon it of Western Europe, the acquiescence of Latin America, and the requirements of newly independent countries whose economics could be developed only with American help. There was also its own powerful economic strength that could support armies and programs too costly to have

F

been imagined by previous great powers. Last, and certainly not least, was the openness of American society that encouraged the most audacious thoughts and actions as well as allowed the free play of primitive opposition and extremist demands. What emerged, despite the alarums, the nonsense, the unspeakable accusations, and the strident demands of the political system, was a policy suitable for the national character and style that could and did secure the national interest. Obviously mistakes were made, and will continue to be made. Clearly there was, and is, a too easy assumption that the American interest is the interest of all free men. Military demands were also excessive, of which more in the next chapter, but it must never be forgotten that the United States pursues a national security and not a foreign policy.

5 The Department of Defense

"Peace is our business."

—UNITED STATES AIR FORCE

"No sane man wants nuclear war, or any kind of war. But war has to be conceivable in support of vital national interests. Otherwise you have no national power."

—ROBERT MCNAMARA
Secretary of Defense (1962)

Americans generally regard themselves as a peace-loving people, but in the first two decades of the Cold War it was the United States and not the Soviet Union which was engaged in most of the wars since the last great war to end wars. Apart from the police actions in East Berlin and Budapest, brutal as they were, not a single Russian soldier heard a shot fired in anger. The United States fought in Korea and South Vietnam. It was the only country to resort to strategic aerial bombing since the American nuclear destruction of Hiroshima and Nagasaki was supposed to have put a stop to that kind of violence. The abortive invasion of Cuba in 1961 was organized by the United States, which also took the world to the nuclear brink during the Cuban missile crisis of the following year. There was the landing of troops in Lebanon, the intervention of the Dominican Republic, and interference in Laos. Pilots were surreptitiously provided for the Congolese army of its choice, and clandestine attempts were made to overthrow governments as far apart as Iran and Guatemala.

It is a mildly astonishing catalogue of martial militancy, a do-it-yourself kit for Communist propagandists on how to condemn the United States for aggressive imperialism. Friendly nations were outraged, and there were anti-American demonstrations in London and Paris as well as in Moscow and Peking. A few Americans shared the outrage, especially in the universities, but the vast majority apparently remained convinced that theirs was a peace-loving country. They condemned the Anglo-French adventure at Suez with a moralistic fervor, but not much of that was evident when the United States intervened in Santo Domingo. There was criticism of excessive use of force, but little of the use of force. Nothing was said of the fine aspirations of President Wilson or President Kennedy, or that passage from the Declaration of Independence on the right of people to overthrow government. In 1965 when President Johnson assured Pope Pius in New York of his devotion to peace, American bombers were devastating large areas of Vietnam. The United States, it could be said, was guilty of both aggression and double standards.

But can it be said? The American certainty of peaceful intention is at least supported by the search for peace uninterrupted by the landings and bombings. It was the first country to establish a Disarmament Agency. National security policy is designed to avoid nuclear war. Many of the martial actions listed above can be defended. If no Russian soldier heard an angry shot outside East Berlin and Budapest, it was because the Soviet Union had realized most of its territorial and ideological ambitions in Eastern Europe in the early postwar years. All Europe east of the Elbe was handed to them in a GI's canteen by unthinking American generals, but the motive was nothing but peaceful. In Korea and South Vietnam the United States responded to Asian Communist aggression. The Soviet Union was dangerously provocative in stationing missiles in Cuba.

Here is the ammunition of the propaganda offensive and counter-offensive which have bored so many people since the Second World War. They remain boring in the extreme, but the assumption that Columbia is the goddess of peace does not really bear close investigation. Many Canadians remember the War of 1812 as their war of independence from early American imperialism. The wars against Mexico and the Indians were expansionary wars to further the American national interest. They made the United States a subcontinental nation from sea to shining sea, and do not have to be rationalized at this late date. They can be said to have been fought for a worthy cause, but it is possible that much the same would have been said of Napoleon if he had not met his Waterloo. In 1922 the War

Department announced that the United States had fought 105 wars since the Revolutionary War, and the subsequent score has maintained the batting average.

The American record is not so different from that of other countries it has chastised in the past. The United States has been, and will continue to be, prepared to use force in defense of the national interest. It is prepared to use nuclear force. This has been the posture of American national security policy since the Second World War, and there is no reason to believe, as the Chinese once said, that the United States is a paper tiger. Nuclear war is irrational, as is any kind of war, but is not seen to be inconceivable. Given a Soviet nuclear capability, the United States must have a credible deterrent. Irrational as nuclear war may be in theory, it is seen to be rational in situations when the alternative might be worse than the risk of nuclear war. An unacceptable alternative is the surrender to Communist aggression, either wholesale surrender or in stages. This position has been stated officially and categorically, and it explains American militancy. Moreover, the United States is doubly determined to maintain the territorial and ideological power balance because a Communist victory, military or political, is unlikely to be reversed by some future election. The belief is that Communist victory must not be permitted to take place. Hence the wars, landings, and the clandestine operations.

This position, despite some apprehension about overextension, has been accepted by the American people, as they have long accepted intervention in the Caribbean. The Marine landings in that area were, and are, seen to be justified by the Monroe Doctrine. As suggested in the previous chapter, it is not fanciful to conclude that the doctrine has been extended to much of the world, but unlike President Monroe the postwar Presidents have had the military power to apply it. It is this power, its organization and command and control, which is discussed in this chapter, but first it is worth looking a little closer at the Monroe Doctrine because it does reflect much of the American attitude to national security.

The Doctrine, enunciated by President Monroe in a message to Congress on December 2, 1823, grew out of a minor clash with Russia concerning the northwest corner of the American continent, and out of the fear that the Holy Alliance would seek to reconquer Latin America. It announced that the United States would view with displeasure an attempt by the European powers to subject the nations of the New World to their political systems. The announcement was regarded in Europe as unwarranted and provocative, and did not find a place in international law. No Congressional action was taken. Nevertheless, over the years it became a fixed and nationalistic principle. In 1895 Richard Olney, the Secretary of State, said, "The United States is practically sovereign on this continent, and its fiat is law upon those subjects to which it confines its interposition." The Platt Amendment, a rider to the 1901 Army Appropriations Bill, provided for intervention in Cuban affairs and practically made the island an American protectorate. The rider still rides the American attitude to that unfortunate country. In 1904 President Theodore Roosevelt expounded his corollary to the Doctrine, stating that continued misconduct in a Latin-American republic might force the United States to intervene, an interpretation of the Doctrine that explained President Johnson's intervention in the Dominican Republic sixty-one years later.

American historians are inclined to condemn the Roosevelt corollary as imperialistic, and there is no other word for it. In suggesting that the Doctrine has been extended to include much of the free world, however, there is no intention of charging the United States with neo-colonialism in Europe and Asia. Instead, I am suggesting that the Doctrine evolved from a rather meaningless bit of diplomacy into a military doctrine that is as applicable in Berlin as in Santo Domingo, or wherever the enemy is next to be seen. The Doctrine can be restated as a determination to intervene militarily wherever necessary when the American national interest is seen to be threatened. Berlin is of course covered by solemn diplomatic agreement as well as the right of conquest. It is no accident, however, that the doctrine was restated by the Secretary of Defense and not the Secretary of State. In declaring in 1962 that the United States must be ready to deal with so-called wars of liberation, guerrilla wars, and subversion, Robert McNamara did more than rationalize his expensive demand for balanced forces. He expounded the latest military global version of the Monroe Doctrine. It was widely accepted, I believe, not as a sophisticated and very persuasive strategic plan to avoid escalation to nuclear war, but simply because the ancient Doctrine had become so deeply embedded in American thought.

What began as an attempt to divide the world into two parts, the old and the new, and slipped into imperialist misuse in the Caribbean, emerged in the divided world of the 1960s as a military strategy the like of which had never been seen before. Not in its greatest imperial period was Britain ever capable or willing to take on great powers such as the Soviet Union and China, and fight battles anywhere along the periphery of an area as large as the non-Communist world. To do it, the United States raised the most powerful military forces in military history, developed more complex and sophisticated doctrines, and revolutionized the defense establishment.

The cost was, and remains, enormous—at least half of the federal budget. The level of forces maintained during the first two decades of the cold war was about 2,500,000, and at least 500,000 were stationed overseas. The over-all strength exceeded three million when troops were committed in Vietnam. The Defense Department also increased its civilian work force to about one million. Two complete naval fleets remained constantly at sea in the Mediterranean and the China seas, and nuclear-powered submarines armed with Polaris missiles stood guard underwater for the Doomsday after the two superpowers had devastated each other in a mutual bombardment of intercontinental ballistic missiles.

These missiles, which replaced the bomber as the main strategic strike force, and their crews were maintained at a constant state of readiness deep in the bowels of the earth impervious to any attack except a direct nuclear hit. The Army, which was at first regarded as a relic of the prenuclear age, assumed new importance when the need was seen to fight smaller wars without bringing about a superpower confrontation. Nevertheless, it was equipped with a vast armory of tactical nuclear weapons. Divisions were raised that could be flown halfway round the world within a few days, and were equipped with helicopters to carry them directly into battle. Special Forces troops were deployed in Europe and Asia for clandestine operations. The Marine Corps, in its tradition of an elite force, was always ready for an immediate landing in the Caribbean or the Pacific.

No country, not even the other superpower, ever attempted such a massive global deployment of armed force, or was faced with so many problems of administration and command and control. In building up this force, the Defense Department acquired physical assets worth more than $150 billion. Some fourteen thousand installations were manned, in every state of the Union and about fifty foreign countries. The large ones, some six hundred in the United States alone, were small towns with their own utilities, schools, hospitals, transport, police, shops, and places of entertainment. The department also operated its own air transport service, larger than any commercial airline, a shipping line, and a communications system comparable to any of the larger commercial companies. It came to dominate large areas of American industry, and led President Eisenhower to his cautionary remarks on the military-industrial complex.

This overwhelming power was built up after the Second World War. The military and industrial mobilization skills were acquired during that war, but the forces were run down during the only too brief years of postwar optimism. Earlier, in the isolationist period, they had been utterly inadequate. In 1938 the Army Chief of Staff reported that the Army strength was only 165,000 men, although 280,000 were authorized under the National Defense Act. The American Army ranked eighteenth among the standing armies of the world. There were isolationists in the armed services, who criticized political leaders for reckless adventurism right up to Pearl Harbor. There were no plans with any application in the world situation as it then existed. Only two plans called for general mobilization: the Red Plan for war against Britain, and the Red and Orange Plan against a coalition of Britain and Japan. Equally odd ideas were entertained about their own country. Harry H. Woodring wrote of the Army in 1934, prior to his appointment as Secretary of War, as the only force to cope with social and economic problems at home. It was the secret weapon against domestic chaos. Fort Bragg, North Carolina, which emerged in the sixties as the military academy for counterinsurgency, was used in those days to train troops to break up strikes and put down mobs.

Much of this simplistic approach to complex foreign and domestic problems survived, but, as we have already seen, the military came into rather more than its own during the war and was allowed to usurp, under Presidential authority, much of the power traditionally reserved for civilians. This was corrected after the war when the Defense Department was established and the armed services were subordinated to the Defense Secretary. The assertion of civilian control over the military led to intense controversy. The process was the usual uproarious American affair, including a so-called mutiny of the admirals, but civilian control in the real sense was achieved to a remarkable extent.

At this point it is perhaps as well to consider the constitutional position and its historical development. Both are clearer in regard to defense than to foreign affairs. For the latter the Constitution merely provides that the President shall have power, by and with the advice and consent of the Senate, to make treaties, provided two-thirds of the Senators present concur. The rather uncomplicated eighteenth-century conception of foreign affairs, with its assumption that the Senate would act as an advisory council or cabinet, exposed subsequent Presidents to assaults on their prerogative of over-all responsibility for the direction of foreign policy. Not so in defense. Article II, Section 2, could not be more specific. "The President shall be Commander in Chief of the Army and Navy of the United States, and of the Militia of the several States, when called into the actual service of the United States. . . ." The constitutional position is unassailable, firmly based as it is on British practice and the example of Washington when he was Commander in Chief of the Revolutionary Army. Washington always scrupulously subordinated himself to civilian authority as expressed by the Continental Congress, despite proposals for a military dictatorship, which on the second occasion came within two votes of passage. When the Congress voted him extensive powers, he returned them intact. His demeanor was one of proper military humility throughout the war.

Civilian authority devolved upon him as the first President and Commander in Chief, and at first his military duties were taken quite literally. The Constitutional Convention and the ratifying conventions of the states were concerned over the propriety of allowing the President to assume command personally. Hamilton devised a plan giving the President power of direction of future wars but not command in the field except with the consent of both houses of Congress. At the Constitutional Convention, William Patterson of New Jersey proposed that the President be given the direction of all military operations, but barred him from commanding troops either as a general or in any other capacity. The proposal was not adopted, presumably because Washington had demonstrated his military talent, and subsequent Presidents were not loath to exert their authority as Commander in Chief. President Andrew Jackson once

F*

threatened to ride out and hang a few rebels. During the Civil War President Lincoln saw his military authority as a source of "inherent powers," divorced from the legislature and virtually unlimited in scope. This was the first modern interpretation of the Presidential role as Commander in Chief, and it was the precedent amplified by President Wilson and President Roosevelt for the conduct of total war in the twentieth century. When the first atomic bombs became available, there was no question under whose command they should be placed.

It can be argued that the principle of civilian control in the United States has never been seriously questioned, although there has long been a national weakness for generals as Presidential candidates. Aversion to military influence preceded the Revolution, and can be traced back to the English Civil War. The early English immigrants remembered the history of the Cromwellian period and the New Model Army. The quartering of troops in colonial homes after the French and Indian Wars became a cause for the Revolution. The Declaration of Independence complained that King George the Third had affected to render the military independent of and superior to the Civil Power. At the Continental Congress of 1787, it was said, despite its earlier lobby for a military dictator, "Standing Armies in time of Peace are inconsistent with the principles of republican Governments, dangerous to the liberties of a free people and generally converted into a destructive engine for establishing despotism."

If the principle was still revered, the high state of preparedness required in the Cold War created obvious difficulties if not dangers. Primarily there were fears, exaggerated but natural in a democratic society, of the emergence of a general staff similar in organization and power to the former German General Staff. They were not realized. The military command and control structure was organized to ensure a unity of military purpose, but not complete unification of the armed services, which retained their separate identities, and to strengthen Presidential authority beyond dispute. The tight structure created tensions, which still exist to a lesser extent, but it became increasingly difficult to assume civilian control with any confidence as the stocks of nuclear weapons multiplied. Civilian control could not be said to exist if the President was unable to ensure that the smallest tactical nuclear weapons—and there were thousands—would not be fired without his express order. Elaborate procedures were worked out for bomber and missile squadrons, but the dangers of nuclear affluence were compounded by technological advances which, for instance, made it impossible to separate the warhead from the missile. Many such problems were overcome by electronic devices, and the most complete command and control system man and money could devise was ready by the sixties. If the United States remains prepared to go to any lengths, even to a nuclear exchange, to defend the national interest, it has been made certain that only the President can order it. Nothing has been overlooked, not even Presidential disability or the possibility of insanity.

The process began in 1947 with the enactment of the National Security Act. This most important piece of legislation established the Department of Defense as an executive department of the government, and brought into being the National Security Council and the Central Intelligence Agency. Its primary objective was not to ensure Presidential command, but rather unification in its widest sense. The experience of the Second World War had driven home a number of lessons. The unification of the armed forces, at least to some degree, was found necessary. Equally important was the realization that the military establishment was but one element in the security of the nation, which was seen to depend as much upon economic growth and the skill and wisdom with which the government conducted its foreign relations. The need was seen for improved organizational means to relate military, foreign, and domestic policies in setting national goals. In possible future conflicts the United States could hardly depend upon time to prepare while allies held back the enemy, and planning for rapid mobilization was seen to be essential.

Much of this, however, combined with nuclear weapons to emphasize the constitutional prerogative of the President as Commander in Chief. The National Security Act therefore provided for the appointment of a civilian Defense Secretary to direct and control the administration of the armed forces under their own departmental secretaries, and to act as the President's principal adviser in all defense matters. The Joint Chiefs of Staff were also established to serve as the principal military advisers to the President, the National Security Council, and the Defense Secretary. The Joint Chiefs, as they are generally known, were to consist of the Chairman, who was to have no vote, the Chiefs of Staff of the Army and Air Force and the Chief of Naval Operations. The Commandant of the Marine

Corps was granted the right to be present whenever the Corps was involved. The Joint Chiefs were given their own staff, the Joint Staff. The Chairman, subject to the authority and direction of the President and the Defense Secretary, was to be responsible for the agenda as the presiding officer, and to inform the Secretary when the Chiefs failed to reach agreement.

Subsequent amendments and the Reorganization Plan No. 6 of 1953 strengthened the office of the Defense Secretary. All functions of the Munitions Board, the Research and Development Boards, and some other agencies were transferred to his office. Six additional civilian Assistant Secretaries of Defense were appointed. The appointment of the Director of the Joint Staff had to be approved by the Secretary. A few months later the Key West Agreement further refined the functions of the armed forces and the Chiefs, and the authority of the Defense Secretary was again increased. It established that no function in any part of the Department of Defense would be performed independent of his direction, authority, and control. There was to be the maximum practicable integration of all departmental policies, short of a merging of the armed forces, to bring about an effective and economical organization ensuring military security. The main objectives were the effective strategic direction of the armed forces, the operation of armed forces under unified command wherever possible, the integration of the armed forces into an efficient team of land, naval, and air forces, and the coordination of operations to promote efficiency and economy and to prevent gaps in responsibility. The agreement also laid down that doctrines, procedures, and plans for joint operations would be jointly planned.

The Secretary, acting for the President, was made solely responsible for defending the Constitution of the United States against all enemies, foreign and domestic. He was to maintain, by timely and effective military action, the security of the United States, its possessions, and areas vital to its interest; uphold and advance national policies and interests; and safeguard internal security. The role of the Joint Chiefs was reduced to one of advice, and their functions were carefully defined. They included the preparation of strategic plans and the provision of strategic direction of the armed forces, including guidance for the operational control of forces and the conduct of combat operations. They were to participate in the preparation of joint plans for logistics and military mobilization, and of combined plans in conjunction with foreign armed forces, as directed by proper authority. They were to establish unified commands whenever necessary, advise the Secretary of Defense and the military departments on the means required for unified commands, and to submit to him for budgetary reasons their requirements based upon agreed strategic considerations, joint war plans, and national security commitments.

It was once bitterly said that the Joint Chiefs were left only sufficient authority to organize military displays and sporting events, but this was something of an overstatement. They cannot move troops except with civilian authority, and the Chairman is a legal anomaly who has no command. They may appeal to the President and Congress, but they are legally dependent upon the judgment of the civilian Secretary of Defense. It could not be otherwise if civilian control is to be something more than a principle, but apart from the Chairman they wear two hats. They are not only advisers. Each is also responsible for the administration and operations of his service, which can hardly be described as a sinecure. Their collective functions are vital to the national security. Upon them depends to a large extent the degree of unification sought, the first objective of the National Security Act. Nevertheless, their subordination to civilian authority is indisputable.

To ensure civilian control, the National Security Act provides that a person who has been on active duty as a commissioned officer shall not be eligible for appointment as Secretary of Defense for a period of ten years. The principle of civilian control, it must be admitted, was not always clear even after the signing of the Key West Agreement until Robert McNamara was appointed as Secretary by President Kennedy. He did not increase the legal authority of the office of the Secretary, but vigorously implemented the broad powers already available. He rejected the essentially passive role of decision-making accepted by some of his predecessors, a mechanistic process of accepting one of the recommendations made by the Joint Chiefs, and instead asserted an aggressive leadership based on questioning, suggesting alternatives, proposing objectives, and stimulating progress. In other words, Mr. McNamara demonstrated that legal authority for civilian control was not enough. The civilian Secretary must exert that authority for the President.

The Defensé Secretary is now the vital link in the civilian chain of command from the White House to the missile sites and the most distant infantry post. He is the second most important Cabinet officer, and the distance between him and the Secretary of State is occasionally too narrow to be measured by the human eye. He is a member of the North Atlantic Council as well as the National Security Council and the National Aeronautics and Space Council. Inside the Pentagon, the real power lies in the Office of the Secretary of Defense, a vast civilian hierarchy dominating the entire defense establishment. Its Director of Defense Research and Engineering, for instance, is responsible for unification where it means most, in basic and applied research, and the development, testing, and evaluation of weapons, weapons systems, and all defense equipment. His authority is wider than even these responsibilities suggest. The interaction of research and national security policy and military strategy is obvious. A recommendation to proceed with a certain weapons system can influence both policy and strategy. It can also cost billions of dollars. Such systems can take years to produce, and a wrong evaluation of its role in the circumstances of the next decade or more could prove to be a national catastrophe.

The responsibility involved in this kind of work has increased over the years. The development of missiles is an example. When the first generation of missiles was being developed, it was necessary, and indeed possible because of the relatively modest cost of these early weapons, to authorize more than one project to ensure success. The intense competition between the services, each anxious to find a role for itself in the nuclear age, was on the whole beneficial for the nation. The need was to produce a missile as quickly as possible, and interservice rivalry was a sharp goad. When the time came to evaluate the second generation, the costs had risen so sharply that decisions had to be made more or less from specifications rather than from actual testing. The pressures did not ease when the second generation was safely delivered. At the time of writing, an antiballistic missile system was being built, at a cost of $5 billion. The impact upon the economy could be as immense as upon national security policy and strategy. The necessity for civilian control had grown immeasurably.

The Director of Defense Research and Engineering ranks third in the civilian hierarchy of the Pentagon, after the Secretary and Deputy Secretary of Defense. His eminence reflects the new position of science in defense, and to some extent of defense in science. His annual expenditure has run as high as $7 billion, at least fifty times as much as the budget of the National Science Foundation. He controls more than 100 research and development centers, employing about 100,000 men of whom about one-third are scientists. Defense grants to university laboratories have run into billions of dollars, thus influencing the direction of American science. It remains that these enormous projects are controlled by civilians.

In recent years much of this effort has been devoted to what are normally described as delivery vehicles for nuclear weapons, such as missiles, and defensive systems. The design and production of warheads is the responsibility of the Atomic Energy Commission, which is again firmly under civilian control. The Director of Defense Research and Engineering must of course consult with the Chiefs, but the decisions are his. He can approve, modify, or disapprove the projects of the military departments, and his judgment is guided by the Advanced Research Projects Agency and the Weapons Systems Evaluation Group, two of the esoteric products of the nuclear and technological revolution of mid-century defense.

The Director must work closely with another civilian, the Assistant Secretary of Defense (Comptroller), who is rather more than a glorified accountant. He is responsible for the military budget, but he has an even more important function. The *Government Organization Manual* describes it as follows:

He assists the Secretary of Defense, the several components of the Department of Defense, and other agencies of the Government in the evaluation of Defense programs by developing measures of resource utilizations and methods of characterizing resource limitations and availabilities in such a way as to make it possible to answer quickly and accurately questions about the costs and feasibility of a variety of alternative programs of force structures, weapons systems, and other military capabilities projected over a period of years. . . .

A translation is perhaps in order. A successful defense program now requires consideration in its entirety. For instance, the Polaris submarine force could not be determined as part of the naval shipbuilding program, but only in relation to the other components of the Strategic Retaliatory Force, and its requirements. The Polaris submarine program was one of the simpler decisions to be made. Other problems are more complex and continuing, and a system of five-year plans was devised to present the proposed force structure and cost estimates in relation to the national security responsibilities of the department. The responsibilities are further analyzed in terms of weapons and equipment and men required, and investment and operating costs. Competing programs and systems are judged on the basis of their contribution to the objective and the defense effort as a whole. Balances are sought, always with the single overriding objective of the defense of the Republic. This, of course, includes the impact of costs upon the economy as well as military effectiveness.

The judgment required can no longer rely on military experience or tuition. When a nuclear missile system is to be evaluated, it is immaterial if an Air Force general has been flying aircraft ever since he left high school. Too much is involved, and is beyond the imagination even of the recent past. The generals have given way not only to civilians and their five-year plans but also to a technique known as systems analysis. It has been described as quantitative common sense, and is a method of isolating a complex problem and separating the many factors. The aim is to assist the Secretary by providing quantitative estimates of both the effectiveness and costs of the alternative courses he could choose. Its tools are computers, and its operatives are mathematicians and physicists.

Thus at the apex of military authority stands the Secretary with civilian assistants with a variety of disciplines except military discipline. They depend upon management tools, such as cost and systems analysis and program budgeting, rather than combat experience. It is no exaggeration to suggest that a young mathematician only a few years out of graduate school can influence the shaping of defense policy more than a full general with a chest covered with medals and memories of a lifetime of military service all over the world. Civilian control within the Defense Department is now complete.

Every year when the Defense Secretary presents his budget to the House Armed Services Committee, he circulates a statement of about two hundred printed pages. The subheadings alone indicate the complexities of modern defense. They include the defense program and the economy, the nature of the general nuclear war problem, civil defense, general-purpose forces, research and development, nuclear testing and detection, space development projects, and management and support. This weighty book is, in fact, a state of the union forces message, and a review of the current five-year plan. It can be a remarkably candid document.

For instance, one year it discussed the possibilities of saving millions of lives in the event of a nuclear war. The estimate was that in 1970 casualties would be 149 million, or almost three-quarters of the estimated population. An investment of $25 billion in an approved damage-limiting program could reduce casualties to 78 million, or one and a half times the population of Britain. The problems posed were not so much whether 71 million lives were worth $25 billion, at $365 a life, but whether such a program would make nuclear war more probable, create economic problems, and adversely affect the spirit of the people. The statement also discusses the effectiveness of various weapons systems, and hints at future technological advance. No other government is so candid or publishes such an extensive and revealing statement of its defenses.

The statement always begins with an assessment of the international situation, which is perhaps the most remarkable section. Changes within the Soviet bloc are discussed along with the economic renaissance of Western Europe. The world is reviewed region by region. Stability is assessed, the economic condition being balanced against political leadership and opportunities for Communist subversion. Communist theological disputes are given the closest attention, as is the Gross National Product of the larger Communist countries. The military alliances and the United Nations are reported upon. There can be no better guide to the national security policy of the United States, but it is not the work of the State Department or the National Security Council. The author of this section is the Assistant Secretary of Defense (International Security Affairs), the department's own Secretary of State.

The ISA Assistant Secretary is invariably a man of considerable stature, and the reasons are understandable. As the department's Secretary of State, he maintains representatives abroad who amount to ambassadors, officers in charge of military aid programs and military aid and advisory groups as well as the military attachés. His budget, if military aid is included, is larger than that of the Department of State. But these are only the beginning of his functions. Disarmament is one of his concerns. He also supports the Secretary in the National Security Council, and is often responsible for implementing its policies. He conducts politico-military studies, and is interested in international political, military, and economic affairs. He is active in the negotiation and monitoring of agreements with foreign countries and international organizations on military facilities, such as bases, operating rights, and status of forces. He advises the Secretary and other members of the department at international conferences. There are few foreign ministers anywhere with so many and far-flung responsibilities.

In a Defense Department subjected to less civilian control, he could be even more powerful. His office is a military Department of State that approaches national security problems from a military viewpoint. Without a civilian bias, the over-all balance could tilt toward militarism. The necessity of such an appointment has been questioned. The argument is that foreign affairs is not the concern of the Defense Department. The Secretary of State is responsible for the conduct of affairs with foreign governments. The supradepartmental organization for national security should be adequate to coordinate foreign policy and defense. The argument is persuasive, but the apparatus of American administration is so complex that more complexity is often required to achieve a measure of simplification at the top. Moreover, the responsibilities of the Defense Secretary are so numerous and demanding that he needs for himself an administration in many ways a small replica of the federal government.

His responsibilities often overlap an area traditionally reserved for the Secretary of State, as became painfully clear for many in South Vietnam. His responsibility for the conduct of that war was obvious, but the war in Vietnam could not be won by military means alone. It was a political, social, and economic struggle. A Saigon government had to be deposed and its successors urged to adopt policies that were not necessarily to their liking. Political unity was seen to be essential. The economy had to be bolstered, entire communities moved from one area to another, refugees to be cared for, transportation and sanitation improved, and there were a hundred and one other programs not usually associated with defense. Many departments of the United States government were involved, but it was the Defense Secretary under the President who was in charge. An interdepartmental committee coordinated and applied policies, but the embryos of many were nurtured first in the Defense Department. The need for an Assistant Secretary of Defense for International Security Affairs was never more obvious.

The Defense Secretary has emerged so far as the principal assistant to the President in all defense matters, with complete control over the armed forces and their arms and equipment, and a member of the National Security Council, where he, and not the Joint Chiefs, speaks for the armed forces. He must necessarily involve himself in foreign affairs. But the picture is not complete. In 1961 the Defense Intelligence Agency was created, which also reports to the Defense Secretary through the Joint Chiefs. Within it were combined most of the intelligence functions previously carried out by Army G–2, Air Force A–2, and the Office of Naval Intelligence. The immediate result was a further diminution of military authority. The service Chiefs lost their seats on the U.S. Intelligence Board, but the ultimate consequences were more far-reaching. When in charge of their own intelligence services, the estimates of the military departments could bring direct pressure to bear on the deployment and armament of forces. For instance, the Air Force demand for a larger missile force carried greater weight when it could estimate a probable increase in Soviet missile strength. Such an estimate led to the so-called missile-gap crisis of 1960, which was afterward found to be nonexistent. The Defense Intelligence Agency subsequently failed to find any evidence of an increase in the strength of the Soviet forces, which led to charges that the Defense Secretary was misusing information to support an economy drive, but the assumption must be that a unified intelligence service under civilian control was primarily concerned with the threat to American security rather than with advancing the cause of any one service department.

The Defense Secretary is also responsible, again under the President, for the formulation of military strategy to a degree that still confounds old soldiers. If there was one area beyond the battlefield where the military ought to be responsible, it was always thought to be in the formulation of strategy. This is no longer the case. Nuclear weapons also changed that. Clemenceau said two world wars ago that war was too important to be left to the generals. The preservation of nuclear peace can only be the responsibility of the President, acting for the most part through the Defense Secretary. It is not even a matter of the Joint Chiefs' proposing and the Secretary's disposing. Quite frequently the Secretary proposes. His proposals, as we have already seen, are to a large extent dictated by political, economic, and above all technological factors, which are in turn subjected to the continuous control of the five-year plans or reviews and the technique of systems analysis. Moreover, it is the Defense Secretary who initiates the studies and evaluates the plans dictated by strategic requirements, with the advice of the Joint Chiefs of course, and presents them for Presidential approval. The organizational plan of the federal bureaucracy as well as the cold logic of nuclear war demands that the Defense Secretary be responsible for strategy.

Again recent history provides the perspective required for a proper understanding of this evolutionary process. The first atomic bombs did not, in fact, change strategy immediately. The Hiroshima and Nagasaki bombs were only terror weapons used to bring a long war to an early end. Subsequently each of the armed services saw the bomb merely as another weapon that would increase its striking power enormously but would not necessarily change its strategic role. This became painfully clear when the Army began to equip its field formations with tactical nuclear weapons with little thought of nuclear escalation. The assumption was that such weapons could be used without creating an entirely new situation beyond the control of the field commander. Prior to this monumental error of judgment, the bomb was primarily seen by those concerned with higher strategy as a counterbalance to what were then the superior mobilized forces of the Soviet Union.

The loss of nuclear monopoly did not immediately change this view. A devotion to economy and a balanced budget persuaded the Eisenhower administration to accept what was known as the strategy of Massive Retaliation. There was much talk of a bigger bang for a buck, but what it amounted to was the commitment of the United States to use nuclear weapons to prevent almost any form of aggression. It was always a dangerous strategy, but the physical danger to the United States became transparently clear when the two superpowers developed intercontinental ballistic missiles. In theory the United States was prepared to risk the destruction of New York and other large American cities in the event of a small Soviet incursion of Western Europe, a posture that was unsettling at home and hardly credible in Moscow.

All this changed, not so much with the inauguration of President Kennedy in 1961 and the appointment of McNamara as Defense Secretary, but rather with the gradual emergence of a distinguished school of nuclear war theoreticians. Most of them were civilians, and came from outside government service. Some were first introduced to their esoteric subject when employed at the so-called think factories, such as the RAND Corporation and the Hudson Institute. RAND was the first of any stature, and was organized by the Air Force, in the words of General Arnold, "to get the best brains and turn them loose on the problems of the future." It was a typical American response to the challenge of new conditions, and its establishment in 1948 was also typically American. The first money came from the Ford Foundation. With headquarters in Santa Monica, California, and a liaison office in Washington, it employed several hundred professional men to think about nuclear war and such diverse subjects as subversion, guerrilla warfare, and astronautics.

Indeed, RAND can claim most of the credit for the organization of the Defense Department as described here. It is usually given to McNamara, the Defense Secretary, but his arrival in office in 1961 coincided with the completion of an investigation of the department first undertaken by RAND ten years previously. McNamara, a corporation manager, recognized its value, and furthermore imported a RAND man to be his comptroller.

RAND and Hudson are only two of the private agencies who do much of the thinking for the Defense Department on a contract basis. One reason for their existence is that government pay scales are often unattractive to men of the required caliber. The outside agency men are paid more than the pay scales allow to think about almost everything concerned with war and peace, and it was these men who first evolved the new strategies. One of the more distinguished, at the time of writing, was Herman Kahn, who served with RAND before establishing the Hudson Institute. His book *On Thermonuclear War* was evocative in substance as well as title of Clausewitz, the Prussian strategist whose masterpiece dominated military thinking throughout the nineteenth century. Mr. Kahn went on to write *Thinking About the Unthinkable* and other works, while others also made valuable contributions.

One remarkable aspect of this creative thinking is that much of it is quickly communicated to the public as well as to the armed services in books similar to those mentioned above, and in popular magazines and learned periodicals. One reason is that RAND encouraged its thinkers to publish, a unique approach to a field traditionally enshrouded in secrecy. The Hudson Institute went one step further by holding seminars, and inviting journalists and other nongovernment people to participate. If the authors were employed by agencies and centers largely dependent upon the Defense Department for funds, the public cross-germination of ideas was generally instructive and nationally rewarding.

At a time when men in and out of government were confused as well as apprehensive about the new weapons, these theoreticians devised logical frameworks for constructive thinking. If constructive appears an odd adjective to use in reference to weapons capable of devastating the world a dozen times over, it is nevertheless applicable because the theories adopted contributed some measure of nuclear stability. If the lack of secrecy bothered the generals, the theoreticians worked under a new discipline. Part of it was that the enemy had to know what the United States was likely to do in any given situation because without broad knowledge of intention there could be no stability. They therefore saw themselves as educators, not only of the Defense Department and the United States generally but also of Moscow, and of Peking if the Chinese cared to listen. The approach was a shrewd extension of the Open Door policy, which has long influenced American policy.

These men are members of a new American Establishment. I must apologize to readers if I appear to be overdoing this idea, but I believe it to be necessary for a proper understanding of the American system. As at the State Department, where the old Establishment men are mainly influential, so the new Establishment men play a similar indispensable role at the Defense Department. The comparison cannot be taken too far. The old Establishment men tend to come from the traditional centers of power, influence, and availability, and most of them have Anglo-Saxon names. The new Establishment men are necessarily drawn from a much narrower section of the population. They are more often mathematicians or physicists, and most of them have German names. It is possible that personally they will not play a continuously influential role. There must be an assumption that like physicists working in laboratories they are capable of producing only one or two new breakthroughs, but their contributions have transformed strategic councils as the new weapons transformed the defense Establishment. If the old Establishment men are largely administrators, the new men are innovators. Their influence has been enormous. Their books can be found on a thousand and one desks in the Pentagon and in the defense ministries all over the world. Their disciples are employed in the office of the Defense Secretary. Their collective monument is the strategy of the United States.

The basic strategic problem was to find alternatives to Massive Retaliation, or what came to be known as the "spasm response," which seemed to condemn the world to some future but inevitable nuclear holocaust. It was useless to hope for disarmament, the diplomatic spasm response to such fears, when clearly neither super-power was in a position to disarm. The new search for alternatives was, in fact, part of the continuing postwar effort to meet changing situations with an applicable national security policy. Prior to Massive Retaliation, the policy of containment had been effective, and indeed remains an essential component of national security policy. This was the brain child of a Foreign Service Officer, George Kennan, and would have been discussed in the previous chapter except that in the wider sense it is essentially a military doctrine. He was also encouraged to publicize his proposal in the quarterly magazine *Foreign Affairs* by the then Defense Secretary, the late James For-restal. The United States could not, as in the past, wait passively until it became involved in a defensive war. It could not afford, the argument continued, to allow the Soviet Union to pursue its imperial-ist policy. The United States had to meet and contain Soviet expan-sionism, even if it meant dangerous collision.

The containment policy was a forward version of the Monroe Doctrine, and worked well enough while the United States enjoyed a nuclear monopoly. It was to some extent a passive policy, despite the possible danger of a Soviet-American collision, and was temporarily superseded by Massive Retaliation and the so-called liberation policy of the middle fifties. Neither met the situation of the time, and the search for a more appropriate national security policy continued. The basic proposition was that if war had to be conceivable in support of vital national interests, it did not have to be suicidal. "We intend to have a wider choice than humiliation or all-out nuclear action," President Kennedy said in July 1961 when the new answers were eventually found. There was also an assumption that the Russians did not want to disappear in a nuclear cloud, but were equally determined to defend what they regarded as their vital national interests. The first requirement was to define the national interest in any given situation. The second was to equip the country with enough military alterna-tives to make a major nuclear exchange less likely.

The first deserves some explanation because the national interest is not always well defined. An example was Berlin. The United States was committed to its defense, but what did the commitment entail? How was Berlin vital to the American national interest? How could it be ensured that the commitment would not expose the United States to dangerous local pressures? Was it committed to go to war if East German guards replaced Russians at the checkpoints on the Berlin road, or if East Germany stopped the disposal of the city's sewage on its territory? The Kennedy administration took eight months to make up its collective mind. Special committees sat, the new Establishment men and other experts, including a former Secretary of State, were called in, and Allies consulted. Eventually the American vital interests in Berlin were defined, and made known to the Soviet Union. They were the security and economic viability of the population of West Berlin, free access to and from the West, and the maintenance of Allied garrisons. For these interests, and for these alone, the United States was prepared to go to war.

The definition was of immense importance, and thereafter influenced the course of events. Backed by a show of force and Presidential determination, they persuaded the Soviet Union that there were limits to the harassment of the city which the United States was prepared to accept. The immediate and major consequences were a return to stability, and a revival of popular morale and modest prosperity in the city. There was a later consequence that deeply influenced American action. The building of the wall dividing the Western and Eastern sectors of the city created a major crisis which could have led to mob violence and armed hostilities if the United States had been less prepared. During that weekend when much of the world trembled, President Kennedy and his advisers met to make a decision that could have ended the years of precarious peace. They met, however, equipped with a vital yardstick. Did the wall violate or threaten the American interests in Berlin? The decision was negative, and the world breathed again. The decision was criticized, of course, because the wall was so hateful. There were charges of appeasement. President Kennedy said afterward in private that the United States Army did not stand guard in Western Europe to guarantee the escape to the West of East Germans who had had more than a decade in which to seek refuge. But the reason for inaction was larger than that. In the nuclear age a superpower must not only defend its national interest; it must also recognize that the other superpower has a similar obligation. Thus the process of defining national interests exerted a powerful discipline in both directions, and became essential to the maintenance of peace.

The second requirement of equipping the country with an array of military alternatives to secure its interests without an inevitable resort or escalation to nuclear war demanded increased military expenditures. The billions of dollars spent would have been of little use, however, without the evolution of a new grand strategy. It actually began in 1954, the year of Massive Retaliation, when members of the old and new Establishments then out of office combined to seek new answers. There was no official support, and in the first instance the work was essentially a private undertaking by bodies and men who had no statutory right to interfere in the business of government and defense. It is not only possible to follow the development of the strategy with reference to books published commercially; it would, in fact, give a wrong impression to do otherwise. Here is a supreme example of how the American Establishments can formulate as well as influence national security policy.

In 1954 the old Establishment, represented by the Council of Foreign Relations, undertook a major strategic study, and appointed as a staff director Henry Kissinger, who represented the new. Three years later he published his analysis in a remarkable book entitled *Nuclear Weapons and Foreign Policy.* The main point was that the United States must retain the ability to retaliate with a massive nuclear attack if sufficiently provoked, but also be prepared to retaliate in a more limited fashion against limited provocations. The book was not well received for a number of reasons, and the Taiwan and Lebanon crises of the following year revealed deficiencies in the ability to meet limited challenges. In proposing the use of small tactical nuclear weapons in limited war, Mr. Kissinger also failed to understand the mechanics of escalation.

It was a beginning, however, and the work was continued and shared by others. Herman Kahn, in *On Thermonuclear War,* argued that the prospect of nuclear war must be squarely faced, and indeed attempted to prove that the world could survive a nuclear holocaust. He nevertheless asked rhetorically, "Will the survivors envy the dead?" He was no bloodthirsty militarist. Rather did he insist, before Mr. McNamara was appointed Defense Secretary, that nuclear war must be conceivable if the national interest was to be defended. He was among the first to think in quantitative terms. How many megatons (nuclear destruction equivalent to one million tons of TNT) would be required to inflict X number of megadeaths (millions of dead)? He advocated a strategy, that came to be known as overkill, calling for enough weapons to permit not only retaliation but survival and victory.

Mr. Kissinger, in *The Necessity of Choice,* saw his previous error, and argued that the failure to achieve a coherent and acceptable definition of the nature of limited war militated against the capability of limiting war. Many such books and hundreds of magazine articles were published, and some people were persuaded that the open discussion of war made war inevitable. In *The Limits of Defense,* Arthur Waskow argued that military strategies were not merely theories for deterrence or defense, but provocations. The only workable deterrent, in his opinion, was "disarmament plus." This conceived of an international level of arms sufficient only for peacekeeping operations.

The whole point of this civilian traffic in military ideas, apart from assuring an adequate national defense, was not to evolve a strategy of escalation. Rather, in seeking to define the various rungs on the escalation ladder, was it an attempt to prevent escalation. Much of the argument was subtle in the extreme, and it was further complicated by the psychology of enemy and ally alike. Caution was required to avoid the possibility of the potential enemy's underestimating the American determination to defend the national interest. Allies had to be persuaded that the United States, in preparing to meet a conventional attack with conventional means, was not unilaterally reducing its commitments. The subtleties were made apparent in 1965 when Mr. Kahn published *On Escalation.* This work envisioned forty-four rungs in the escalation ladder from "Ostensible Crisis" to "Spasm or Insensate War." Equally important, Kahn saw a number of thresholds, or rungs, where the two superpowers should pause before escalating further from political crisis to conventional war, from limited to total nuclear war. He chose some graphic names, from "Don't Rock the Boat Threshold" and "Nuclear War Is Unthinkable Threshold" to "City Targeting Threshold" and "Aftermaths."

This, if you like, was the sophisticated gloss. The lessons of the civilian strategists had been well learned in the Pentagon, and long before, in the early sixties, the Doctrine of Controlled Response had been announced. Fundamentally, it required American forces to be equipped to give the President a variety of alternatives or responses before resorting to nuclear war. They were to be equipped to meet subversion with countersubversion, conventional attacks with conventional defense, a nuclear attack with a nuclear response. All this sounds very simple and obvious, but the complications are as numerous as the nonofficial civilian sources of the doctrine. For instance, nuclear war had to be conceivable without violating the national traditions. If the United States could not, because of its humanistic traditions, launch a pre-emptive nuclear war or surprise attack, a second-strike capacity was vital. In other words, the United States had to have sufficient missiles in protected sites to survive a nuclear attack and respond. Such a capability was seen to discourage an enemy surprise attack, and changed the entire conception of nuclear deterrence.

In creating this new balance of terror the promise of nuclear stability was achieved for the first time. It was acknowledged to remain only a promise. Circumstances were possible, if only because men do not always react rationally, when a nuclear exchange could conceivably take place. The need was seen for an extension of the doctrine to limit the damage in such an event. The counterforce and countervalue concepts were added. They have since become known collectively as the "Option of No-Cities Response," which was explained by Robert McNamara, the Defense Secretary, in a speech at Ann Arbor in 1962:

The United States has come to the conclusion that to the extent feasible, basic military strategy in a possible general nuclear war should be approached in much the same way that more conventional military operations have been regarded in the past. That is to say, principal military objectives, in the event of a nuclear war stemming from a major attack on the Alliance, should be the destruction of the enemy's military forces, not of his civilian population.

In other words, the United States offered the Soviet Union the option of bombing its missile sites rather than American cities, and in return Soviet cities would be spared in the retaliatory bombardment. A mutual attack on missile sites would, of course, kill millions of people on both sides, but it would not be insensate war or utter destruction. The No-Cities Response was therefore seen as one of the final steps on the escalator.

This is the military strategy of the United States, and as with American diplomacy it has become the strategy that dominates the world. At the time of writing, only China appeared to reject it, but it was in fact in no position to do very much, and there was an assumption that Peking might learn to accept the discipline of superpower should that status ever be achieved. Once again, the United States has succeeded in imposing its ideas on the world. They might be resented elsewhere, but no other attempt has been made to meet the problems of the nuclear age. It is recorded here because it is as much a part of institutional America as is civilian control of the military. There will no doubt be further refinements, but it is likely to survive as long as the teachings of Clausewitz. No understanding of the American national security policy is possible without knowledge of it.

In passing, one might add that it is essentially American. It is a civilian product, but more than that. It is American because of the means used to produce it. A most complex problem was seen to exist, and the best available minds in and outside government were called in to resolve it. No money or effort was spared. Intelligence apparatus such as U-2 aircraft and surveillance satellites were used to identify Soviet missile sites, and banks of computers employed to work out the equations of targeting. Discussion was free and far-ranging, no seemingly outlandish idea was rejected because it seemed to be outlandish. There was no flinching over the costs when the decisions were finally made. The costs were, and remain, higher than any country now and in the past could support. They are higher than are perhaps strictly necessary, because of the allowance for a margin of error. Above all, the national security policy is peculiarly American because only the Americans could afford the superiority demanded.

Effective command and control of the armed forces have always been necessary in all countries and under any kind of political system. Napoleon lost at Waterloo because he had no contact with one-third of his forces. In 1914 Kaiser Wilhelm of Imperial Germany had to accept the von Schlieffen Plan for an attack in the West because the alternative for an Eastern attack was not divulged by the General Staff. Here are two historical examples, one military and the other political, of what can happen when command and control are not assured. The ambitions of history's most famous general and most vainglorious emperor, both with enormous authority, were brought to nothing.

If an efficient command and control system has always been a necessary adjunct to martial valor and political authority, for the United States in the mid-twentieth century it became absolutely vital. It is vital if the President is to carry out his constitutional responsibilities as Commander in Chief. It is vital to ensure that not one single nuclear weapon can be used without his command. It is vital to the strategy or Doctrine of Controlled Response. Without it, the civilian control would be meaningless and nuclear doom inevitable.

The issues are obvious, and the most casual newspaper reader is aware that in the vicinity of the President, no matter where he goes, there is always a man with the codes that must be used to order a nuclear bombardment. He is the monkey on the President's back, a constant reminder of awful responsibilities. But command and control do not begin with nuclear weapons. If they did, the man would probably have produced the codes long ago. Apart from the constitutional requirement, the President must be assured that not a single aircraft, warship, or infantry company will be involved in a military conflict without his knowledge. The dangers of escalation in certain conditions are too evident for reiteration. Aircraft straying off course have created major diplomatic incidents. Under special circumstances, as in the Gulf of Tonkin in 1964, the President assumed total command of retaliatory operations, even to the extent of selecting targets. All this requires elaborate communications, electronic and computer systems as well as discipline and well-rehearsed procedures. Alternative systems and command headquarters must be constantly available, as must the hot line to Moscow in the event of some untoward development. The communications facilities of the White House are now said to be such that little more equipment could be moved into the basement.

These facilities are connected with the National Military Command System (NMCS), the primary component of a world-wide command and control system. The other centers are the National Military Command Center at the Defense Department, the Alternate National Military Command Center, the National Emergency Command Post Afloat, and the National Emergency Airborne Command Post. The two emergency command posts, as the names suggest, are aboard ships and aircraft. At least one aircraft is always aloft and in sight of the Strategic Air Command's headquarters at Omaha, Nebraska. If those headquarters go up in a nuclear cloud, the commanding general in the aircraft knows that he is in command. All are linked to unified or special commands by warning, sensor, and communications networks. The intention is to provide, according to Robert McNamara, who was responsible for its creation, "a standardized, highly survivable, non-interruptible command capability for a wide range of possible situations, and will provide the authorities with a number of alternatives through which they may exercise their command responsibilities."

Various systems are used within the National Military Command System. Their function is not merely to transmit information and orders. Command and control have been defined as running the show. Implied in this definition are the traditional military functions of intelligence, planning, operations, and logistics as well as command. They must dispel the fog of war and provide alternative courses of action. They must encompass any foreseeable situation, and be flexible enough to reach the most unlikely parts of the world.

A good example is the Dominican crisis of 1965. A communications network was immediately established between President Johnson, the American Ambassador in Santo Domingo, the Defense Intelligence Agency, and the Joint Chiefs, who in turn were in constant communication with the U.S. Strike Command. This was only the upper layer of the command and control system. Strike Command, which with all other commands is always in direct voice communication with the Joint Chiefs through the Joint Chiefs of Staff Alerting Net, was well equipped to meet the emergency. Operational procedures were already outlined in the Strike Emergency Action File, complete with messages already composed and with blanks for information such as times, numbers, and units. Contingency plans were on file for the Emergency Action Team. Computers processed all data relative to the plan, and immediately made available such information as the location and strength of the forces required. Other information, such as airfield facilities and municipal services, was stored on high-speed discs and tape. Only the correct button had to be pushed to project the information on a screen. All this was instantly available to land a few thousand Marines on a beach, or rather the exact number ordered by the President.

This astonishing array of devices was available to the President at a moment's notice for what was essentially a very minor operation. The array was only one part of the national system. The Air Force commands and controls its world-wide forces and facilities for the President with an electronic and computer system that can assess and analyze situations and resources, generate and evaluate plans, and monitor operations. It can instantly provide information on the status of units, material, facilities, personnel, and the like. A special computer language has been invented for the operator to find his way about more than a thousand programs and eighty million characters. The Army has developed a system that will control and coordinate the maneuvering of troops, direct artillery firepower, and support combat units.

If much of this is an extension of command arrangements for troops, it is nevertheless essential if the President, with the assistance of his advisers, is to control the response to meet any given emergency. That it is both necessary and workable in a larger conflict than the Dominican crisis was proved in the war in Vietnam. The system gave President Johnson, in Washington, the capability of directing the bombing of targets only a few miles from his own troops in a country half a world away. The commander of the American forces in Saigon recommended targets to Washington. There the Joint Chiefs, generally acting under the broad directions of the President but often under his personal command, approved or disapproved the recommendations. Copies had already been sent from Saigon to Pacific Command in Hawaii, the Seventh Fleet, and the nearest Air Division of the Strategic Air Command, and the bombers were ready when the decision was made in Washington. The staff officers of the bombardment wing or the Seventh Fleet worked out the flight plan, but the actual bombing was done by radar, even in the finest flying weather.

It can almost be said that the President actually did the bombing. In a sense never before contemplated, the bombers were an extension of Presidential power. The President was not only the Commander in Chief but the bombardier. Certainly very little more than electronic equipment came between his decision and the actual bomb detonations. The President is back on the battlefield where George Washington began. This is especially true in the command of the ultimate weapons, the intercontinental ballistic missiles and the Polaris submarines. Should these weapons ever be used, the mutual bombardment will be a duel between the President and whoever is in command in Moscow. The targets have already been selected, the necessary computations have been made, and the computers stand ready to report and assess. The President will, of course, be supported by a staff, as was George Washington, but the decisions will be his, and nothing will stand between him and the missiles and submarines except a few technicians. So the principle of civilian control has been developed from the White House to the battlefield.

It is a remarkable development that is perhaps not well understood, and of course the burden for the President is immense. It helps to explain the powers of the Defense Secretary because the President ultimately cannot depend upon the advice of the Joint Chiefs. There is no suggestion here of possible disloyalty. Few men can be more dedicated to the defense of the United States than the Joint Chiefs, but the principle of civilian control can only be applied by civilians. Only a civilian can ensure the traditional subordination of the military. Only the Defense Secretary with the Secretary of State and other civilians can assist the President in deciding whether or not the national interest requires resort to arms. The decision, of course, always rests with the President.

In writing this chapter, I have been constantly aware of the possibility of the future election of a weak President, or the more likely possibility of the appointment of a weak Defense Secretary. The system I have tried to describe depends upon men, as do all systems. It is probable that the relationship between the civilians and the soldiers will change, if only marginally, but whatever the caliber of future Presidents or the amount of marginal change, the final decisions will always rest with the President. The final and intangible factor is the will of the President. It is a factor that cannot be quantified, run through the computers, or exposed to systems analysis. Behavorial studies have been made in the most unlikely areas, but no university will receive a grant to assess the will of the White House incumbent.

The new Establishment men have produced procedures that may help him and his advisers to determine every imaginable situation. Every effort has been made to ensure that he will be furnished with all information, and that his decisions, when made, will be acted upon. But they will be his. There can be no certainty, should the time ever come, that the President will bring himself to trade, say, Philadelphia for Murmansk, or New York for Leningrad. No man before has been expected to accept the nuclear annihilation of one city for another. The new Establishment men have visualized such an eventuality as part of the Doctrine of Controlled Response. The logic of such a trade has been clear in many exercises and rehearsals, but will logic be sustained if and when the moment comes?

There can be no certain answer. Only the American President and the Soviet Prime Minister, and perhaps the British Prime Minister, can really comprehend the final meaning of nuclear command and control. It is not a matter of having exclusive access to information on the effects of nuclear blast. Such information is available to all through the courtesy of the U.S. Atomic Energy Commission. But with the best information, no one can hope to understand the effects of the power of nuclear life and death except those who have that power. The record shows that those burdened with this power seek relief in accommodation between the superpowers and the expectation of eventual arms control and disarmament. The assumption must always be that they will be reluctant to use their power. The basic logic of nuclear deterrence is that the power will not be used, but some kind of nuclear exchange must be conceivable in support of the national interest. There may come a time when the President will have to decide if the annihilation of millions of Americans serves that interest. Should that time ever come, it will be a very lonely decision that cannot be shared. But the President will not be alone. The arrangements devised for final decision-making are as comprehensive as could be devised, and will be discussed in the next chapter.

Before moving on to the apex of the American national security system, it is as well to look at four of its main instruments, the armed forces of the United States. Some critics have it that they are the only instruments, that the first reaction of Presidents or Secretaries of State to trouble in the Caribbean or Central America is to send in the Marines. This is an exaggeration, despite the efforts of some Presidents to have it otherwise, but clearly the efficiency of the armed forces is always an important factor in the pursuit of national security objectives. It can be decisive, even in times of what has passed for peace since the Second World War. The Berlin Airlift is an obvious example. The technological affluence of the United States made the aircraft available, but it was the staff work of the Air Force that

G

forged the squadrons of transport aircraft into a bloodless weapon that saved the old German capital and stabilized Central Europe.

The first thing to be said is that they are distinguished by a remarkable degree of professionalism. This is perhaps surprising to some readers. Tradition has it that the Americans are not a martial people. History shows that when they are compelled to fight, the armies raised have invariably been civilian hosts. The large civilian armies of the First and Second World Wars also resisted much of the customary military trappings and attitudes. If the very size of these modern armies diluted the professionalism at the battalion level, it was always very much evident at the command and staff levels. This military professionalism in a society traditionally suspicious of most things military and previously impatient with foreign adventure is well worth examining because it explains a great deal of the tension that has existed from time to time between the armed services and civilian authority.

Oddly enough, it was a direct product of civilian indifference after the Civil War. What status the professional soldier had enjoyed disappeared when the South, the cradle of the officer class, went down in defeat. The subsequent business pacificism of the North nurtured civilian indifference, and even hostility. Military expenditures were progressively lowered. In the last quarter of the nineteenth century the strength of the Army averaged about 25,000 officers and men, and that of the Navy and Marine Corps about 11,000. Until 1890 the Army was strung out along the frontier fighting Indians, a strenuous and often heroic task rarely recognized, perhaps because recognition would have diminished the later frontier myth. Intellectual isolation also increased as the Military Academy at West Point gradually lost touch with the American education movement. Officers were rarely received in polite society. The United States Army, one officer complained at the time, was an alien army existing in practically complete separation from the lives of its own people.

The armed forces, it can be seen, suffered much the same fate as the diplomatic service, but American historians have noted that the very isolation and rejection, which reduced their numbers and hampered technological advance, helped to foster military professionalism. Civilian rejection perversely encouraged pride and interest in the profession of arms. Physical and social isolation permitted the officer corps to develop a distinctly military character. The soldiers also had more to build on than the diplomats. The Civil War was the first of the great modern wars, and it produced some superb generals. They emerged from that war better equipped, and with a more certain understanding of large-scale maneuver and the logistics it required, than any other existing army.

General Sherman especially nurtured the military virtues, and in establishing the infantry and cavalry school at Fort Leavenworth provided the necessary specialized instruction. He also insisted upon the divorce of the military from politics. Three of the six generals commanding before him had become Presidential candidates, but he began the tradition of political neutrality which, with the sole exception of General Wood, was maintained until after the Second World War. Less unenthusiastic Presidential possibilities have long quoted his refusal to run: "I will not accept if nominated and I will not serve if elected." His successors continued the trend toward professionalism and increased the military isolation from civilian society.

One contributing factor was that much of their inspiration came from foreign military institutions, although American military professionalism continued to differ from foreign varieties because it was concerned entirely with military ends. It played no part in the development of the nation as did the Prussian Army. Prussia was, however, the main source of inspiration. It may have begun with von Steuben, the Prussian who fought in the Revolutionary War, but in the latter part of the nineteenth century there were visits to Berlin, and exchanges with men such as von der Goltz and von Moltke. Clausewitz was translated into English in 1873, and there was correspondence with the *Militarische Gesellschaft*. All this well served the American armed forces, although it perhaps explains the military absolutism of the mid-twentieth century. This is reflected in the acceptance of total nuclear war and a ruthlessness which continually surprises the British.

Herman Kahn, the American nuclear theoretician, argues that British nuclear strategy is based on pre-emptive surrender. That is, in the event of a conflict Britain would tread all the rungs of the escalation ladder until a nuclear exchange threatened, when it would immediately seek a negotiated solution. Mr. Kahn is undoubtedly correct. The British people were more than prepared to fight an invading Nazi Army on the beaches with Winston Churchill, but that was before the advent of the nuclear age. British humanism is revolted by the absolutism that has led the United States to accept the necessity in certain circumstances of a nuclear war. Similarly most Britons were revolted by the conventional bombing ordered by the then Prime Minister, Sir Anthony Eden, during the Suez intervention of 1956. In Malaya Britain fought Communist guerrillas with what were essentially police methods. I have the impression that few armies other than the German Army, and I am not referring to the Nazi *Wehrmacht,* would have used the force the American Army brought to bear in Vietnam. The French Army was less indiscriminate.

I realize that I am on tricky ground here, and in any case it is only a personal view after observing the United States Army in the Korean War and previously in Asia during the Second World War. As for the historical reasons for the professionalism of the armed forces and the tensions between them and civilian authority, one military writer, Samuel P. Huntington, recently wrote:

The withdrawal of the military from the civilian society at the end of the 19th Century produced the high standards of professional excellence essential to national success in the struggles of the 20th Century. If the officer corps had not been rejected, if the Army and Navy had not been reduced to the bone in the 1870s and 1880s, the United States would have had a more difficult time of it in 1917 and 1942.

The military officer who, at the end of the period of isolation, rejoined civilian society in World War I and World War II, was a fundamentally different creature from his ancestor who had withdrawn in the 1860s. When he left, he was a citizen-soldier, an accepted member of the liberal family. When he returned, he was a stranger in his own household. His membership in the national family was no longer free, easy, and relaxed. The years of isolation had remade him into a professional with values and outlook basically at odds with those of the mass of his countrymen. They had interjected steel into his soul which was missing from that of the community. His return marked the beginning of the real problem of American civil-military relations: the tension between the conservative professional officer and the liberal society.*

Even the most casual visitor to military libraries cannot but be impressed by the contributions of American officers. Upton's *Armies of Europe and Asia* and *The Military Policy of the United States* are

---

* *The Soldier and the State: The Theory and Politics of Civil-Military Relations,* Cambridge, Harvard University Press, 1959.

obvious examples. Admiral Luce brought the same exacting standards of professional excellence to the United States Navy, and was
responsible for the early foundation of the Naval Institute and the
Naval War College. Rear Admiral A. T. Mahan had a much wider
impact. *The Influence of Sea Power upon History, 1660–1783* and
*The Influence of Sea Power upon the French Revolution and Empire,
1793–1812* were first delivered as lectures when Mahan was president
of the Newport War College, but they were widely read in Britain,
Germany, and Japan. He was among the first to see the interrelation
of naval power and commerce, and was convinced of the interdepen-
dence of naval and political power. It is no exaggeration to suggest
that he provide the intellectual framework for the big navies of the
twentieth century. His conception of the fleet in being dominated
American and British naval doctrine for decades. Mahan also became
an ardent advocate of Manifest Destiny, as American colonialism was
euphemistically described, and as such greatly influenced political
thought in Washington.

On the whole, however, American military professionalism led to a
corporate jealousy of military prerogatives and widespread distrust of
politics. The military mind is, of course, more often than not distrustful of the democratic process, which is essentially one of compromise.
In Imperial Germany the army rejected what passed for democracy
there. During the Franco-Prussian War even Bismarck was kept
waiting by the General Staff. That did not happen in the United
States. American soldiers have always been Americans first, but
distrust of politicians appears to have been more prevalent in the
American armed forces than in the British. The reason may well have
been that in Britain the officer corps, if such a corporate body ever
existed in the accepted sense of the word, was at least part of society.
It could not be isolated when so many officers came from families
often actively involved in political life and providing recruits for other
professions.

It is perhaps necessary to emphasize that at no time in the history
of the United States has civilian authority ever been seriously questioned by the military. Its loyalty to the Constitution and national
political institutions has always been beyond question. The great
generals such as Washington and Grant were men of political modesty. Only General MacArthur saw himself as a man of political
destiny. If the tensions have been disturbing at times, the generals

have not been Bonapartes as much as affronted professionals. The resistance of the old Indian-fighting generals to the Root reforms was an early example. The reforms were the beginning of a lengthy process culminating in the reorganization of the military establishment after the Second World War.

Prior to the Root reforms of 1903, the separation of the American military from civilian society was curiously reflected in the organization of the then War Department. The general commanding the Army was responsible for the efficiency, discipline, and conduct of troops in peace and war, and the Secretary of War for the budget, supplies, and transportation. This system of dual and separate responsibility led to discord and inefficiency, and was almost disastrous in the Spanish-American War. Elihu Root, who has been described as the father of the modern State Department, could also claim paternity for the modern Army. His General Staff Act of 1903 did the obvious by creating a General Staff of forty-four officers, but it also abolished the office of General Commanding and provided for a Chief of Staff subordinate to the President or his representative, the Secretary of War.

As Secretary, Mr. Root reported:

It will be perceived that we are here providing for civilian control over the military arm, but for civilian control to be exercised through a single military expert of high rank, who is provided with an adequate corps of professional assistants to aid him in the performance of his duties, and who is bound to use all his professional skill and knowledge in giving effect to the purposes and general directions of his civilian superior, or make way for another expert who will do so. In this way it is hoped that the problem of reconciling civilian control with military efficiency with which we have been struggling for so many years will be solved. . . .*

Affronted professionalism explains much of the antics which went on in Washington during the debates after the Second World War. There were other factors; as previously noted, the generals and admirals had wielded immense politico-military power during the war, and the Cold War was seen to require a high degree of military participation in the formulation of policy as well as military preparedness. This approach to some extent reflected the traditional American attitude to war and peace. In peace, the military should be

* Report of the Secretary of War, 1903.

small in size and divorced from power. In war, when the goal is victory, military needs should be overriding. Perhaps it also reflected the American respect for experts and expertise, or what the military describe as professionalism. No other development caused so much pain as when this was affronted by the reassertion of civilian authority.

There was a further blow, and that was the Presidential decision to fight a limited war in Korea. Even victory as a war objective was denied to them. Many years later, retired military gentlemen and their political allies on the extreme right were claiming that there was no substitute for victory, but of course there was: national survival with honor in the nuclear age. To understand the military predicament it must be remembered that there were no intercontinental ballistic missiles or fusion weapons when the Korean War began. The disciplines of Korea prepared the United States for the nuclear age, but in 1950 there were other reasons for a limited war. The Korean War began because of a monumental miscalculation on the part of the Communists, who sought a limited objective by a limited use of force. They probably did not expect the United States to react because the independence of South Korea had not been declared essential to American national security. It was also preoccupied in ensuring the survival of Western Europe with what was then inadequate force. President Truman, however, was convinced that the failure of the League of Nations to provide collective security had brought about the Second World War. He was determined to avoid another failure.

The prevention of a Third World War was essentially the American objective in Korea. Hence the limited nature of the war. It was successful to the extent that the Soviet Union did not launch a diversionary attack elsewhere. It was a partial failure because of pressure from General MacArthur to extend the war into North Korea. The United Nations forces advanced toward the Yalu River and China intervened. The uniqueness of the Korean experience raised a number of questions regarding national security policy. Many Americans felt that the President, despite his authority as Commander in Chief, ought not to have waged war without the consent of Congress. The dismissal of General MacArthur revealed military impatience with limited war, despite the violent Chinese reaction to his forward policy, but confirmed American respect for Presidential authority. It led to violent disputes over the civilian and military roles in national security, and when they subsided, the military discovered that the MacArthur incident was merely the dramatic froth brought about by a sudden and fundamental change in the command and control of war.

In a way, Korea was the Spanish War of the nuclear age. No nuclear bombs were dropped, and few if any new weapons were tested as aerial bombing and tanks were tested in Spain. What was garnered from the rice paddies, however, was far more fundamental than a little experience in the use of new weapons. The need for constant civilian control was evident from the beginning, and became all the more necessary when President Truman in effect found himself Commander in Chief of a varied and polyglot United Nations force. What was learned, in fact, was how much remained to be learned if limited wars were to be fought successfully and without resort to nuclear weapons. It was a problem far beyond the military experience and the resources of military intelligence agencies.

Worse was to follow. The complexity of national security problems and situations continued to increase as the relevance of the old distinctions between land, sea, and air warfare decreased. The old professionalism, apart from the maintenance of discipline and military skills, seemed more and more meaningless. As already noted, civilians secured effective control of the Defense Department, took charge of weapons development, and dictated strategy. There were other forced military withdrawals. One was especially painful, and came after the Farewell Address of President Eisenhower in 1961. The former Supreme Commander of the Allied Forces in Europe said, "In the councils of government, we must guard against the acquisition of unwarranted influence, whether sought or unsought, by the military-industrial complex. The potential for the disastrous rise of misplaced power exists and will persist."

No one was absolutely clear as to the precise meaning of this Delphic warning at the time, but it did give expression to a widespread concern over the relationship between the military and big business. With about 10 percent of the Gross National Product devoted to military purposes, the Defense Department had become big business' biggest customer. Its procurement officers had also become experts, or had developed a new military professionalism. Few corporation managers have had similar experience in the tendering, testing, and ordering of a variety of equipment, from missiles to belt buckles, costing billions of dollars. The experience dated back to the Second World War when miracles of arms production had been performed largely under military direction. For instance, the Manhattan District Project, which produced the first atomic bomb, was under the over-all command of General Leslie Groves. This was a new kind of professionalism, vital in the new technological age, and it was mastered by the American military to a degree unmatched elsewhere.

It gave them a new form of power, shared by industry and to some extent by Congress, and it could perhaps have been dangerous. There is reason to believe that President Eisenhower issued his warning because he regarded his successor as a youthful and inexperienced man. The warning enhanced the impression of military domination, which was wrong and dangerous, especially abroad, and in any case unnecessary. The new situation had already been appraised by civilians. Charles Hitch of the RAND Corporation had written a book on the subject entitled *The Economics of Defense in the Nuclear Age,* and his appointment in the Defense Department as Comptroller brought to an end the latest form of military professionalism. From 1961 procurement was firmly in civilian hands.

The military did not take this and other diminutions of power quietly. Political neutrality is the American tradition, but the generals had their friends in Congress. The ties had increased as Senators and members of the House of Representatives scrambled for arms contracts and other defense expenditure for their states and districts. The forces had each in turn long lobbied Congress for a larger share of the defense budget. Their information services were as efficient as most commercial public relations firms, and a good deal larger. The procurement battle was largely fought for them by the chairman of the House Armed Services Committee. The battle against limited war was continued on a wider front, by Congressmen, the service leagues, friendly columnists, and retired generals turned journalists. General Thomas White, a former Chief of Staff of the Air Force, wrote:

It seems to me the old strengths still apply. In my opinion the two that count for most in the nuclear space age, regardless of academic cerebrations, are national determination and military forces designed to achieve victory, not tailored to obtain compromise. Professional military teaching teaches the philosophy of victory, whereas politics is based on compromise.

G*

There was also military opposition to the partial nuclear-test-ban treaty, the first formal evidence of the partial eclipse of military absolutism in American Cold War strategy. Its ratification demonstrated without a shadow of doubt that the executive branch and Congress, while determined to defend the national interest by nuclear arms if necessary, were also determined to seek peaceful accommodations with the Soviet Union. The treaty followed upon the Cuban missile crisis of 1962, and also upon a rather blatant attempt by some officers to influence troops and civilian audiences with militant ideas normally associated with the radical right wing and McCarthyism.

The most infamous case was that of Major General Walker, a divisional commander obsessed by the nightmare of an international Communist conspiracy at home and abroad. An Army investigation confirmed that he had tried to influence the voting of his troops in the 1960 Presidential election. During the subsequent Congressional investigation, the general suggested that President Eisenhower had been a dupe of the Communists. The Secretary of State was said to be influential in the control apparatus that frustrated military anti-Communist activity.

There were more insidious attempts to influence public opinion against national security policy by military participation in public seminars and so-called freedom forums. They were brought to light in 1962 by Senator William Fulbright, chairman of the Senate Foreign Relations Committee, who proved that most of them were dominated by radical right-wing speakers. Their central theme was that internal Communist infiltration was the primary danger, and American appeasement was said to be responsible for most of the country's international problems. Federal social legislation was equated with socialism, and socialism with Communism.

Such antics would be unthinkable in other advanced democracies, and elsewhere might well have presaged a military *coup d'état*. In American terms, they certainly amounted to a crisis, but one quickly resolved by Congressional investigation and prompt Presidential action. No heads rolled. It was accepted that the average military officer was by nature a conservative animal, and that the United States was a wide-open society, even an unbuttoned one. It was further recognized that the military, despite its pervading conservatism, reflected to some extent civilian political differences. Nevertheless, the older disciplines were reasserted, and the military stepped smartly back into line.

If these and other incidents were painful, they were perhaps inevitable. In less than two decades, the armed forces had lost much of the political influence they had enjoyed during the Second World War, and the old professionalism had come to mean less and less. Frustration was understandable, if many of its manifestations inexcusable. The armed forces, it can perhaps be said, were the victims of the new superdiplomacy as well as technological change and the reassertion of civilian authority. The lesson was largely learned, however, although impatience with limited objectives became obvious again during the war in Vietnam. The change was most evident among younger officers as they learned the new expertise, and in so doing found a new professionalism. The lessons of the civilian nuclear theoreticians were learned, and the new management tools mastered. In the field, new tactics were evolved to apply the latest ideas on counterinfiltration and counterinsurgency. Whatever disgruntled retired officers may have said in their memoirs, the new professionalism made the American armed forces a suitable instrument for the national security policy of the United States in the nuclear age.

6 The National Security Council

"The heads of the various departments are in a position to carry on during such times with full knowledge of the continued validity of the broad policy concepts established by the President in the cumulative experience of the National Security Council. . . . The continued functioning of Government in such periods under a body of established policy exemplifies, in a real sense, the principle which John Adams wrote into the Massachusetts Constitution in 1780—that ours is a Government of laws and not of men."

—DILLON ANDERSON
Special Assistant to President Eisenhower for National Security Affairs

"Agreement by exhaustion."

—DEAN ACHESON
Secretary of State (1949–53)

The President, by law and practice, has total responsibility for national security. He is responsible for the conduct of foreign affairs, he is the Commander in Chief, and he proposes the federal budget. He alone must finally weigh all the domestic, foreign, and military factors that contribute to security and the country's position in the world. The National Security Council was created by statute to help him in meeting these responsibilities. The 1947 Act says:

The function of the Council shall be to advise the President with respect to the integration of domestic, foreign, and military policies relating to the national security so as to enable the military services and the other departments and agencies of the Government to cooperate more effectively in matters involving the national security. . . .

The Council was one of the answers to the frustrations of the Second World War that bedeviled those responsible for the coordination of military and foreign policies. It can claim a mixed descent from such temporary bodies as the State-War-Navy Coordinating Committee and the former British Committee on Imperial Defense. Its creators, however, were well aware of the constitutional differences between Britain and the United States. There could be no question of Cabinet or group responsibility. The Council is not therefore a decision-making body, nor does it make policy. It can only hope to serve in an advisory capacity to the President. He alone can make the decisions.

By 1953 when the 1947 Act had been amended to suit the requirements of President Eisenhower, the membership was as follows: the President, the Vice President, the Secretary of State, the Secretary of Defense, the Director of Mutual Security, and the Chairman of the National Resources Board. These were the inner group, and they were assisted by the Secretaries and Under Secretaries of other executive departments and of the military departments, the Chairman of the Munitions Board, and the Chairman of the Research and Development Board, when appointed by the President, by and with the advice and consent of the Senate, to serve at his pleasure.

The Reorganization Plan No. 6 of the same year quickly abolished the National Resources Board and appointed the Director of the Office of Defense Mobilization as a member of the Council. The Munitions Board and the Research and Development Board were also abolished and their functions transferred to the office of the Secretary of Defense. Other changes were made, and the membership of the Council was eventually reduced to the President, the Vice President, Secretary of State, Secretary of Defense, and Director of the Office of Emergency Planning. These were not the only changes. Although the Council was created by statute, each successive President was perforce allowed considerable latitude in deciding how to use it. The essential weakness of the Council, at least for three of the four Presidents, was that it appeared to trespass upon their Constitutional prerogatives. President Truman clearly resented the trespass.

All new bodies, especially sensitive ones such as the Council, have growing pains, but after two decades there was little evidence to suggest that it would ever achieve full stature. Experience explains why. President Truman, especially in the few years prior to the outbreak of war in Korea, showed a strong concern for the authority, responsibility, and prerogatives of the chief executive. He questioned the constitutional power of Congress to require the President to seek advice from specific individuals or officeholders, and recognized the dangers of imitating a British model with the possible diminution of Presidential authority. "There were times during the early days of the National Security Council when one or two of its members tried to change it into an operating super-cabinet on the British model," he recalled later. He attended only one in five of the meetings before the Korean War to emphasize its advisory role. The Council was seen as a useful facility to study and appraise continually military, diplomatic, and resources problems, but it was kept at a distance.

Nevertheless, under President Truman the Council drew up for the first time in the nation's history formal statements on national objectives and methods of achieving them. Although the effort was not always successful, it served an important purpose in a period when the United States was assuming new responsibilities overseas. Policy papers were produced dealing not only with national security problems and strategy, but with mobilization, arms control, trade, and organizational questions including intelligence and internal security. The long-range effect of these papers on policy as well as organization was probably greater than successive Presidents cared to admit.

It might also be said that the Council, for all President Truman's jealousy for his constitutional authority, played an indispensable role in organizing the United States for superpower, and, as with other bodies organized to meet an emergency, could have been allowed to fade away gracefully. This well could have happened if President Kennedy had been elected in 1952. Instead, President Eisenhower, with a lifetime of orderly staff work behind him, criticized Mr. Truman's use of the Council during the election campaign, and on coming to power institutionalized it. More than that, by developing and expanding the structures and procedures of the Council he created a National Security Council system of which the Council itself was but a component.

By the end of his administration, the Council system was a highly complicated but apparently smoothly operating machine with clear lines of authority and elaborate staff work. The Council met regularly on Thursday mornings, and was attended not only by its statutory members but by a score and occasionally two score of officials and advisers. The Chairman of the Joint Chiefs and the Director of the CIA were invariably in attendance. There were two special assistants supporting the President, one responsible for National Security Affairs and the other for Security Operations Coordination. The first had enormous bureaucratic authority and was chairman of two subsidiary organizations, the Planning Board and the Operations Coordinating Board.

The Planning Board, which was manned by Assistant Secretaries of the various departments and agencies, developed studies and policy recommendations for the Council's consideration. The second, which began as the successor to the old Psychological Strategy Board, integrated the work of that body in the over-all strategy. More importantly, it acted as the coordinating arm of the Council in implementing national security policy. It had no authority to direct or control the activities of departments executing policy, but it provided a means by which they could consult and cooperate with each other. It also initiated proposals within the existing framework of national security policies.

The National Security Council system under President Eisenhower included interdepartmental committees for intelligence and internal security, and other special committees. It looked most impressive on paper, and the Council was described as the top of "policy hill." Recommendations moved up one side of the hill and through the Planning Board to the Council. When approved by the President, the new policies traveled down the other side to the departments and agencies. In the first three Eisenhower years, the Council met 145 times and took 829 policy actions compared with 128 meetings and 699 policy actions in more than five years under President Truman. The neatness and mechanical orderliness of the process were highly praised by some as the most efficient means of transacting pressing business. These were the golden years, but there were plenty of critics, and charges of mass production, packaging, and distribution. Others questioned whether truly effective policy could be developed by a form of standardized bulk processing. The system was seen to suffer from all the weaknesses of committees. Representatives of departments were said to defend their departmental positions at the cost of the national interest, and to indulge in horse-trading. The result, according to one critic, was agreement by exhaustion.

Whatever the merit of the orderly conduct of business—and it is considerable—the system as it evolved under President Eisenhower was said to be largely restricted by its very nature to continuing and developing established policies. It became increasingly difficult to introduce new ideas. Moreover, it prevented the normal exchange and cross-fertilization of ideas within the government, and shut out the lively public debates that have long distinguished the American process of formulating policy. There was even a suggestion that the constitutional authority of the President was compromised. During one of the President's illnesses, one of the staff members said that the departments could act within the broad policy concept established in the Council by the President.

The thought that contingency planning could replace the President was rather breath-taking. Subsequently Senator Henry Jackson, the chairman of the Senate Subcommittee on National Security, began his study of the system. The subcommittee rejected the idea of a policy-making machine, and offered a number of recommendations to "de-institutionalize" it. The Council should be an intimate forum for the President to meet his chief advisers in the discussion and debate of a limited number of critical problems. It should offer alternative courses of action, and not spare the President the necessity of choice. The Operations Coordinating Board should be abolished, the staff of the Council reduced, and more reliance placed on the Secretary of State.

President Kennedy acted on much of this and other advice. The bureaucratic battalions of the Planning Board and the Operations Coordination Board were replaced by a small commando unit, numbering no more than an ordinary infantry platoon, under the Special Assistant for National Security Affairs. This was an intensely personal staff, many of them young men who specialized in regional affairs but were assumed capable of generally helping the President. "Generalist" was very much a favorite word. They were supported by so-called task forces organized on an *ad hoc* basis to tackle specific problems or crises. The Council remained, but it was reduced to its statutory membership except for the President's brother, Robert Kennedy, who regularly attended, not as Attorney General but as a personal adviser. These arrangements suited President Kennedy, and were supposed to express the spirit of the New Frontier.

To some extent they continued in the early years of President Johnson's administration. Both Kennedy and Johnson were activists, and with President Truman were jealous of their authority. It seems safe to conclude therefore that the National Security Council will continue in most future administrations to play a lesser role than was first visualized for it. The main reason will not necessarily be efficiency or performance, but because Presidents on the whole are not prepared to have their authority diminished, or have it appear to be diminished. There can be no argument with this. Whatever Congress cares to legislate, the President will continue to have the last word on the organization as well as the direction of national security. Nevertheless, it is perhaps not entirely unprofitable to wonder if greater efficiency and dependability could not be achieved without diminishing or appearing to diminish Presidential authority.

If performance is any guide, a case could be made for the system of President Eisenhower, or something like it. In his eight years, the United States was not involved in any war, and the Lebanon intervention, if logistically weak, was carried out with dispatch once the troops were landed. Sputnik surprised his administration in 1957, but in its three remaining years the first generation of missiles was made ready and the second generation was well on the way. The Minuteman and Polaris missiles and the nuclear-powered submarines, the basic weapons of the new strategy of the Kennedy administration, were started during the previous administration. President Eisenhower was afterward ridiculed for his supposedly primitive nuclear strategy, but his conception of a limited deterrent was eminently respectable.

The weakness of the National Security Council under President Eisenhower was not so much due to organization as to his respect for a balanced budget and his demands for economy. President Kennedy was more in tune with the American character in his determination to have a deterrent superior to that of the Soviet Union despite the cost. Few Americans would settle for less than first place, but the fact of the matter is that Soviet security is no less because its missile strength is limited as compared with that of the United States. What largely distinguished his defense policy was a readiness to outspend the Soviet Union to achieve maximum security.

President Kennedy's performance was at best spotty. No one can say that the large national security system of President Eisenhower would have avoided the disaster of the 1961 Cuban invasion, but good staff work has saved inexperienced leaders in the past. We have it from a sympathetic biographer, Arthur Schlesinger, Jr., that the United States drifted into the Vietnam war because "he had never really given it his full attention." The 1962 Cuban confrontation was handled better. It was essentially simple as a command operation, but the so-called Executive Committee of the National Security Council was much larger, 16 to 5, than the Council's statutory membership. It was much closer to what Congress visualized when it voted on the National Security Act and the amendments than the usual commando operation of the Kennedy team. This performance comparison may be unfair, the demands of their time were perhaps different, but no doubt operational analysis would produce a similar conclusion.

President Kennedy's system was best defended by his Special Assistant for National Security Affairs, McGeorge Bundy, in a letter to the Senate Subcommittee on National Security in July 1961. He said that three changes had been made in the inherited system. First, the Council met less often because the President preferred to convene it only after a particular issue was ready for discussion. The Council had never been and should never become the only instrument of counsel and decision available to the President. This could not be overemphasized. It was likely to continue as a major channel through which broad issues of national security policy came forward for Presidential decision, but the President continued to meet the Secretaries of State and Defense, and other officials at frequent intervals, together or alone.

Second, the Operations Coordination Board was abolished because it did not match the style of operation and coordination of the administration. Without unanimity it had never had authority, and was not a truly Presidential instrument. The President preferred to rely on the leadership of the State Department, and he did not want a large separate organization between him and the Secretary. The clear authority and responsibility of the Secretary, not only in his own department, but as the agent of coordination in all major policies toward other nations, must be established.

Third, planning and operation were to be combined because their separation tended to break down in the business of decision and action at the Presidential level. The Council staff, which was essentially a Presidential instrument, should be composed of men capable of both functions. The staff was smaller than before, and its job was to help the President and not to supersede or supplement the departmental Secretaries. Their task was that of all staff officers: to extend the range and enlarge the direct effectiveness of the man they served. The rest could be left to the State Department and other agencies.

There remains a crushing burden of responsibility, and of sheer hard work, on the President himself; there remains also the steady flow of questions, of ideas, of executive energy which a strong President will give off like sparks. If his Cabinet officers are to be free to do their own work, the President's work must be done—to the extent that he cannot do it himself—by staff officers under his direct oversight. But this is, I repeat, something entirely different from the interposition of such a staff between the President and his Cabinet officers.

It is a compelling view, because it is essentially a Presidential view, and in the field of national security the President will always prevail. There is also a certain logic about it. As the two previous chapters have tried to illustrate, the two great departments most concerned with national security have been reorganized to ensure not so much civilian control of the departments as over-all Presidential control. The interposition of some super-Cabinet system would be intolerable. The weakness of the system was, as it remains, that the leadership of the State Department was not established. The task force system also cut across the Secretary's lines of authority. In such a force the State Department representative was only one of many, and the presence of a Presidential assistant was inhibiting.

On the whole, I am persuaded that the various arguments for or against the National Security Council are largely irrelevant if not spurious. The President will always make the decisions, in or outside the Council, and its statutory membership is at present so small that it makes little or no difference whether the President meets the Secretaries of State and Defense in its chamber or at the White House luncheon table. What is important is that the system provides the necessary information and the judgment of experts. The system devised under President Eisenhower was probably too elaborate, but President Kennedy perhaps went too far in the other direction. He appeared to rely too heavily on his immediate assistants, and in one instance with terrible consequences. I refer to the decisions made for Vietnam in 1961.

The situation which President Kennedy inherited there was murky, to say the least, as indeed it was in Cuba. He accordingly sent out two representatives, a distinguished general, who had resigned from the

Army over a policy disagreement and joined the President's staff, and a special assistant. They reported that South Vietnam could be saved for the local variety of democracy with more military, technical, and economic aid and some twelve thousand American military advisers. This became the policy for the next four years, during which time the situation steadily deteriorated. Eventually the general rather engagingly admitted that he had been wrong, and American divisions were committed to prevent a shattering defeat. What was worse, the long slide downhill, although doggedly reported by the American press, was ignored or not understood by Washington. The Defense Secretary had first responsibility for Vietnam under the President despite the leadership claimed for the State Department. He looked confidently to Christmas 1965, when all American advisers would be withdrawn. In actual fact, about 175,000 American troops spent that Christmas in Vietnam, and American bombers had by then devastated the South Vietnamese countryside and much of the transport system in the North. By 1967 there were about 500,000 troops committed.

The United States had suffered military reverses in the past mainly because of unpreparedness, but it was not unprepared in the early sixties. No country had ever been better prepared in time of peace for all kinds of conflicts. The unavoidable conclusion is that something was radically wrong with the national security system. When Mr. Schlesinger recorded that President Kennedy had never really given it his full attention, it was another way of saying that he was not properly informed or advised. He was certainly aware of the dangers of so-called wars of liberation, which he discussed with Khrushchev in Vienna in 1961. The modern version of the Monroe Doctrine was extended to meet the threat of such wars in the following year.

Some errors were tragic. The administration persuaded itself that improvements were possible if the then President of South Vietnam dismissed some of his advisers, especially his brother. Officials promoted the idea of a military *coup d'état,* and eventually President Kennedy appeared on television to suggest a change of personnel. The South Vietnamese President was quickly assassinated, and a series of military juntas followed under which political stability disappeared. It is no exaggeration to say that much of the work of the Vietcong was done for them by Washington.

A reverse would have been possible, of course, under a much improved national security system, but it would have been less likely.

An example is the British experience in Malaya. The Communist uprising there began in 1948, when Britain, the imperial power, was in no condition to fight such a war, militarily, economically, or psychologically. Nevertheless, the uprising was quelled within five years, although incidents continued sporadically for another two or three years. In comparing Vietnam with Malaya I am not claiming a greater intelligence for Britain. What I am suggesting is that the British cabinet system was a good deal more efficient than the American national security system. Mistakes were made. I reported many of them as a foreign correspondent. For instance, helicopters were used only at a late stage, and never extensively. The Labour government of the time never proclaimed Malayan independence a war objective. Oddly enough, that was left to the succeeding Conservative government, but London under both was always more responsive to the local situation.

Americans have said in their defense that no fair comparison can be made. The Malayan conflict never developed beyond the guerrilla stage. Britain, as the imperial power, was in complete control, unlike the United States, which perforce had to work through an independent government with an inefficient and corrupt administration. The Malayan conflict certainly did not develop, but largely because of the successful counteractions. Britain certainly was the imperial power, but Malaya was a protectorate and not a crown colony. The existence of a number of separate states, each with its ruler, was a complicating factor. In any event, colonialism, even the attenuated form practiced in Malaya, was hardly popular, and the conflict raged when all Southeast Asia was in a turmoil. It might also be added that the British cabinet system failed during the Suez affair of 1956 only because the then Prime Minister refused to use it, and instead acted as if he were an American President.

At this late stage in the development of the Republic, I am not about to recommend the wholesale transfer of the British system to Washington. I doubt that there are sufficient states prepared to ratify the abolition of the United States Constitution, even if it were legally possible. It is nevertheless worth noting that the British Prime Minister makes do with four private personal secretaries and a Cabinet secretary, compared with whom even President Kennedy's small national security staff looks excessive.

It could be that an efficient and continuing national security system is impossible under the American Presidency. The office is too personal and the President's constitutional powers too explicit to permit such a system. Certainly a good many wise and imaginative Americans, in and out of government and Congress, have tried to bring it about without much success. The hearings of the Senate Subcommittee on National Security continued after the changes made by President Kennedy. They were intelligently run, and produced a wealth of material. The subcommittee made many astute observations and recognized what ought to be avoided, but its recommendations did not pretend to add up to a complete answer.

A proposal for an Office of National Security Affairs, similar to the Bureau of the Budget, was considered, and rejected for fear it might grow into another barrier between the President and his Secretaries of State and Defense. A larger National Security Council staff found small favor because it could diminish for the President the utility of the Special Assistant for National Security Affairs. The hearings did add, however, to the growing support for returning to the Secretary of State much of his traditional responsibility. The Subcommittee noted that the department was becoming three-dimensional in its collective thinking, and paying more attention to the economic and military aspects of problems.

There are obvious drawbacks. The United States generally pursues a national security rather than a foreign policy. The Secretary of State would have little time for running his department if he were to become the President's first national security adviser. The Secretaries of Defense and the Treasury would not relinquish part of their statutory and traditional responsibilities without a struggle. Nevertheless, many Americans are attracted by the prospect of the Secretary of State's assuming greater responsibility, largely because future Presidents may be less disposed to change a system based on an established department.

Recommendations have been made, although rejected, to appoint a Permanent Under Secretary of State, similar to the senior civil servant in the British Foreign Office, who could relieve the Secretary of much of the work that modern diplomacy entails. The department would benefit from the continuity such an official could provide, and leave the Secretary free to advise the President. He would be responsible, under the President, for policy, and the permanent official for operations. There are objections, but also a belief, fairly widely held, that the present system must be improved.

At present it is not so very different from Hitler's *Oberkommando der Wehrmacht*. The OKW was a military headquarters, of course, but it did have a few of the characteristics of the American National Security Council system. The most obvious, in terms of performance, is that in national security the President is as much a dictator as the former *Reichsführer*. He can be ousted from office at the polling booth, or by impeachment, but Congress does not have to enact enabling laws for him to assume dictatorial powers. Congress can deny him money, but he can still plunge the world into a *Götterdämmerung*.

It is an improbable thought. The McCarthys and Goldwaters never had a chance of winning a Presidential election, although one cannot altogether forget Harding. There is the possibility, no matter how slight, of a weak President coming to power again. If that now seems to be more than remote, because American election campaigning is thought to expose the personal weaknesses of candidates, Presidents can die in office. Four have been assassinated, and Vice Presidents are frequently chosen for political reasons, such as balancing the ticket, rather than for their abilities. Certainly their experience or interest in national security is not normally part of the calculation.

Vice President Johnson proved to be a powerful chief executive when he assumed office after the assassination of President Kennedy. At first his handling of national security affairs was very tentative. Much the same can be said of most of his predecessors, which of course strengthens the case for continuity in national security affairs. He did, however, take up the earlier proposal to improve the National Security Council system, and give it some permanence by placing it under the direct charge of the Secretary of State.

A directive was issued on March 4, 1966, authorizing the Secretary, as Presidential agent, to assume responsibility for the over-all direction, coordination, and supervision of official activities overseas to the full extent permitted by law. The qualification may seem unnecessary, but departments and agencies in Washington are each subject to laws, often complex, which regulate their operations. They cannot be changed by Presidential directive, and resort to Congress would be asking for trouble. But the statutory framework can be a prison for reformers, which helps to explain why reforms are rarely comprehensive.

Under the 1966 directive a group known as the Senior Interdepartmental Group (SIG) was established to assist the Secretary, with the

Under Secretary of State as executive chairman. He was given a casting vote in the event of a division of opinion, and the power to make any decision final, although the other members were given the right to appeal to the President. The regular members were the deputies of the Secretary of Defense, the Chairman of the Joint Chiefs of Staff, the Directors of the Central Intelligence Agency, the Agency for International Development, and the United States Information Agency, and the ubiquitous man from the President's personal staff.

Immediately below SIG were five Interdepartmental Regional Groups under the chairmanship of the Assistant Secretaries of State for Africa, Europe, Latin America, Middle East and Southern Asia, and the Far East. Collectively these groups were the apex of the organizational pyramid reaching down to embassies and other missions overseas, whose internal reorganization is mentioned elsewhere.

Thus President Johnson tried to put his own stamp, or LBJ brand, on the National Security Council system. It was not so cumbersome as the Eisenhower model, but at the time of writing a good deal of cynicism, not all of it unhealthy, was evident in Washington. If four organizations under four Presidents were par for the course, the supposedly comprehensive organization did not cover some important areas of national security. Disarmament was often left out in the cold, although President Johnson paid even more attention to it than did his predecessors. Vietnam had its own interdepartmental group, but remained a personal Presidential responsibility.

Vietnam, of course, raises the question of whether the National Security Council system is effective at its present state of development. At the time of writing the war was the cause of considerable internal division partly because the United States was seen to have stumbled blindly into the rice paddies and jungles of that unfortunate country. The United States was also said to have defeated the objectives of its national security policy. In contesting a so-called war of liberation in order to maintain the global ideological balance and avoid a superpower confrontation, it escalated the conflict to a large-scale war. A confrontation with China, if not the Soviet Union, seemed at times to be dangerously close.

In fact, the record of the system was not all bad. It is my opinion, and after years of military service and reporting wars I am almost a pacifist, that it demonstrated much of the system's strength as well as weakness.

To some extent, Vietnam was not a fair test. The rot set in under President Kennedy, whose main contribution to the National Security Council system was to strip it of staff and influence. President Johnson came to office in tragic circumstances, and his first responsibility was to demonstrate the continuity of Presidential rule. This he did superbly both at home and abroad, and I hope historians will be more appreciative than some members of his own party. Within a few months he had to campaign for election, and with help from Mr. Goldwater this was also an immense success. He saw his unprecedented victory as a mandate for change at home. But, as he once said in private conversation, a President has at the most a nine-month mandate to put his major programs on the statute books, and he was determined to lay the foundations for the Great Society.

During that period the distant little war steadily deteriorated. The political changes in Saigon brought about by President Kennedy eventually put the South Vietnamese Army in charge. The political and economic sides of the war, as important as the military in such a situation, were largely ignored by the local generals. In Washington the situation was confused because the President's representatives in Saigon were not united. The Central Intelligence Agency went its own way, and at one period had more authority than the State Department. North Vietnam began to infiltrate troops as well as supplies into the South, which of course changed the situation completely, and by the end of 1964 the war was almost lost.

Defeat was narrowly avoided by the bombing of North Vietnamese supply routes and the dispatch of American divisions. Once again the armed forces demonstrated their superb logistical capability, and 100,000 troops and equipment were flown halfway round the world and committed to battle within 120 days. New tactics were evolved, and the world's first Airmobile Division flew into battle aboard more than four hundred helicopters. If they were not immediately successful, the course of war was reversed. A year after the first troops had been landed, it was apparent that the fighting war could not be lost.

Much of this was to be expected. With armed forces in excess of three million and given the strength of the American economy, the impossible of yesteryear was not much more than routine. Vietnam, and the Dominican landings, demonstrated beyond doubt the strength, flexibility, and superb staff work of the armed forces. The bombing and some of the tactics used in the South were ruthless, but again this was to be expected for reasons discussed elsewhere in this book. American military efficiency has been well tested in Vietnam, and not found wanting.

Criticism was directed elsewhere, and much of it, as in the Korean War, and indeed the War of 1812, was evident in the strident battles between the hawks and the doves. Their demands ranged from bombing North Vietnam back into the Stone Age to the adoption of an enclave or Maginot Line strategy. The hawks were ignored because the United States was fighting a limited war, but this did not placate the doves, who seemed to think that a two-pistol Texas Ranger was sitting in the White House.

This is not a detailed review of President Johnson's conduct of the war, but the doves did him a disservice. "Limited" is a comparative word; nowhere in the new textbooks is there a definition in terms of troops or the weight of bombs dropped. Its only application in the nuclear age is when a war such as Vietnam is fought without escalation to a superpower confrontation and conflict. As much as I objected to the bombing, and especially to official claims that somehow it was discriminate, which is a contradiction in terms, at the time of writing President Johnson had been successful in limiting the war.

The Russians and Chinese had not intervened with troops. Indeed, Soviet-American *détente* diplomacy had become very active and successful. The Chinese were of course involved in their so-called cultural revolution, but the successful limiting of the war was not an accident. No step was taken to intensify the war without considering the probable Russian and Chinese reactions. In every case the vast apparatus for collecting and assessing information was fully used. Bombing operations were often controlled directly from the White House. It was a process calling for strong nerves and an efficient National Security Council system, and neither was found wanting.

This was superpower diplomacy. Nothing quite like it had happened before, with the exception of Korea, and that was too recent to be widely understood. Its lessons had been well learned in Washington, but there were also some lessons to be learned in Vietnam. One was that the discipline and methodology of the nuclear age could lead to a dangerously mechanistic view of international affairs. Computers and what are called management tools are essential in the Defense Department. For instance, proof of their worth was evident in Vietnam, where in spite of the sudden and immense expansion of

American forces no serious shortages of arms and equipment were evident. A computer mentality was, however, hardly appropriate to the modern decision-making process, which must be concerned with variables and unknown factors such as national pride. It was unfortunately rarely absent after the think factories such as the RAND Corporation and the Hudson Institute devised their esoteric discipline and methodology. Vietnam demonstrated the unwisdom of applying disciplines suitable for military planning to politico-military affairs.

One such method is the game theory, which reduces problems to what are known as scenarios. Antagonists are pitted against each other in a confrontation, and logical responses to given moves analyzed and escalated to a showdown. The perception of international politics is thus changed. Confrontation is implicit, as is the existence of two opposing sides with some irritating interruptions by bit players. The real stuff of international relations, the peculiarities of the several players, is ignored. Professor William Polk, writing in the *Bulletin of the Atomic Scientists,* said, "A sort of world-man, who logically and coolly understands and rightly plays the game, was posited. That this school of thought deeply affected our thinking on the Berlin and Cuba crises is evident." In other words, foreign affairs was reduced to a duel between the superpowers, the irritating bit players being Britain and France, East and West Germany, and other, lesser breeds.

The method was devised by the new generation of nuclear theorists to equip the President with the means and discipline to control and use nuclear weapons. It was extended to politico-military affairs with the realization that the nuclear balance could be disturbed by so-called wars of liberation. Nuclear war can, of course, only be waged by commanders on what amounts to a games board. The strength and the location of the enemy's missiles are fairly well known, and the unknown factors of conventional war such as leadership and the courage of troops are absent. Given electronic efficiency, the only questionable factor is the courage of the President and his closest advisers—hence the so-called games to prepare them for the superhuman authority to destroy much of the world.

The games of superpowers are, however, ill-suited for dealing with the pygmies of this world. The extension of the game theory to Vietnam simplified policies to the point that they were misleading. This was evident in the strategy with its steady escalation to the probable limits of limited war, and in the political rationalization. The game theory approach could not be applied to a civil war, therefore Vietnam had to be a power confrontation between the United States and North Vietnam. Methodology demanded simplification. Buddhist politics could not be programmed for the computers.

Even terminology became a trap. To write of the decision-making process, as I have done, should be only a useful piece of shorthand, meaning no more than the men and apparatus required to reach decisions. But it has taken on a special and misleading meaning. There is an assumption of a formula suitable for making decisions in peace and war, in reference to the Soviet Union or India, France or Vietnam. Most politicians, indeed most shrewd men, would reject the assumption as arrant nonsense, but, alas, many of the President's advisers were led into the trap.

Some of them admitted it privately, long before it became publicly evident as the war dragged on. A few went back to those special centers of study at the older universities to wait out the consequences of their mistakes. In a way, it was the unfortunate issue of the marriage of the two American Establishments, the old and the nuclear, the Anglo-Saxon and the German. I use these labels cautiously, but I believe that they signify something more than the national origins of the two Establishments, the Harrimans and Mc-Cloys in one, the Kahns and Kissingers in the other. The thought processes and ruthless logic of the latter are very German.

The lesson was learned while the Vietnam war was still being fought. General Maxwell Taylor passed on part of it in his book *Responsibility and Response*. It was his report that persuaded President Kennedy to commit American military advisers in 1961, and subsequently he served in Saigon as ambassador. Few men could have been so aware of their own mistakes. "One of the most significant political developments in this decade has been the progressive dissolution of the bipolar nuclear confrontation of the United States and its allies with the Sino-Soviet Communist bloc and its replacement by a multipolar power relationship." It was, alas, a development that the game theory approach had to ignore.

Congress has not been overlooked in this discussion of the President's authority in national security affairs. The fact of the matter is that most of the time it can bring remarkably little influence to bear.

There are two qualifications to this apparently sweeping statement. Congress holds the purse strings, and the Senate must ratify treaties and confirm the nominations of ambassadors and other high officials. These can be considerable powers, but in recent years Congress has often voted more money than was requested, especially for defense. In refusing these gifts, Presidents may have amazed the country with their moderation, but they were merely defending their unique authority. It is possible that Congress may be less generous in future, but hardly likely because of the pressure of public opinion. Policy may not command unanimous support; nevertheless, a price has never been put on national security.

The full power of the Senate, implicit in the advice-and-consent clause of the Constitution, has of course never been fully exercised. The Founding Fathers clearly intended the upper chamber to act as a privy council, to advise on the formulation of policy as well as to consent to treaties. But efforts to establish this constitutional relationship in foreign affairs have always failed. Even Washington, with the best will in the world and a much smaller Senate, found it irksome. The failure of successive Presidents to seek the advice of the Senate before embarking upon a new foreign or national security policy created a long-standing predicament that was well stated by Senator Elbert Thomas in 1942 before the United States was fully aware of the shape of its future responsibilities: "The practice of considering advice and consent as a single act makes it possible for an executive to conduct foreign policy which becomes law in such a way as to leave the Senate with the single power of accepting or rejecting."

It does indeed, and no future President is likely to change it. Rather is he likely to extend still more the use of Executive Agreements which have further diminished the constitutional power of the Senate. No reference is made in the Constitution to such agreements, authority for which can be found by the President only in his inherent or assumed powers as Commander in Chief and in his primary responsibility for foreign affairs. The first was the Rush-Bagot Agreement of 1817 demilitarizing the border with Canada, and there have been many more since then. With these inherent powers, the President can do almost anything with a written Executive Agreement or Order, as long as it does not include a special Congressional appropriation. The special contingency fund, established after the Second World War, often weakens that limitation of his freedom.

The Senate consent to treaties, with the requirement of a two-thirds majority of those present, remains a powerful brake on the President's activities. It creates obvious difficulties for American negotiators and it has had serious consequences in the past. The rejection of the Treaty of Versailles, with its exclusion of the United States from the League of Nations, was the most tragic, but it was a costly victory. Edward Corwin wrote:

The Senate's triumph in 1919 was the most spectacular in its history; but that indeed was its fatal defect. For as the years wore on . . . people —who always look for a devil to blame—began pointing the finger of reproach at the body that had so lightheartedly assumed the responsibility for keeping the United States out of the League, the one great nation with comparatively detached outlook and hence the one whose participation, it was said, was absolutely indispensable.*

Much has been learned since then at both ends of Pennsylvania Avenue. The Senate has been more responsible and responsive to the requirements of the nation and the world outside, and President Wilson's successors have learned to be less disdainful or rigid. Nonpartisanship, the label for private negotiations between the Secretary of State and leaders of both parties, certainly secured prior support for the postwar settlement. This is one explanation why the Secretary spends so much of his time on the Hill. But cooperation is hardly a substitute for power, and the Senate did not abdicate without a struggle that share of authority in national security affairs which many of its members believed was theirs by right.

The so-called Bricker Amendment, which after extensive debate in 1953 and 1954 was defeated by only one vote, sought to subordinate the treaty-making powers of the President to Congress and the states. It harked back to the classic case of *Missouri* v. *Holland* heard by the Supreme Court in 1920. The heart of the controversy was in the second and third sections of the Senate resolution proposed by Senator Bricker. Section 2 provided that "a treaty shall become effective as internal law in the United States only through legislation which would be valid in the absence of a treaty." Section 3 sought to give Congress "power to regulate all executive and other agreements with any foreign power or international organization." There was

* *The President: Office and Powers*, New York, New York University Press, 1957.

little agreement about the precise meaning of Section 2, but President Eisenhower complained that the federal government would be so shackled that it would no longer be sovereign in foreign affairs. Section 3 was no less objectionable because it struck at the President's power to make Executive Agreements without the consent of the Senate.

It can be argued, although few Presidents would do it publicly, that the two-thirds majority vote required for ratification is no longer really valid. The Founding Fathers were obviously concerned more with domestic matters and interstate jealousy than with foreign affairs. The states or combinations of states then feared that other combinations might be willing to barter away their interests or upset the balance of regional power. Such particularism or sectionalism warranted a two-thirds majority at a time when some of the young states had to be persuaded of the benefits of unity. It was very much evident when the New England states objected to Jefferson's purchase of Louisiana. States' rights can be questionable in more immediate circumstances. They would appear now to have little relevance in foreign affairs or national security, but of course the Senate is unlikely to relinquish its power and no President would propose the necessary constitutional amendment to remove it.

The rejection of the Bricker Amendment was a turning point in more ways than one, but most of all it gave what must be regarded as final recognition, no matter how reluctant, to the inherent as well as textual constitutional powers of the President. Congressional impatience with the restrictions on its role in national security policy continues, however, in the form of riders to appropriations bills, most of which are intended to deny aid to countries which have incurred its displeasure. They can be irritating.

One of the more unfortunate consequences of this further aggrandizement of Presidential power has been the loss of prestige and effectiveness of the Senate Foreign Relations Committee. The power of Congressional committees depends to a large extent upon their ability to thwart or treat with the executive, and thus in recent years the Senate Foreign Relations Committee has not amounted to much in Presidential calculations. For instance, the advice of the chairman was ignored by President Kennedy before the disastrous Cuban invasion of 1961. His doubts about the Dominican intervention of 1965 only angered President Johnson. The chairman, Senator William Fulbright, at the time of writing, admitted that he could not hope to influence policy when the President was clearly the dominant personality in the government. He was rarely if ever consulted, but only informed of a policy decision and then often but a few minutes before its public announcement. He saw the increase in Presidential power as inevitable because of the growing complexity of international relations, nuclear power, and the rapidity of communications. He did not object; foreign relations were, in his opinion, not so well suited for Congressional action as were domestic matters. Clarification of issues was the more important role for the committee chairman.

At best, it can be said that the Senate can influence the direction of national security policy by withholding consent, but once the course has been set with the ratification of a treaty it is more often than not powerless to intervene. It might also be noted that treaties fundamental to basic policy are rare. The massive defense establishment and national security apparatus, and the direct responsibilities overseas, came about after the Rio and North Atlantic treaties, and the administration has not felt the need for others.

In the circumstances it is misleading to speak of a government of laws and not of men when discussing American national security policy. More than one President has waged war without a formal declaration by Congress. Constitutional advisers can be, and are, ignored in the conduct of policy. Three out of four Presidents resented the National Security Council. If the President is not above the law, it is only because the law and practice have conceded him an almost unchallengeable position. Few other democratic countries would permit one man to wield so much power.

One can see in this cool relationship with Congress a fierce determination to defend Presidential authority. This is, of course, standard practice, even now when the balance of power within the American system is tilted so much to the advantage of the executive branch, but it is rather more than the ancient tension brought by constitutional checks and balances. One suspects a certain jealousy of executive authority that presses most Presidents to extend it even further. As an earlier age would have had it, they have the bit between their teeth.

Indeed, apart from the infrequent occasions when treaties are to be ratified, it is not much of an exaggeration to say that the main limits to Presidential authority in national security affairs can be found in the direct relationship he establishes with the American people. This is one reason why the President can be more interested in the latest public opinion polls than in the *Congressional Record*. First, there is the widespread belief that only the President has all the necessary information to formulate policy and make decisions. This acceptance of omniscience and omnipotence, both rather surprising in a political democracy, is the President's strongest and most comforting support.

Second, there is the national consensus, established since the immediate postwar years. On the whole it is eminently respectable in that it has formed round what I have chosen to see as the extensions of the Monroe Doctrine, but it does have some weaknesses worth exploring. Some are intrinsic to the Doctrine.

President Monroe's work has generally served the nation well, but it nevertheless assumes a world divided, if you like, between them, the Communists, and us, the free world. It was an American instinct before President Monroe raised it to the dignity of a doctrine. It was evident in Hamilton's warning to Washington against the dangers of European connections. It helped to explain the isolationist period, and is now applied to the Soviet Union, China, and most other Communist countries.

By the mid-twentieth century, the American "us" had come to include Western Europe and other areas collectively known as the free world. The term is meaningless, encompassing as it does a variety of political dictatorships and unjust economic systems. Indeed, many Americans are more suspicious of the genteel social democracy of Western Europe than of the military juntas of Latin America or the Asian client states. The majority have little interest in the countries of the so-called free world except as allies. The Western European democracies are not much more than Teutonic tribes holding the Eastern imperial glacis against the barbarian. (So much for the vanity of those Europeans, especially the British, who believed they were the Greeks of the American Rome.) Their destiny is to hold the line with the American legions. Holding the line has become the most recent expression of the American instinct for separateness. I believe that this relic of the past continues to influence American attitudes, and that this influence has been enhanced by the disproportionate power of the United States.

H

Not every American, of course, is aware of the Monroe Doctrine, except as a sacred revelation that gives the United States divine right of intervention in Latin America. For them, anti-Communism is a sufficient, if erroneous, explanation. There is certainly no wide understanding of the assessments that helped the architects of the postwar national security policy to define its objectives. They saw Communist aggression and not Communism as the enemy, an enemy, moreover, not to be defeated in war but to be contained and perhaps converted to the pursuit of peace. Peaceful coexistence was their ultimate objective before Mr. Khrushchev coined the phrase. If there was an ideological fervor in Moscow at the time, there was very little in Washington. But a similar fervor had to be encouraged if the President was to achieve the freedom of action required. Public opinion had to be mobilized as well as material resources for defense purposes. A very blatant form of anti-Communism became the main driving force.

It was not without internal danger, witness the McCarthy period and the violent reaction to any objective approach to the problems created by the emergence of the Soviet Union as a superpower and China as a great power. A patriotic outlet was provided for the prejudiced, the forces of the radical right were strengthened, and the moderate center moved perceptibly to the right. The differences between the United States and Western Europe, which was directly threatened by Soviet aggression and internal Communism, could not have been more striking. On the eastern rim of the Atlantic during that period there was, if anything, a move to the left, and Christian and Social Democracy introduced their most remarkable social reforms. Not so in the United States, where many saw themselves as crusaders against the Antichrist of Communism, social justice, and even the fluoridation of drinking water, with Adam Smith's *Wealth of Nations* as their bible.

No doubt those who encouraged the spurious rallying cry—and for some the decision was quite calculated—comforted themselves with the thought that American common sense would prevail eventually. They have been vindicated to a large extent, but a sizable section of public opinion remains deeply antagonistic to Communism, whether or not it threatens American national security. It is a vocal minority, amplified by party politics, and the President is very much a prisoner. In the conditions of the sixties, it was imperative for President

Johnson to intervene in the Dominican Republic. There was little choice open to him that was politically acceptable. It was easier to extend the war in Vietnam in 1965 than to accept the Vietcong as a political force with whom the United States had to come to terms to secure peace.

The McCarthy period was also harmful within the State Department. The failure of President Eisenhower and his Secretary of State, Mr. Dulles, to defend it from the attacks of the extreme right demoralized a whole generation of Foreign Service officers. Too many good men were destroyed professionally for truthful diplomatic reporting and outspoken but unpopular advice. Circumspection was a condition for survival, and many became more militaristic than the military. The balance between the diplomat and the soldier, who is often an ally of the extreme right, has been to that extent upset. It is possible that the rising generation within the department will be free of such inhibitions and fears, but collective morale is a somewhat mysterious thing. It did not improve much under President Kennedy, when the department was exposed to attack and ridicule from the liberal wing. Attacks from one side or the other will no doubt continue, but the assumption must be that the heaviest will continue to come from the right. In self-defense, the State Department will assuredly remain right of center.

Senator McCarthy has been dismissed as a passing phenomenon. Perhaps it is more accurate to remember him as a recurring American phenomenon. Whatever he was, he could not have done so much damage at a period of maximum danger without some public support. He must have expressed some deep apprehension or fear. As it emerged, the fear was of an internal Communist conspiracy. This conspiratorial view of history and the mass emotions aroused were certainly not new, witness the Palmer raids and deportation of aliens after the First World War, to mention only more recent incidents. Presumably it could have been an expression of the insecurity to be expected among certain groups in an immigrant society. Members of the State Department could not afford to take the long view after the Communist revolution in China. They were too painfully aware that the so-called China lobby prevented the Truman administration from coming to terms with the new regime. President Eisenhower was also frozen in a position of immobility, although his Secretary of State had earlier favored recognition. All room for diplomatic maneuver was lost, and President Kennedy made little effort to regain it. The only direct channel of communication was the ambassadorial meetings in Warsaw.

The pressures of small extremist organizations can still distort public opinion. Their members are the permanent opposition to the Establishment men. They are political primitives, the provincials from the big rectangular states, especially those in the Southwest, which at times appear to have only tenuous links with old centers of civilization. They are nationalistic, with little or no comprehension of the rapid changes in superpower diplomacy, technology, and strategy. They do, however, influence the national consensus, and in so doing limit the President's freedom of action. They have often vulgarized American diplomacy.

These extremists did not disappear under the electoral avalanche that swept Mr. Goldwater into ignominious defeat in 1964. Indeed, at the time of writing organizations such as the John Birch Society, the Liberty Lobby, and the Christian Nationalist Crusade were still very active. They were supported by wealthy men and a few corporations, and their propaganda was incessant and not unsuccessful. They could claim to have postponed, if not frustrated, the grand design of achieving superior military power in order to negotiate after that power was achieved.

Nevertheless, there was a gradual change in the late sixties. President Kennedy lived to see the Senate ratify the partial nuclear-test-ban treaty, and under President Johnson further steps were taken toward arms control, if not disarmament. The Soviet-American consular treaty was ratified after more than two years of delay. President Johnson was firmly committed to improving relations with the Soviet Union, and not finding it too unpopular.

In its mysterious way the national consensus was performing its customary wonders. The defeat of Goldwater in the 1964 Presidential election, largely because of his casual approach to war and peace, was a factor as well as evidence of change, and there were others. Senator William Fulbright, who had accepted the diminution of his authority as chairman of the Senate Foreign Relations Committee, re-emerged from the shadows as a considerable influence on public opinion. His warnings about the arrogance of power were perhaps unfair, but subsequently the beginnings of moderation became evident.

This new moderation was not confined to a more purposeful rejection of the radical right. Moderation was at least discernible in the official and Establishment attitudes toward national security policy as it had evolved over the first two decades after the Second World War.

There were many causes. Increasing confidence in relations with the other superpower was one, and the realization that China could not become a third and dangerous superpower in the foreseeable future was another. These led to second thoughts on the global extension of the new Monroe Doctrine, but there were third thoughts not directly concerned with what was once known as the international Communist threat. Superpower was no longer seen to be limitless.

It was not that the United States was seen to be incapable of maintaining a decisive lead in nuclear power or maintaining hundreds of thousands of men in Europe and fighting a war on the other side of the world. All this was done without emergency measures, and with a relatively slight impact upon the economy. But domestic policies had suffered, and not only because of the lack of money. Few countries can successfully pursue more than one or two major policies at the same time, and the United States cannot be counted among them. The Presidential system, in spite of the enormous system devised to extend Presidential power, is an administrative bottleneck. It cannot be otherwise when the interest and energy as well as the authority of one man are required if anything important or difficult has to be done. The bottleneck is all the more restrictive because so many domestic issues are now funneled through it. The constant preoccupation with internal politics and running for re-election are stoppers that can block the bottleneck.

In the late sixties the desperate need for attention to domestic problems, such as the plight of the Negroes and the poor, the decay of the cities, the inadequacies of social services, and the relations between the federal government and the states, could no longer be ignored. The war in Vietnam continued at the time of writing to divert funds and attention, but it also helped to emphasize the limitations of superpower.

In that area of national security policy not directly concerned with the Soviet Union and China there was a perceptible falling off of interest and money. Vietnam was responsible in part, but official thinking no longer assumed that the line between "them" and "us" must be eternally manned by American legions and local levies. The thought was ventured that some countries could be allowed to misgovern themselves without the line being breached by the Communist hordes. It was not universally shared, the physical security of the United States was still seen to depend largely upon the balance of power and ideology, but it was no longer treasonous or irresponsible to entertain such a thought.

Moreover, it was nurtured by larger understanding of the strategic consequences of superpower nuclear stability and of the causes of unrest and revolution in third-world countries. Official and Establishment thinking, while cautious, was becoming more relaxed.

I happen to believe that American national security policy is again approaching a corner that may be as momentous for the future of mankind as the one turned after the Second World War.

As already suggested, Vietnam was a factor at the time of writing. The war revealed the remaining weaknesses of the national security system as well as the human frailties of President Johnson. It was a painful reminder that the authority of the President depends upon a broad consensus; that it diminishes with a loss of public confidence. There was dissension, and proposals in Congress reminiscent of the Bricker Amendment. There were demands for unlimited war, but the movement to moderate the more Germanic characteristics of the national security system also gathered strength.

Above all, Vietnam was a reminder that the system with its doctrines and geopolitical view of the world must change with the world and the requirements of the American people. As Adlai Stevenson said at Harvard in 1954, the quest for peace and security is not a day's or a decade's work. For the United States it may be everlasting. Much will depend upon the Soviet Union and China (hence the abiding caution), and American extremism will not be ineffectual. There will, of course, be no return to isolationism, and the new Monroe Doctrine will remain as long as the balance of ideology is seen to be fundamental to American national security.

Nevertheless, I believe that gradually the United States will accept the notion that technological change, even a technological balance of sorts between the now developed and underdeveloped countries, is of greater significance than ideology for the peace of the world, and in turn American security.

Part III

New World Symphony

"The moral latitude is so very wide in America: if there is abnormally much that is very bad, there is also unusually much that is extremely good."

GUNNAR MYRDAL
An American Dilemma

7 The States and Cities

"The first and most natural attachments of the people will be to the governments of their respective states."
— JAMES MADISON

"To a deplorable degree, the public lacks confidence in state government, particularly the legislature."
— ADLAI STEVENSON III

There is nothing quite like an American state anywhere in the world, although American federalism has been the example for younger countries. They are hardly sovereign in the accepted sense of the term, despite the chauvinistic protestations of white Mississippians. They are clearly more than mere administrative units or components of the American common market. The original thirteen were briefly sovereign as Britain or Somalia are now sovereign. Texas was an independent republic before the annexation of 1845. Each freely renounced a part of its sovereignty and accepted federal authority as defined in the Constitution. But at best the Constitution is a set of Queensbury rules under which a continuing struggle for power is fought. Reference to the Constitution will not necessarily explain past struggles, victories, and defeats. For instance, it was not the founders but the Civil War, or the War between the States as it is more accurately remembered in the South, which quashed once and for all the lingering thoughts of nullification and secession.

The original thirteen and Texas can claim a residual sovereignty, but this is not really the case with the remaining thirty-six. They are the creation of the United States, and previously they were federal territories. The Constitution allows for the admission of new states, but their genesis was not preordained. The Northwest Territory could have been divided between claimant states such as Connecticut, Massachusetts, New York, and Virginia. The Ordinance of 1787 could have provided for its eventual admission into the Union as one state, and not six. Similarly, Louisiana might have been admitted after the purchase as one and not thirteen states, or fourteen if Florida is included.

The explanations for the creation of so many states are varied. An obvious one is necessity because it was virtually impossible to administer such vast areas from a few centers. The original thirteen (Massachusetts, New Hampshire, Connecticut, Rhode Island, New York, New Jersey, Pennsylvania, Delaware, Maryland, Virginia, North Carolina, South Carolina, and Georgia) ceded the Western territories to the United States to resolve one of the most pressing problems that troubled the Congress in the Articles of Confederation, but the cession of territories could not divorce their future development from the past of the thirteen. They had been sovereign, and jealously retained a large measure of independence. Autonomy if not the sovereignty briefly enjoyed, or rather suffered, by the thirteen had to be bequeathed upon later entrants. Finally, the new states had been settled and developed not by administrative fiat, but by free Americans, by individuals, who naturally demanded equality.

This they now enjoy. Despite the disparity in size and population, all are equal. The population of California is about eighteen million and that of Alaska a sparse 250,000, or much less than one of California's thirty-eight electoral districts, and they have equal representation in the United States Senate. In that chamber the vote of Alaska or Wyoming is not less weighty than that of California or New York. Again, in ratifying an amendment of the Constitution, the grandest exercise of state authority, all fifty are equal.

This contrived equality has influenced American politics to a degree that other free men would only reluctantly accept. Equality has led to inequality. Bills and constitutional amendments can be defeated or foisted upon the nation by Senators representing a popular minority. This is the price of federalism, but it is more than that. Haphazard as the process had to be—and the rectangular shapes of some states suggest that it was also mechanistic—the sum of statehood is a monument to American political wisdom and empiricism. If it has left a legacy of political and regional conflict, the legacy could have been more burdensome. In hindsight, it is difficult to see how a subcontinent could have been much better organized politically in the piecemeal process of development and settlement. A by-product of the conflict, moreover, is the political sophistication acquired over the years and essential to keep such an enormous country and pluralistic society on an even keel.

Today the United States, except for territories such as Guam, the Virgin Islands, American Samoa, and the Trust Territory of the Pacific Islands, is what its name suggests, a nation of states. Puerto Rico, ceded to the United States after the war with Spain, is a commonwealth represented by a Commissioner in the House. Each state possesses all the machinery of independent government, with the exception of a foreign ministry, and much of the trappings. Each has an independent executive under an elected governor, and a legislature with two chambers, except Nebraska which has one. Each has a complete judicial system crowned by a supreme or superior court, full police powers and military and paramilitary forces to enforce them. Each has a state capital, flag, nickname, motto, flower, bird, and anthem.

If the trappings tend to raise smiles on foreign faces, they at least demonstrate the local patriotisms and variety of the Union. The flag of Hawaii, the last state to be admitted, bears the Union Jack in one quarter. The nickname of Missouri is the Show Me State. The motto of Michigan is *"Si Quaeris Peninsulam Amoenam Circumspice"* ("If you seek Pleasant Peninsula, Look Around You"). The flower of distant Alaska is the forget-me-not. The bird of Florida is the mockingbird, and of course the anthem of Oklahoma is "Oklahoma." Each has the power of taxation, and the budgets of some are larger than those of most members of the United Nations. At the time of writing, their combined annual revenue was nearly $60 billion. This impressive figure does not, however, tell all. Subordinate units within the states, such as cities and counties, also levy taxes.

There is also not one American constitution, but fifty-one. Each state has its own, and some have direct antecedents older than the United States Constitution. The first written constitution of a self-governing people, the Fundamental Orders of the townships of Wethersfield, Hartford, and Windsor in Connecticut, was written in 1639, and Connecticut's later constitution was based on it.

The internal power of a state is considerable. A citizen charged with common murder is tried in a state court, not a federal court, and the punishment is meted out by the state. There can be no appeal to federal courts unless the fundamental rights of the accused are in question. When justice is not seen to be done, as in some Civil Rights murder cases, alas, the Attorney General of the United States cannot order a retrial. He can only charge the defendants in federal court with denying the Civil Rights of the victim. It is not a matter of double jeopardy, although that is one of the cornerstones of Anglo-American law. In such cases the power of the state courts is absolute.

The distribution of power between the federal government and the states was effected in two ways, by the original abdication of power to the United States and the imposition of restrictions on the states. Both are liable to constitutional amendment, but meanwhile a state in many instances is free to decide whether justice will be done and see that it is done. It can also educate its children superbly well or release them from school ill-equipped for the modern world. It can legislate modern labor laws or permit itself to be dominated by a giant corporation. It can build or subsidize decent housing or let the poor exist in a squalor long since forgotten in Western Europe. It can respond to the demands of enlightened citizens or permit the exploitation and oppression of minorities and the unlettered. The best and the worst of American life flourishes and festers within the jurisdiction of the states.

Their residual power is exercised under the Tenth Amendment: "The powers not delegated to the United States by the Constitution, nor prohibited by it to the states, are reserved to the states respectively, or to the people." In theory the federal government exercises no power not expressly granted, but the reality is somewhat different. Nor should the last qualification of the Tenth Amendment be overlooked. The nondelegated and nonprohibited powers are not reserved to the states alone, but to the states or to the people, and the people, or peoples, of the several states have in their constitutions reserved varying but considerable degrees of power for themselves. In some the building of an airport requires constitutional amendment, which can mean reference to the people. The states are, in fact, caught in the conflict of the increasing authority of the modern Presidency demanded by the modern triple revolution of rising expectations, technology, and race, and the sturdy and suspicious resistance to authority of an earlier America. The resistance is not all questionable because it continues to be used in defense of some questionable interests.

The relationship of the federal government and the states can only be understood when one accepts the fact of the theory that all power stems from the people, and not from their elected representatives. Some see a single triangular relationship, a pyramid of delegated authority. At the base, the people authorize the state to provide for the protection of property and punish those who threaten it, to educate their children, to build roads, and the like. In turn, the state authorizes the federal government to provide for its protection against foreign aggression, to represent its interests abroad, to perform such functions as may be required by interstate relationships, and so on. It is not so simple as that.

There is, of course, a basic, if complicated, structure. Bryce described it well, although the traditional structure was less encumbered in his day. He distinguished between five classes of governmental powers.

They were the powers vested in the national government alone and those vested in the states alone. They are more or less indicated in the Constitution, and are straightforward enough from a fundamentalist constitutional viewpoint, but only conservatives out of office can afford to be fundamentalist these days. We have seen how the Supreme Court has crossed this neat dividing line in defense, for instance, of the rights of the individual and by requiring the reapportionment of electoral districts for the House of Representatives and state legislatures. Federal legislation providing funds for education and other services which are state responsibilities has brought much federal intrusion. Money appropriated has to be accounted for, and standards must be maintained. The federal government is often not slow to take advantage of these requirements, and there are complications. It is, for instance, obliged under the Civil Rights Act of 1964 to ensure that federal funds do not support programs perpetuating racial segregation. Indeed, the entire Civil Rights struggle demands frequent federal intervention in state affairs.

Bryce next listed those powers exercised concurrently by the national government and the states. These include powers of legislation on specified subjects, of taxation, direct or indirect, judicial powers, and powers to determine matters relating to the election of Representatives and Senators. Where there is conflict, the federal government takes precedence. State legislation is effective only in the absence of federal legislation, and is null and void when declared unconstitutional by the Supreme Court.

Then came the powers forbidden to the national government and those forbidden to the state governments. Some are listed in the United States Constitution, and many more in the various state constitutions. Finally, Bryce recognized the residual power of the people thus:

What the Constitution had done is not to cut in half the totality of governmental functions and powers, giving part to the national government and leaving all the rest to the states, but to divide up this totality of authority into a number of parts which do not exhaust the whole, but leave a residuum of powers neither granted to the Union nor continued to the states but to the people, who, however, can put them in force only by the difficult process of amending the Constitution.

The process of amending the Constitution is indeed difficult, but with nature politics abhors a vacuum, and the forces of the modern triple revolution cannot always be denied. The instances are almost innumerable, but one can suffice. The President can and does intervene constitutionally in the maintenance of law and order. The National Guard is under the control of the state government, but the President can use it against the people of its own state in times of disorder. So much is clear, but the recent internal exercise of the President's authority as Commander in Chief has led to some odd situations.

Some Alabamians who rioted against Negro freedom riders one morning in the summer of 1961 were called up in the evening to defend them against the mob. Their National Guard unit wore the old Confederacy flag, but it was under the command of the President of the Union. One moment they were fighting for the Heart of Dixie, as Alabama describes herself, in the streets of Montgomery, the state capital, which is known as the Cradle of the Confederacy. The next moment, as it were, they were loyally if reluctantly putting down another manifestation of Southern resistance to one of the three modern revolutions. On the face of it, the President was only restoring order, which the state had signally failed to do. Every citizen of Alabama, from the governor to the most disreputable redneck in the mob, knew, however, that he was furthering the cause of the Negro and other minorities.

The justice of the President's intervention in Montgomery is incontestable, but how can it be justified within a system that gives the national government no more right to trespass upon the domain of a state than it does to a state to trespass upon the federal domain? The theory and the fact of the federal-state relationship are that it is not the concern of the federal government if a state chooses to misgovern itself unless federal authority is infringed or the grand purposes of the Union frustrated. The sentiment behind the fact and the theory is not unlike the Gandhian principle of the right of a people to misrule themselves. The assumption is that they will learn in time, and that it will be their bad luck if they do not. This sturdy independence, which helps to explain the occasional inhumanity of American life, is all very well when men can combine to defend their interests or right a wrong. It is not when the people wronged belong to a minority or cannot defend themselves.

The federal government then intervenes, but not always. It can do so with legislation, Supreme Court decisions, the constitutional authority of the President to execute them, and the very occasional exercise of his inherent powers, or it can choose to remain silent. Intervention can be, and often is, necessary, just, and sensible, but what of the theory that all authority flows from the people? The Governor of Alabama who permitted violence to occur in 1961, whose announced policies made violence inevitable, was elected by the people. Why federal intervention? The prosaic answer is that the President intervened under the commerce clause and the relevant constitutional amendments. The freedom riders rode interstate buses and claimed their constitutional right to use refreshment facilities at interstate bus depots unlawfully segregated on the basis of race. Their constitutional right had to be protected.

The constitutionality as well as the justice of the President's intervention in Montgomery is again incontestable, but a contradiction naggingly remains. I can remember trying to explain it to a colleague from a Communist country outside the town's Trailways bus depot while members of the Alabama National Guard and the local sheriff's posse held back the mob somewhat depleted by their call to duty. He was better trained in dialectics than American metaphysics, but it seemed perfectly clear to me. The American political animal is two people: a citizen of his state, in this case Alabama (motto: "We Dare Defend Our Rights"), and a citizen of the United States. He has delegated part of his supreme authority to Alabama and part to the United States. The part delegated to the state represents, as it were, his fallible, occasionally wrongheaded self. That being can be dominated or torn by very human prejudice, and concerned largely with intensely personal matters such as the color of his neighbor's skin, the economic threat of a lower-paid race, and in some counties its political dominance. That being can be regrettably wrong, but very human.

As citizen of the United States, however, he associates himself with the nobility of the opening periods of the Declaration of Independence and the Bill of Rights. He is expected to be ennobled by what the Union stands for. This metaphysic can exert a powerful discipline, and when it fails, Americans must be prepared to accept a temporary retribution. This probably explains the belief, widespread among themselves, that Americans are more moral than other people. The evidence is not obvious, at least not to me, but I think I can understand why the belief is so widespread. As citizen of the United States, our American political animal accepts an authority claiming a higher moral principle than he can be prepared to observe.

The federal government is not, of course, a sublime godhead. Some very odd things occur in the corridors of federal power. The President is also human and a politician. There are 535 very human politicians in Congress, and ten of them represent the state and people of Alabama. The Supreme Court is a body of nine mortals, and the record shows that it has not always handed down enlightened justice. The President can act for the most sublime reason or for the most questionable political motive, or he can refuse to act. The Congress can fail to legislate, and the Court refuse petitions. All governments can move in mysterious ways their wonders to perform, and movement can be especially tortuous when the powers of a government are separated, even under the modern Presidency.

When it does act, however, it takes precedence over the states and claims the loyalty of the citizenry, or a majority of it until the next elections. If I may stay with Alabama a little longer, the loyalty of most of its citizens in an intense racial situation will be claimed by the state. The claim will not avail much in confrontation with the federal government when it is supported by a majority of American citizens, although a confrontation such as our Montgomery example is rarely a permanent defeat for the state. The interstate bus depots may be desegregated, but the resistance of prejudice throws up other barriers.

The conflict appears to be endless. Nevertheless, as with the old medieval magnates the state must compromise when the federal government is strong, that is, when it is seen to act with the full authority of the national majority. Then Presidential power is invariably extended. The growth of federal departments is one yardstick of this process. In the beginning there were only the Post Office and the departments of State, Treasury, Army, and Navy. The Attorney General was a member of the Cabinet but did not have a department. The Department of the Interior was founded in 1849, largely to take care of land, Indian affairs, pensions, and patents. The Agriculture Department followed in 1862, Justice in 1870, Commerce and Labor in 1903, Health, Education, and Welfare in 1953, Housing and Urban Development in 1965, and Transportation in 1966.

The full impact of these departments was not immediately felt in the states. The Department of Justice is an obvious example. In 1870 the new department was concerned primarily with enforcing federal law, furnishing legal counsel and advice, and supervising United States attorneys and marshals in the judicial districts. The Antitrust Division followed in 1903, Civil Rights in 1957, and Internal Security in 1954. In the Department of the Interior the Bureau of Mines was established in 1910, the Bureau of Land Management in 1946, and the Oil Import Administration in 1959. The Commodity Credit Corporation was first organized as an independent agency in 1933 and transferred to the Department of Agriculture in 1939.

Many of these and other subdepartments were for the most part established to help as well as regulate industries and other interests, but invariably impinged upon state authority. The regulatory agencies such as the Interstate Commerce Commission, the Federal Communications Commission, the Federal Power Commission, the Federal Reserve System, the Federal Trade Commission, and the National Labor Relations Board also reduced state authority. They are independent of the federal structure of government, and essential to the maintenance of the American common market and the very essence of federalism in modern circumstances, but they emphasize the subordination of the states.

The Fundamental Orders of the townships of Wethersfield, Hartford, and Windsor may be the oldest written constitution of a free-governing people, but it is not the fountainhead of the numerous

American efforts to secure the fundamental liberties of the citizen by documentary means. The origins go back to Magna Carta and beyond, of course, but there were more recent documents that provided examples for Thomas Hooker and the other early settlers in Connecticut when they met in Hartford more than three centuries ago.

Their English ancestors did not consider a written constitution vital for their liberties, but they were well acquainted with contracts or compacts. The charters issued to the medieval trading guilds were early examples, and similar commercial documents were the legal foundation for the colonization of North America. For Hooker the charter issued by King Charles the First to the Governor and Company of the Massachusetts Bay in Newe-England in 1628 was the obvious guide, although the first Plymouth Company was chartered in 1606. This was mainly due to the efforts of Sir Ferdinando Gorges, who, alas, seems to have been forgotten by all the Americans who came after him. Years before the Pilgrim Fathers set sail, Virginia was established under his charter, entitled "The Treasurer and Company of Adventurers and Planters of the City of London for the first colony in Virginia."

The Massachusetts charter created a governor, deputy governor, and eighteen assistants, and required them to hold four general meetings a year.

The Governor or deputie Governor, and such of the assistants and Freemen of the Company as shall be present, shall have full power and authority to choose other persons to be free of the Company, and to elect and constitute such officers as they shall thinke fit for managing the affaires of the saide Governor and Company, and to make Lawes and Ordinances for the Good and Welfare of the saide Company, and for the Government and Ordering of the saide Landes and Plantasion, and the People inhabiting and to inhabite the same, soe as such Lawes and Ordinances be not repugnant to the Lawes and Statuts of this our realme of England.

This rudimentary frame of self-government was extended by the new charter issued by King William in 1691, only two years after he was required to accept the ancient rights and liberties of Britain codified in the Bill of Rights. Under William's charter, the assistants received the title of councilor, and their numbers were increased. They were selected by the general court, which included freeholders elected by the towns and settlements. The governor was empowered to appoint judges, and the general court to pass laws and provide for all civil offices. Appeals from the courts were heard by the King in privy council.

As Bryce observed, this was a true political constitution. It profoundly influenced the Constitutional Convention in 1787, and much of it was incorporated in the Massachusetts constitution in 1780, which still remains in force. The respect for other colonial charters is indicated by the fact that, with some alterations, they served as state constitutions for Connecticut until 1818 and for Rhode Island until 1843. Nevertheless, they were all profoundly changed by the acts of independence. Before, the superior authority was the British Crown or Parliament. Afterward, that authority passed not to the state legislatures but to the people whose will was exercised through the state constitutions as previously the will of the Crown had been exercised through the charters.

With very few exceptions, the state constitutions have not withstood the test of time as successfully as the United States Constitution. Rather more than half of the states, twenty-seven to be precise, have had more than one constitution. Louisiana has had ten, Georgia eight, and Alabama and South Carolina six. Even when one allows for the fact that these were secessionist states, the number of discarded constitutions is rather excessive. Altogether 135 state constitutions have been ratified, thirteen of them in this century although in that period only five new states were admitted to the Union. Some three thousand amendments have been adopted. Louisiana leads again with 460, and California has had 350. Some constitutions tend also to be verbose, with Louisiana once again leading with a tome of 236,000 words.

All these changes and this verbosity are due to the fact that all power stems from the people. They suggest that the people of the states find it hard to make up their collective minds, which may be another way of saying that the desire for perfection has led them to constant experiment and improvement. This supports the idea that the states are powerhouses of innovation—there is, alas, little else to support it—but it would be wrong to be content with the suggestion. The fact of the matter is that the people do not trust their elected state representatives. They must be restrained, and constitutional restraint is the first direct weapon.

The result is that some constitutions make little or no distinction between constitutional and general law. They can be rag bags of provisions and prohibitions that can only be explained by distrust of the legislature, and of the judiciary in some cases, and a fondness for direct action. Observers see in this evidence of a healthy participatory democracy. History suggests that it is rather a very American attempt to keep government at a distance. Frederick Jackson Turner, the historian of the frontier, has it that the frontier was antisocial and antipathetic to direct control. I am not personally convinced of the prevailing power of frontier memory, as opposed to myth, especially as in recent years the Southwestern states, the most antipathetic to control, have become the haven of middle-age refugees from the bleakness of the Middle West. Whatever the reason for distrust, the states suffer.

In restraining the legislatures, the people reduce their scope and efficacy, but that is not all. The second direct weapon is a resistance to taxation. Demands for higher taxes can be regarded as political suicide by governors and lesser state officials, and have proved to be. Past experience exerts a powerful discipline on them. Sixteen states do not have income tax, and twelve are without corporate income tax. Generally speaking, state taxes have been increased in recent years, but they are still inadequate. Total indebtedness of state and local government rose to about $100 billion in 1966. This was much less than the national debt, but it represented a fortyfold increase over a decade. In all state capitals there are complaints of too little revenue, and many are starved for funds urgently required to provide minimal services. But in reducing the effectiveness of the states, the people invite, and in some cases demand, federal intervention.

The lack of revenue is the real predicament of the states in their relations with the federal government. They are now in a subordinate position, where they should be co-equal or independent, because much that is considered necessary in advanced industrial societies would be ill done or left undone without federal grants, which have increased enormously. In the last decade they have moved from 10 to 14 percent of state and local revenues, and from 4 to 7 percent of federal expenditures. The proportion is increasing under the Great Society program, which can be assumed not to be the final legislative response to the revolution of rising expectations.

The tax collector is hardly a welcome visitor in any country, and people are of course something more than an abstract constitutional concept. There are people and people. They range from conservatives to liberals, with their diametrically opposed ideas of the functions of government, and from those liable to large tax assessments to others who stand most to gain from tax-supported services and programs. At the national level an acceptable balance can be struck often enough in the interaction of the three branches of government supported or opposed by lobbyists and pressure groups. That interaction is moreover under the closest possible scrutiny, and the demands of politics can be supreme.

This is not necessarily the case in the states, cities, and counties, where the local establishment, power structure, or call it what you will has more abiding influence than most of the national forces or combinations of forces in Washington. State legislatures can be, and frequently are, legislative instruments or defenses of corporate entities more concerned with private profit than with the public welfare. Their secret constituencies can include banks, insurance companies and savings and loan companies, industry, mining and lumber companies, and public utilities. Their lobbyists are active in state capitals. They can be more persuasive than their big brothers in Washington in part because most state capitals are small secluded cities situated well away from the larger urban centers and the scrutiny of metropolitan newspapers. Paradoxically perhaps, fewer Pulitzer Prizes would be awarded to newspapers for revealing some scandal if their scrutiny was more sustained.

State legislatures can also be ill-equipped to deal with the press of modern problems. Those of thirty states still meet only every other year, which may explain why they do not arouse sustained interest. Most sessions are relatively brief, and thirty-seven have no means of recall. Only seventeen states have unlimited sessions, and the regular sessions of a few are limited to a mere thirty days. Such brief sessions hardly encourage calm and thorough debate, but can allow considerable skulduggery in the hurried drafting of legislation. In most states legislation is a part-time occupation with small remuneration. It is $200 in New Hampshire, where the legislature meets every other year, and the average is about $4,000. Corruption is inevitable. For instance, a recent report of the Massachusetts Crime Commission said: "We have observed with disgust, indignation, and shame the ways in which some of the most highly placed and powerful political figures in the state have betrayed, actively or passively, the public trust."

The dominance, often overwhelming, of rural constituencies in state legislatures also helps to explain their lack of responsiveness to the problems of urban dwellers, who now are much more numerous in most states. The reapportionment orders of the Supreme Court will eventually correct this unfair imbalance, but it remains that representation in most legislatures has been essentially undemocratic. The rural legislators, uninterested in urban problems because they are not directly accountable, have with their undemocratically weighted representation often become willing and effective partners of local economic interests.

There should be little wonder why the people of most states are distrustful of their legislatures. Such devices as the referendum, initiative and proposition, and the recall of officials and judges are common, but the people's desire for direct action can in many ways be detrimental to the dignity and efficiency of state government. Constitutional prohibition and the demand for direct federal action have already been noted. Conversely it has led to the perpetuation of smaller administrative units within the state. There are fifty states, each with the organization and trappings of autonomous power, but there are also 3,049 counties enjoying some kind of exclusive authority and some 80,000 local governments. That is not all. At the time of writing, there were 24,534 operating school systems, and a further 2,668 classified as nonoperating. This generally meant that they had contracted their responsibilities to the operating variety. According to the International Association of Police Chiefs, there are 43,200 separate police forces, an average of fourteen to a county. The fissiparous tendencies of American internal administration are endless, and at times they appear to be a negation of government.

Some of this could be commendable. It is regarded by many as evidence of healthy democracy at the grass roots, although the majority of Americans have less interest in local than in federal government. It has produced some fine school systems as well as a good many indifferent ones. It has, alas, exposed the United States, for the most part a beautiful country, to the spoliation of land and building speculators because zoning regulations are a county responsibility. One county can legislate and enforce enlightened town and country planning, and have it ruined by a neighboring county without zoning regulations.

The predicament of the modern American state is plain to see. The distrust of the citizen has led to restraint of the legislature, demands for federal action, and the splintering of local government. Fiscally, it is caught in a pincer-like grip of local parsimony and federal benevolence. There are those, however, who prefer to see it defended by rugged individualism against big government, and rush to defend what are known as states' rights. These have been a burning issue since the time of Jefferson, but in the field of Civil Rights there are many who take the name of the states in vain, not to save them from federal intervention but to prevent the relief of the Negro. Others are more concerned in defending privileged economic positions against what they choose to see as the ominous flood of welfare statism. There are also people genuinely concerned with the parlous condition of the states, and really believe that the solution is a return to what they see as the verities of an older and simpler America.

Clearly states' rights is not always the battle cry of the scoundrel, but it is more frequently heard along the last-ditch defenses against the modern triple revolution, against the revolutions of technology and rising expectations as well as the Negro revolution. It can be a corruption of political intelligence and ideals perhaps more corrosive of the American system than the old-fashioned variety still practiced with such grace and artistry in Massachusetts. The fact of the matter is that the states have never had rights as such. The Tenth Amendment speaks only of powers reserved to the states. It is only the people who have rights. As James Madison said in the *Federalist* papers, "The ultimate authority resides with the people alone, and it will not depend on the comparative ambition of the different government, whether either, or which of them, will be able to enlarge its sphere of jurisdiction at the expense of the other."

A former governor of Florida, Leroy Collins, recalled in a paper published by the Center for the Study of Democratic Institutions that states' rights had been most generally used as a political weapon. Throughout American political life it had been an expression of protest or a defensive tactic rather than a sincere call for constructive effort. States' rights had always been, he added, a favorite haven of refuge for special interests in fear of government regulation.

Governor Collins also said that when state legislators speak of state and local rights they are often concerned with the rights, or rather preferential advantages, of the special interests they seek to serve. He referred to minimum wages as an obvious example. The economic interests which opposed federal legislation in the name of states' rights had not encouraged state action. They were opposed not so much to federal encroachment as to minimum wages. Lost somewhere in this maneuvering were the human rights and needs involved. The long struggle for medical insurance for the aged, it must be added, is another example. To avoid a federal scheme, the opposition earlier succeeded in enacting in Congress a program dependent upon state participation. The majority refused to participate.

Another former governor, Orville Freeman of Minnesota, in a similar paper condemned as a myth the very potent notion long exploited by the defenders of states' rights that local government is more democratic and efficient than federal government. At least, local government might be more democratic and responsive simply because it was more accessible. Nevertheless, it could be easily documented that the nearest thing to dictatorship in America was the petty tyrannies of local political bosses, some of whom had survived for decades while the control of state and national governments had frequently changed hands. It was far easier for a citizen to be intimidated by the local power structure than by those who ruled from afar. As for efficiency, the most monumental examples of waste and corruption, in relation to the size of the budgets, had been in local governments.

Oddly enough, states that claim to defend states' rights and rugged individualism, whatever that may mean for the majority in an industrialized and computerized country, are among the first to accept federal help. For instance, Texas is one of the wealthiest and has the sixth largest population. A recent investigation showed that it was seventh in the amount of federal taxes paid, but third in the amount of aid received from Washington. The absence of a state income tax helps to explain this dependence upon federal bounty. Nevertheless, although Texas at one time received more federal aid than any other state for child welfare services, forty-three other states spent more on such services. Perhaps this is what is meant by rugged individualism, but much of this explains what for Europeans is the most striking American phenomenon, the coexistence of great private wealth and public squalor.

The rugged individualism of Texan oilmen also flourishes with the help of federal tax deductions for oil depletion. The confusion wrought by states' rights at the national level is immeasurable. At the state and local level, it has clearly not produced the purer forms of democratic government that many Americans insist flourishes away from Washington. Nevertheless, it is a fact that many, perhaps a majority, for good and questionable reasons, cling to the notion that state and local governments are more democratic, honest, and responsive than the federal government. It is true, alas, that Washington was at one time not the most honest city in the United States. If the old muckrakers (God bless their memory) did occasionally exaggerate, there was a long and bitter legacy of suspicion. The occasional scandal still erupts, but the policing machinery is now more efficient than anything a state government possesses. There are also rather more than fourteen hundred reporters, ably assisted by specialists and researchers of all kinds, to keep an eagle eye on the goings-on in Washington, which proportionally is much more than any newspaper group that descends upon a state capital during the legislative session.

Presidential politics now makes corruption less likely, and Presidential power exceeds that of the fifty governors combined. It is also supported by the largest administrative machine in a non-Communist country. If some of the bureaucrats are as bureaucratic as they are supposed to be, Washington also attracts considerable administrative and technological talent. The country, despite the belief that local government is the best, is learning more and more to look to Washington as the imperatives of the modern triple revolution are better understood.

To draw attention to the deficiencies of state and local government, and the increasing authority and efficiency of Washington, is not to condemn decentralization, or what American political scientists prefer to see as noncentralization. State and local government ought to be more democratic and responsive simply because they are more accessible. Noncentralization is clearly preferable if man is to be regarded as a human being with the right to share in the shaping of his future and immediate environment rather than as a cipher in an efficient but impersonal system. Nearly 200 million people and 3,615,211 square miles of land cannot be efficiently or democratically administered from the federal capital. Noncentralization is not only desirable but essential.

Americans, for all their love of red meat, are a people traditionally devoted to farinaceous foods, and it is not surprising that they compare their system of government to cake. At one time federal-state-local relationships were seen to resemble a three-layer cake, each layer of government a part of the whole, but separated. Morton Grodzins improved on this misleading metaphor. For him, the relationships were like a marble cake with chocolate strands of government functions intertwined from top to bottom. It is as good a description as any, and recent scholarship also suggests that the federal government was never allowed to rest at the top in splendid isolation on a bed of cakey goo.

With land grants, occasional cash grants, and participation in joint stock companies, the federal government early became involved in many functions that were hardly federal in the strict sense of the term. These ventures amounted to federal assistance for schools, canals, and roads. Lunatic asylums were also supported. Together they can now be seen as the rudimentary beginnings of a modern welfare state. Federal authority was afterward also exerted over business, previously policed after a fashion by the states, under the Interstate Commerce Act of 1887 and the Sherman Antitrust Act of 1890. Conversely, local government was rarely if ever free of state authority. Local autonomy was strong in the New England states, but less so in other regions. Almost everywhere state authority was exerted downward, especially in the field of taxation. There was also a good deal of state-local cooperation.

Nevertheless, most of the nineteenth-century Presidents subscribed to the principle of strict construction of the Constitution. President Madison, for instance, vetoed an internal improvements bill in 1819 which Calhoun, the champion of the states, had shepherded through Congress. President Jackson subsequently vetoed a post road bill. The Southern states, prior to the Civil War, were allowed to defend their peculiar institution of slavery, and after Reconstruction the Union was content to leave the Negro very much to his own devices and local white prejudice.

The present situation is different largely to the extent that the federal government appears as the wooer rather than the wooed. The modern triple revolution is, of course, responsible for the reversal, as it is for the aggrandizement of Presidential power at the expense of Congress. State and local government, with Congress, have simply failed, or have been unable, to meet its demands.

I have noted the resistance to the revolutions of rising expectations and of the Negro, but the states, apart from the poor performance of many legislatures, have been the victims of the technological revolution. Only a few are big enough to tackle most of its problems, and not one is capable of meeting all of them. Water, electrical power, and road construction, for instance, are vital needs that cannot all be met by individual states. Political boundaries cut across physical and industrial entities, and are largely ignored by a restless population made more mobile by the demands of industries recognizing few of the lines drawn on the map. Smog and industrial waste, with their pollution problems, drift across state lines. Even crime has, as it were, gone federal.

Praiseworthy attempts have been made to solve many of the attendant problems by interstate cooperation. The Council of State Governments, a joint agency created, supported, and directed by all the state governments, helps in the first place to improve state legislative, administrative, and judicial practices. It is also an agency for cooperation in solving interstate problems, both regional and national, and in facilitating and improving state-local and state-federal relations. The interstate organizations affiliated with it run from the National Governors' Conference to the National Association of State Purchasing Officials. Then there are interstate compacts concerned with such diverse matter as fishing, pest control, unclaimed property, air pollution, and regional planning. These have led to the establishment of multistate agencies, the first of which was the Port of New York Authority in 1922.

Other multistate bodies have established permanent patterns of interstate relations governing rights, benefits, and duties, as in the allocation of water and the apportionment of interstate transport registration and weight fees. They also help to bridge jurisdictional barriers that invariably arise in compacts covering forest fires and civil defense, juvenile and mental health cooperative services, and even such matters as prison parole. If much of this does not sound particularly exciting, it remains that they are problems that could be painfully exacerbated by the federal system. If the states had not acted, the federal government would have been forced to intervene. Performance has not always lived up to promise, and federal legislation has been required, but the marbling of the cake has become even more convoluted.

State-local relations have also improved, but the need for federal assistance is painfully obvious at the bottom of the cake. Most cities are decaying, and more than half of the counties reported a decline of population in the last decade. Many small towns, once the ideal of American social life, are literally dying. Main Street can often be a row of empty stores. One bank may survive where three flourished before. The decline in taxable resources has left rural jurisdictions without the means to support normal public services. The flight from the land has often shifted an insupportable burden upon the cities, especially as their better-paid citizens have moved to the suburbs beyond reach of the local tax collector. Northern cities have also been almost overwhelmed by successive waves of Negroes and poor whites from the South, which of course has hastened the flight to the suburbs.

Here, if you like, is another variety of marbling, a demographic marbling which again makes nonsense of state and local boundaries and can create some very difficult problems. Few states, cities, and counties can cope alone. Most have to turn to the federal government, including those who shout about states' rights. Federal urban renewal programs are generally accepted simply because the money required is beyond local resources. If many of the small towns are not to become deserted villages, they must seek inclusion in the rural areas development programs.

Gigantic as many of these problems are, a political solution would not appear to be beyond the wit of politicians. Nevertheless, a solution, or rather a general acceptance of requirements, has not been reached. Men such as Barry Goldwater may think that federal help for the depressed is morally wrong and must sap the moral fiber of Americans, but as Senator he saw nothing paradoxical in his search for billions of federal dollars to irrigate his desert state of Arizona. The Southern states want their share of federal funds for education, but only for the white children. The paradoxes of demand are numerous, and the causes of conflict are not all from one side.

It is perhaps necessary to give some idea of the shape, scope, and the constitutional position of federal assistance before indicating its deficiencies and the problems it can create for federal-state-local relationships. While modern Presidents insist that they always act in the spirit of the Constitution, it remains that the principle of strict construction is no longer adhered to. The reason can be found somewhere in another variety of marbling.

The recent liberalism of the Supreme Court is part of the mix, although a decision of an earlier period was perhaps determinative. Certainly the New Deal could not have got very far without *Massachusetts* v. *Mellon*, 1923. In that decision, the Court held that since a state was not forced to accept the offer of federal funds for welfare purposes, grants involving the acceptance of federal requirements did not infringe state sovereignty. The President, moreover, has always had considerable constitutional authority to support him in relations with the states, the key provisions being the general-welfare including taxing and spending power, commerce, supremacy, reserve powers, due process, and equal-protection clauses. In the thirties, after declaring unconstitutional much of the New Deal, the Court broadened its interpretations of the general-welfare and commerce clauses to accept federal legislation covering labor relations, agricultural subsidies, social security, and other programs.

With *Helvering* v. *Davis*, 1937, the Court recognized for the first time the power of Congress to provide for the general welfare by legislation not specifically covered by the Constitution. The majority opinion said, in regard to the limits of federal power under the general-welfare clause:

The discretion however, is not confined to the courts. The discretion belongs to Congress, unless the choice is clearly wrong. . . . Nor is the concept of the general welfare static. Needs that were narrow or parochial a century ago may be interwoven in our day with the well-being of the nation. What is critical or urgent changes with the times.

This and other decisions brought about a fundamental change in federal-state relations. In 1956 the Commission on Intergovernmental Relations said:

Under judicial doctrine since 1937 the Supreme Court has largely removed itself as a practical factor in determining the economic policies of the states and the nation . . . under present judicial interpretations, especially of the spending power and the commerce clause, the boundaries of possible National action are more and more subject to determination by legislative action. In brief, the policy making authorities of the National government are for most purposes the arbiters of the federal system.

A minority report went further:

The effect of these decisions has been to create a situation under which the Congress may by the expenditure of money enter virtually any sphere of government. There exists little restraint on Congress other than that which it determines to exercise over itself. These decisions have fundamentally altered the balance of power designed by the architects of the Constitution.

The authors may have exaggerated a little, but clearly there was not much left of the principle of strict construction unless a President was anxious to pick up the pieces. President Eisenhower, in fact, had a try when he established the Commission.

The Commission was to examine the proper roles of the federal government "to the end that these relations may be clearly defined and the functions concerned may be allocated to their proper jurisdiction." Behind these terms of reference was the strong Presidential conviction that the federal government was too big, had usurped too many state functions, and spent too much money. Two years later, the Commission admitted that functions could not be allocated, but insisted that the duties could. The general principles proclaimed combined to strengthen the state governments and give them a large role. When it tried to deal with separate areas of activity, however, it was unable to recommend any drastic decentralization, and had the grace to apologize. The President was not to be gainsaid, and challenged the Governors' Conference in 1957 to set up a Federal-State Action Committee to select the functions and revenue sources that could be transferred from the federal government to the states. Four recommendations were made, the most important of which was that the federal government should abandon its aid for the building of sewage plants. The project was quietly dropped, perhaps into one of those plants, and when President Eisenhower left office the federal government was bigger, spending more money and involved in more projects.

It can be seen from this that Presidential ambition, or lack of it, is not necessarily a determining factor in the increasing internal authority of the federal government. The doors of the White House, or of the Capitol for that matter, cannot be closed against the forces of the modern triple revolution. The confusion of Congressional demands produces conflict, of course, but it also blurs some constitutional edges. Only the fundamentalists can complain when they see poor children drinking milk paid for from federal funds, and very few have objected to the interstate highways they have helped to build.

Federal grants amounted to $1 billion in 1946, $10 billion in 1964, and about $15 billion in 1966, a phenomenal increase over the $3 million provided at the turn of the century. The rate of increase has not been constant but it has been dramatic in recent years. On a per capita basis, grants rose from about $38 in 1962 to $52 in 1964, and $78 in 1966. Most of the money went to highways, education, public welfare, employment security, and health and hospitals. There were 115 federal aid programs in 1964, and 170 in 1966, after two years of Great Society legislation. They will undoubtedly increase in numbers and cost.

A structural change of great significance emerged with the postwar growth of direct federal-local relations. The states played little or no part in this, although they have constitutional jurisdiction over local governments. Indeed, cities and counties do not have a constitutional existence. The change was dramatic in the sixties when the new Department of Housing and Urban Development began to deal directly with the cities, and the Office of Economic Opportunity with groups that could be considered rivals to elected local governments. They did, in fact, only follow the trail blazed earlier by the Department of Agriculture, which had reached down through the governmental cake to individual farmers. The technological revolution was primarily responsible.

The twentieth-century revolution of agricultural technology began after the depression and gained increasing momentum during the Second World War, when apart from military demands much of what was left of the free world had to be fed. The chief features of the revolution were mechanization, the widespread use of fertilizers and insecticides, and the spread of specialized and scientific farming. The department was one of the revolutionary activists, and then moved into a position of almost Draconian control when demand fell off after the Korean War and production continued to increase. At one time this process appeared to dominate American politics. A consensus was never found in the debate over a free market or a managed farm economy, but what emerged was something very close to central planning and control, which is supposed to be anathema to all Americans, and the first of the structural changes in federal-local government relations.

The problem was seen to be primarily the support of farm income, and this was more or less achieved by two programs. The first was concerned with technical advice, cheap credit, pest control and crop improvement, and soil and water conservation. The second was more direct. It included price supports, surplus disposal, and production controls. The federal government accepted the responsibility of taking specified crops off the market at the support price, which was fixed by Congress or by the Secretary of Agriculture acting within limits set by Congress. The crops supported included beans, cotton, corn, dairy products, peanuts, tobacco, wheat, and wool. These surpluses were disposed of through various foreign aid and internal welfare programs, and the former became a useful weapon in diplomacy. The remainder was stored in huge granaries and warehouses. Guaranteed prices naturally stimulated production, and production controls such as acreage allotments and marketing quotas were enforced.

By the mid-sixties some surplus stocks had disappeared, largely because of the generous response to the appeals of hungry India. The growth of large efficient farms seemed to make unnecessary much of these programs. But by that time North America had become the world's granary. Only its surplus capacity stood between much of the world and a dreadful Malthusian fate. Controlled agricultural production had in fact become vital to the well-being and peace of nearly every continent.

These programs brought the federal government right into the fields and county courthouses without so much as a by-your-leave of the state governments, but the department has not been content with managing these enormous programs. It claims to serve the consumer as well as the farmer and rancher. The logic is indisputable, but it has taken the department into some odd corners of American life. After perusing the list of services and specialized advice offered, I am forced to conclude that it now reaches into almost every corner. It gives advice on house building, painting, termites, lighting, heating, air-conditioning, and how to plan a modern kitchen. Furniture and rugs, tools and cars, cooking and refrigeration, mortgages and installment credit, life, fire and car insurance, health care and services, gardens and patios, vacations and books, clothes and dry-cleaning have not escaped its benevolent attention. It is all very helpful, but for a writer from a welfare state it seems to take the constitutional welfare clause a little further than the founders anticipated.

It is not the only federal department that now deals directly with the people. For those Americans who do not realize what the federal government is prepared to do for them, without the benefit of state and local government, I suggest a visit to the nearest post office or federal building. There, under the Stars and Stripes, very much like a United States Embassy in a foreign land, sit federal officials ready to advise and help on almost everything, from weed-killing to loans for small businessmen.

Again this is not all, not by a long chalk. I have shown how, in the opinion of many Americans, the balance of power between the federal, state, and local governments as designed by the architects of the Constitution has been fundamentally altered. I have also shown how the federal government reaches over the heads of the states to city and county governments and to the citizen. All this is, to say the least, surprising in a country dedicated to rugged individualism and respectful to the point of obeisance to an eighteenth-century Constitution. Nevertheless, it has done much more and without the awareness of those who passionately defend states' rights. For most purposes, it has suborned many servants of the states.

The Commission on Inter-Governmental Relations had another word or term for it. "Vertical functional autocracy" was used to describe the close relations at all three levels between administrators of highway, welfare, education, employment, and health programs. The autocracy can be easily explained. The specialized county official prefers to work directly with the specialized state and federal official rather than with the local authority. To that extent he becomes more a component of a national official or professional network, and less a county official. As a consequence, some state governors felt that their administrators were closer and more loyal to the federal fountainhead of funds and advice than those who appointed them.

This smudging of the lines of authority and loyalty is partly explained by increasing professionalism, which in turn is part of the technological revolution, and by the increase in state employees. The expansion of state civil services has been more extensive and rapid than in Washington. The major reason of course is money, or the federal grants-in-aid, which make much of their professional, technological, or administrative work possible. These transfers of federal funds to state and local government are for specified purposes. There are flat grants made available to state governments regardless of local requirements and conditions, and proportionate grants the sum of which depends upon the amount the recipient government is prepared to spend. There are some variations, but generally speaking federal

I

grants do more than suborn state and local officials. They can be fiscally disruptive, and they tend to dictate the policies and programs of the states.

The state governor must subscribe to federal objectives, standards, and guidelines or do without the money. The latter is not usually an attractive or politically acceptable alternative. Thus state or local government, as well as the specialized civil servant, tends to become less of an initiator of policy and programs and more an administrator, or an appendage of the national system. The demotion was almost inevitable. He who pays the piper calls the tune, and the federal choice can be as seductive as the tune played by the Hamelin piper.

This further internal aggrandizement of Presidential or federal power has, however, not been brought about without cost. Unlike in the days of the New Deal, the dangers and weaknesses of centralization are better understood in Washington, but the administrative mess is still considerable and costly. It also makes for ham-handed inefficiency. This is perhaps understandable in a system haphazardly put together to circumvent the constitutional limitation of federal power and yet encompass the workings of the federal government, fifty state governments, numerous interstate agencies, and some eighty thousand local governments. Bureaucratic jealousy and the Congressional appropriations system have also made sensible coordination more difficult.

For instance, in 1966 the 170 federal aid programs were financed from 400 appropriations. They were administered by 21 federal departments and agencies, assisted by 150 bureaus in Washington and 400 regional offices. To this mess must be added the various state agencies all looking to Washington, and often only dimly aware of the larger situation in their own states. In this muddle, mess, or maze, the local agencies could be utterly lost, and federal control was at best clumsy. Much of the blame no doubt belonged to the states for failing to fulfill their role in what should be a noncentralized system. But once they became part of a supraconstitutional network of federal-state-local offices it became the responsibility of Washington to devise some reasonably efficient administrative machine.

How to establish such a machine and a workable balance of power and division of responsibility between the three levels of government are problems that engaged many minds in the sixties. There was considerable talk of creative federalism, which was often little more than a slogan. Nevertheless, the old facility of political inventiveness was also apparent. The importance of revenue was quickly recognized, and there were proposals that a proportion of federal revenues should be made available to the states without strings. It was an attractive idea if only because of the immediate prospects. While states taxes were unlikely to be raised to the level required to return political leadership to gubernatorial mansions, federal revenue was bound to increase as a consequence of national economic growth. If defense expenditures remained constant even at a high level, and the country was not plunged into a large war or economic depression, Washington would have at least $5 billion more to spend each year on domestic programs.

There were some who questioned the constitutionality of the proposals. Others warned against corruption or inequity within the states. At the time of writing, there appeared to be small chance of the proposals' being accepted and attention was turning to methods of improving the administrative efficiency of the existing ramshackle system. One Congressional proposal was the establishment of a national intergovernmental affairs council within the executive office of the President to coordinate planning and provide information. This could lead to a further aggrandizement of Presidential power, which appeared inevitable to many if only because the President had the ultimate responsibility for making the American system work.

Whatever happens, Presidential power may well increase. The Great Society programs of President Johnson were further extensions, notably into hospitals and schools. Medicare and the Elementary and Secondary Education Act of 1965 provided much-needed funds, but they also imposed federal standards. They were not all concerned with the quality of health care or teaching; the states had to provide proof that hospital wards and schools had been desegregated. Moreover, Medicare is seen as the thin end of a federal wedge. Medical insurance under Social Security will almost certainly not be limited to old people, but eventually will be extended to everyone as in most other industrialized democracies.

The growth of the great American cities, said Bryce in 1888, was among the most significant and least fortunate changes in the character of the population of the United States since 1787. It was certainly significant. The census of 1790 showed only five cities with a population of more than 8,000. In 1880 there were 19 with populations exceeding 100,000. There were 130 by 1960, 21 of them with more than 500,000 inhabitants. To put it another way, in 1790 only 5 percent of the population were townsfolk, and by 1960 it was 70 percent.

The significance is obvious, and in more ways than the figures would suggest. The urban populations of Britain and other Western European countries also increased with industrialization. It was inevitable, but urban growth in the United States was something more than the by-product of industrialization. The real significance of American cities is that they absorbed more than 25 million immigrants between the Civil War and the First World War.

Whether or not this was unfortunate is of course a matter of opinion. Presumably it is for those who regret the passing of the old white Anglo-Saxon America with its simple rural certainties and moral smugness. I for one do not regret it for some rather selfish reasons. Without the deluge of immigrants, the United States would not have become powerful enough industrially to assume world leadership, without which the kind of world that I want might well have been lost. Next time the city fathers of New York feel that they must express themselves in monumental imagery I suggest that they erect a monument to the poor immigrant as a companion to the Statue of Liberty.

There should be few regrets for the Anglo-Saxon Protestants whom Bryce knew so well. The later immigrants (it is strange that the WASPs did not always remember that they were also of immigrant stock) not only provided the necessary manpower for industrial greatness. They were also a cushion in the process of industrialization, and absorbed most of the shock. They suffered much of the injustice and indignity that were apparently inescapable in the early years of industrial growth. The United States was two nations in those days, and the immigrant city dwellers were the second and rather ill-used nation. The general-welfare clause of the Constitution was rarely extended to them. Yet they gave the established Americans something denied to the citizens of other industrializing countries, time to adjust to the new economic world.

In so doing, the immigrants helped to extend the old order that passed much more quickly in Western Europe. I think that this is a historic fact given too little attention. The United States is an enormous country, and much that happened in the cities at the turn of the century in any case would not have been immediately felt in many areas. The new industrial workers were not all immigrants, but fewer poor whites and Negroes were attracted to the new industrial centers because of the availability of cheaper foreign labor. Industry might not have expanded so quickly if it had been less numerous, but small-town attitudes would not have been so dominant when *Main Street* was written. It might have been a very different book.

The innocence of so many Americans—and that is how their unruffled acceptance of provincial certainties and standards struck Europeans—could not have been sustained for so long in a period of social and technological revolutionary change without the immigrant shield or cushion. The United States might now be a less conservative and perhaps more united country, further down the road toward an acceptable resolution of the race problem. All this is mere supposition. What is undeniable is that the government and the very nature of American cities cannot be understood if the tidal waves of immigrants which almost overwhelmed them are forgotten.

In the nineteenth century the antagonism to the immigrant arrivals was evident in the abuse of state control. The cities and other local government systems are not mentioned in the Constitution, and the states have constitutional responsibility. Cities everywhere were at their mercy. Franchises for utility services were bought and sold, and financial burdens imposed without reference to the inhabitants. In Pennsylvania, for instance, the legislature created a commission in Philadelphia authorized to collect revenue and spend it regardless of the city government. Such interference and corruption were constant.

The conflict between state and city is as old as the American city. Much of it can be explained by the preponderance of rural legislators tucked away in the distant state capital. In the past the expectations of their constituents were few. Their legislative experience did not encompass the problems and challenges of the city, and to be fair to them, the growth of American cities was unprecedented. If they backed away from the problems, it was perhaps understandable. The antipathy of the settled rural communities to the cities with their foreign languages, religions, and social habits was perhaps just as understandable, if regrettable, and much older.

The early colonists, many of them appalled by the goings-on in London, were convinced that country life was good and city life evil.

Later intellectual and political leaders found justification in French philosophy for this weird and wrongheaded simplification of the human experience. Jefferson wrote in his *Notes on Virginia:* "Those who labour in the earth are the chosen people of God. . . . Corruption of morals in the mass of cultivators is a phenomenon of which no age or nation has furnished an example."

This was a rather sweeping statement, even for one whose vantage point was as elevated as his hilltop home above Charlottesville. The Bible furnishes many examples to the contrary, but in spite of its wide American readership the ideal of an American Eden and Canaan persisted for generations. Contrary evidence, as in Garland's reports of the awfulness of life in the Western territories, was attacked by city-bred critics and ignored by the country. Long after the social and economic possibilities of industrialization were at least comprehended in Europe, the virtues of rural life were assumed in the United States.

By the beginning of the twentieth century, there was, alas, more to rural antipathy than outmoded romanticism and indifferent Biblical scholarship. I refer elsewhere to the growth of Americanism with its admixture of reaction, anti-intellectualism, and xenophobia. There was also local radicalism and progressiveness when the hard truths of American rural life could no longer be ignored, but the conspiratorial theory of politics and history took a greater hold on many more people. Indeed, rural radicalism was invariably xenophobic. The devil was Wall Street for the farmers hard-pressed to meet mortgage payments, and for the great majority of Protestants he was the Catholic or Jew in the cities. The immigrants were, of course, defenseless aliens in a foreign land, and it is little wonder that they turned to the city political bosses for help. In so doing, they helped to establish the most notable American contribution to city government, the machine.

The oldest and most famous is Tammany Hall, the Democratic organization of New York County. It is older than the Constitution, and began as a benevolent and fraternal organization. It was named after an Indian chief, and entered politics in the Presidential campaign of Thomas Jefferson in 1800, since when it has always been associated with the Democratic Party. This association of Tammany and the rural philosopher of Charlottesville is one of those endearing American paradoxes which makes the still occasional smugness bearable, but I digress. Tammany flourished, especially in the period of massive immigration, until the New York political uprising of 1937 when Fiorello La Guardia was elected mayor. Many other cities have also been ruled by machines, including Chicago, Kansas City, New Orleans, St. Louis, and San Francisco. Most, but not all, were Democratic.

They flourished because of the help they gave to the poor, especially the immigrant. The kind of help, and why it was given, was well described by George Washington Plunkitt of Tammany Hall:

What holds your grip on your district is to go right down among the poor families and help them in the different ways they need help. I've got a regular system for this. If there's a fire in Ninth, Tenth or Eleventh Avenue, for example, any hour of the day or night, I'm usually there with some of my election district captains as soon as the fire engines. If a family is burned out I don't ask whether they are Republicans or Democrats, I don't refer them to the Charity Organization Society, which would investigate their case in a month or two and decide they were worthy of help about the time they are dead from starvation. I just get quarters for them, buy clothes for them if their clothes were burned up, and fix them up till they get things running again. It's philanthropy, but it's politics too —mighty good politics. Who can tell how many votes one of these fires brings me? The poor are the most grateful people in the world, and, let me tell you, they have more friends in their neighborhoods than the rich have in theirs.

The machines did not wait for disaster to strike to win votes. Immigrants were often met at the dockside to be enrolled. Jobs were found, and sports and social activities, ranging from ball games to the celebration of national heroes, were encouraged. Thus in a rough and ready fashion was the immigrant provided for and made to feel less alien. It may have been politics, but it was also mighty good philanthropy.

The only direct payment expected from the immigrant was his vote, and with these enormous blocs of votes the machine boss could run the city, do business with contractors and party chieftains, and make his profit. This was the final pay-off of the machine, and its *raison d'être*. The boss was not in politics for civic improvement or for personal prestige. Usually he did not hold public office, because it was sufficient to control nomination to public office and in turn the elected or appointed officials. He was in politics to make money, and this he did by acting as broker for those representatives of a more respectable America, the businessman in search of city contracts and the Presidential or gubernatorial candidate in search of votes. The first paid with kickbacks and the second with patronage.

The immigrant paid indirectly, and unwittingly, for the favors and services received. Some of his tax money disappeared in bribes and inadequate municipal services. More seriously, because machine politics was necessarily the politics of the *status quo,* the relief from a city government interested in civic improvement was rarely available.

Reformers still win elections by campaigning against machines and bosses, but it is widely assumed that machine politics was killed by the New Deal and the introduction of national politics in local elections. There is an assumption that it is just as much a victim of the aggrandizement of Presidential power as other parts of the American political system. The evidence is not entirely persuasive. It is true that there are very few obvious successors to the Crockers, Pendergasts, and Tweeds, and, as with the Kennedys, their sons and grandsons may have gone on to bigger and better things, including political and social respectability. Clearly the larger requirements of machine politics, unrestricted immigration, poverty, and official indifference have gone, or have been diminished. Patronage is not what it was before civil services were introduced, although it can remain considerable, as in Chicago. Primary elections have also loosened the machine's control of nomination to public office.

Nevertheless, if it can rarely control a big city, it can still be powerful in its political subdivisions. Machine politics can be largely ethnic politics. Not all the ethnic groups have found, or feel that they have found, complete social and economic acceptance. The internal migration of Negroes and Puerto Ricans also helps to keep the machine alive. Machine politics is also political organization, and aspirants for higher office can still hardly afford to ignore it. There were some machine politicians on board the wagon train, if tucked out of sight, that headed for the New Frontier in 1960. The New Deal may have sounded their ultimate doom, but President Kennedy needed their support for the Democratic nomination as much as did President Roosevelt nearly thirty years earlier.

The city machines (there are also rural machines) have spanned a long period of American politics, first because they filled a need and later because the opposition was so weak. The various reform parties that sprang up over the decades achieved some success, but only limited success because they were more interested in honest government than in the condition of the poor. They were expressions of middle-class indignation, and rarely survived because they were not broadly based. A fairly recent development has been the Democratic reform movement, which tries to work within the parent party. It is ideological, largely liberal, and differs from earlier reform movements in that it is not exclusively concerned with administrative honesty and efficiency. Its sights are set on improved housing, transport, and the services and amenities that only good government can provide for the majority. It is also passionately interested in national issues, such as Civil Rights, and at times the parent party and not the city government appears to be the objective of its reforming zeal. Whatever their future, the machines have strongly influenced national politics and city government.

There are three basic systems of city government, and the machines flourished with the first, and brought about the development of the third. The first, that of the mayor and council, is the oldest, with attenuated roots reaching back beyond colonial times to the English medieval city. It is still the most popular, especially in big cities. The mayor and the council are elected, but unlike his English ancestor the mayor is not a figurehead. He is the city's chief executive. It is unsafe to generalize, but he usually enjoys legislative, budgetary, administrative, and police powers. He can have veto power and appoint officials, although many of the higher posts are elective. The mayor can assume national political prominence if he governs a great city. The mayor of New York can be regarded as a man of possible Presidential stature.

The second system, that of the city commission, enjoyed wide esteem after it was first introduced at the turn of the century in Galveston, Texas, but is now the least popular of the three systems. It is a government comprising a mayor-president and commissioners for the various departments, all of whom are elected at large. The chief characteristic is that the commission acts as both a legislative and an executive body. Each member has executive responsibility for his department. The promise of prompt executive action inherent in such a small body has not been generally fulfilled. In fact, there has more often been diffusion of power and factional strife. The concentration

I*

of power has also been resented, leading in some cities to a system of referenda, which, to say the least, can be slow and clumsy.

The third, the city-manager, system is supposed to banish politics, especially machine politics, from municipal administration. It is more often found in smaller cities. The distinctive feature is that an elected council or commission appoints a professed expert to manage its affairs. The city managers have achieved professional status, and some move on to larger cities as their fame spreads. An essential part of the system is the nonpartisan ballot. This is an electoral system designed to remove political parties or machines from between the voter and the candidates. The voter is supposed to vote for a man and not a party or machine. However, machines are known to have flourished under the city-manager system. On the whole it has improved efficiency and reduced corruption, but there are some weaknesses. The question of political leadership can be left unresolved, and there is a tendency to appoint local men whether or not they have had sufficient experience.

For an Englishman, the second and third systems appear to be a little too far removed from the democratic process for comfort. Efficiency is not everything, but there are city councils in Britain and West Germany and other Western European countries, proving that democratic government can be efficient and honest. One reason in Britain is the constituency party, especially the Labour Party, which gets out the vote and is a training ground for local and national candidates. The Reform Democrats are rather similar. It is too early to pass judgment on their efforts, which in any case are somewhat circumscribed by the nonpartisan ballot which is mandatory in many cities.

Moreover, another generation, as it were, of cities is reaching the painful stage of adolescence, and it is not at all certain that the lessons learned in the old ones are applicable. Los Angeles is the obvious example, and ought to be seen as a new departure in the development of the city. New York has more in common with ancient Athens than with Los Angeles. The city's essential structure is a system of motor roads, or freeways. There is no obvious civic focal point, and it has been dismissed as a collection of suburbs in search of a center. There is also little civic life. It is an American phenomenon, and possibly the prototype of the megalopolises now being formed elsewhere as urban sprawl joins existing cities and communities together.

Los Angeles is the third largest city in the United States with, according to the 1960 census, a population of about 2,500,000. It is also the nucleus of a metropolitan area of some 450 square miles and 7 million inhabitants. Los Angeles County comprises seventy-four incorporated municipalities and stretches of unincorporated county land. Some municipalities exist only to avoid local taxation. There can be small justification for the existence of others, and Angelenos profess ignorance of the jurisdiction within which they live.

Apart from the city's boosters, there is little or none of the civic pride which can still flourish fiercely in the squalor of New York. One reason is that the majority of the inhabitants come from elsewhere, and tend not to stay in one municipality when they settle, if that is the word, in Los Angeles. The mobility is extraordinary even by American standards. There are also large Negro and Mexican populations, for the most part segregated. More important, each household tends to be a complete and segregated social unit living on its patio, or about the swimming pool if it is in the middle or upper classes. Not even the city's single and powerful newspaper reaches a majority of them. Suburban papers flourish, not as an expression of local community feeling or pride but because of the fissiparous tendencies of the city and its dwellers. They meet each other for the most part only on the freeways, each boxed in his car, like so many ships passing in the night.

The car and the freeway have made possible this personal freedom, or anonymity. The Angeleno and his city could not possibly exist without the car. In some parts of the city he is likely to be arrested as a vagrant if he walks. Those who have to walk or use public transport can be condemned to a life not much better than vagrancy. The relative immobility of the Negroes of the Watts district largely explained the awful riots in 1965. If New York slums are squalid, they at least have some of the warm, intimate life that has sustained slum dwellers all over the world. In Los Angeles alienation can be more than attitude, color, and poverty. It can be space, almost uncrossable space for the man without an automobile.

There was a city machine of sorts once, but it could not survive the explosion of the city along the freeways. Nor, for that matter, could the usual pyramid of classes and local interests with a civic leadership at the apex. There are powerful families and interest groups in the city still, but no establishment or local power structure as the terms are normally understood. There cannot possibly be any local version of traditional American city government and society in such a decentralized, unled, unbossed, pluralistic society. This is Los Angeles, the American city of the future according to many expectations, most of them pessimistic.

Yet in one way its growth has been a repetition of the nineteenth-century experience of other cities. It has not just grown, but has attracted, absorbed, and been almost overwhelmed by immigration. The difference, of course, is that the vast majority of immigrants are from other American states. The few foreigners who came, especially before the Second World War, were largely an elite of professional people escaping Hitler or the war. The internal immigrants were of all sorts and conditions, Okies escaping the dust bowl and the grinding poverty of the old rural life, retired people seeking the sun, and the usual run of Americans with their atavistic yearning to move westward. Hollywood attracted its own, and the defense industries established largely during the Second World War attracted waves of industrial workers. This movement continued almost unabated after the shooting ceased, partly because of the demands of the Cold War and also because of aerospace and other new industries.

Apart from the 335,000 Negroes and 260,000 Mexicans, who together comprise rather more than a quarter of the population of the city, the Angelenos are generally better-off and better educated than the average American city dweller. Collectively, they must be the most creative group outside of New York, but their intellectual interests have not been reflected in local politics. Their voting record in state and federal elections is higher than the national average, but the turnout for a local election is dismally low. As one writer put it, politics simply has a low visibility in Los Angeles.

One reason, of course, is that people generally do not organize themselves politically until there is some pressing problem to be resolved, and until recently Angelenos have escaped from the usual urban problems by simply moving down the freeway. The restless mobility and private way of life in the sun do not lend themselves to political organization, although organization is not impossible, as the Goldwater forces demonstrated in 1964. Simply by ringing doorbells and working like old-time precinct captains they managed to deliver a victorious vote for their candidate. He was, of course, running for the Presidency and not for local office, but they made an interesting discovery. Many families isolated on their patios were intensely lonely. There was often a pathetic eagerness for communion with their fellow men, even a political canvasser. An old machine boss would have instantly recognized the situation.

Since the collapse of the so-called Shaw machine in the thirties, Los Angeles has in fact enjoyed a reputation for good local government. One reason is the long years of distinguished service of Mayor Fletcher Bowron. Another is that it enjoys a strong city council, a large civil service, and an efficient police force. These bodies, together with nonpartisan local elections which are common throughout California, are generally held to be characteristic of good local government. Angelenos can point to the ever-unrolling freeways, and the nation's most efficient anti-air-pollution regulations required by their carbon monoxide canopies, as futher evidence of good government. At least they could until Watts exploded in 1965, and after three days of rioting left thirty-four dead on its dreary streets.

Subsequent investigations, notably that of the McCone Commission, revealed that one-quarter of its Negro families was on relief. One out of every ten men in Watts was unemployed, and family incomes had actually decreased in the previous five years while elsewhere the incomes of nonwhite families had risen. The bus services were discovered to be the worst of any large American city. There was no public hospital, not even a cinema. State psychologists reported that the inhabitants spoke of Watts as a prison, and went on to explain the riot pattern along the lines of a prison riot. An altercation with the police was the fuse for the explosion, and afterward it became evident that the police was a paramilitary elite force of five thousand, highly mechanized, and applying modern control technology developed by space and defense industries for law enforcement.

There is something radically wrong behind the façade of good government if such a force is considered necessary for the maintenance of law and order in a democratic society. Much of it is the anonymity of the city, which can lead to indifference to or ignorance of the condition of others. It can be explained in political terms by a lack of organization. Whether one makes the other impossible is perhaps the essential question for younger American cities. New York has had racial troubles, and has felt obliged to form a small paramilitary force, but the humanity of its citizens has been involved, largely because of its political structure. Little evidence of this could be found in Los Angeles after the Watts riots when the voters refused to approve a $12 million bond issue to build a public hospital. The city council was also reluctant to operate a human relations council, and once again the federal government had to intervene.

Los Angeles is the urban expression of the technological revolution, and as yet has created more problems than it has solved. It is also clearly reluctant to face up to the question of race, which is not so much a problem as a serious threat to the future prosperity of many American cities, old and new. Washington, D.C., already has more Negro citizens than white, and by the seventies many other large cities will be in a similar predicament, of which more in a later chapter.

8   The Political Parties and Elections

"There are now two great and several minor parties in the United States. The great parties are the Republicans and the Democrats. What are their principles, their distinctive tenets, their tendencies? . . . This is what a European is always asking of intelligent Republicans and intelligent Democrats. He is always asking because he never gets an answer. The replies leave him in deeper perplexity. After some months the truth begins to dawn on him. Neither party has anything definite to say on these issues; neither party has any principles, any distinctive tenets. Both have traditions. Both claim to have tendencies. Both have certain war cries, organizations, interests enlisted in their support. But those interests are in the main the interests of getting or keeping the patronage of the government. Tenets and policies, points of political doctrine and points of political practice, have all but vanished. They have not been thrown away but have been stripped away by Time and the progress of events, fulfilling some policies, blotting out others. All has been lost, except office or the hope of it."
—JAMES BRYCE
The American Commonwealth

The American political system is the oldest in the world. Party politics is, in fact, an American invention. Despite Washington's admonition that the spirit of party was the worst enemy of popular government, two factions were very sensibly struggling for power before the first President was buried. When the House of Commons in Britain was still controlled by factions, the Americans had established at least one popular organization in support of a Congressional faction. The United States has another political claim to fame. It is the only democratic country I know that has a one-and-a-half-party

255

system. This is a fact of American history, and not a bad anti-Republican joke.

The one or whole party is of course the Democratic Party; it can trace its unbroken history back to Jefferson, and is therefore the world's oldest popular political organization. The early Democrats first appeared on the hustings as Republicans, fought their first successful Presidential election as Democratic Republicans, and finally decided to call themselves Democrats more than a hundred years ago. This confusion of labels did not reflect interruptions in its steady organizational progress. In Congress the Democrats were an identifiable group by 1792, and a nationwide party by 1800, when they elected their first President, Jefferson.

There was also a one-party system with the demise in 1816 of the Federalists, the first half-party. It did not last long—from 1816 to 1824, when groups that were to form the Whig Party in 1836 appeared in opposition to Jackson's Democracy. The Whigs went the way of the Federalists by the early 1850s, but during its existence emerged the modern party system with national conventions, state and local organizations, and patronage.

The abiding strength of the Democrats is that they have always remained a national party. This was first achieved by combining the rural South and its slave economy with the free laboring masses of the Northern cities. On the face of it the combination was an impossible one, even allowing for the mutual antipathy between it and the commercial and banking interests, but it survived the Civil War and the Civil Rights movement a century later. In between it absorbed the Populists and most of the more recent immigrants. It is the genuine American party, and even the Republicans should be grateful for its long service to the Republic.

They had their ups and downs of course, and the national organization encompassed, supported, and depended upon much to deflate party pride. There was gross corruption and inefficiency, although the spoils system has since been proved necessary for American government. Some of the practices of the city machines were disgraceful, and courthouse politics added to the tragedy of the South. It was a party run by professionals, often cynical and self-seeking, but outside the South it has always been a genuine popular democratic party. Bryan and the Populists stirred the national conscience, and the seeking of immigrant votes eased the harsh process of assimilation. If there was political calculation in their concern for the poor, there was also humanity. The party is responsible for much of the social legislation that now graces the statue books. In other words, it more often than not, certainly more often than the Republican Party and its predecessors, harked to the demands of the majority.

This is enough to explain why the Democrats are now the majority party, a whole party. They often appear to be a very confused party torn by inner strife, but this too holds a lesson for half-parties. The causes of confusion and strife are not to be found in the party but in the circumstance and condition of American society. Democrats manage to remain more or less united, if confused, and thus give true unity to the country, because of compromise and accommodation. In the United States the politician's gifts to mankind, it would seem, have been largely monopolized by the Democrats.

The half-parties can be explained largely by the absence of one or more of these Democratic characteristics, especially national unity. The Federalists fought the good fight for the adoption of the Constitution, but they failed to make the change from a government faction to a party with broad popular support. They were nativists in a land whose destiny depended upon immigration. They represented the established order, especially the commercial and financial interests. They were apprehensive of the revolutionary consequences of independence, and after the transfer of power were anxious to resume profitable and friendly relations with Britain. They were political dinosaurs, doomed to extinction because they were incapable of adjusting to the evolution of political and social America.

The Federalists were the first American political faction, but it never became an organized party, and the main link between it and the Whigs was that its followers had no other place to go. The Whigs were not unlike the Republican Party of 1964 under the leadership of the then Senator Barry Goldwater. They sought the most unlikely alliances to defeat Jacksonian Democracy, and unlike the Goldwaterites achieved some success. At least they elected two Presidents, General Harrison, the hero of the Battle of Tippecanoe, and Tyler. "Tippecanoe and Tyler too" is one of those old American campaign slogans that will probably never be forgotten, but the Whig victories were as indecisive as the battle. The party, or rather alliance, split over slavery, as did the Republicans in 1964 over Civil Rights. The pieces were never put together again. They had some notable Congressional leaders, Clay and Webster, but lacked what the Democrats have somehow nearly always maintained: the gifts of compromise and accommodation, broad national appeal and organization, and some concern for the individual.

The Republicans are of course the party of Lincoln, and since the sixteenth President there have been twelve Republicans and eight Democrats in the White House. Not a bad record for a half-party, I can hear Republicans growling menacingly. They did depend for victory upon popular war heroes such as Grant and Eisenhower, but it is an impressive record. They are now very much the minority party, but at the beginning it was an authentic popular movement, democratic and even radical, at least in its dealings with the South. Slavery and its extension into the new territories were the sparks that set the grass roots afire, and the blaze was so great that Lincoln was elected President within six years of the party's inception.

Inevitably the early party was a coalition of Whigs, Abolitionists, Free-Soilers, Know-Nothings, local parties, and even Democrats. The choice of the name "Republican" was a salute to Jefferson, the first Free-Soiler. In taking their stand against Southern slavery they perforce became a sectional party, and the record of the radical Republicans after the Civil War has denied them to this day the opportunity of becoming a truly national party.

The Republicans were the majority party for many years after the Civil War, and it was during this period that they became identified with conservatism and industrial and financial interests. There were, of course, exceptions. President Theodore Roosevelt was a man of vision, although his liberal record at home was blemished by jingoistic patriotism. Senator Robert La Follette led the Progressive Republican group which favored social legislation, but the group splintered from the parent party and fought two Presidential elections as the Progressive Party.

Senator La Follette was perhaps too much of a reformer for his times, but the defections of the Progressive Republicans left the party in the firm control of those who gave priority to economic interests over social requirements and justice. Industrial violence and agrarian unrest were rarely absent, but the Republican Party prevailed largely because it represented both the opportunity of America and an older America yet to be overwhelmed by the political consequences of immigration. It prevailed until the depression.

This long period of dominance persuaded many Republicans that they were the natural leaders of the nation. The assumption grew out of class and race as well as wealth. Bryce wrote:

If you find yourself dining with one of "the best people" in any New England city, or in Philadelphia, or in Cincinnati, Cleveland, Chicago, or Minneapolis, you assume that the guest sitting next to you is a Republican, almost as confidently as in English county society you would assume your neighbour to be a Tory; that is to say, you may sometimes be wrong, but in four cases out of five you will be right.

Bryce went on to say that in the Republican Party were to be found the men of substance who desired to see things go on quietly, with no shocks given to business confidence by rash legislation.

An American contemporary, Senator George Frisbie Hoar of Massachusetts, said:

The men who do the work of piety and charity in our churches, the men who administer our school system, the men who own and till their own farms, the men who perform skilled labor in the shops, the soldiers, the men who went to war and stayed all through, the men who paid the debt and kept the currency sound and saved the nation's honor, the men who saved the country in war and have made it worth living in peace, commonly and as a rule, by the natural law of their being, find their places in the Republican party. While the old slave-owner and slave-driver, the saloon keeper, the ballot box stuffer, the Ku Klux Klan, the criminal class of the great cities, the men who cannot read or write, commonly and as a rule, by the natural law of their being, find their cogenial place in the Democratic party.*

There is more than the confidence of wealth and class in this statement. There is the arrogance, which always surprises Europeans, including the English, of those described by demographers as white Anglo-Saxon Protestants, native-born of native parentage. In the Census Bureau they are known as WASP-NN. Ben Wattenberg, co-author of *This U.S.A.* (with Richard Scammon, then Director of the Bureau of the Census), wrote in 1965:

Some day someone will write an inspiring piece about one of America's greatest and most colorful minority groups. They came here on crowded ships, were resented by the natives and had to struggle mightily for every advance they made against a hostile environment. Despite these handicaps, despite even a skin color different from native Americans, this hardy

* Theodore H. White, *The Making of the President, 1960,* New York, Atheneum, 1961.

group prospered and, in prospering, helped build the nation. They fought in her wars, guided her commerce, developed her transportation, built her buildings. The debt that the country owes to their particular group of immigrants can never be over-estimated. In short, like most American minority groups, they made good citizens.

The only thing different about the group is that it is the one traditionally viewed as the "American majority." For the minority group described is of course the "White Anglo-Saxon Protestant," further qualified today as "native-born of native parentage." The key point is that neither the WASP–NN, nor any solidified ethnic or religious group constitutes an "American majority." That America is indeed still a nation of immigrant and minority groups can be clearly seen from these numbers, taken from the 1960 Census and from *Current Population Survey* reports:

11 percent of our population is non-white: 14 percent of our population is of foreign or mixed foreign parentage: 5 percent of our population is foreign-born: 26 percent of our population is Catholic: 3 percent of our population is Jewish: 65 percent of our population is not of Anglo-Saxon derivation.

In Senator Hoar's day the WASPs were probably still the majority, and they were certainly the most dominant group. In the Forty-fifth Congress (1877–79), chronologically the halfway Congress, there was only a handful of members whose names suggest that they were not of Anglo-Saxon origin. Perhaps even in those days the largest single concentration of WASPs was in the South, but in the eyes of the Republican North they were rebels, old slaveowners and Klansmen. They were also economically depressed. In their heyday the Republicans had another source of strength. They were the victors of the Civil War. They dominated the South until the disputed Presidential election of 1876, but for long after they could depend upon the support in the North of the Grand Army of the Republic. This veterans' organization was supposedly nonpolitical, but its 400,000-odd members formed a reliable bloc for the party from 1872 to 1904. Pension legislation was enacted with their support in mind, and they were the backbone of the party organization in the states.

All this has gone. The last GAR veteran to march in patriotic parades was buried long ago. The WASPs still mainly make up the American Establishment, and wield a pervasive influence, but they are an electoral minority. Much of the old idealism has gone. It was the Democrats who introduced the great Civil Rights legislation of the 1960s, despite the interparty strife and the earlier but brief emergence of the Dixiecrats, a segregationist splinter group. In the 1964 Presidential campaign, the Republicans, the party of Lincoln, sought victory in alliance with white supremacists in the South, and suffered the most overwhelming defeat in American history.

The decline began long before, mainly because of the party's indifference toward social problems and disdain of immigrants from Eastern and Southern Europe. In a way, the party was rather like the giant corporations of bygone days whose interests it still represented. For decades they ignored the social and environmental problems created by their expansion, and had to be reminded the hard way. For instance, industrial unrest was endemic and violence brutal, but eventually they came to terms with organized labor. The increased purchasing power from higher wages contributed, if only indirectly, to their further expansion. Many corporations are now supergiants because they adjusted themselves, no matter how unwillingly, to the revolutions of technology and rising expectations. Not so the Republicans, and the party declined as would any corporation that ignored the facts of modern life.

The evidence is in their failure to attract the urban vote. The reasons are well understood by the moderates in the party, but they have yet to persuade the conservative majority of the need for change. Men such as Governor Nelson Rockefeller of New York and Senator Edward Brooke of Massachusetts, who is a Negro, have demonstrated the connection between a concern for the cities and electoral victory, but they can be charged with "me-tooism."

It is a catchy but misleading label. Successful liberal and moderate Republicans do not so much emulate the Democrats as show an intense awareness of what is required of the party in the second half of the twentieth century. The vast majority of Americans are now city dwellers and wage earners. Their requirements, from job security to clean air, from better education for the children to slum clearance, can for the most part be met only by concerted action by city, state, or federal government and private initiative. The traditional laissez-faire attitude of conservative Republicans is largely irrelevant to their needs.

The party ought also to strengthen its position in the South if it is to be a truly national party. The so-called Southern strategy of the 1964 campaign, which called for electoral gains in the old Confederate states to balance Democratic strength in the cities, threatened to set it on a disastrous lily-white course. Much of the Southern support it now enjoys is undoubtedly racist, but the possibility exists of a two-party system in the South. Both the party and the South would gain.

The Republicans will remain what I chose to describe as a half-party until they broaden their popular and regional support. In any event, there will be Republican Presidents in the future, and they are not condemned to minority status in Congress. Both can be assumed with confidence. Parties in power exhaust themselves or lose touch with the electorate. They become tarnished with corruption, or the suspicion of it. The independent vote cannot be forgotten, nor the encyclical nature of the two-party system.

A majority can decide that the time for political action has come, as in 1932 and 1960. It can also decide that a pause is required, as in 1952 and perhaps in 1968 and 1972. The Great Society programs of President Johnson carry the seeds of political defeat. Democrats also have something of a reputation of being the war party, and wars are rarely popular, as they were reminded by the 1966 mid-term elections. The political pendulum must swing in political democracies, even in socialist Scandinavia, and a popular Presidential candidate adds weight to the pendulum. President Eisenhower is the obvious example, but the Republicans managed to lose control of Congress under his benign Presidency. At the time of writing, they still lacked a *raison d'être* in the new American pluralistic society, except the necessity for an alternative party.

Brief accounts can be misleading, especially when the subject is as amorphous as American political parties. Lines cannot be sharply drawn. There have always been some Republicans in the South, and wealthy Episcopalians with proud Anglo-Saxon family trees are Democrats. The contradictions of human nature are no less numerous in the United States, but three out of four Americans are said to inherit their political allegiances.

Theodore Roosevelt McKeldin, the Republican Mayor of Baltimore, said it rather better one wet night as he waited at a helicopter pad to pledge fealty to President Johnson, a Democrat, during the 1964 campaign: "An American takes his religion from his mother, and his politics from his father." Americans are not known for ancestor worship, and it is safe to assume that they are largely influenced by their economic, ethnic, and regional backgrounds.

Generally speaking, the rich or well-to-do and professional people vote Republican, as do many of the older Protestant stock in the North. The converse is held to be generally true of the Democrats, although race rather than the lack of patrimony is supposed to explain much of its appeal. With the exception of its Southern section, the Democrats are the immigrant party. The Irish, the Italians, the Poles, and the Slavs tend to be Democrats. A few tend to change parties as they scale the economic and social ladder. The vast majority of wealthy Irish-Americans vote Republican with other members of the country club, despite the Kennedys, except of course when an Irish-American is a candidate. There are exceptions. Jews, rich and poor, used to vote Republican, but now, with Negroes, tend to vote Democratic.

As noted in an earlier chapter, the Democratic right wing is often more conservative than the Republican left. As much can be said of the Labour and Conservative parties in Britain. There is nothing odd about this when a nation the size of the United States has to divide into two or one and a half parties despite regional, economic, racial, and social differences. Conditions have also changed. The South was once against high tariffs, one of the first political objectives of the commercial and industrial North, but has become increasingly protectionist with partial industrialization. Its Congressmen, moreover, have combined with their Republican colleagues from the Midwest to defend their mutual agricultural interests. Similar changes have occurred in traditionally Republican areas. Eastern Republicans have long been internationalists, and their support of the postwar foreign and national security policies moved them to the left of their party. A few generations of wealth have also liberalized their social attitudes.

This tendency to meet and overlap at the center, although not unknown elsewhere, presumably explains the belief widely held in Europe that there is little or no difference between the parties. It is erroneous. I have noted here some of the tendencies that help to distinguish Democrats and Republicans, many of which have become increasingly evident as the triple revolution has taken effect. They now have characteristics—it is difficult to think of a more specific word—almost amounting to ideologies in the American circumstance. The Democrats on the whole depend upon federal action. The Republicans tend to be suspicious of Washington, and oppose what they choose to see as federal interference in the affairs of the states.

The reasons can, of course, be found in the platforms and memberships of the two parties. It is true that in their resistance to racial progress the Southern Democrats are ardent supporters of states' rights. Nevertheless, the liberal objectives pursued by the party, from conviction as well as the need to keep the voters happy, demand federal action. Social Security, medical care for the aged, assistance for education, the alleviation of poverty, and urban renewal can only be effectively launched and administered on a federal scale. Equally clearly, the innate conservatism of the Republican regulars can best be defended in state legislatures. With very few exceptions, history proves that Republicans seek the Presidency in order to diminish the involvement of the federal government in internal affairs.

The most notable exception was, of course, Theodore Roosevelt, who was not exactly popular with the party regulars. His nomination for the Vice Presidency was an obvious attempt to put him on the shelf, but he became President when McKinley was assassinated. He was a forerunner of the modern President, who sensed the greatness of the country, and also recognized the growing demand for social reform. Party resistance was evident when he sought the Presidential nomination again in 1912 against Taft. The conservative forces proved to be superior, and he withdrew from the party to be nominated as the Progressive candidate at the Bull Moose Convention.

At more recent Republican conventions, the moderates managed to influence the nomination of the Presidential candidate, but the radical right wing and conservatives prevailed in 1964. It was an unmitigated disaster, but there was some logic in the rejected program of Senator Goldwater. For reasons that have already been explained, he in fact ran against federal government. His program was extreme, in that he even wanted to divest the President of the control of nuclear weapons and hand it over to Army commanders, the military equivalent of state governors, but it appealed to many conservative Republicans.

The radical right wing, whose capture of the Republican party in 1964 surprised so many people, is not a recent phenomenon. It is, in fact, representative of the one real political ideology the country has ever produced: Americanism. It is nationalistic and intemperate, and some of the modern ideologues have been compared with Fascists and Nazis. That is a slight exaggeration, but they are not dissimilar to the later shoguns of Japan. Apart from their narrow nationalism and racialism, they are as terrified of outside influences as were the Japanese when Commodore Perry anchored off Yedo. In their extremism, however, they are very American.

The Puritans were extremists, as were those who practiced genocide against the Red Indian. The War of 1812 would not have been fought if extremists had been less numerous. Extremism on both sides made the Civil War inevitable and the Reconstruction period unnecessarily damaging. In more recent times there was industrial violence and the "Red scares" with their deportation of innocent immigrants. The Ku Klux Klan, McCarthyism, and perhaps the brinkmanship of the Dullesian period and the so-called liberation policy are all variations on a very old American theme. This is not to suggest that all Americans are violent or extremists. The vast majority are amiable, moderate, and unassuming. Professor Jacques Barzun said that Americans were the prosperous poor, who have inherited from the European poor a diffused amiability, a restraint in social intercourse, and an inbred recognition that they must live together and had best be pleasant to one another.

Extremism and violence are nevertheless more evident in the United States than in comparable democratic societies, and history and recent experience suggest that extremism at least is a characteristic of the White Anglo-Saxon Protestant. The suggestion that this pillar of propriety is extremist is perhaps outrageous, but the evidence cannot be denied. Cotton Mather was clearly a WASP, as were the circuit preachers who helped to strip American Protestantism of much of its intellectualism. They perhaps explain why more extremists are found in the fundamentalist religious sects. The extremism and anti-intellectualism of the early WASPs reappeared at the 1964 Republican National Convention. Tens of thousands cheered Senator Goldwater when he said, "Extremism in the defense of liberty is no vice. Moderation in the pursuit of justice is no virtue."

In spite of the sophistry, the statement provided a key to one form of American extremism. Much depends upon individual definitions of liberty, but at the 1964 convention it was variously defined as liberty to continue the oppression of the Negro and to return to untrammeled individualism in industry. Goldwaterism was in part a return to the nativism of the earlier Know-Nothings. That curious movement of the 1840s was an extreme reaction to unlimited immigration and Roman Catholicism, and in turn gave birth to the Native American and

American parties. Senator Goldwater was of course defeated, but his defeat was not accepted by the extremist groups, who continued to flourish.

Americanism is a mildly astonishing phenomenon, and I have often looked for the differences in the direction and intensity of extremism in this and other democratic countries. I excluded Nazism, not because I subscribed to the view that it was a national aberration but because until that time Germany had never tried democracy.

History again appears to provide part of the answer. The Puritan religious revolution made extremism almost respectable, and it was subsequently fostered by the exaggerated conception of individual liberty. The formulation of Jeffersonian ideals, noble as they are, can serve to provide a respectable mandate for extremism. The restraints required by modern industrialized life can still be bitterly resented. The resentment is the basis for the latest manifestation of Americanism. In Mencken's time the *American Mercury* said that if Fascism came to the United States it would come in the guise of Americanism. Fascism has not come and its arrival is not expected, but right-wing Americanism is now the most powerful expression of political extremism in the United States. It is anti-intellectual, middle and upper-middle class, and essentially defensive. A prominent American historian once said that it is the product of frustration, and destructive. A lonely survivor of the political left, a victim of McCarthyism, said that at the turn of the century the extremist was a frustrated poor man, but today he is a frustrated rich man.

There are some who claim that the modern extremist is defending something that never existed except in his hot imagination or perhaps on the old covers of the *Saturday Evening Post*. They are not altogether correct. The opposition to uncontrolled immigration, an early manifestation of Americanism, was an emotional defense of the Anglo-Saxon Protestant culture against Catholics, Jews, Slavs, and Latins. The Ku Klux Klan incidentally still lists them as enemies. Today the extremists are resisting most of the manifestations of the triple revolution. The resistance takes some odd forms, against the graduated income tax and the fluoridation of drinking water, for instance, but it has a weird kind of fundamentalist logic.

The modern extremist is, of course, a fervent anti-Communist. Much of the hatred he once had for Catholics has been transferred to Communists, but not necessarily against Moscow or Peking. They talk excitedly of the international Communist conspiracy, but once again their attitude is local. The American liberal, or comsymp (Communist sympathizer), to use the jargon of the John Birch Society, is feared more, although some groups have formed armed bands to continue the struggle for freedom in the hills when the Russians land. These are part of the lunatic fringe, but the conservative right wing cannot be easily dismissed even if it remains a minority. It keeps alive the old Cold War hatreds and fears, as well as the earlier animosities, and perceptibly swings public opinion to the right.

Most Americans, in fact, still appear to be more apprehensive of the left, which amounts to a considerable propaganda victory for extreme conservatism. The visiting Englishman is inclined to ask, "Which left?" and certainly American liberals are not an impressive lot. History may have conspired against them. Populism was a genuine agrarian protest movement, but it was helpless in the period of unrestricted capitalism, divided by racialism in the South and eventually absorbed by the Democratic Party. The brutalities of earlier industrial life produced a strong trade union movement, but for a number of reasons it remained apolitical. The older leaders are leading Cold War warriors.

In the hopelessness of the depression period some intellectuals turned to Communism, proportionately more than in Britain, and the subsequent witch hunts cowed the entire left. Americans for Democratic Action managed to purge the intellectual left of Communists after the Second World War. The party was subsequently routed by unconstitutional measures and witch hunts. If the measures were regrettable, they at least demonstrated the temper of the American majority.

The absence of a non-Communist left, such as the Labour Party in Britain and the Social Democrats in West Germany, is nevertheless a peculiarity of American politics. The suspicion of most things foreign is partly responsible. The development of social democracy elsewhere coincided with mass immigration to the United States, and was therefore suspect. But all third parties have failed to establish themselves, mainly because the Democrats and Republicans were able to accommodate almost every shade of opinion. Even the Republicans absorbed social democracy in Wisconsin. The Democrats of course were more accommodating, and absorbed the majority of those who elsewhere would have joined a more radical party. Hence their greater numerical strength.

The New Left, which began in Britain in 1957 and soon after crossed the Atlantic, is first and foremost a youth movement. Most members are attracted by its activism, mainly against war, racialism, and what is seen as liberal hypocrisy. There is little organization and no common ideology. The young grow up; their movements rarely do, especially when they lack organization. There must be something to replace cooling ardor, and at the time of writing there was little to suggest that the movement could survive the present generation of undergraduates.

All the evidence suggested that the New Left was a symptom of the distemper of modern American society, and not a possible instrument for its reform. Alas, it has already been rejected in turn by young Negro activists. One must assume, unless it can learn to work as a racially-integrated movement, that the death knell has already tolled for the New Left.

Much that I have written about party politics here would be dismissed as irrelevant by the politicians, who have little interest in ideologies and social philosophies. Issues are entertained at election time, but for the most part politics is seen as an organizational problem. They can be forgiven in a country where the national parties hardly exist between elections, and where each national party is, in fact, a committee superimposed on fifty state parties and one from the District of Columbia. Federalism is faithfully and painfully reflected in the parties, and Professor James MacGregor Burns has seen another division. According to his analysis, each national party is also divided into what he described as the Presidential and Congressional parties or wings. The professor, as I recall, took a dim view of this further division, but it was unavoidable with the ascendancy of the modern Presidency.

The first include the men concerned with national and international affairs, who understand that these can best be dealt with by the Presidency. The second include those who are preoccupied largely with state and regional questions and their representation in Congress, the state legislature, and city council. This is not another way of describing the national committees and state parties. The national committees are primarily concerned with organization, and most of their members are nonentities, at least at the national level. Presidential candidates have also emerged from state politics. They can generally hope for party nomination only if they successfully straddle the two internal parties or wings. This gymnastic feat can look ludicrous because it is a matter of seeking the support of organizational men largely concerned with bread-and-butter problems, and at the same time appealing to the electorate with issues that sound noble and can offend the interests of the professionals. Their support must also be paid for in some way, and this gives American politics an earthy realism.

Promissory notes invariably bring the two together, but it can be a shot-gun marriage for the Congressional wing. The banns are read by the Presidential candidate, and generally the Congressional wing acquiesces because the Presidential election is what American politics is all about. There are thousands of other elective offices, ranging from governors, Congressmen, state legislators to village selectmen, and victory is often more likely if the candidates share the ticket with a successful Presidential candidate. The party regulars ignore this political fact at their peril. The Republicans paid the price for ignoring it in 1964.

The marriage of the two wings can be resented. Apart from the candidate, the men who belong to the Presidential faction rarely run for elective office. Resentment in the Congressional wing is especially strong among men who come from the small towns beyond the Eastern seaboard. They mutter about the Eastern Establishment, and the mutterings are often not without some foundation. The Republican Party especially has long been dominated from the East, in the first place because that is where the money came from and in recent years because the East has provided leadership and ideas. It was largely Easterners, or those who had attended Eastern universities, who first accepted the world role of the United States and the need for social reform. The financial center of gravity for the party has moved westward, but for the time being at least the Presidential wings of both parties bear an unmistakable Eastern stamp.

The resentment is enhanced because the Congressional wings do most of the donkey work in maintaining the party machines and getting out the vote. Presidential candidates also enjoy the support of various citizens' committees, which are parallel if temporary political organizations. They tend to strengthen the personal position of candidates, and attract funds which the regulars feel should go to the party. The published contributions to both parties in the 1964 campaign prove their point. About half of the contributions at the national level went to the various citizens' committees, ranging from the President's Club for Johnson Committee ($2,732,577) to the Goldwater Radio-TV Fund in San Francisco ($353,951).

The regular party organization cannot, of course, be ignored. Bryce, who had a poor opinion of American parties, also said that they were like two bottles. Each bore a label denoting the kind of liquor it contained, but both were empty. This was an overstatement, but the Congressional wing with its party organization can be said to be the bottle, and the Presidential wing the liquor. The organization, or bottle, is, however, indispensable even for supposedly idealistic groups such as the New Frontiersmen in 1960. Mr. Kennedy stirred his audiences with calls for duty and sacrifice, but his family traded and treated with political bosses who regarded such calls as empty rhetoric to be forgotten after election day. The prime party task, accepted by both wings, is to get out the vote as well as nominate candidates.

The first is not at all easy because of the widespread lack of interest in politics. Interest has grown in Presidential elections with the aggrandizement of Presidential power, as the statistics prove. In 1964 the proportion of the estimated electorate that cast a vote was 62 percent compared with 44.2 percent in 1920. There were larger turnouts in 1960 and 1952, respectively 63.8 percent and 62.6 percent, but the over-all record is miserable compared with most European elections. In Britain, France, the Scandinavian countries, and West Germany, the average vote is between 75 and 80 percent.

The mid-term elections are even more disappointing. In 1966 the turnout was 48 percent and 32.4 percent in 1922. There are, or rather were, some peculiarly American reasons for these poor polls. Negroes were often prevented from voting, and others were denied the right to vote by poll taxes and residential requirements. In traditionally one-party states the reason for a lack of interest is obvious, and their average polls, often not much more than 30 percent, reduce the national average. Recent Civil Rights legislation and reapportionment orders issued by the courts will presumably increase the vote, but apart from the Negroes interest in politics is not expected to increase.

The American political party, as defined by most states' laws, comprises the registered voters, but comparatively few play an active part in its affairs. The British constituency party, with its volunteer activists and dues-paying members, is almost unknown. In reality, and especially since the rise of the rival citizens' committees, the party is its officials. They man a pyramid of organizations from the precinct to the national committee.

There are some 175,000 precincts, or electoral subdivisions, and the Democrats claim to have an organization in all of them. The Republican National Committee prefers to think in terms of voting places, of which there are some 200,000 and claim about 80 percent representation. The size of the precinct varies, from a handful of people to tens of thousands, and in the larger ones there is more than one voting place. However, with an estimated electorate of 115 million the average precinct has about 650 voters. Of these about 400 can be expected to vote in a Presidential election, and about 300 in a mid-term election. The precinct leader or captain can generally swing the election in his division if he delivers about one-quarter of the vote. In the urban precincts, with their tradition of machine politics, the captain depends upon personal acquaintance, petty patronage, and other favors. The messy side of American politics therefore begins at the bottom of the pyramid.

Immediately above the precincts come the county committees, some three thousand of them to each party, and then the fifty state committees. The latter, which have paid officials, can be a real power within the state, although few of them make much of an impression at the national level. The state chairman can be the creature of the governor or a Senator. They are responsible for voter registration, and must nurse the local organizations, maintain unity, and raise funds. They direct election campaigns within the state in cooperation with the national committee and local organizations. In the past they controlled the nomination of candidates for office through convention or informal caucuses, but abuses led to the introduction of primary elections.

The primary is an election within the party by the voters, registered or unregistered, for the purpose of electing candidates. The first state laws were passed in California and New York in 1866, and about two-thirds of the states had some kind of primary election law by the turn of the century. The first mandatory law, placing the primary on the same plane as a general election and uniformly applicable throughout the state, was enacted in Minnesota in 1889, and was subsequently adopted by most states. By 1964 forty-four states nominated candidates for the United States Senate and House of Representatives by direct primary election. There were sixteen Presidential primary elections.

There is considerable variation. In ten states conventions or state committees of one or both of the parties endorse candidates before the primaries, and where the practice is recognized by law, the endorsed candidate is given a prominent place on the ballot. Most primaries are closed, that is, only registered party members can vote, but eight states have open primaries. In these the voter, registered or not, can choose at the polling place to cast a Democratic or Republican ballot, and until 1959 the cross-filing system in California made it possible for supporters of one party to win the primary election of the other.

The party regulars are not exactly enthusiastic about the primary because it diminishes one of their functions, the nomination of candidates. The old state convention system is still defended on the grounds that delegates are better equipped to judge the qualifications of candidates, and moreover can be held accountable. The state parties, in fact, still retain a large measure of control, direct or indirect, over the nomination of candidates. At the precinct level, for instance, an independent must contend with the local captain, who can deliver a block vote to the official candidate. At the county and state levels, the independent more often than not has to compete with united and well-financed machines.

The primary elections are clearly a more democratic way of nominating candidates, and therefore more untidy and unpredictable. For Presidential hopefuls they can provide a high road to the nomination. In 1960 they proved to be a royal road for Mr. Kennedy, who might not otherwise have been considered because of his Catholicism, when he won every primary he entered. In 1964 Mr. Goldwater, who hardly enjoyed the full support of the Republican Party, did badly in the early primaries, but disposed of his first rival, Governor Nelson Rockefeller of New York, by winning the California primary. The best advice ever given to ambitious politicians is to run for office hard and early, and if they are not Eisenhowers the primaries are the best route.

They have had other consequences. The electoral campaigning season is painfully extended. The first Presidential primary is held in New Hampshire in early March, eight months before the general election, and candidates must be fairly well established before they seriously begin to tramp its snow-covered hills in January or February. Obviously primaries increase the expense of campaigning. Very few Presidents were born in a log cabin, despite the local mythology, and now they must be very rich men or have wealthy backers. In 1964 the two parties declared their total contributions to have been $32,663,587, but this was perhaps only a third or quarter of the actual money received, and $100 million would be a better guess. Not every contributor is altruistic or a loyal party member. Some contribute to both parties, and not because they support bipartisanship in foreign policy. The messy, or, if you like, realistic, side of American politics reaches up from the precinct to the Presidential level.

The high cost of American politics has led to demands for reform, but previous attempts have not been altogether successful. The Corrupt Practices Act of 1925 and subsequent legislation are riddled with loopholes. Further legislation was enacted in 1966, in the form of a rider to a foreign investment bill, that was at least novel. It recognized that election spending was impossible to control, and instead provided for contributions from the income tax. Taxpayers were given the opportunity to direct that one dollar of their tax money be paid into a central fund which would be shared equally between the two parties, or with a third party if it fulfilled certain conditions.

The law was repealed; its constitutionality was in question because it appeared to encroach upon Congressional authority. It also seemed to be a dangerous precedent. If taxpayers could direct that their tax dollars be spent on the political parties, why should they not decide that the remainder be spent on roads and the like and not on foreign aid? If it had survived, considerable power would have been returned to the national committees. With anything up to $60 million to spend between them, they could considerably weaken extraparty organizations such as the citizens' committees.

Reported political spending at the national level has increased twelvefold in the last half-century. The electorate has been more than quadrupled, and the dollar is not what it was. Television and radio are costly, but the primaries are an expensive factor. One Senatorial

K

candidate admitted privately to spending more than $600,000 in a California primary. Senator Hubert Humphrey's Presidential campaign ground to a halt in the 1960 primaries for lack of funds. He operated from a bus and plunged heavily into debt, while his wealthier rival, Mr. Kennedy, had the convenience of the family's private aircraft and the support of its millions. It can be argued that money does not win elections. In 1964 the Republicans admitted to spending $19,314,796 and were shamefully defeated by the Democrats, who admitted to spending $13,348,791. But very few candidates can hope to win without money. Even Mr. Eisenhower, a national hero who appeared in politics as the pendulum of public support was usefully swinging from twenty years of Democratic rule, spent $12,229,239 in 1952 and $13,220,144 in 1956.

The primaries are an expensive way of circumventing the smoke-filled rooms of party conventions, but, as noted, they have become one of the main instruments of the Presidential wings of both parties. A candidate who proves his vote-getting capability in the sixteen Presidential primary elections cannot be ignored by the party regulars, whose first objective is victory. The primaries give candidates nationwide publicity, that most precious commodity for politicians and soap manufacturers. Held in states as far apart as New Hampshire and California, they can prove whether the candidate has a national appeal. They also prove whether he has physical and mental stamina, and of course he can pick up convention votes. It is argued that they are the one sure test of a man's fitness for the Presidency, and there are certainly few others before he is nominated as candidate at the national convention. Not least, they are wonderful fun.

If that remark appears to be irrelevant, it remains that the hoopla of American campaigning is an indispensable part of the function of nominating two men to contend for the world's most powerful elective office. By the time the national conventions are held in July the choice of probable candidates is narrowed, but the field is wide open to the pack at the beginning of the primaries. A pack often takes to the field, and for a brief moment the shadow of power crosses small villages and crossroads, and the candidates are suitably humble.

The parades, the music and the harangues, the coffee and doughnuts in the local firehouse, and the flowered hats of prominent ladies in front parlors are all part of getting out the vote. They seem utterly inconsequential, especially when repeated a thousand times, but the television cameras and reporters are watching and nobody can be certain that yet another repetitious speech and a dozen handshakes may not move the candidates a little closer to the seat of power.

The primaries serve another purpose. If American politics is basically a matter of organization, the candidate must have an issue. It is not enough to wind oneself in the flag and take a strong stand for God and motherhood, although moral decay is always a good stand-by, especially for Republicans. The Democrats, who are perhaps too involved in politics and mankind to afford a high moral tone, are inclined to pretend apprehension over the Republic's prestige overseas. It is perhaps the only time when Americans are expected to worry about what foreigners think of them.

All candidates have at least the framework of a platform months before they can hope to accept the nomination at the national conventions, but they normally do not arouse too much interest. Hence the search for an issue, or issues, and their careful testing during the primaries. The object is in the first instance to attract publicity, and not to take a firm stand. At first the issues can be only vicariously connected with reality, and might be acceptable to candidates of both parties. Nevertheless, the candidates must establish some kind of political identity, and, in a process perhaps impossible even for the most diligent political scientist to explain, a profile of that identity does often emerge. It often borders on caricature, but it is identifiable. More than that, if the candidate becomes President, it can influence his future policies.

Finally, the primaries have a consequence unthought of by the early reformers who did not like the smell of cigars in those smoke-filled rooms. The men who begin with the candidate at the beginning of the campaign trail, and those who join or declare for him before his nomination, become candidates for executive office. The governor who rallies round when the end of the trail is still out of sight establishes a claim to a seat in the Cabinet or some other high office. The campaign staff men are obvious choices for White House jobs. The rewards are not always so obvious, but as the candidate works toward the national convention his future administration as well as his policies begin to take shape. Much of the cement holding the loose pyramid together is personal loyalty, all the more fierce because of shared trials and tribulations, but there is also a good deal of calculation. At its lowest level, a future judgeship can be the price of some favor done in a primary.

The primary is a distinctive American political institution. Nothing quite like it exists in the other Western political democracies. In Britain the selection of candidates for Parliament is formally a matter for the constituency parties. The central office has its list of suitable candidates who can be pressed upon the constituencies (a Member of Parliament does not have to live in his constituency), but many local men are elected. There is no separate election of the Prime Minister. The leader of the victorious party is invited by the monarch to form a government. In the United States the Constitution makes no direct reference to the procedure for the nomination of Representatives and Senators, and the original purpose of the Electoral College has long since been forgotten. The primary elections just grew out of the American circumstance, and for that reason must be regarded on the whole as beneficial.

The President, one tends to forget, is still actually elected by the Electoral College, in which each state is represented by electors equal to the number of its Senators and Representatives. Each elector has two votes, and originally the candidate receiving a majority was elected President and the runner-up Vice President. The system worked in 1788 and 1792 because Washington was the unanimous choice and the Federalists were in the ascendancy, but in 1796 the votes went to John Adams and Jefferson, who belonged to different parties. This rather delicious situation could not be allowed to remain unchanged (otherwise Mr. Goldwater might have been Vice President to President Johnson), and in 1804 the Twelfth Amendment was duly ratified. It requires the electors to vote separately for President and Vice President.

The Constitution left to the states the method of choosing the electors, and they were first appointed by the legislatures because the people, despite the constitutional rhetoric, were thought to be unfit to participate directly. In the early nineteenth century, however, a majority of states decided under political pressure that they must be elected by popular vote. Most of them were at first elected from districts, but to avoid a split vote and to strengthen the power of the state parties, the unit rule or general ticket system was adopted. That is, all of a state's electoral votes go to the party which wins a popular majority or plurality in the general election. This is the law, but in a few Southern states, notably Alabama, the nominally Democratic state has gone to a Dixiecrat or segregationist candidate. Such gestures were, of course, no more than a protest against the national Democratic Party's policy of integration.

The electors, most of them men of little political consequence, are therefore now nothing more than counters in an elaborate system devised to maintain federalism. Efforts to reform the college or replace it with a direct federal popular vote have failed. The voter still does not vote for a Presidential candidate but for a state slate of electors pledged to a candidate. In fact, from 1820 to 1964 only eight of the 14,554 electors cast their votes contrary to instruction. In the event that no candidate receives a majority of electoral votes the election is decided by the House of Representatives. Each of the state delegations is allowed one vote. Nevertheless, fourteen Presidents have been elected who did not receive a popular majority vote, most of them in three- or four-corner fights. Three actually won fewer popular votes than their leading opponents.

State legislation providing for the unit vote could not, of course, provide for the election of national candidates. The first answer was the caucus, but in 1824 three candidates campaigned without party endorsement, and in 1828 Jackson appealed successfully to the country through a combination of state caucuses, informal conventions, and public campaigning. The first nominating convention was held in 1831 by the now almost forgotten Anti-Mason Party at Baltimore, and by 1840 the national party convention was established to nominate Presidential candidates and agree upon the platforms. The national conventions are therefore an old and well-tried institution.

They are also what American politics are all about because, as Hamilton prophesied, every vital question of state is now merged with the question of who will be the next President. The stakes are enormous and obvious, and not only for the country as a whole or for the world. There are the spoils of victory for the parties, and for candidates in marginal Congressional seats an attractive Presidential candidate can make all the difference between victory and defeat. The record shows that being swept into office on the coat tails of the Presidential candidate is no empty figure of speech.

The late Will Rogers said that the national conventions were the Fourth of July celebrations of national politics. They are indeed a colorful spectator sport commanding universal attention, but their prime function of nominating Presidential candidates has been somewhat diminished. The nomination is now more often fought for and won in the primaries, and the convention confirms rather than confers the nomination upon the most successful man. If the number of ballots required to nominate a candidate is any guide, the last real contest at a Democratic convention was in 1924 at New York. No less than 103 ballots were taken to break the deadlock between Alfred Smith and William McAdoo by nominating the unfortunate John Davis. For the Republicans it was in 1920, when Warren Harding was chosen after ten ballots. At subsequent conventions all but two Democratic candidates were nominated on the first ballot or by acclamation (Franklin Roosevelt in 1936 at Philadelphia), and the Republican record is similar.

This demonstrates the far-reaching consequences of the primary elections, which have removed much of the nominating process not only from the legendary smoke-filled room but almost from the conventions. What is left can be little more than an elaborate ritual. One reason for instant nominations is that few leaders of state delegations want to be on the losing side, and a candidate who has established himself in the primaries or by any other means therefore begins with an enormous advantage. Nevertheless, calculation and bargaining remain to be done at the convention, although generally not on the floor. The candidate must call on state delegations with favorite sons to trade, and the party leaders have to decide whether the nomination is possible on the first ballot. To that extent the final phase of the nominating process can still return to smoke-filled hotel rooms.

The conventions, however, are not so mechanical as the record would suggest. They are open by invitation to the public, which on occasions in the past has marginally influenced the nomination. Lincoln's supporters packed the galleries at Chicago in 1860, and contributed to his victory over Seward. In a more recent decade, the galleries influenced the nomination of Wendell Willkie, a dark-horse candidate who came to the fore when the front runners were deadlocked. The conventions keep alive the romantic idea that lost causes are not irrevocably lost, and deadlocks could appear again. They also serve the most important function of welding the parties into a concentrated state of national unity.

This is not for public demonstration purposes only. The first fundamental step toward unity is the seating of state delegations.

Each party has its own formula for apportioning delegates. The Republicans are stricter than the Democrats to the extent that their formula is stipulated by the preceding conventions and may not be changed by the national committee. At the Republican National Convention in San Francisco in 1964 each state was apportioned four delegates-at-large, two for each of its serving members in the House of Representatives, six for states which voted for the previous Presidential candidate or elected a U.S. Senator or state governor, and one or more delegates for districts which voted with various degrees of enthusiasm for the previous candidates to the Presidency and House of Representatives. With special allotments for the District of Columbia, Puerto Rico, and the Virgin Islands, the total was 1,308. At their national convention at Atlantic City in 1964, the Democrats rewarded past services more handsomely. Their formula was three delegates for each electoral vote, one for every 100,000 votes cast for the 1960 Presidential candidate, and a bonus of ten for each state which awarded him its electoral votes. Special allotments brought the total to 2,316 voting delegates.

Each national committee issues a tentative list of delegates, which is referred to the credentials committee of the convention. The committee hears contesting claims, and makes recommendations to the floor. The convention is the final arbiter of all disputes. The seating contests are often important in that they can demonstrate the degree of control the leading candidate exercises over the convention. They often reveal a conflict between the two wings of the party, as at the 1952 Republican Convention at Chicago. Eisenhower's nomination was assured by the Presidential wing when some contested delegations supporting him were allowed to be seated. At the 1964 Democratic Convention a compromise was reached to allow some representation of Negroes who had been excluded from the Mississippi delegation.

The preliminaries of the convention last two or three days, and include the presentation of the platform by the resolutions committee and much internal party business. Generally speaking, the committee produces a platform upon which all candidates for elective office can stand without too much discomfort, but there can be excitements. Platforms nevertheless bear the unmistakable stamp of the leading candidate, and are another indication of the almost inevitable result of the long nominating process begun months earlier in the primaries.

The convention then proceeds with the nomination of "the next President of the United States." The state roll is called, and in alphabetical order each state places a name in nomination, passes, or seconds an earlier nomination. The nominating speeches are short but flamboyant, and are always followed by carefully arranged spontaneous demonstrations of support on the floor. These tribal dances serve no other purpose than to release tension. They are strictly partisan, and throughout competing delegations sit stolidly and silently on their little hard seats. With all the names placed in nomination, the state roll is called again and usually the candidate is quickly and formally nominated. There is nothing more to do except to nominate the Vice Presidential candidate, hear the acceptance speeches, and try to gargle away the taste of too many cigarettes and hot dogs and go away to prepare for the final election campaign.

The national conventions have their critics, but I am not one of them. There is nothing wrong with the hoopla, and it is little enough reward for the work horses of the parties. They are expensive, but the United States is wealthy, politics attracts money, and in any event convention cities offer what amount to enormous subsidies for the honor and profit of providing a hall. Atlantic City offered $625,000 and the free use of its Convention Hall to the Democrats in 1964, and an identical amount was offered by San Francisco to the Republicans to use its Cow Palace. The credentials committee can exert some discipline on the state parties, although not necessarily beneficially, and those ambiguous platforms do re-establish the characters and tendencies of the parties. Occasionally they do more than that. The Civil Rights plank of the 1948 Democratic platform may have produced the Dixiecrat revolt, but it also helped to ignite a social revolution.

The nominating process may be largely usurped by the primaries or the selections of the Presidential wings of the parties, but the final act of nomination still rests with the national conventions. The sovereign state parties, and their internal principalities, have to nominate a man who can capture the Presidency under the joint banner. For each of the loose alliances the brief masquerade as a united national party is the final act of political compromise, and it is no less vital because the choice has been almost unavoidably narrowed to one man. They could opt out of the national party, but in choosing to remain they give the country as well as the party an essential unity.

Bryce had a chapter entitled "Why Great Men Are Not Chosen Presidents," in which he suggested that the only remarkable thing about most Presidents was that being so commonplace they should have climbed so high. He saw several reasons for this. The proportion of first-rate ability drawn into politics was smaller in America than in most European countries. The methods and habits of Congress gave fewer opportunities for personal distinction. Eminent men made more enemies, and were therefore less desirable candidates than obscure men.

Fiercer by far than the light which beats upon a throne is the light which beats upon a presidential candidate, searching out all the recesses of his past life. Hence, when the choice lies between a brilliant man and a safe man, the safe man is preferred. Party feeling, strong enough to carry on its back a man without conspicuous positive merits, is not always strong enough to procure forgiveness for a man with positive faults.

Much of this remains. Adlai Stevenson perhaps had small chance of beating Eisenhower, but it was further diminished because he was divorced. Governor Nelson Rockefeller is assumed to have committed political suicide when he was divorced. Worse than that, according to some critics, he broke up another man's home.

A candidate must be more than a loving husband if he is to entertain any hope of victory. The Constitution requires that he be at least thirty-five years old, and a natural-born citizen fourteen years resident within the United States. An unwritten constitution demands that he must be male, white, and Christian. Until 1960 it was assumed that he could not be a Catholic, but one American in five is now a Catholic, and religious prejudice can be overcome if he has other qualities. It helps if he is of British descent, and must almost certainly be of Northern European stock. A good war record is an asset. These are the personal requirements. Politically, he ought to come from a large Northern or Western state, and be what is known as a pragmatist. He must be a good campaigner with an attractive public and television presence. A President who has served one term with reasonable success has, of course, the greatest advantage.

The personal requirements would appear to rule out the vast majority of the population, although it must be assumed that men of Italian, Polish, or Slavic origins will in the future be as acceptable as Irish Catholics. But once again the greatest change in recent years has been brought about by the primaries. They afford to men of wealth

K*

the opportunity to try their luck, and the financial cost of the primaries has curiously made extreme riches an added advantage. It is argued that a man of wealth, especially old wealth, does not seek office for private gain, and that he will be above corruption. More than that, those Americans who help to shape public opinion appear to have become quite class-conscious. They argue that the rich have the opportunity to prepare themselves for office, that they are cultivated men who can bring great personal style to the Presidency (style is a favorite word), and that they are better educated. In other words, the working-class American is not fit for high office.

Of the modern Presidents, Franklin Roosevelt and John F. Kennedy clearly had more style than Harry Truman and Lyndon Johnson, who of course both reached the White House first through the Vice Presidential back door. The recent record proves little or nothing, except that it is doubtful that the thirty-third or thirty-sixth Presidents would have got the nomination without first serving as Vice President. One must assume, however, that in most cases wealth is necessary not only to fight the primaries but to satisfy the new class consciousness. This recent snobbery, not unexpected in a country of such great affluence, was evident in American press reports of the 1966 British general elections. Their egalitarian authors made much of the fact that Harold Wilson had what they described as a working-class background.

The primaries and wealth have in fact transformed the political scene since the days of Bryce. Apart from weakening the hold of the party regulars, they do allow candidates to test some of the old dogmas. Intellectualism, once regarded as anathema, does not have to be disguised, and if the approach must be tentative, the level of debate can be raised. A great many Americans also realize that the global responsibilities of the United States require special qualities that can amount to greatness. Despite Mr. Goldwater's nomination, it is just possible that the days of the Fillmores, Hardings, and Pierces are over, and that future Presidential candidates will have to possess the qualities, refurbished for modern times, of the early giants.

It is to be hoped that future Lincolns will not be excluded, but the evidence suggests that they will. If wealth is now a requirement for Presidential candidates, middle-class affluence is almost as essential for lesser offices. The difference between republican America and monarchical Britain is astounding. Lawyers, businessmen, and banking men dominate Congress, while the House of Commons has many journalists, teachers, miners, and industrial workers. Britain, it might be added, has had one Jewish Prime Minister, admittedly an apostate, and a transport worker as Foreign Secretary. Politically speaking, Britain is the land of opportunity. Increasingly in the United States, national politics is becoming the special reserve of the moneyed classes.

The election campaigns of Kennedy in 1960 and Goldwater in 1964 are likely to be prototypes for the future. Both are worth considering, although the Republican suffered the worst defeat in American electoral history. The two candidates had much in common. They were wealthy men, even if Goldwater was more dependent upon wealthy backers. They began as outsiders. Kennedy was a Catholic and Goldwater was a conservative extremist. His home state of Arizona, with its five electoral votes, is moreover politically insignificant, but an apostate Jewish father did not appear to be a factor. Neither was the choice of the party leadership at the beginning. Kennedy had to overcome the opposition of some of the most powerful men in the Democratic Party, including Mr. Truman, the former President. Goldwater was regarded as something of a bad joke. Both made the decision to run for the Presidency without party encouragement.

If they had been born in Britain, it is doubtful that either of them would have become Prime Minister. Both were Senators, but their records in the chamber were indifferent. An English or Anglo-Irish Kennedy would have fared better in the House of Commons than a Goldwater, who at best could have been a backwoods Conservative condemned to the back benches, but probably not much better. It may be necessary to add here that the failure of an English Kennedy to rise to the top would have been Britain's loss, but it is difficult to imagine him accepting the disciplines Westminster exerts on personal ambition.

Their campaigns also had much in common. There were enormous amounts of money to be spent, and both set up powerful organizations. Organization was to prove to be the key to the nomination, but organizations parallel to or separate from the parties and intensely personal. Few military campaigns could have been planned so meticulously, with refinements such as investigation in depth of regional, ethnic, and class differences, ambitions, and prejudices. If military metaphor can be continued further, before the nomination both men led cavalry raids against the flanks of their parties, but their forces could be compared to modern airborne and armored divisions rather than a few troops of horse.

Kennedy took the royal road of the primaries, but only after nearly four years of careful preparation. They paid off, with seven primary victories and intense publicity which made him nationally known. By the time he arrived at the national convention it was estimated that of the 761 votes required to win the nomination he could count on 620. He had a lot going for him, as the saying goes, apart from the family fortune and political connections.

Of the other candidates for nomination, Adlai Stevenson was still available after two electoral defeats, but was indecisive. Symington and Johnson were traditionalists in seeing the convention as the arena for the nomination struggle. Johnson, who did not announce his candidacy until five days before the convention opened, depended upon his Congressional connections. They were unsurpassed, but the former Senate Leader was passed over by the convention. Symington had sought the support of the party leaders, and to avoid antagonizing any of them decided not to enter the primaries. Humphrey did, but he was not a wealthy man and hardly pragmatic in his approach to social problems. The calculations of an older generation of politicians proved to be of little use, although there was excitement enough at the convention. The first ballot total was 806 for Kennedy and 409 for Johnson, before the inevitable switches were announced.

A great deal was subsequently written about Kennedy's organization, and of course it was indispensable. But the most interesting aspect of his campaign was how closely it resembled the workings of the modern Presidency. As candidate for the nomination he appealed directly to the people over the heads of the party, as later he was to appeal to them over the heads of Congress.

Goldwater did much the same four years later, although his situation was rather different. None of the usual classifications applied to him as a party politician. Although a Senator, he was no more a member of the Congressional wing of his party than Kennedy. He was certainly not a member of the Presidential wing, but the Republican Party also defied the usual classifications in 1964. Resistance to the Presidential wing had been steadily growing throughout the Eisenhower and Kennedy years, and not only from the party regulars. The conservatives had convinced themselves that the party and the country were going to the dogs, and looked for one of their own to save them. Goldwater was the obvious choice, not only because he was one of them but because he had clearly demonstrated the fact in years of steady campaigning. After those years of campaigning, he did not so much win the nomination as capture the party.

Goldwater also had a lot going for him, apart from money and organization. The Presidential wing obviously miscalculated the strength of the conservative revolt. It anticipated a deadlock between Goldwater and Governor Rockefeller, who had a first-class organization but was, alas, divorced. Almost until the convention began it hoped that a compromise candidate, one of its own, would be nominated. The miscalculation was of monumental proportions. Long before Governor Scranton of Pennsylvania announced himself belatedly and diffidently, Goldwater's organization had overshadowed many state parties and taken over some of them.

There was some excuse for the Presidential wing at the beginning of the campaign. Goldwater did not do well in the primaries. He was even beaten by Henry Cabot Lodge, who at the time was Ambassador in Saigon. There was little of the usual evidence of the strength of his following until the California primary. The margin of his victory over Governor Rockefeller was small, but it was enough to demonstrate his vote-getting capabilities in the largest state against another wealthy and well-organized candidate. It was also the signal, as it were, for all the cells so painstakingly built up across the country to rise in revolt. For election purposes there was no longer a Republican Party but a Goldwater party.

The organization of the campaigns of Kennedy and Goldwater were remarkably similar after they had won their nominations. Goldwater also absorbed the operations of the Republican National Committee into his own campaign organization. His own men occupied most of the key posts in the committee. The casualty list of the old party regulars was reminiscent of a bad London blitz, and was certainly without parallel in modern American politics. The national committee's business and labor divisions were abolished and then re-established as arms of the Citizens for Goldwater movement, which in turn created a network of subsidiary movements from Ham Radio Operators for Barry to Byelorussian-Americans for Goldwater.

The Byelorussian-Americans were not, of course, the only ethnic group to receive special attention. The nationalities division of the campaign organization actually set out to woo forty-one groups. The list of hyphenated Americans reads almost like a gazetteer, and is worth recording: Albanian-American, American Indian, Armenian-American, Bulgarian-American, Byelorussian-American, Chinese-American, Carpatho-Russian-American, Croatian-American, Cuban-American, Cossack-American, Czech-American, Dutch-American, Estonian-American, Filipino-American, Finnish-American, French-American, Georgian-American, German-American, Greek-American, Hispanic-American, Hungarian-American, Japanese-American, Ideo-Ural-American, Italian-American, Korean-American, Latvian-American, Lebanese-Syrian-American, Lithuanian-American, Norwegian-American, Polish-American, Portuguese-American, Puerto-Rican-American, Rumanian-American, Russian-American, Serbian-American, Slovak-American, Swedish-American, Turkestan-American, Turkish-American, and Ukrainian-American.

For the party of White-Anglo-Saxon Protestants it was quite a list. Only the Negro-American and the WASPs themselves were not represented. The Negroes were not wanted. The Goldwater movement was after all a rebellion against the Negro and other tedious mid-twentieth-century problems, and the WASPs were in charge. The Goldwater organization spanned the country, which it divided into seven regions. Each was the charge of a politically experienced director, who controlled the state coordinators. There was the usual women's division, and one to take care of the big cities. Policy was formulated by Goldwater men and implemented by the subordinated national committee. The organization of the Nazi Party could not have been more efficient.

The capture of the party was complete. The fairly liberal-minded Presidential wing which had controlled the nominations since 1940 was utterly routed, and the rather weird political ideas of the candidate became party doctrine. The country was faced for the first time in many years with a major party going to the people with a candidate and platform that rejected the established domestic and foreign policies of the United States. They were more sharply rejected by the people on election day, but for the purposes of this review that is not the point.

The point is that the nomination of the Presidential candidates is no longer necessarily in the control of the parties the candidate is to lead. The Presidential wing, which has long been regarded as the usurper of party control, is no less open to attack and defeat. Almost any man with some of the physical characteristics of a Presidential candidate can, if he is wealthy enough, set out to capture the nomination. He does not require a record of public service, but money and organization. He need not have a program or fire in his belly for reform. He can pick up ideas along the road, or men with ideas, because by the time the last primary has been held there are relatively few candidates in the field. Men who want to serve their country cannot shop around for some worthy leader. If an outside candidate makes the running, he cannot be ignored. Men who feel they have something to contribute to the country must make a choice or remain in political limbo for another four years.

The old checks and balances within the party system can no more be assumed than they can in government, and the reason, of course, is clear. Presidential power is so immense that the substance or the promise of it is hard to contain. In the end, of course, the people decide, the Ideo-Ural-Americans and the Lebanese-Syrian-Americans as well as the WASPs. It is a comforting thought, but nevertheless the system of nominating a candidate is now a little more open to abuse. The nomination of Mr. Goldwater at San Francisco was a very unpleasant event, a ruthless and spiteful *putsch* all the more disquieting because the campaign was strictly democratic and legal.

9 The People

> "America is God's crucible, the great Melting Pot where all the races of Europe are melting and re-forming! Here you stand, good folk, think I, when I see them at Ellis Island, here you stand in your fifty groups, with your fifty languages and histories, and your fifty blood hatreds and rivalries. But you won't be long like that, brothers, for these are the fires of God you've come to— these are the fires of God. A fig for your feuds and vendettas! Germans and Frenchmen, Irishmen and Englishmen, Jews and Russians—into the Crucible with you all. God is making the American."
>
> —ISRAEL ZANGWILL
> *The Melting Pot*

The two main characteristics of the American political system are of course the constitutional separation of powers and federalism, and I would add a third. For want of a better term it must be described as ethnic politics. Its elevation to a place of honor might be objected to because of the unsavoriness of the past, but it has been a great unifying force and still has a great part to play. The evidence is indisputable.

As one must always remind oneself that the United States is a big country, so is it necessary always to remember the diverse origins of Americans. Very few Americans are directly descended from eighteenth-century English gentlemen. Two out of three are non-Anglo-Saxon. One out of every five is listed by the Census Bureau as of foreign stock. To put it another way, 34 million are first- or second-generation Americans. Rather more than one in ten is a Negro, and the proportion will increase for reasons explained later. The Jewish community is larger than the population of Israel. There are more

Puerto Ricans in New York than in San Juan, and those left behind are free to emigrate to the United States whenever they feel inclined. Altogether more than 42 million immigrants have been more or less successfully absorbed in spite of social rejection in the past. The world's largest pluralistic society now flourishes with a minimum of internal friction, for which ethnic politics can claim a large part of the credit. The reasons for my admiration of American politicians were never more apparent.

It has become fashionable in recent years to pretend that ethnic politics no longer exists. Most of the immigrants who came from Europe since the beginning of the century are certainly passing successfully through the various stages of assimilation. The early crude practices of ethnic politics, such as bloc votes and undisguised appeals to ethnic interests, are generally confined to a few industrial cities in the East and Middle West, but they have become part of the political system. Southern politics is largely race politics, which is merely a more demanding form of ethnic politics but in reverse. The Negroes, the Puerto Ricans, the Mexican-Americans, and other racial minorities are still outside American society. The most critical period of ethnic politics lies ahead. One can only hope that its practitioners in the future prove to be as adept as they have been.

Politicians were not, of course, always conscious of the larger role they could play. They sought power, and the basis was the vote. In seeking ethnic votes they brought the groups into American political life, one of the main steps toward assimilation. For those with a larger understanding, the problem was essentially familiar. Pluralism, in this sense, assumes fragmentation, division, and separation that can be accommodated, a process by no means novel in the United States. The Constitution separates power, federalism divides the land into fifty states, and immigration fragments society. The pluralistic society therefore is no more than a further complication in the quest for unity and political power.

So much has been obvious to Democrats for many years; hence their party's success since they accepted the emergence of the immigrants of the early twentieth century as a political force that could not be fully accommodated by the old city machines. The first resounding victory was won by President Roosevelt in 1932. If this appears to be a rather belated recognition of a new political force, some of the blame must go to Israel Zangwill, an English Jew who believed that poor European immigrants of all nationalities and persuasions would magically become as American as white Anglo-Saxon bankers. His play, *The Melting Pot,* is about a young Jewish composer from Russia writing a symphony expressing the wonder of this anticipated metamorphosis. The hero falls in love with a gentile between bouts with the muse, and the play ends with the triumphant performance of the masterpiece and his marriage with the refined and beautiful WASP. The play was an immediate success, and the phrase passed into the language, perhaps because total assimilation was then the imperative of the dominant Anglo-American community. (I use the term in the same way as one refers to Americans of Italian extraction as Italian-American.) The phrase is now outdated as Mr. Zangwill's histrionics because total assimilation in the foreseeable future is seen to be impossible and not necessarily desirable.

The early behavior of the Anglo-Americans hardly helped. They combined social rejection of most immigrants from Eastern and Southern Europe with a demand for complete conformity with Anglo-American standards. Everything was to be accepted, from the Constitution and rib roasts to the Puritan ethic and the Ku Klux Klan. Most of the immigrants were docile enough and eager to please, but it did not work for some very human reasons. Confused by the new environment and language, they invariably sought the comfort and help of their own kind and most continued to live their old way of life. All over the country, but especially in the industrial areas of the East and Middle West, ethnic communities were established. Their social development produced distinctive institutions such as fraternal associations, their own churches and synagogues, and sectarian schools and hospitals. They perpetuated ethnic differences, and still do.

The second generation was often impatient with these ties with the past. They were eager for assimilation, but occasionally they tripped over obstacles as subtle as anything to be found in the old English class system. The second generation, however, did achieve what is known as behavioral assimilation. Many continued to live in areas largely populated by their own ethnic groups, but mixed freely outside. English became the common language, of course, although there are still some four hundred foreign-language newspapers. They saluted the flag, ate turkey at Thanksgiving, and shared the same public manners and most of the popular attitudes.

With this experience, the melting pot was not rejected so much as multiplied. Three pots were seen to be simmering over the American fire, one each for Protestants, Catholics, and Jews. The suggestion was that ethnic backgrounds were discarded within the three religious groups as mixed-ethnic marriages occurred. It remains a valid theory, but only Jews appear to have achieved almost total assimilation within their own religion. One obvious reason is that theirs is a relatively small community with a large concentration in New York. Whatever the reasons, Jews of different congregations and national backgrounds have come together more successfully than Protestants and Catholics.

The Catholic melting pot has produced an Irish stew, as it were, but with large Polish, Italian, and sundry other dumplings difficult to digest. The mess in the Protestant pot is better stirred, but it is not homogenized because of sectarian and social differences. They can be identical. The old remark that an Episcopalian is a well-to-do Presbyterian, and a Baptist is a Presbyterian without shoes, is very American, and there is still some truth in it. The various ethnic groups can also still be physically separated, although their enclaves have diminished in size and number.

Some Protestant churches—the Lutheran come to mind—also tend by their very survival to maintain ethnic differences, as do Catholic churches with congregations with similar ethnic backgrounds. Niebuhr has demonstrated that religious divisions and values can be influenced more by class, ethnic group, race, and region than by theological dispute. This may well explain the bewildering proliferation of religious sects in the United States, and the record church attendances in an increasingly secular age. About 60 percent of the population regularly attends church or synagogue compared with about 20 percent in 1900, which is probably a neat reversal of the trend in Britain. It is possible that Americans are more God-fearing, but clearly the churches can serve as convenient ethnic centers and thus protract assimilation.

These melting pot theories consign hyphenated Americans into a rather unsatisfactory limbo, but they are not in accord with the reality of modern American life with its wide fulfillment of personal hope and ambition. In 1966 it was still necessary for the police chief in Washington, D.C., to warn his men not to address the citizens as wop, kike, Dago, Polack, bohunk, and kraut, but on the whole an easy relationship between the white ethnic and religious groups has been established. The United States accepts the undeniable fact that it is a pluralistic society, and with acceptance much of the old friction has gone.

The vague shape of the present was perceived long ago by Horace Kallen, who coined the phrase "cultural pluralism." He saw the United States as a federation of national cultures as well as a political union:

> The common language of the commonwealth, the language of its great tradition, would be English, but each nationality would have for its emotional and involuntary life its own particular dialect or speech, its own individual and inevitable esthetic and intellectual forms. The political and economic life of the commonwealth is a single unit and serves as the foundation and background for the realisation of the distinctive individuality of each. . . .*

He did not, however, perceive the extent of American accommodation, perhaps because he was of recent immigrant stock. Few besides the intellectuals have been completely assimilated, but the lines are now much more blurred. If one must speak of melting pots, there is also the economic pot. The cruder form of ethnic politics is essentially proletarian, and it has less meaning when Americans move up into the middle class. This has been especially true for Jews. The middle-class suburbs are a super-melting pot. The movement out of the city can break many ethnic bonds, and in the anonymity of the suburb, often with its emphasis on income and age-group equality, the hyphenated can lose much of his past. (Money undoubtedly helps, but is not all, as President Kennedy's father discovered when he tried to join an exclusive Boston club.)

I cannot agree that the United States is a classless society. As an Englishman long resident in the United States, and with some modest claim to knowledge and experience of class, I have been constantly aware of attitudes and degrees of exclusiveness, which is what class is all about. Much of it, but not all, springs from ethnic differences. Professions commanding considerable social prestige, such as some forms of banking, are still almost exclusively WASP. Jews as well as Negroes are prevented from occupying houses and apartments in

* *Culture and Democracy in the United States,* New York, Boni & Liveright, 1924, p. 124.

many areas. It is illegal in many states and in Washington, D.C., but in the capital city Semites, defined as Jews, Syrians, Greeks, and Cypriots, are still unwanted in some sections. Clubs can be more exclusive than in Britain, and again ethnic background and religion can be decisive factors. The escalator to high places in government is always switched on for the sons of the established.

American society, in the exclusive social sense, is of course provincial. There is not one but many. They are therefore not so obvious from abroad, but they can be painfully restrictive. An Englishman with the right accent can move more easily into most of them than many cultivated Americans with impeccable manners but the wrong name or face. There are other restrictions apart from the ethnic background. For instance, much can depend upon the school attended, and American private schools perhaps because they are relatively few, are more exclusive than most British public schools. These restrictions are some of the partially submerged divisions of the American pluralistic society. They cause pain and social tension, perhaps because American society has been more mobile than others, and certainly because class or exclusiveness is not supposed to exist.

The tension is especially obvious among cultivated and intelligent Jews. If their fate in Diaspora is any guide, one must conclude that Britain is a less exclusive society. There are fewer barriers to social and professional advancement for Jews there than in most parts of the United States. The structure of the old British aristocratic and class system still survives, as it probably must because of the monarch and court, but it means very little to the average Englishman. The postwar social revolution has had a greater impact than many foreigners would imagine when they see the trappings of royalty or read the social columns. If the American rural minority is still blessed with an assured egalitarianism, London is a much friendlier city than New York, Chicago, or Los Angeles. There is a marked reserve in some American attitudes, all the more surprising for an Englishman perhaps because he does not expect them.

All this suggests that the American pluralistic society is as complicated as its politics, and that foreigners should beware. It is, however, less important than the fact that a greater degree of unity has been achieved than in Canada, between the English and the French, and in such mixed European societies as Belgium, Finland, and Spain. Ethnic politics is at least in part responsible, and the Democrats continue to have a constant awareness of the need to accommodate minority groups. I can recall taking luncheon with a member of President Kennedy's personal staff just before the mid-term elections of 1962, when more than one reference was made to the President's apparent anxiety over the polls. I was somewhat at a loss because Mr. Gallup and Mr. Harris had reported that the Democratic Party was shaping up nicely. I drew attention to their findings, and the staff member impatiently said, "Poles, not polls." Goldwater also showed at least an organizational interest in ethnic politics in 1964, all of which suggests that it is still a potent factor.

The process of accommodation has worked both ways, of course. We have seen how the requirements of the immigrant poor have helped to develop the modern Presidency, further its power, and bring about social reform long overdue. Other consequences have not been confined to St. Patrick's Day and Christopher Columbus Day parades, or jobs for the boys. In foreign policy the popular distrust of Britain was kept alive by Irish-Americans, and required a Churchill to counterbalance it. The Jews largely influenced policy in regard to Palestine. The German community helped to postpone the American entry into two world wars, although most of them have been so long settled that they can hardly be regarded as a separate ethnic group. Efforts to improve relations with Eastern European countries can count on the support of Congressmen of Polish, Czech, or Hungarian origin.

With the exceptions of the Irish-Americans and Jews, ethnic groups have had only a marginal influence in foreign affairs, although they can be rarely ignored. Their influence in specific internal affairs, however, is beyond dispute. Ethnic groups now have a fairish share of representation in the House of Representatives. There were very few foreign names in the Forty-fifth Congress, but the election results for the Ninetieth read like a gazetteer: Addabbo, Conte, Derwinski, Fuqua, Harsha, O'Konski, Pucinski, Rodino, Zablocki, and of course Mrs. Patsy Mink from Hawaii. Many of them represented districts where a majority or a sizable number of the voters belonged to one ethnic group. The House of Representatives is certainly representative of the American pluralistic society, which also helps to explain the delegate status of Congressmen. The Senate has its Fong and Pastore, but Senatorial names still remain overwhelmingly Anglo-American. The public dominance of the WASPs is even more evident when one reads the list of Presidents, but change is inevitable.

In that part of the political world dominated by men appointed by the President, the ethnic balance is better maintained. For instance, it is generally assumed that at least one Jew should sit on the bench of the Supreme Court. Elsewhere in the appointed world of politics an ethnic as well as regional balance is now expected. This goes far beyond the old concept of jobs for the boys. It is seen to be necessary in maintaining the balance and the unity of the parties, and in turn the country. A special assistant to President Johnson once remarked that the Heren Theory of the modern Presidency as a medieval monarchy was no better demonstrated and proved than in appointments to high office. Leaders of ethnic groups had also joined the other magnates who could not be ignored by the King-President.

The political good sense of the country cannot be better demonstrated than in this acceptance of a pluralistic society, and the confidence in continuing political and social accommodation. Something splendid has emerged from the early mire of ethnic politics for the United States, and perhaps for the world. Pluralism is surely essential for peace in the world and domestic tranquillity at home, and the American experience, incomplete as it is, has demonstrated that it is not beyond the wit of man. To me, it does not seem to matter whether the pluralistic society existing in the United States today is but a stage in the transition to complete structural assimilation, to use the scientific jargon, or the more or less finished product. As far as white Americans are concerned, a very stable society exists.

It is more stable than the federation of national cultures anticipated by Kallen, and the wonder of it is that the great Anglo-American traditions, and not only the English language, have survived. They may be served, observed, or spoken in some odd foreign ways, but the character as well as the institutions and traditions remains essentially unchanged. No matter what his ethnic background or religion, the average American identifies himself with a white Anglo-Saxon Protestant ideal, even to the Brooks Brothers suits and button-down shirts. He may remember his old national heroes, but Miles Standish, George Washington, and Abraham Lincoln are claimed as his own. Some, indeed, have become ultrapatriots, more American than anyone whose descendants may have come across in the *Mayflower*. Early American characteristics that may have been influenced by the passage of time have been enhanced and perpetuated, and they can be divisive at home and abroad.

The obvious example is the glorification of what is known as the

American Way of Life. Presumably it was considered necessary to give newcomers a sense of national as well as personal identity, but the patriotism demanded is something more than simple love of country. The insistence on the superiority of all things American may occasionally be defensive, but it can also be offensive. It explains the shrillness of some American rhetoric. There are constant undertones of ultranationalism, which have risen to crescendos of hate. Mc-Carthyism was the obvious example. It would seem that the old paranoiac Americanism, which was often an emotional response to immigration, has been transformed into an inclusive faith during the process of accommodating immigrants. Anti-Americanism, whatever that may be, has become the major heresy, with the House Committee on Un-American Activities acting as the inquisitor. It is enthusiastically assisted by unofficial patriotic bodies, many of them beneficiaries of tax rebates.

After more than six years of close and sympathetic observation, I must admit failure in perceiving an essential difference in the quality of American life and that of other Anglo-Saxon countries. I can only conclude that, in fundamentals such as the rule of law, respect for the individual, and fair play, it is remarkably similar to that of Britain, Australia, Canada, New Zealand, and the Scandinavian countries, except where it is threatened and cheapened by this clamorous nationalism. My conplaint of the glorification of the American Way of Life is that it has distorted American values.

It is perhaps impossible to assess the influence of the non-Anglo-Saxon majority on the very Anglo-Saxon American system. The structure has remained unchanged because of the Constitution, as the non-Anglo-Saxon immigrants were eventually defended by the Bill of Rights. There can be no better defense of a written constitution in such unprecedented circumstances. The national leadership and Establishment remain very much Anglo-Saxon. This will change, and if there are to be changes in the spirit with which the Constitution is read, they do not have to be anything but beneficial. The Anglo-Saxons cannot assume that they have a monopoly of political wisdom and social morality. I am prepared to be persuaded, however, that the Brooks Brothers suit and the takeover of early American heroes are symbolic. The pluralistic society may long continue, but the metamorphosis of the melting pot may work to the extent that the American system, in spirit as well as structure, will remain essentially unchanged.

The ultranationalism I have complained about will probably diminish as the assimilative process continues and the country grows more accustomed to its new power and affluence. In any case, it has yet to be proved that too high a price has been paid for what remains a remarkable chapter in the American success story. Immigration continues at a controlled annual rate of about 350,000. It is but a ripple when compared with the earlier tidal waves, but the Immigration Act of 1966 removed the old national quotas favoring Britons and other Northern Europeans. In the future the numbers of Eastern and Southern Europeans will be proportionately greater. The present ethnic balance will continue to change, and it will not favor the Anglo-American minority. The act itself is evidence of the growing political weight of the non-Anglo-Saxon majority, which is anxious to reunite families divided under the old legislative controls. But immigrants will long be welcomed because, as the Act recognizes, the United States is still dependent upon a steady flow of talent and skill from abroad.

For instance, the nuclear power and space programs would have been delayed without European knowledge, as the building of the railroads would have been without European muscle. From 1949 to 1966 about 100,000 scientists, engineers, and doctors arrived, most of them from Britain and other Western European countries. In one year, the new arrivals were the equivalent of 11 percent of all American engineering graduates, and 29 percent of the new medical enrollment. The American journal *Science* estimated that the brain drain, as it is known in Britain, has saved the United States some $4 billion in educational and training costs. It suggested that total savings and contributions to American life could have been worth more than all American foreign aid during the same period.

The dependence is rather surprising. Professor Walt Rostow has a theory explaining the economic progress of underdeveloped countries. Their march towards self-sufficiency is seen to take five steps, the last being the point of economic take-off when they generate sufficient resources to maintain future development without external help. Clearly the United States has not yet reached the point of educational take-off, despite some magnificent universities, and must still depend upon foreign aid in the form of immigrant talent from what Professor Rostow presumably regards as more advanced countries such as Britain and West Germany. Their continued arrival will not, however, much influence the one really significant ethnic change since immigration was curtailed. Proportionally the Negro population is increasing at a much faster rate than any other group.

When independence was declared, about one American in five was a Negro, but by 1940 the ratio was rather less than one in ten despite the higher Negro birth rate. The reason, of course, was that immigrants from the Old World had redressed the potential racial rivalries of the New. At the time of writing, however, one in every six babies born was a Negro, and the reduction of white immigration can only help to bring about a larger Negro minority. Some demographers are persuaded that it will amount to as much as 15 percent of the population by the end of the century. The problem it has created is therefore increasing steadily in quantitative terms. If the country is to escape further violence, and perhaps disaster, ethnic politics must rise to the occasion.

The peculiarity of the Negro condition in the United States is not racial prejudice, of which there is no American monopoly. The evidence is only too painfully obvious. The Indian word for caste means color, which suggests that the sanctified segregation and discrimination of the caste system are fundamentally racial. The Chinese have always felt themselves to be superior to the red-haired devils and high-nosed barbarians, as the first Englishmen to set foot on their shores discovered to their mortification. The English were also found to be only too human when colored immigrants from the Commonwealth came crowding in after the Second World War. The same prejudice exists even in deepest, darkest Africa. I can recall meeting a very intelligent but unhappy American Negro in Ethiopia, who had emigrated in the hope of escaping discrimination. Alas, the Ethiopians may be of dark complexion, but they have fine features and despise the Negro of the plains where the American's ancestors were captured and transported by Arab slave traders. Only countries without minorities of another color appear to be free of racial prejudice.

The peculiarity of the American Negroes' condition, which does not seem to be shared by racial minorities elsewhere, is political. The Indian untouchables can vote, but the Negroes have been willfully excluded from political life. It began in colonial times with slavery, and was continued after independence. Slavery is a denial of political rights as well as a crime against humanity, and the denial of those rights was evident in the Constitution. The discriminatory passage is still there, although it is invalidated by the Thirteenth Amendment (ratified December 18, 1965). Article I, Section 2, reads in part, "Representatives and direct Taxes shall be apportioned among the several States which may be included within this Union, according to their respective Numbers, which shall be determined by adding to the whole Number of free Persons, including those bound to Service for a Term of Years, and excluding Indians not taxed, three fifths of all other Persons."

Thus slaves were established to be not whole men but three-fifths persons for the apportionment of political representation that did not represent them, and excluded them from the political process. Slavery was abolished as a consequence of the Civil War, but the Negroes were soon excluded once again. The Accommodation of 1876, which was supposed to heal the wounds of the Civil War, returned to the Southern states the mastery of their political fate. It also marked the end of Northern concern for Negroes, most of whom then lived in the South. It was a political deal, perhaps understandable and even unavoidable in the circumstances of the time, but nevertheless a calculated act which led to the exclusion of Negroes from political life for almost another century.

Negro disfranchisement was not part of the deal, but was made inevitable when the federal government withdrew its forces from the South without requiring special safeguards. Even so it was not quickly achieved because the South was not then solidly Democratic, and Republicans, Populists, and other candidates for political office were not disdainful of the Negro vote. However, the conservative Democrats, the Bourbons, also had economic motives for disfranchisement. As representatives of the plantation owners, they were determined to ensure a docile colored work force. Few free men would willingly work in the cotton, tobacco, and rice fields on the wages then offered. They were equally anxious to reduce the political threat of the poor upland farmers, many of whom had been remarkably unenthusiastic about the Civil War and afterward had even less cause to defend King Cotton.

The opposition to the constitutional conventions of the former Confederate states in the Reconstruction period was vigorous, and the first attempt to call a convention in Virginia was opposed by two-thirds of the electorate. The reason was obvious. The conventions were called to approve amendments requiring literacy tests for voters and the poll tax, and these measures were designed to disfranchise most of the poor and often illiterate poor white farmers as well as the Negroes. The amendments thus also rendered agrarian rebels politically impotent.

The Bourbons eventually won, largely by fraud, intimidation, and blatant racialism, although one radical leader, Pitchfork Ben Tillman, led the disfranchisement movement in South Carolina because he was afraid that the conservatives would capture the Negro vote. Thereafter the politics of the South was primarily concerned with the maintenance of political control by a small minority among the whites under the dominance of the state Democratic parties. One-party rule in the South became essential for the defeat of any attempt in the U.S. Senate to protect Negro rights. Thus the degradation and oppression of Negroes were ensured by perfectly legal means in a country dedicated to Life, Liberty, and the Pursuit of Happiness. In Congress the authority of others to deny Negroes their political rights became but another special interest to be defended in combination and bargaining with other special-interest groups.

One-party rule was equally essential to defend the special interests of the white dominant minorities within the Southern states. First it was necessary to ensure that further discriminatory legislation could be enacted by the state legislatures, and that Negroes could not seek redress in the state courts. There was also the special economic interest, which became more apparent with the later rise of trade unions in the tobacco, textile, and oil and gas industries. Most Southern states still have the so-called right-to-work laws, which hinder and often prevent the organization of unions. Strike-breaking and other punitive measures against labor organizers remain common under benevolent state law enforcement agencies.

Another significant consequence of one-party rule was the stifling of political life and activity. Until recently, there have been no competing parties in the South, but only factions within the Democratic Party. Once the primaries were fought, the actual elections were a mere formality. This is still largely true in some Southern states, and helps to explain the apathy in politics, its degradation to courthouse intrigue or to smoothly functioning machines or demagogues. It also explains the awful social backwardness of most of the Southern states as well as the continued violence against Negroes.

In a review as necessarily brief as this, the differences in the South must be left unexplored. They are considerable, ranging from small groups of liberals and the occasional crusading newspaper editor to law enforcement agencies armed with electric cattle goads and water hoses. Arkansas has produced Senator William Fulbright, and Alabama was governed by the archsegregationist George Wallace. Huey Long pursued a perverted form of Populism in Louisiana, and for decades Senator Harry Byrd ruled Virginia through a machine that was no less effective because he was a country gentleman with beautiful manners.

The South is still dominated by the racial question, and in spite of progress here and there it remains an outstanding example of ethnic politics in reverse. It would be idle to wonder what would have happened if ethnic politics had been allowed to work, if the old constitutional conventions of the Reconstruction period had been defeated and the Populists had sought the Negro vote even for their own purposes. Slavery and the tragedy of the Civil War bequeathed the curse of poverty, illiteracy, and prejudice.

The words of Mr. McIlvaine, a delegate to the Virginia convention of 1901, are worth recalling:

The need is universal, not only in the country, but in the cities and towns; not only among the blacks, but among the whites, in order to deliver the state from the burden of illiteracy and poverty and crime, which rests on it as a deadening pall . . . it is not the Negro vote which works the harm, for the Negroes are generally Republicans, but it is the depraved and incompetent men of our race, who have nothing at stake in government, and who are used by designing politicians to accomplish their purposes, irrespective of the welfare of the community.*

The Southern whites still pay a price for the reversal of ethnic politics, in spite of the delayed but growing industrial expansion of their region. The Negroes suffered infinitely more, of course, and in the North, where so many of them emigrated during the depression and Second World War. Chaim Weizmann once said that Jews carried anti-Semitism in their knapsacks, and the American Negroes carried racial prejudice with them when they moved to Harlem, Chicago's South Side, and other Northern ghettos. In escaping the Southern prejudice they seemed to create a national epidemic. There

* V. O. Key, Jr., *Southern Politics,* New York, A. A. Knopf, 1949.

were race riots in many Northern cities, and by the sixties some members of the Civil Rights Commission were inclined to believe that the racial problem would first be resolved in the South.

In spite of violent manifestations of racial prejudice, there was one vital difference for Negroes living in the North. They could vote. They have won elections to city councils, the House of Representatives, and in 1966 even to the Senate. The election of Senator Edward Brooke, the first Negro to sit in the Senate since Reconstruction days, was of special significance because Massachusetts has a Negro minority much smaller than the margin of his victorious vote. If his election was unusual, recent experience does indicate that ethnic politics can also work for the Negro. It can work with white politicians representing districts and states with a sizable Negro vote as well as in the election of Negroes.

For the last it has proved to be a much slower and less complete process than it was for Eastern and Southern European ethnic groups. For instance, one such group could elect one of their own even if it was a numerical minority in an electoral district. For Negroes, the assumption is that generally they must be a majority. Nevertheless, a start has been made in the North, and there would appear to be no reason why it should not continue. Ethnic politics has already begun to work its magic in the appointed world of politics, if only because Presidents cannot afford to ignore one-tenth of the national electorate. There are Negro judges and federal officials. At the time of writing, there was a Negro Cabinet officer and an associate justice of the Supreme Court was also a Negro. Presidential pressure has also opened some doors to them in industry and commerce. Their leaders tread the national stage with confidence, and are invited to dine at the White House. They share the credit for recent Civil Rights legislation.

Of course they have a long way to go, much longer than their most percipient leaders at first imagined. The Civil Rights Acts of 1964 and 1965, which were enabling laws for the federal government to assert rights already guaranteed by the Constitution, were largely intended for the South. They had little relevance elsewhere. The 1966 Bill did, and it was not enacted. The main reason was its open-housing provision, and not enough Senators outside the Southern bloc voted to close the usual filibuster. They knew that the average white American was not prepared to live next door to a Negro. They were also aware that white support for the Civil Rights movement had declined drastically after years of intense interest.

The reason went beyond normal racial prejudice. If that human frailty must be accepted as a fact of life, no matter how regrettable, there was little of the anticipated white backlash to the Negro demands in the 1964 and 1966 elections. Racist candidates were defeated in most states outside the South. White Americans were disturbed by racial violence, much of it Negro violence against whites, but there was more to it than that. During the early years of President Johnson's administration the awful facts about the Negro poor were given in a federal report on the disintegration of Negro family life. The Moynihan Report did little more than bring together available statistics, but the findings were devastating. About a quarter of Negro children were fatherless, and a similar proportion were known to be illegitimate. A third lived in broken homes, and desertion was commonplace. The social instability, which these and other statistics indicated, was moreover increasing. The report concluded somberly that the United States was approaching a new crisis in race relations.

Another federal report said that the problem was not being improved by education, and a Senate subcommittee investigation provided some dreadful insights. Here are some excerpts from the record of the exchanges between Senator Abraham Ribicoff of Connecticut and Claude Brown, a writer, and Arthur Dunmeyer, both young Negroes from Harlem:

RIBICOFF: How old were you when you had your first child?
DUNMEYER: Fifteen.
RIBICOFF: You were fifteen. And how old was your daughter when she had her first child?
DUNMEYER: Twelve.

After establishing that Mr. Dunmeyer was a grandfather before he was thirty, and that this was by no means uncommon, the subcommittee tried to find out why.

BROWN: Both of my parents had to work to make $50 a week—you know, eight hours a day. That is why at the age of six I was left out on the street to be brought up by the criminal elements, prostitutes, the hustlers, the pimps, and stick-up artists, the dope dealers, the fences and this sort of thing. I had to learn about sex because like—and this was at the age of six—everybody else was doing it, you know. It was the biggest. This was the most we had.

The subcommittee was then told why Negroes emigrated to the North.

BROWN: They were told that Negroes lived in houses with bathrooms, electricity, running water, and indoor toilets. To them, this was the Promised Land that Mammy had been singing about in the cotton fields for many years. Going to New York was good-bye to the cotton fields, good-bye to "Massa Charlie," good-bye to the chain gangs, and, most of all, good-bye to those sunup-to-sundown working hours. . . .

They felt as the Pilgrims must have felt when they were coming to America. But these descendants of Ham must have been twice as happy as the Pilgrims, because they had been catching twice the hell. Even while planning the trip, they sang spirituals such as "Jesus, Take My Hand" and "I'm on My Way" and chanted, "Hallelujah, I'm on my way to the Promised Land."

It seems that when Cousin Willie (he is the one who had gone before and written back) told about the Promised Land he exaggerated it extensively. Anyway, it seems that Cousin Willie, in his lying haste, had neglected to tell the folks down home about one of the most important aspects of the promised land. It was a slum ghetto. . . .

Before the soreness of the cotton fields had left Mama's back, her knees were getting sore from scrubbing Goldberg's feet. Nevertheless, she was better off; she had gone from the fire into the frying pan. The children of these disillusioned colored pioneers inherited the total lot of their parents —the disappointment, the anger. To add to their misery, they had little hope of deliverance. For where does one run to when he's already in the Promised Land?

Mr. Brown went on to describe how family life broke down under economic pressures the fathers could not understand, in the old tenement flats the mothers could not keep clean, and in the crowded schools which tried to teach subjects often beyond the comprehension of the children. But this and other testimony has not had the effect expected. There is no universal sympathy for the plight of the Negroes. One reason perhaps is that too many Americans can remember the hard beginnings of their immigrant past, and wonder why most Negroes cannot make good as they or their parents did. They seem to assume that if the Negro family collapsed under pressure the reason must be some deficiency of the Negro. I have run into this utter lack of comprehension many times, even among Americans with the kindest of hearts.

I can recall one elderly doctor, a good man who freely gave much of his skill and time to poor patients, many of them Negroes, asking why the Browns and Dunmeyers did not seize the opportunities offered by the United States. He arrived as a poor boy from Germany, and lived in a fourth-floor cold-water flat. His father was a tailor and his mother had to work, but there were books from the public library and he was helped with his homework. He, with literally hundreds of thousands of others, had worked their way through college and armed with degrees had successfully launched themselves on professional or business careers. He told me of his achievements with pride while we sat after dinner in his weekend place in New England, a lovely old colonial house, trim with white paint and filled with every modern convenience.

The house was a measure of the success achieved by many new Americans, but he was misled by his immigrant past. He just could not understand that the immigrant from the South is not only a Negro, but a man from another world. He comes to the industrial North from a primitive agrarian society where chopping cotton was about the only permissible employment. He leaves behind a cabin with no sanitation, a segregated and impoverished school, and the Jim Crow customs and laws which have reduced his self-respect and the respect most other fathers can reasonably expect from their children. He knows little or nothing about the public services that could help him because none existed or were within reach in the rural South. He has no savings, no skills, and nothing to offer except manual labor, of little use in modern America. A man from Mars could be better equipped.

There has been nothing in history like the Negro migration from the South except perhaps, and in much lesser degree, the arrival of West Indian, Indian, and Pakistani immigrants in Britain after the Second World War. Their experience has been rather different. They met prejudice of course, but little or no violence. The vast majority has found work, and, unwelcome or not, most of them are reasonably well established in a number of industrial cities. There would appear to be a number of reasons for this relatively painless if involuntary absorption of about one million colored people, Hindu and Muslim as well as Christian, of whom many could not speak English on arrival.

L

Work was available for them. Much of it was unskilled or semi-skilled, but it was work. They also moved into a welfare state, which was prepared to provide for them, without charge or questioning, from the cradle to the grave, or rather from the womb to the tomb. It might not be good for the British economy, but it made the promised land of Bradford or Smethwick a good deal less ghastly for immigrants than it could have been.

Full employment and the welfare state explain much of their peaceful absorption, but not all. Equally important, the average West Indian, Indian, and Pakistani immigrant may have grown up in poverty perhaps worse than that of the rural South, but very few of them were ever victims of calculated brutality and oppression. Whatever may be said for British colonialism, and I have little to say for it, the law was largely color-blind and it was enforced. Redress was invariably available. If India and Pakistan were denied political independence until 1947, there was a long history of political reform. The Government of India Act of 1935 provided for autonomy and full elections. The immigrants to Britain therefore came from countries which enjoyed many political rights denied to American Negroes in the South. I recall this not to suggest any moral or political superiority, but only to show that the circumstances were different in Britain.

The American Negro immigrants did not find full employment or a welfare state in the North. There were welfare programs, but applied in a fashion that often hastened the disintegration of their family life. In Washington, for instance, welfare payments were not made if there was a man in the house, a policy which would seem to be calculated to destroy a family. What they did find was an overriding importance attached to material success, the reverse side of which was often an indifference to the welfare of others.

With the possible exception of West Germany, I cannot think of a country in Western Europe where material success commands so much respect or motivates so many people. There it is possible to be a failure without losing the regard of friends or the local community. In Britain it is possible for a man such as Lord Butler, who was twice denied the leadership of the British Conservative Party, to state with dignity that nevertheless he had lived a fulfilling and, he hoped, a useful life although he was denied his ultimate ambition. The warm public response suggested widespread popular agreement.

The preoccupation with material success in the United States can persuade foreigners that the old charge of American materialism is true. The charge is misleading by any standard, but material success does remain as a motive force and a measure of American life. Ruthless competitiveness continues, if the industrial violence of the past and the bitter resistance to social reform, both unparalleled in other industrial countries, have somewhat abated. It is perhaps understandable in an immigrant society, where economic opportunity was at least as powerful an attraction as political freedom. The later immigrants from Europe were the early victims, of course, but in taking advantage of the prevailing social-economic climate they have prolonged the transition between the past and what should be a kindlier present.

The defenseless go to the wall in such a climate, as have the American poor in general and the Negroes in particular. Their condition is therefore especially critical. They must contend with racial prejudice, with their own lack of skills and ignorance, and what can be described as a thoughtless or careless society. I stress society rather than individuals because the average American is anything but thoughtless. But what is often described as the system—the combination of political institutions, traditions, attitudes, arrangements, compromises, opportunities, and ambitions which no President, Prime Minister, or Chancellor can hope to control—has in the United States tended to work against those who cannot defend themselves.

Personally, I see no grounds for the Negro pessimism prevalent during the sixties. Clearly some kind of emergency action is required, perhaps the $100 billion Liberty program proposed by the Negro leader A. Philip Randolph, if another Negro generation is not to be lost and a national crisis avoided. But once some semblance of economic balance and opportunity is established, there is no reason why ethnic politics should not continue to work its magic. The presence of federal voting registrars must improve the Negro political strength in the South. There are signs in most of the old Confederate states that some politicians will seek their support, and in so doing will represent their interests after a fashion. This process will be hastened as more Republicans enter what were once one-party elections. In the North there is no reason to assume that the Negroes will not continue to increase their own representation in Congress, state legislatures, and city councils. It is indeed inevitable, unless an attempt is made to subvert the electoral process, which is surely unthinkable.

One advantage enjoyed by the Negroes is superior leadership. As with most movements denied early fulfillment of their ambitions, there have been some rivalries at the top. There have been differences of approach, ranging from the cool legalism and political sophistication of Roy Wilkins to the mystical evangelism of Dr. Martin Luther King. There has also been some understandable impatience, which has produced or revived curious movements such as the Black Muslims who preach segregation in reverse. They were not the first. Soon after the First World War, Marcus Garvey launched a movement for an autonomous Negro state.

In divorcing themselves from American society, the Black Muslims rendered themselves politically impotent, but elsewhere the cry for Black Power did considerable harm to the Negro movement as a whole. Young leaders such as Floyd McKissick and Stokely Carmichael were intemperate of speech. There was nothing exceptional in their demand for Black Power—other minorities had organized themselves politically in the past—but they appeared to be threatening the white community, which was politically disastrous.

Nevertheless, the United States can be thankful for its Negro leaders. They are good, loyal Americans, with faith in their national institutions, and are well aware of what can and cannot be done. Most of them come from the growing Negro middle class, who disprove the nonsense that somehow the Negro is an inferior being. Many have been dismissed by their fellow Negroes as Uncle Toms because they have come to terms with the Man, or the white majority. Some are undoubtedly overly cautious, but they remain a promise for the future.

That said, it would seem to be required of Negroes to temper their demands. I am thinking more of extreme advocates of Black Islam and Black Power, but even some of the levelheaded leaders seem occasionally to forget that the reverse of unconstitutional segregation is not necessarily complete integration. Many white parents will continue to reject enforced integration in schools by moving into white suburbs until such time as the presence of Negro children does not depress educational standards. More are still unwilling to accept Negro neighbors. The Constitution is a closed book on open housing, and if enforced segregation offends the spirit, one cannot honestly say that it blesses enforced integration. Americans, with all free men, are entitled to be prejudiced as long as they do not seek legal sanction for their prejudices.

The defenders of the *status quo* like to recall that European immigrants lived in their own neighborhoods for two or more generations, and that some still do. They ask why the Negro cannot be content to stay in his own neighborhood. Their objectives may not be above suspicion, but the argument cannot be altogether dismissed. If Negroes have been in the United States longer than most of the whites, in cities outside the South they are immigrants, stranger and perhaps more worrisome than the Eastern and Southern European immigrants were half a century ago. When they reach the degree of equality the law can provide and defend, they will certainly have to exercise the political common sense demanded by the American system. If this means some restraint, it would appear to be the price of being a colored minority.

Kallen's federation of national cultures may well be the Negro future, despite the talk of Black Power. The Negro community can only aspire to the power of a minority, a power further circumscribed by racial prejudice, at least for the foreseeable future. This is certainly appreciated by some of the leaders. I can remember a conversation with one of them at the White House conference. He was a cultivated and shrewd man, well dressed and articulate. He could have graced any corporate board room, if it had not been for the color of his face. I referred to the lot of other depressed minorities, and suggested the possibilities of joint action. He heard me out, and in dismissing such action indicated the depths into which Negroes had been thrust. Why, he said without a trace of bitterness, the Red Indians, Mexican-Americans, and Puerto Ricans would never cooperate with Negroes.

All political power in the United States stems from the people. It is the theory and often the fact of the American system. These last pages therefore are mainly devoted to the extent of that power.

On the face of it, the people are omnipotent. They certainly have more opportunity to exercise their power than do most other democratic peoples. The federal structure, with its separation of powers and numerous jurisdictions, provides frequent occasions to vote. Americans can participate in local, state, Congressional, and Presidential elections. They can also directly elect a variety of local and state officials, even judges. Their power is not limited to the polling booth. Consensus politics is seen to require the approval of about two-thirds of the nation before the government can launch a major program. Opinions and preferences are therefore constantly sought. Public opinion polls have become an industry, and their findings enter into most political calculations. The people can also amend state constitutions, and decide a number of state issues by referenda. The primary elections give them the opportunity to decide who shall run for a variety of offices, including the Presidency in many states.

Representation of their particular interests is also believed to be strengthened by the tradition—it is no more than that—requiring a Congressman to be a resident of his electoral district. Bryce took a poor view of this. "In Britain and France, a man seeking to enter the higher walks of public life has more than five hundred seats for which he may stand. If his own town and county is impossible, he goes elsewhere. In the United States he cannot. If his own district is already filled by a member of his own party, there is nothing to be done. . . ." The tradition certainly keeps many good people out of Congress, although the distaste for carpetbaggers did not prevent Robert Kennedy, a native of Massachusetts, from being elected to the Senate from New York. My viewpoint here, however, is that of the voters, and they are assumed to believe that the tradition does protect their interests.

Moreover, they can feel that those interests are represented in Washington even when their own party is in the minority in Congress. The political wilderness is much less bleak for Congressmen than for politicians in parliamentary democracies from London to Canberra. They generally retain their committee assignments, and in the other party there are always men willing and anxious to strike bargains. The conservative coalition of Midwest Republicans and Southern Democrats may be a travesty of party politics, but it is assumed to defend their constituents' prejudices, which can be more important than their interests. The delegate status of a Congressman is said to serve the same purpose, and, as we have seen, constituents are quick to remind them of their primary duties.

That said, there are clearly many deficiencies in the system. A true democracy is, of course, impossible. Plato concluded that the ideal democratic state should have no more than 5,040 households, and

Aristotle thought that this was obviously too many. The number of American households runs into millions, and is steadily increasing. The United States is consciously dedicated to Life, Liberty, and the Pursuit of Happiness, but there are always inequities, as President Kennedy once said with infinite sadness.

Some American inequities are obvious. A sizable minority, the Negroes, have long been denied their sovereign power and their self-respect. The recent rediscovery of poverty in the midst of plenty suggests that the interests of a large minority have not been properly represented. The question for Americans, now that the country has reached its present high plateau of power and plenty, is whether the present residue of inequity can be further reduced, and if not why not.

I am not convinced that it can be much reduced in the foreseeable future, because of political and constitutional factors. The first is more susceptible to change than the second, but further progress will be necessarily slow. This is not to suggest that life for the vast majority of Americans is anything but tolerable. The high standard of living satisfies many, although the revolution of rising expectations can diminish contentment. Equally important, most Americans, even oppressed Negroes, seem to be convinced that theirs is the best possible of countries. It may well be. I venture no opinion if only because standards of comparison are too uncertain or illogical.

The inequities are recognized, but the innate optimism of the Anglo-Saxon, which has also been acquired by other Americans, nearly always has it that they will be overcome. This may explain why the troubles of others can be so easily borne. The sturdy belief in self-help can also assuage any sense of personal guilt. It may be misleading, and indeed cruel in a modern industrialized society. To argue, for instance, that the high and continuing rate of unemployment in recent years is due to a widespread refusal to work is patently nonsensical, but it can be a successful therapy for the majority. Those in government who accept, say, a 4 percent unemployment rate as long as the economy continues to expand have, to say the least, confused the priorities of democratic government.

For Western Europeans, the United States is socially a backward country. It has certainly been slow to accept social reforms and security long common in their countries. More important than the judgment of visiting foreigners, however, is that the United States has not lived up to the preamble of the Constitution. I am not dreaming Utopian or American Dreams, but of all countries it is physically best endowed to promote the general welfare and secure the blessings of liberty. I know that envy is one of the deadly sins, but even with the discipline of a sound English Christian education I cannot avoid an occasional twinge when flying over its vast cornucopia of natural wealth. It can be, and ought to be, God's own country. It is not, in the first place because the political representation of the people is by no means what it is supposed to be.

I am perhaps old-fashioned in my belief in the ultimate good of equal political representation. I do not subscribe to the American heresy of the essential goodness of man, but this is not a contradiction. The Anglo-Saxon political experience simply demonstrates that equal political representation is the first protection of majorities and minorities against man's imperfections.

The fault lies mainly in Congress and the state legislatures, where the people are supposed to rule. This explains why Americans have turned to the Presidency and the Supreme Court. The first has led to far-reaching improvement; the second to the social revolution launched by the 1954 school desegregation decision, and much more. All this suggests that where there is a way the Americans have a will. It is also a reminder of the wisdom of the founders, and the prescience of early Chief Justices such as John Marshall. In separating power, the founders provided alternative ways for exercising the will of the people.

Obeisances must be made to the founders, with commendations for those modern Presidents who seized their opportunities. Nevertheless, the awkwardness of such a concentration of power, if not the alleged dangers, is a warning that the Presidential way ought not to be pursued too far. Despite the excellence of the Court, there is surely something rather preposterous about intelligent and politically sophisticated people turning so frequently to nine men for the resolution of their problems like so many children turning to teacher.

In the American scheme of things there will always be a vital role for the Supreme Court. The power of the modern Presidency is here to stay. Both are indispensable, but so is Congress, where the founders assumed that the sovereign power of the people would be exercised. There is no reason to believe that the gentlemen of Philadelphia were guilty of a gross error of political misjudgment, or that the subsequent non-Anglo-Saxon majority has somehow perverted the pure Anglo-Saxon political process. The sin of Congress is original, or at least it was long evident before the great demographic changes of recent decades.

Part of the explanation is the dominant place given in American politics to business. I can understand why it was accepted often without question by the American laity. To some extent, the wheel has turned in Western Europe, where the old class struggles are gradually being forgotten. In the United States it was very early evident that industry and commerce could unlock the country's riches and create history's most productive economy. In the industrialized modern world, from Los Angeles to London, Bonn, Tokyo, and Canberra, there is now an assumption that what is good for General Motors, the British Motor Corporation, and Volkswagen is indeed good for the United States, Britain, and West Germany, with of course appropriate safeguards. I make this point to avoid the charge of reading a socialist tract from the American experience.

It is a historical fact, however, that American industry did not perform its miracles without federal or state help. The early legislative history of the United States turned on protection, which remains the underlying theme in one way or another of much modern legislation and political activity. What has been forgotten from time to time by Congress and the state legislatures is that individuals can be in greater need than giant corporations for help and protection. The harsh joke of American legislative history is that rugged individualism has long been demanded from those who are least fitted to stand on their own. If the Supreme Court, in the words of the American Bar Association, has eschewed the jurisprudence of interests, Congress is still attached to the politics of interests.

Much of its business, to continue using the language of the A.B.A. report, still amounts to a positivistic effort to spell out in legislative terms the property and power priorities of society. In the process, the general welfare is not so much overlooked, but the assumption that it is adequately served by what comes out of the competition of power priorities has at best not been proved. The obvious example for a European is that it took forty-five years to force through Congress an essentially modest measure such as medical insurance for the aged, although it had overwhelming popular support. There was no sinister reason for this, no conspiracy, international or domestic, Communist

L*

or Fascist. Whatever the United States is, a republic or a democracy, and unanimity has yet to be reached on this basic point, it is a remarkably free country. There is one simple reason. Political representation is not what it is said to be, in spite of all those elections, primaries, public opinion polls, and the constitutional rights to assemble peaceably and to petition the government for redress of grievances.

Most of the structural barriers in Congress and the state legislatures to optimum political representation can, I think, be found in this book. There is no reason to repeat them. Many can be removed, and ought to be removed, but it remains that the people, or rather those whose interests do not directly coincide with the property and power priorities of American society, are generally ill-equipped for the fierce competition of American politics. It is often unfair competition, and they can be handicapped from the beginning.

For instance, the sovereign power of the American people can be limited in the election of candidates for state, Congressional, and Presidential office in spite of the primaries and public opinion polls. As we have seen, one reason is the very high cost of American politics, which tends to make many elective offices the preserve of the well-to-do, or those supported by economic or special interests. There are campaign contributors motivated by higher patriotism, but most are human enough to expect some return on their investment. The political machines are by their very nature supporters of the *status quo,* and generally have their own arrangements with those who benefit most from it.

The unmoneyed can, of course, work their way to the top of the local party, and they are not all hacks. Financial support for candidates in industrial areas is forthcoming from trade unions and various action groups, but they more often support an available candidate rather than run one of their own. The ordinary interested American voter cannot hope to have the same degree of control over the selection of candidates as that wielded by the very democratic constituency parties in Britain. If the central offices of British parties provide lists of prospective candidates, the local parties have the last word.

Once elected, Congressmen must participate in the process of accommodation which makes American politics so fascinating and demands admiration for most of the participants. Nevertheless, the process is rather like the formulation of American foreign policy. We have seen how the Secretary of State is primarily concerned with alliances and not countries, with multilateral ventures and not bilateral relations, with entire regions where political boundaries are seen to be meaningless. The sheer complexity of these world-wide relationships requires a continual process of adjustment and compromise, and there can be occasions when other countries feel that their interests have been compromised or adjusted out of existence.

This description, borrowed from an earlier chapter, fits the Congressional process. Indeed, it is infinitely more difficult to govern the United States than to run a number of world alliances. The Southern bloc can be more resistant and inflexible than President de Gaulle, and it cannot be ignored. Congressmen representing special interests can be more demanding than Dr. Adenauer was during his imperious career as the West German Chancellor. It is little wonder that concern for the general welfare can be diminished, and necessary reforms or the redress of grievances ignored or long delayed.

It is also rather ironical that the constitutional provision for redress should be used more by the giants of industry and commerce than by some ill-used citizen. The available facts are irrefutable, and as with most Washington facts they by no means tell the whole story. Reported expenditures of registered lobbyists show that well over half went into furthering business and professional interests. This does not include money spent on advertising and other indirect ways of bringing pressure to bear on Congress. For instance, in the first three months of 1965 the American Medical Association reported spending $122,086 on lobbying against medical insurance for the aged. It also spent $829,484 on press, radio, and television campaigns designed to bring pressure on Congressmen from constituents.

It is a free country, and doctors have the right to defend their interests even if the price, apart from the millions spent over the years in lobbying and advertising, is inadequate medical treatment for millions. The right is shared by trade unions as well as industry. Nor can the arms industry be denied its basic constitutional rights, although it will be recalled that one President of martial background warned against the unwarranted influence of the military-industrial complex in his farewell address. Mr. Eisenhower also said earlier that obviously political and financial considerations rather than strict military needs were influencing arms purchasing.

This and earlier warnings of President Eisenhower had no effect, and for obvious reasons. A Congressional investigation established that fourteen hundred retired officers were employed by the hundred largest defense contractors as lobbyists and Washington representatives. The corporation employing the largest number, 187, including 23 retired generals and admirals and a former Secretary of the Army, received the largest share of defense orders. Rivals could not be expected to ignore its success.

Such business for local companies had also become too important for Congressmen to ignore. A very basic view was honestly expressed at the time by Representative Ken Hechler: "I am firmly against the kind of logrolling which would subject our defense program to narrowly sectional or selfish pulling and hauling. But I am getting pretty hot under the collar about the way my state of West Virginia is short-changed in Army, Navy and Air Force installations. . . . I am going to stand up on my hind legs and roar until West Virginia gets the fair treatment she deserves."

It is possible to argue that lobbying as practiced in Washington reflects all the national interests, and therefore serves the country well and equitably. Certainly lobbying appears to be a national pastime. The veterans' organizations are very active, as are church groups, especially when Civil Rights legislation is being considered. The lobbying of a group of scientists, who were alarmed by the possible misuse of nuclear energy, was largely responsible for persuading Congress in 1946 to establish the civilian Atomic Energy Commission. Similar if more modest victories have been scored by citizens' groups. Nevertheless, all the evidence suggests that lobbying is generally for special privilege, and that the influence of lobbyists does not depend upon the strength of their case or its relevance to the public interest. Since lobbying was regulated by law, there has been little evidence of corruption, but opportunities remain for discreet deals and pressure.

The Bobby Baker case was an obvious example. At his trial, on charges of income tax evasion, his defense counsel did not dispute evidence that large sums of money from savings and loan companies passed through his hands for Congressional services rendered; or that Senatorial opposition to efforts to reduce a major tax increase for such companies was subsequently withdrawn.

Another example was a foreign investors tax bill passed at the end of the 1966 session. It was better known as the Christmas Tree Bill because of the presents for importuning companies hung on it by obliging Senators in the form of amendments. Among them was a tax rebate bill for an aluminum company, higher depletion allowances for three other aluminum companies and the clay, shale, slate, and mollusk industries, special tax advantages for an importer of Scotch whisky and relief of a holding company tax for an electrocoating company. There was also an excise tax reduction for manufacturers of hearses, perhaps a vital aid for a dying industry. Just before the overloaded tree went into conference with the House committee, a lovely present was hung on it for stockholders who wanted to diversify their holdings without paying capital gains tax. This discreet business had been arranged by a Democratic party fund-raiser, and attacked by Treasury officials as a glaring tax loophole.

Even the House committee balked, and it looked as if the tree would tumble into oblivion under the sheer weight of goodies. What saved it, oddly enough, was another present from the House Ways and Means Committee for doctors, lawyers, and other self-employed professional men in the shape of tax reductions on pension contributions. The Treasury Department, which also opposed this measure, estimated that it would cost some $60 million a year, and mainly benefit men with minimum annual incomes of $25,000. The Senate also did not like it much, but gracefully acquiesced to save the tree. Thus is the wonder of Congressional compromise.

The present dimensions of lobbying are due to the postwar expansion of federal activities. Those who benefit most are often the most opposed to big government, but as yet they have apparently not seen a conflict of interest. Lobbying is, of course, only one consequence of this concentration of power. The aggrandizement of Presidential power, as we have seen, is due largely to the quest for better political representation. This has been provided. As is often said in Washington, only the President represents the nation. But there are clear limitations to representation through the White House rather than Congress. One is unavoidable in the American Constitutional scheme of things.

Although many Americans have the unalienable right to elect dogcatchers, they do not elect members of the Cabinet. Yet these men, and many others of sub-Cabinet level, are not mere Presidential assistants. The Cabinet rarely has much influence as a body, but its individual members can and do initiate policies vitally important for the country. The retort that the President is ultimately responsible is correct, but hardly comforting for those who believe in direct political responsibility as well as equal representation.

The President is certainly responsible for what goes on in the numerous departments and agencies. They are administrative extensions of his office. No other person can be responsible, but he cannot possibly be in complete charge. This applies in varying degree to the heads of other governments. Everywhere decisions are made at most levels of government without the prior knowledge or consent of the President, Prime Minister, Chancellor, or whoever is in charge. The increasing power of civil services is a problem that ought to engage most democracies. The difference in parliamentary democracies, however, is that Cabinet officers and lesser government leaders involved in making policy and capable of controlling the bureaucracy are elected. They have at least passed the basic test of being elected by one constituency.

It is true that Prime Ministers, Chancellors, and Cabinet members are not elected to their offices, but in fact voters in parliamentary democracies have a very clear idea of who will lead the government should the party of their choice win. Most candidates for high office have long been in the public eye. Often they have served in shadow cabinets, and have been the leading opposition spokesmen on matters that become their responsibility when the new government is formed. Their views are known, and all voters have the opportunity of considering them before deciding who to vote for in the local constituency.

To that extent the office of Prime Minister has come more closely to resemble the American Presidency. A general election can be a contest for supreme office by two party leaders, with members returned on the implied condition that they are members of an electoral college. The difference is that British voters also help to elect the Cabinet men who share responsibility for governing the country with the Prime Minister. It might even be argued that those whose party loyalty has not been decided by family background and economic conditions can play the three-dimensional chess game of American Congressmen. That is, in the polling booth they can take into account the national and regional as well as constituency interest.

American voters do not wield this indirect control over the future administration. No Presidential candidate has ever campaigned, at least to my knowledge, with a list of prospective Cabinet members in his hand. There is rarely any mention of those who will become the King's Men. Candidates have a position on every imaginable issue or problem. The voters can pick and choose, but not the men who will translate those positions into policies and programs, and initiate their own. No President can be expert in foreign affairs, defense, economics, finance, and agriculture, to mention only some of his over-all responsibilities. Cabinet members and other appointed officials can also hold strong views of their own which inevitably shape national policies, and often they are not members of the President's party. Recent defense and foreign policies are obvious examples.

President Kennedy, a Democrat, appointed Robert McNamara, a nominal Republican, as Defense Secretary. Apart from readers of the automotive trade press, few of Kennedy's supporters could have been aware of the existence of this Detroit executive until after he was appointed. McNamara quickly proved to be an efficient Defense Secretary, but the radical changes he made in military strategy and national security policy came as a complete surprise to the electorate. The need for those changes had been discussed in learned magazines of limited circulation, but they got small mention during the campaign. Indeed, Kennedy campaigned on the necessity to close the missile gap, only to be told later by McNamara that the gap did not exist. The Secretary's policy for maintaining the nuclear balance and preventing it from being endangered by so-called wars of liberation also led inexorably to the war in Vietnam. It is possible that fewer Americans would have voted for Kennedy if this and other probable consequences had been discussed during the campaign. I am not suggesting that such a subtle policy could have been fully discussed in any electoral campaign, but the most intelligent American voters could not even ponder the possibility because they did not know who would be appointed Defense Secretary.

George Ball, who was appointed to the State Department by President Kennedy, is my second example. He was a very good Under Secretary, but he had one personal objective which he passionately pursued, European unity. The policy was fully supported by Kennedy, but it was Ball who was largely responsible for framing and implementing it. He was responsible for the Trade Expansion Act, which he drafted in such a way as to influence Britain to join the European Economic Community. He could not influence President de Gaulle, and the Act lost much of its value when the general decided that Britain was not a fit candidate for Europe. This was only one aspect of Ball's struggle for Europe. It was a worthy struggle, even if it did worsen Franco-American relations, but the point I am trying to make is that few voters knew of Ball or his European passion before the election, and had no say whatsoever in his appointment or policy.

I have purposely chosen for examples two men who would grace any government, but, alas, some appointed by Presidents have been anything but worthy or adequate men. Many appointments are disposed of as Presidential patronage for a variety of cogent reasons, but the preference of the electorate is not one of them except to the extent that regions, states, or groups are rewarded for campaign services. I can also think of some inadequate Cabinet officers in parliamentary democracies, but their possible elevation to high office was not unknown prior to the elections. The American voter can, of course, always express his dissatisfaction at the next Presidential election, but if he is moved to support the opposition's Presidential candidate he must still give him what amounts to a blank check.

The fact that officials of the executive branch must be appointed incidentally explains why the American Establishment flourishes. I have nothing against its members, who on the whole have served the Republic well, but their continuing influence is hardly democratic. Conservative Republicans have a point when they complain of the Republican Eastern Establishment. Professor Kenneth Galbraith has said that Britain is the most egalitarian society in the non-Communist world, which must have surprised Americans. He may not have had in mind the American Establishment, of which he is a proud ornament, but it remains that in Britain official tasks left largely to the upper reaches of the American Establishment are entrusted only to men who are elected.

From the viewpoint of popular representation, I do not believe that the nonelective character of the administration can be overemphasized. I am aware of the Jacksonian tradition of men moving in and out of government, and of the contributions many of them have made, but the practice still strikes me as undemocratic. Too much power is now concentrated in Washington to be wielded by men who are not elected by the people. The apparatus evolved to extend

Presidential authority is ingenious, and on the whole works well. It remains that decisions are made without the President's prior knowledge. It could not be otherwise in the absence of a parliamentary cabinet. Even Presidential decisions can be cloaked in mystery. He cannot possibly initiate all the larger policies. His personal staff protects him from departmental domination by seeking alternatives, or options, to use the jargon. He can keep his options open, but very few are originally his own. The process of Presidential decision-making is a classic example of competing elites, but the electorate had no choice in selecting the leaders.

The appointment of Cabinet officers and other senior administration officials requires the consent of an elected body, the Senate. This constitutional requirement disciplines the President's selection of officials, but the Senate in turn is fully aware of the constitutional authority of the President to choose the men he wants. That authority is rarely questioned, although unsuccessful attempts have been made in the past to dismiss officials. Hearings are held when a nomination comes up before the appropriate committee for confirmation, which provide the opportunity to inquire into the man's background and qualifications. Nevertheless, when the nomination is made, the Senate is often just as ignorant of the man as the voter, unless he has been pressed upon the President by its members.

The press, as in other democratic countries, keeps an eye on the administration and other arms of government between elections, and to that extent is a guardian of the public interest. As a journalist, I cannot be expected to denigrate the press, and American newspapers are as good and bad as most others. Nevertheless, I am not persuaded that they are able to perform all the tasks expected of them. They are unable to disseminate news thoroughly on a national basis because they are regional or local newspapers with limited geographical circulation. Even the best of them, such as the *New York Times,* Baltimore *Sun,* or Washington *Post,* do not have national distribution on any meaningful scale. In many states the most omniverous reader would be hard put to find out what is going on in Washington. Most cities are also one-newspaper towns, and the lack of competition, so un-American, hardly nurtures excellence. The television and radio networks are generally unable to fill the gaps, as was admitted by TV news commentators during the New York newspaper strikes.

Most Washington newspaper bureaus are much too small to do

the job that is expected of them. Necessarily, the reporters go to where the action is, to the White House and perhaps the great departments. Congress is not well reported, except on spectacular occasions such as important committee hearings. The smaller newspapers, most of which have only one man in Washington, or share one with other publications, tend to concentrate on their Congressional delegations and regional interests. But even the larger bureaus are unable to deliver comprehensive and prompt reports because the government is now too big and its activities too numerous. The news agencies are somewhat better placed, but they must perforce avoid controversy.

I am not suggesting that foreign newspapers could do better, but only that they are not expected to do what is probably an impossible job. In the House of Commons and Commonwealth legislatures, question times exert a strong discipline on the government and can be a fruitful source of information. The questions are asked by elected representatives, and answered by responsible ministers. The system is by no means perfect, but it is more responsive to the electorate.

The American press does its best to ferret out information, and act as a communications medium between the arms of government. It is a good best, but if the confusion can be enjoyable, the opportunity to prevaricate and mislead is greater. Questions cannot be answered off the record in Parliament. There are the Presidential press conferences. They are, however, infrequently and irregularly held, and not even the toughest reporter dares to treat his President as roughly as the Prime Minister is treated at Westminster. In the Commons the Prime Minister is among his peers. The President is peerless.

This criticism may sound carping when compared with the achievements and over-all success of the American system, but some of it does perhaps help to explain why the United States can reach for the moon and accept an infant mortality rate that would shame other industrialized democracies. The inadequacies of the Congress led to greater Presidential power, but there are limits to what can be done from the White House even when the incumbent has fire in his belly and large majorities in Congress. One that became increasingly evident by 1967 was the mechanics of administering federal programs in a federal system. In his State of the Union message, President Johnson said that the Eighty-eighth and Eighty-ninth Congresses had enacted an unprecedented amount of social and economic legislation, but that it would all come to nothing unless it reached the people.

He called for improved federal-state-city relations, but there were doubts that even the most modern administrative methods could help much. This could be taken as further evidence of the wisdom of the founders in accepting the noncentralization of federalism. But if the Great Society was too great to be administered from Washington, fifty state governments had painfully demonstrated that they were unable or unwilling to do it alone. This is the basic dilemma, the real American Dilemma of which the Negro problem is but a part. Federalism and sheer bigness create problems that may well be beyond the wit of man to solve.

Americans are unlikely to accept this, and the problems posed afresh by federalism and bigness could be great opportunities brilliantly disguised, to quote John Gardner, who was appointed Secretary of Health, Education, and Welfare in 1965. I am certain that new arrangements will be made without doing damage to the Constitution, but it will take time, much more time than in man-size countries with unitary systems such as Britain.

The majority of Americans appear instinctively to understand this, which is fortunate because impatience can harm the most stable systems. They believe that they live in the best possible of societies, and for the majority life can indeed be comfortable and rewarding. The issue is not only the condition of the minority, but the opportunity for compassionate Americans to further develop their society through the political process, or if you like, to make it God's own country. Patience is not always a political virtue, it can tend toward indifference and smugness, but nevertheless it is essential in the United States because the country's unity is at stake. The North cannot travel too far ahead of the South, or for that matter the East too fast for the West and Southwest. Consensus politics must rule in the formulation of policy. Delays must be longer and compromises more generous to the opposition than in most parliamentary democracies in the cause of union.

Americans must also pay the price of being a superpower rather than a man-size country. Defense spending accounts for about half of the federal budget even when a war is not being fought. National security policy and alliance leadership demand even a larger share of Presidential attention. The price is recognized, and there are those who argue that the country can afford to help as well as defend its people. They are correct, but ignore the facts of American life and politics, and the simple human failure to realize that the United States is rich enough to do both. The failure can be excused. Never before in history has this been possible.

As I bring myself reluctantly to finish this book, the writing of which has been a sustaining joy for more than two years, I am struck again by the American paradoxes. The United States is old when it is supposed to be young. It is immensely stable, but even Americans worry about an assumed lack of steadfastness. It has enormous resources of patience, but its people can be restless. It can be careless and indifferent, although if charity is ever rewarded in a higher place, surely many prizes will go to Americans. It is a land of opportunity which has denied opportunity to many. It is fiercely dedicated to equality and has accepted oppression with remarkable equanimity.

Paradox can be defined as a statement seemingly absurd and self-contradictory, but really true. I am aware of the apparent contradictions in this book, but believe them to be true. They are inevitable in a country which has achieved so much so quickly, and in unprecedented circumstances. But I am certain that within the limits of federalism and bigness the less pleasant paradoxes will be resolved largely because of the greatest paradox of them all.

I refer to my original contention that the modern Presidency makes sense as a political system only when seen as a latter-day version of the English medieval monarchy. In the constant conflict of the Union's many parts, only the President's constituency is the Union, as the monarch's was the realm. With the early monarch, he is more than the chief executive, commander in chief, and all the other vital roles that had to be assumed. In the third era of the United States his leadership is essential. I can think of no better way of closing this book than with the old English toast suitably amended in order not to offend American republican sensibilities: *The President, God Bless Him.*

Appendix A

THE CONSTITUTION OF THE UNITED STATES

Preamble

We the People of the United States, in Order to form a more perfect Union, establish Justice, insure domestic Tranquility, provide for the common defence, promote the general Welfare, and secure the Blessings of Liberty to ourselves and our Posterity, do ordain and establish this Constitution for the United States of America.

Article I

Section 1. All legislative Powers herein granted shall be vested in a Congress of the United States, which shall consist of a Senate and House of Representatives.

Section 2. The House of Representatives shall be composed of Members chosen every second Year by the People of the several States, and the Electors in each State shall have the Qualifications requisite for Electors of the most numerous Branch of the State Legislature.

No Person shall be a Representative who shall not have attained to the Age of twenty five Years, and been seven Years a Citizen of the United States, and who shall not, when elected, be an inhabitant of that State in which he shall be chosen.

Representatives and direct Taxes shall be apportioned among the several States which may be included within this Union, according to their respective Numbers, [which shall be determined by adding to the whole Number of free Persons, including those bound to Service for a Term of Years, and excluding Indians not taxed, three fifths of all other Persons.][1] The actual Enumeration shall be made within three Years after the first Meeting of the Congress of the United States, and within every subsequent

[1] Superseded by the Fourteenth Amendment.

Term of ten Years, in such Manner as they shall by law direct. The Number of Representatives shall not exceed one for every thirty Thousand, but each State shall have at Least one Representative; and until such enumeration shall be made, the State of New Hampshire shall be entitled to chuse three, Massachusetts eight, Rhode-Island and Providence Plantations one, Connecticut five, New-York six, New Jersey four, Pennsylvania eight, Delaware one, Maryland six, Virginia ten, North Carolina five, South Carolina five, and Georgia three.

When vacancies happen in the Representation from any State, the Executive Authority thereof shall issue Writs of Election to fill such Vacancies.

The House of Representatives shall chuse their Speaker and other Officers; and shall have the sole Power of Impeachment.

Section 3. The Senate of the United States shall be composed of two Senators from each State, [chosen by the Legislature thereof,][2] for six Years; and each Senator shall have one Vote.

Immediately after they shall be assembled in Consequence of the first Election, they shall be divided as equally as may be into three Classes. The Seats of the Senators of the first Class shall be vacated at the Expiration of the second Year, of the second Class at the Expiration of the fourth Year, and of the third Class at the Expiration of the sixth Year, so that one third may be chosen every second Year; [and if Vacancies happen by Resignation, or otherwise, during the Recess of the Legislature of any State, the Executive thereof may make temporary Appointments until the next Meeting of the Legislature, which shall then fill such Vacancies.][3]

No Person shall be a Senator who shall not have attained to the Age of thirty Years, and been nine Years a Citizen of the United States, and who shall not, when elected, be an Inhabitant of that State for which he shall be chosen.

The Vice President of the United States shall be President of the Senate, but shall have no Vote, unless they be equally divided.

The Senate shall chuse their other Officers, and also a President pro tempore, in the Absence of the Vice President, or when he shall exercise the Office of President of the United States.

The Senate shall have the sole Power to try all Impeachments. When sitting for that Purpose, they shall be on Oath or Affirmation. When the President of the United States is tried, the Chief Justice shall preside: and no Person shall be convicted without the Concurrence of two thirds of the Members present.

Judgment in Cases of Impeachment shall not extend further than to removal from Office, and disqualification to hold and enjoy any Office of honor, Trust or Profit under the United States: but the Party convicted shall nevertheless be liable and subject to Indictment, Trial, Judgment and Punishment, according to Law.

[2] Superseded by the Seventeenth Amendment.
[3] Modified by the Seventeenth Amendment.

Section 4. The Times, Places and Manner of holding Elections for Senators and Representatives, shall be prescribed in each State by the Legislature thereof; but the Congress may at any time by Law make or alter such Regulations, except as to the Places of chusing Senators.

[The Congress shall assemble at least once in every Year, and such Meeting shall be on the first Monday in December, unless they shall by Law appoint a different Day.][4]

Section 5. Each House shall be the Judge of the Elections, Returns and Qualifications of its own Members, and a Majority of each shall constitute a Quorum to do Business; but a smaller Number may adjourn from day to day, and may be authorized to compel the Attendance of absent Members, in such Manner, and under such Penalties as each House may provide.

Each House may determine the Rules of its Proceedings, punish its Members for disorderly Behaviour, and, with the Concurrence of two thirds, expel a Member.

Each House shall keep a Journal of its Proceedings and from time to time publish the same, excepting such Parts as may in their Judgment require Secrecy; and the Yeas and Nays of the Members of either House on any question shall, at the Desire of one fifth of those Present, be entered on the Journal.

Neither House, during the Session of Congress, shall, without the Consent of the other, adjourn for more than three days, nor to any other Place than that in which the two Houses shall be sitting.

Section 6. The Senators and Representatives shall receive a Compensation for their Services, to be ascertained by Law, and paid out of the Treasury of the United States. They shall in all Cases, except Treason, Felony and Breach of the Peace, be privileged from Arrest during their Attendance at the Session of their respective Houses, and in going to and returning from the same; and for any Speech or Debate in either House, they shall not be questioned in any other Place.

No Senator or Representative shall, during the Time for which he was elected, be appointed to any civil Office under the Authority of the United States, which shall have been created, or the Emoluments whereof shall have been encreased during such time; and no Person holding any Office under the United States, shall be a Member of either House during his Continuance in Office.

Section 7. All bills for raising Revenue shall originate in the House of Representatives; but the Senate may propose or concur with Amendments as on other Bills.

Every Bill which shall have passed the House of Representatives and the Senate, shall, before it become a Law, be presented to the President of the United States; If he approve he shall sign it, but if not he shall return it, with his Objections to that House in which it shall have originated, who shall enter the Objections at large on their Journal, and proceed to reconsider it. If after such Reconsideration two thirds of that House shall

[4] Superseded by the Twentieth Amendment.

agree to pass the Bill, it shall be sent, together with the Objections, to the other House, by which it shall likewise be reconsidered, and if approved by two thirds of that House, it shall become a Law. But in all such Cases the Votes of both Houses shall be determined by yeas and Nays, and the Names of the Persons voting for and against the Bill shall be entered on the Journal of each House respectively. If any Bill shall not be returned by the President within ten Days (Sundays excepted) after it shall have been presented to him, the Same shall be a Law, in like Manner as if he had signed it, unless the Congress by their Adjournment prevents its Return, in which Case it shall not be a Law.

Every Order, Resolution, or Vote to which the Concurrence of the Senate and House of Representatives may be necessary (except on a question of Adjournment) shall be presented to the President of the United States; and before the Same shall take Effect, shall be approved by him, or being disapproved by him, shall be repassed by two thirds of the Senate and House of Representatives, according to the Rules and Limitations prescribed in the Case of a Bill.

Section 8. The Congress shall have Power To lay and collect Taxes, Duties, Imposts and Excises, to pay the Debts and provide for the common Defence and general Welfare of the United States; but all Duties, Imposts and Excises shall be uniform throughout the United States;

To borrow Money on the credit of the United States;

To regulate Commerce with foreign Nations, and among the several States, and with the Indian Tribes;

To establish a uniform Rule of Naturalization, and uniform Laws on the subject of Bankruptcies throughout the United States;

To coin Money, regulate the Value thereof, and of foreign Coin, and fix the Standard of Weights and Measures;

To provide for the Punishment of counterfeiting the Securities and current Coin of the United States;

To establish Post Offices and post Roads;

To promote the Progress of Science and useful Arts, by securing for limited Times to Authors and Inventors the exclusive Right to their respective Writings and Discoveries;

To constitute Tribunals inferior to the supreme Court;

To define and punish Piracies and Felonies committed on the high Seas, and Offences against the Law of Nations;

To declare War, grant Letters of Marque and Reprisal, and make Rules concerning Captures on Land and Water;

To raise and support Armies, but no Appropriation of Money to that Use shall be for a longer Term than two Years;

To provide and maintain a Navy;

To make Rules for the Government and Regulation of the land and naval Forces;

To provide for calling forth the Militia to execute the Laws of the Union, suppress Insurrections and repel Invasions;

To provide for organizing, arming, and disciplining, the Militia, and for governing such Part of them as may be employed in the Service of the United States, reserving to the States repectively, the Appointment of the Officers, and the Authority of training the Militia according to the discipline prescribed by Congress;

To exercise exclusive Legislation in all Cases whatsoever, over such District (not exceeding ten Miles square) as may, by Cession of particular States, and the Acceptance of Congress, become the Seat of the Government of the United States, and to exercise like Authority over all Places purchased by the Consent of the Legislature of the State in which the Same shall be, for the Erection of Forts, Magazines, Arsenals, dock-Yards, and other needful Buildings;—And

To make all Laws which shall be necessary and proper for carrying into Execution the foregoing Powers, and all other Powers vested by this Constitution in the Government of the United States, or in any Department or Officer thereof.

Section 9. The Migration or Importation of such Persons as any of the States now existing shall think proper to admit, shall not be prohibited by the Congress prior to the Year one thousand eight hundred and eight, but a Tax or duty may be imposed on such Importation, not exceeding ten dollars for each Person.

The Privilege of the Writ of Habeas Corpus shall not be suspended, unless when in Cases of Rebellion or Invasion the public safety may require it.

No Bill of Attainder or ex post facto Law shall be passed.

No Capitation, or other direct, Tax shall be laid, unless in Proportion to the Census or Enumeration herein before directed to be taken.[5]

No Tax or Duty shall be laid on Articles exported from any State.

No Preference shall be given by any Regulation of Commerce or Revenue to the Ports of one State over those of another; nor shall Vessels bound to, or from, one State, be obliged to enter, clear, or pay Duties in another.

No money shall be drawn from the Treasury, but in Consequence of Appropriations made by Law; and a regular Statement and Account of the Receipts and Expenditures of all public Money shall be published from time to time.

No Title of Nobility shall be granted by the United States: And no Person holding any Office of Profit or Trust under them, shall, without the Consent of the Congress, accept any present, Emolument, Office, or Title, of any kind whatever, from any King, Prince, or foreign State.

Section 10. No State shall enter into any Treaty, Alliance, or Confederation; grant Letters of Marque and Reprisal; coin Money; emit Bills of Credit; make any Thing but gold and silver Coin a Tender in Payment of Debts; pass any Bill of Attainder, ex post facto Law, or Law impairing the Obligation of Contracts, or grant any Title of Nobility.

No State shall, without the Consent of the Congress, lay any Imposts

[5] Modified by the Sixteenth Amendment.

or Duties on Imports or Exports, except what may be absolutely necessary for executing its inspection laws; and the net Produce of all Duties and Imposts, laid by any State on Imports or Exports, shall be for the Use of the Treasury of the United States; and all such Laws shall be subject to the Revision, and Control of the Congress.

No State shall, without the Consent of Congress, lay any Duty of Tonnage, keep Troops, or Ships of War in time of Peace, enter into any Agreement or Compact with another State, or with a foreign Power, or engage in War, unless actually invaded, or in such imminent Danger as will not admit of delay.

Article II

Section 1. The executive Power shall be vested in a President of the United States of America. He shall hold his Office during the Term of four Years, and, together with the Vice President, chosen for the same Term, be elected, as follows.

Each State shall appoint, in such Manner as the Legislature thereof may direct, a Number of Electors, equal to the whole Number of Senators and Representatives to which the State may be entitled in the Congress: but no Senator or Representative, or Person holding an Office of Trust or Profit under the United States, shall be appointed an Elector.

[The Electors shall meet in their respective States, and vote by Ballot for two Persons, of whom one at least shall not be an Inhabitant of the same State with themselves. And they shall make a List of all the Persons voted for, and the Number of Votes for each; which list they shall sign and certify, and transmit sealed to the Seat of the Government of the United States, directed to the President of the Senate. The President of the Senate shall, in the Presence of the Senate and House of Representatives, open all the Certificates, and the Votes shall then be counted. The person having the greatest Number of Votes shall be the President, if such Number be a Majority of the whole Number of Electors appointed; and if there be more than one who have such Majority, and have an equal Number of Votes, then the House of Representatives shall immediately chuse by Ballot one of them for President; and if No Person have a Majority, then from the five highest on the List the said House shall in like Manner chuse the President. But in chusing the President, the Votes shall be taken by States, the Representation from each State having one Vote; A quorum for this purpose shall consist of a Member or Members from two thirds of the States, and a Majority all the States shall be necessary to a Choice. In every Case, after the Choice of the President, the Person having the greatest Number of Votes of the Electors shall be the Vice President. But if there should remain two or more who have equal Votes, the Senate chuse from them by Ballot the Vice President.][6]

The Congress may determine the Time of chusing the Electors, and

[6] Superseded by the Twelfth Amendment.

the Day on which they shall give their Votes; which Day shall be the same throughout the United States.

No Person except a natural born Citizen, or a Citizen of the United States, at the time of the Adoption of this Constitution, shall be eligible to the Office of President; neither shall any Person be eligible to that Office who shall not have attained to the Age of thirty five Years, and been fourteen Years a Resident within the United States.

In Case of the Removal of the President from Office, or of his Death, Resignation, or Inability to discharge the Powers and Duties of the said Office, the Same shall devolve on the Vice President, and the Congress may by Law provide for the Case of Removal, Death, Resignation or Inability, both of the President and Vice President, declaring what Officer shall then act as President, and such Officer shall act accordingly, until the Disability be removed, or a President shall be elected.

The President shall, at stated Times receive for his Services, a Compensation, which shall neither be encreased nor diminished during the Period for which he shall have been elected, and he shall not receive within that Period any other Emolument from the United States, or any of them.

Before he enter on the Execution of his Office, he shall take the following Oath or Affirmation:—"I do solemnly swear (or affirm) that I will faithfully execute the Office of President of the United States, and will to the best of my Ability, preserve, protect and defend the Constitution of the United States."

Section 2. The President shall be Commander in Chief of the Army and Navy of the United States, and of the Militia of the several States, when called into the actual Service of the United States; he may require the Opinion, in writing, of the principal Officer in each of the executive Departments, upon any Subject relating to the Duties of their respective Offices, and he shall have Power to grant Reprieves and Pardons for Offenses against the United States, except in Cases of Impeachment.

He shall have Power, by and with the Advice and Consent of the Senate, to make Treaties, provided two thirds of the Senators present concur; and he shall nominate, and by and with the Advice and Consent of the Senate, shall appoint Ambassadors, other public Ministers and Consuls, Judges of the supreme Court, and all other Officers of the United States, whose Appointments are not herein otherwise provided for, and which shall be established by Law: but the Congress may by Law vest the Appointment of such inferior Officers, as they think proper, in the President alone, in the Courts of Law, or in the Heads of Departments.

The President shall have Power to fill up all Vacancies that may happen during the Recess of the Senate, by granting Commissions which shall expire at the End of their next Session.

Section 3. He shall from time to time give to the Congress Information of the State of the Union, and recommend to their Consideration such Measures as he shall judge necessary and expedient; he may, on extraordinary Occasions, convene both Houses, or either of them, and in Case of Disagreement between them, with Respect to the Time of Adjournment, he may adjourn them to such Time as he shall think proper; he shall receive Ambassadors and other public Ministers; he shall take Care that the Laws be faithfully executed, and shall Commission all Officers of the United States.

Section 4. The President, Vice President and all civil Officers of the United States, shall be removed from Office on Impeachment for, and Conviction of, Treason, Bribery, or other high Crimes and Misdemeanors.

Article III

Section 1. The judicial Power of the United States, shall be vested in one supreme Court, and in such inferior Courts as the Congress may from time to time ordain and establish. The Judges, both of the supreme and inferior Courts, shall hold their Offices during good Behaviour, and shall, at stated Times, receive for their Services, a Compensation, which shall not be diminished during their Continuance in Office.

Section 2. The judicial Power shall extend to all Cases, in Law and Equity, arising under this Constitution, the Laws of the United States, and Treaties made, or which shall be made, under their Authority;—to all Cases affecting Ambassadors, other public Ministers and Consuls;—to all Cases of admiralty and maritime Jurisdiction;—to Controversies to which the United States shall be a Party;—to Controversies between two or more States;—between a State and Citizens of another State;[7]—between Citizens of different States;—between Citizens of the same State claiming Lands under Grants of different States, and between a State, or the Citizens thereof, and foreign States, Citizens or Subjects.

In all cases affecting Ambassadors, other public Ministers and Consuls, and those in which a State shall be Party, the supreme Court shall have original Jurisdiction. In all the other Cases before mentioned, the supreme Court shall have appellate Jurisdiction, both as to Law and Fact, with such Exceptions, and under such Regulations, as the Congress shall make.

The Trial of all Crimes, except in Cases of Impeachment, shall be by Jury; and such Trial shall be held in the State where the said Crimes shall have been committed; but when not committed within any State, the Trial shall be at such Place or Places as the Congress may by Law have directed.

Section 3. Treason against the United States, shall consist only in levying War against them, or in adhering to their Enemies, giving them Aid and Comfort. No Person shall be convicted of Treason unless on the Testimony of two Witnesses to the same overt Act, or on Confession in open Court.

The Congress shall have Power to declare the Punishment of Treason, but no Attainder of Treason shall work Corruption of Blood, or Forfeiture except during the Life of the Person attainted.

[7] Modified by the Eleventh Amendment.

Article IV

Section 1. Full Faith and Credit shall be given in each State to the public Acts, Records, and judicial Proceedings of every other State. And the Congress may by general Laws prescribe the Manner in which such Acts, Records and Proceedings shall be proved, and the Effect thereof.

Section 2. The Citizens of each State shall be entitled to all Privileges and Immunities of Citizens in the several States.

A Person charged in any State with Treason, Felony, or other Crime, who shall flee from Justice, and be found in another State, shall on Demand of the executive Authority of the State from which he fled, be delivered up, to be removed to the State having Jurisdiction of the Crime.

No Person held to Service or Labour in one State, under the Laws thereof, escaping into another, shall, in Consequence of any Law or Regulation therein, be discharged from such Service or Labour, but shall be delivered up on Claim of the Party to whom such Service or Labour may be due.

Section 3. New States may be admitted by the Congress into this Union; but no new State shall be formed or erected within the Jurisdiction of any other State; nor any State be formed by the Junction of two or more States, or Parts of States, without the Consent of the Legislatures of the States concerned as well as of the Congress.

The Congress shall have Power to dispose of and make all needful Rules and Regulations respecting the Territory or other Property belonging to the United States; and nothing in this Constitution shall be so construed as to Prejudice any Claims of the United States, or of any particular State.

Section 4. The United States shall guarantee to every State in this Union a Republican Form of Government, and shall protect each of them against Invasion; and on Application of the Legislature, or of the Executive (when the Legislature cannot be convened) against domestic Violence.

Article V

The Congress, whenever two thirds of both Houses shall deem it necessary, shall propose Amendments to this Constitution, or, on the Application of the Legislatures of two thirds of the several States, shall call a Convention for proposing Amendments, which, in either Case, shall be valid to all Intents and Purposes, as Part of this Constitution, when ratified by the Legislatures of three fourths of the several States, or by Conventions in three fourths thereof, as the one or the other Mode of Ratification may be proposed by the Congress; Provided that no Amendment which may be made prior to the Year One thousand eight hundred and eight shall in any Manner affect the first and fourth Clauses in the Ninth Section of the first Article; and that no State, without its Consent, shall be deprived of its equal Suffrage in the Senate.

Article VI

All Debts contracted and Engagements entered into, before the Adoption of this Constitution, shall be as valid against the United States under this Constitution, as under the Confederation.

This Constitution, and the Laws of the United States which shall be made in Pursuance thereof; and all Treaties made, or which shall be made, under the Authority of the United States, shall be the supreme Law of the Land; and the Judges in every State shall be bound thereby, any Thing in the Constitution or Laws of any State to the Contrary notwithstanding.

The Senators and Representatives before mentioned, and the Members of the several State Legislatures, and all executive and judicial Officers, both of the United States and of the several States, shall be bound by Oath or Affirmation, to support this Constitution; but no religious Test shall ever be required as a Qualification to any Office or public Trust under the United States.

Article VII

The Ratification of the Conventions of nine States, shall be sufficient for the Establishment of this Constitution between the States so ratifying the Same.

[AMENDMENTS]

ARTICLES in addition to, and Amendment of the Constitution of the United States of America, proposed by Congress, and ratified by the Legislatures of the several States, pursuant to the fifth Article of the original Constitution.

[The first ten articles proposed 25 Sept. 1789; declared in force 15 Dec. 1791]

Article I

Congress shall make no law respecting an establishment of religion, or prohibiting the free exercise thereof; or abridging the freedom of speech, or of the press; or the right of the people peaceably to assemble, and to petition the Government for a redress of grievances.

Article II

A well regulated Militia, being necessary to the security of a free State, the right of the people to keep and bear Arms, shall not be infringed.

Article III

No Soldier shall, in time of peace, be quartered in any house, without the consent of the Owner, nor in time of war, but in a manner to be prescribed by law.

Article IV

The right of the people to be secure in their persons, houses, papers, and effects, against unreasonable searches and seizures, shall not be violated, and no Warrants shall issue, but upon probable cause, supported by Oath or affirmation, and particularly describing the place to be searched, and the persons or things to be seized.

Article V

No person shall be held to answer for a capital, or otherwise infamous crime, unless on a presentment or indictment of a Grand Jury, except in cases arising in the land or naval forces, or in the Militia, when in actual service in time of War or public danger; nor shall any person be subject for the same offense to be twice put in jeopardy of life or limb; nor shall be compelled in any criminal case to be a witness against himself, nor be deprived of life, liberty, or property, without due process of law; nor shall private property be taken for public use, without just compensation.

Article VI

In all criminal prosecutions, the accused shall enjoy the right to a speedy and public trial, by an impartial jury of the State and district wherein the crime shall have been committed, which district shall have been previously ascertained by law, and to be informed of the nature and cause of the accusation; to be confronted with the witnesses against him; to have compulsory process for obtaining witnesses in his favor, and to have the Assistance of Counsel for his defense.

Article VII

In Suits at common law, where the value in controversy shall exceed twenty dollars, the right of trial by jury shall be preserved, and no fact tried by a jury, shall be otherwise re-examined in any Court of the United States, than according to the rules of the common law.

Article VIII

Excessive bail shall not be required, nor excessive fines imposed, nor cruel and unusual punishments inflicted.

Article IX

The enumeration in the Constitution, of certain rights, shall not be construed to deny or disparage others retained by the people.

Article X

The powers not delegated to the United States by the Constitution, nor prohibited by it to the States, are reserved to the States respectively, or to the people.

Article XI [proposed 5 Mar. 1794; declared ratified 8 Jan. 1798]

The Judicial power of the United States shall not be construed to extend to any suit in law or equity, commenced or prosecuted against one of the United States by Citizens of another State, or by Citizens or Subjects of any Foreign State.

Article XII [proposed 12 Dec. 1803; declared ratified 25 Sept. 1804]

The Electors shall meet in their respective states, and vote by ballot for President and Vice-President, one of whom, at least, shall not be an inhabitant of the same state with themselves; they shall name in their ballots the person voted for as President, and in distinct ballots the person voted for as Vice-President, and they shall make distinct lists of all persons voted for as President, and of all persons voted for as Vice-President, and of the number of votes for each, which lists they shall sign and certify, and transmit sealed to the seat of the government of the United States, directed to the President of the Senate;—The President of the Senate shall, in the presence of the Senate and House of Representatives, open all certificates and the votes shall then be counted;—The person having the greatest number of votes for President, shall be the President, if such number be a majority of the whole number of Electors appointed; and if no person have such majority, then from the persons having the highest numbers not exceeding three on the list of those voted for as President, the House of Representatives shall choose immediately, by ballot, the President. But in choosing the President, the votes shall be taken by states, the representation from each state having one vote; a quorum for this purpose shall consist of a member or members from two-thirds of the states, and a majority of all the states shall be necessary to a choice. And if the House of Representatives shall not choose a President whenever the right of choice shall devolve upon them, before the fourth day of March next following, then the Vice-President shall act as

President, as in the case of the death or other constitutional disability of the President.—The person having the greatest number of votes as Vice-President, shall be the Vice-President, if such number be a majority of the whole number of Electors appointed, and if no person have a majority, then from the two highest numbers on the list, the Senate shall choose the Vice-President; a quorum for the purpose shall consist of two-thirds of the whole number of Senators, and a majority of the whole number shall be necessary to a choice. But no person constitutionally ineligible to the office of President shall be eligible to that of Vice-President of the United States.

Article XIII [proposed 1 Feb. 1865; declared ratified 18 Dec. 1865]

Section 1. Neither slavery nor involuntary servitude, except as a punishment for crime whereof the party shall have been duly convicted, shall exist within the United States, or any place subject to their jurisdiction.

Section 2. Congress shall have power to enforce this article by appropriate legislation.

Article XIV [proposed 16 June 1866; declared ratified 28 July 1868]

Section 1. All persons born or naturalized in the United States, and subject to the jurisdiction thereof, are citizens of the United States and of the State wherein they reside. No State shall make or enforce any law which shall abridge the privileges or immunities of citizens of the United States; nor shall any State deprive any person of life, liberty, or property, without due process of law; nor deny to any person within its jurisdiction the equal protection of the laws.

Section 2. Representatives shall be apportioned among the several States according to their respective numbers, counting the whole number of persons in each State, excluding Indians not taxed. But when the right to vote at any election for the choice of electors for President and Vice President of the United States, Representatives in Congress, the Executive and Judicial officers of a State, or the members of the Legislature thereof, is denied to any of the male inhabitants of such State, being twenty-one years of age, and citizens of the United States, or in any way abridged, except for participation in rebellion, or other crime, the basis of representation therein shall be reduced in the proportion which the number of such male citizens shall bear to the whole number of male citizens twenty-one years of age in such State.

Section 3. No person shall be a Senator or Representative in Congress, or elector of President and Vice President, or hold any office, civil or military, under the United States, or under any State, who, having pre-

M

viously taken an oath, as a member of Congress, or as an officer of the United States, or as a member of any State legislature, or as an executive or judicial officer of any State, to support the Constitution of the United States, shall have engaged in insurrection or rebellion against the same, or given aid and comfort to the enemies thereof. But Congress may by a vote of two-thirds of each House, remove such disability.

Section 4. The validity of the public debt of the United States, authorized by law, including debts incurred for payment of pensions and bounties for services in suppressing insurrection or rebellion, shall not be questioned. But neither the United States nor any state shall assume or pay any debt or obligation incurred in aid of insurrection or rebellion against the United States, or any claim for the loss or emancipation of any slave; but all such debts, obligations, and claims shall be held illegal and void.

Section 5. The Congress shall have power to enforce, by appropriate legislation, the provisions of this article.

Article XV [proposed 27 Feb. 1869; declared ratified 30 Mar. 1870]

Section 1. The right of citizens of the United States to vote shall not be denied or abridged by the United States or by any State on account of race, color, or previous condition of servitude.

Section 2. The Congress shall have power to enforce this article by appropriate legislation.

Article XVI [proposed 12 July 1909; declared ratified 25 Feb. 1913]

The Congress shall have power to lay and collect taxes on incomes, from whatever source derived, without apportionment among the several States, and without regard to any census or enumeration.

Article XVII [proposed 16 May 1912; declared ratified 31 May 1913]

The Senate of the United States shall be composed of two Senators from each State, elected by the people thereof, for six years; and each Senator shall have one vote. The electors in each State shall have the qualifications requisite for electors of the most numerous branch of the State legislatures.

When vacancies happen in the representation of any State in the Senate, the executive authority of such State shall issue writs of election to fill such vacancies: *Provided,* That the legislature of any State may empower the executive thereof to make temporary appointments until the people fill the vacancies by election as the legislature may direct.

This amendment shall not be so construed as to affect the election or term of any Senator chosen before it becomes valid as part of the Constitution.

Article XVIII [proposed 18 Dec. 1917; declared ratified 29 Jan. 1919; repealed by the 21st Amendment]

Section 1. After one year from the ratification of this article the manufacture, sale, or transportation of intoxicating liquors within, the importation thereof into, or the exportation thereof from the United States and all territory subject to the jurisdiction thereof for beverage purposes is hereby prohibited.

Section 2. The Congress and the several States shall have concurrent power to enforce this article by appropriate legislation.

Section 3. This article shall be inoperative unless it shall have been ratified as an amendment to the Constitution by the legislatures of the several States, as provided in the Constitution, within seven years from the date of the submission hereof to the States by the Congress.[8]

Article XIX [proposed 4 June 1919; declared ratified 26 Aug. 1920]

The right of citizens of the United States to vote shall not be denied or abridged by the United States or by any State on account of sex.

Congress shall have power to enforce this article by appropriate legislation.

Article XX [proposed 2 Mar. 1932; declared ratified 6 Feb. 1933]

Section 1. The terms of the President and Vice President shall end at noon on the 20th day of January, and the terms of Senators and Representatives at noon on the 3d day of January, of the years in which such terms would have ended if this article had not been ratified; and the terms of their successors shall then begin.

Section 2. The Congress shall assemble at least once in every year, and such meeting shall begin at noon on the 3d day of January, unless they shall by law appoint a different day.

Section 3. If, at the time fixed for the beginning of the term of the President, the President elect shall have died, the Vice President elect shall become President. If a President shall not have been chosen before the time fixed for the beginning of his term, or if the President elect shall have failed to qualify, then the Vice President elect shall act as President until a President shall have qualified; and the Congress may by law pro-

[8] Superseded by the Twenty-first Amendment.

vide for the case wherein neither a President elect nor a Vice President elect shall have qualified, declaring who shall then act as President, or the manner in which one who is to act shall be selected, and such person shall act accordingly until a President or Vice President shall have qualified.

Section 4. The Congress may by law provide for the case of the death of any of the persons from whom the House of Representatives may choose a President whenever the right of choice shall have devolved upon them, and for the case of the death of any of the persons from whom the Senate may choose a Vice President whenever the right of choice shall have devolved upon them.

Section 5. Sections 1 and 2 shall take effect on the 15th day of October following the ratification of this article.

Section 6. This article shall be inoperative unless it shall have been ratified as an amendment to the Constitution by the legislatures of three-fourths of the several States within seven years from the date of its submission.

Article XXI [proposed 20 Feb. 1933; declared ratified 5 Dec. 1933]

Section 1. The Eighteenth article of amendment to the Constitution of the United States is hereby repealed.

Section 2. The transportation or importation into any State, Territory, or possession of the United States for delivery or use therein of intoxicating liquors, in violation of the laws thereof, is hereby prohibited.

Section 3. This article shall be inoperative unless it shall have been ratified as an amendment to the Constitution by conventions in the several States, as provided in the Constitution, within seven years from the date of the submission hereof to the States by the Congress.

Article XXII [proposed 24 Mar. 1947; declared ratified 26 Feb. 1951]

Section 1. No person shall be elected to the office of the President more than twice, and no person who has held the office of President, or acted as President, for more than two years of a term to which some other person was elected President shall be elected to the office of the President more than once. But this Article shall not apply to any person holding the office of President when this Article was proposed by the Congress, and shall not prevent any person who may be holding the office of President, or acting as President, during the term within which this Article becomes operative from holding the office of President or acting as President during the remainder of such term.

Section 2. This article shall be inoperative unless it shall have been ratified as an amendment to the Constitution by the legislatures of three-fourths of the several States within seven years from the date of its submission to the States by the Congress.

Article XXIII [proposed 16 June 1960; ratified 29 Mar. 1961]

Section 1. The district constituting the seat of government of the United States shall appoint in such manner as the Congress may direct:

A number of electors of President and Vice President equal to the whole number of Senators and Representatives in Congress to which the District would be entitled if it were a State, but in no event more than the least populous state; they shall be in addition to those appointed by the States, but they shall be considered, for the purpose of the election of President and Vice President, to be electors appointed by a State; and they shall meet in the District and perform such duties as provided by the twelfth article of amendment.

Section 2. The Congress shall have power to enforce this article by appropriate legislation.

Article XXIV [proposed 27 Aug. 1962; ratified 23 Jan. 1964]

Section 1. The right of citizens of the United States to vote in any primary or other election for President or Vice President, for electors for President or Vice President, or for Senator or Representative in Congress, shall not be denied or abridged by the United States or any State by reason of failure to pay any poll tax or other tax.

Section 2. The Congress shall have power to enforce this article by appropriate legislation.

Appendix B

The States and Territories

Very few people can recall the names of all the states without some difficulty, and on my part a little cheating. It is perhaps useful to list them with the territories, together with a few vital statistics and brief mention of their origins. The information is given in the following order: capital, area, population (1960 census), when organized as a territory (where applicable), when admitted to the Union, chronological order of admission, and origin.

ALABAMA; Montgomery; 51,060 sq.m.; 3,266,740; Mar. 3, 1817; Dec. 14, 1819; 22nd. Mississippi Territory, earlier ceded by Britain to the United States under the Treaty of Paris 1783, portion ceded by Spain 1813.

ALASKA; Juneau; 571,065 sq.m.; 226,167; Aug. 24, 1912; Jan. 3, 1959; 49th. Purchased from Russia 1867.

ARIZONA; Phoenix; 113,575 sq.m.; 1,302,161; Feb. 24, 1863; Feb. 14, 1912; 48th. Ceded by Mexico 1848, portion obtained by Gadsden Purchase 1853.

ARKANSAS; Little Rock; 52,499 sq.m. 1,786,272; Mar. 2, 1819; June 15, 1836; 25th. Louisiana Purchase 1803.

CALIFORNIA; Sacramento; 156,573 sq.m.; 15,717,204; no territorial status; Sept. 9, 1850; 31st. Ceded by Mexico 1848.

COLORADO; Denver; 103,884 sq.m.; 1,753,947; Feb. 28, 1861; Aug. 1, 1876; 38th. Louisiana Purchase 1803, portion ceded by Mexico 1848.

CONNECTICUT; Hartford; 4,899 sq.m.; 2,535,234; one of the original 13 colonies; Jan. 9, 1788; 5th. Royal charter 1662.

DELAWARE; Dover; 1,978 sq.m.; 446,292; one of the original 13 colonies; Dec. 7, 1787; 1st. Swedish charter 1638, English charter 1683.

FLORIDA; Tallahassee; 54,252 sq.m.; 4,951,560; Mar. 30, 1822; Mar. 3, 1845; 27th. Ceded by Spain 1819.

GEORGIA; Atlanta; 58,274 sq.m.; 3,943,116; one of the original 13 colonies; Jan. 2, 1788; 4th. Royal charter 1732.

HAWAII; Honolulu; 6,415 sq.m.; 632,772; June 14, 1900; Aug. 21, 1959; 50th. Annexed 1898.

IDAHO; Boise; 82,708 sq.m.; 667,191; Mar. 4, 1863; July 3, 1890; 43rd. Treaty with Britain 1846.

ILLINOIS; Springfield; 55,930 sq.m.; 10,081,158; Feb. 3, 1809; Dec. 3, 1818; 21st. Northwest Territory 1787.

INDIANA; Indianapolis; 36,185 sq.m.; 4,662,498; May 7, 1800; Dec. 11, 1816; 19th. Northwest Territory 1787.

IOWA; Des Moines; 56,032 sq.m.; 2,757,537; June 12, 1838; Dec. 28, 1846; 29th. Louisiana Purchase 1803.

KANSAS; Topeka; 82,048 sq.m.; 2,178,611; May 30, 1854; Jan. 29, 1861; 34th. Louisiana Purchase 1803, portion ceded by Mexico 1848.

KENTUCKY; Frankfort; 39,863; sq.m.; 3,038,156; no territorial status; June 1, 1792; 15th. Part of Virginia until admitted as a state.

LOUISIANA; Baton Rouge; 45,106 sq.m.; 3,257,022; Mar. 26, 1804; Apr. 30, 1812; 18th. Louisiana Purchase 1803, portion acquired from Spain 1812.

MAINE; Augusta; 31,012 sq.m.; 969,265; no territorial status; Mar. 15, 1820; 23rd. Part of Massachusetts until admitted as a state.

MARYLAND; Annapolis; 9,874, sq.m.; 3,100,689; one of the original 13 colonies; Apr. 28, 1788; 7th. Royal charter.

MASSACHUSETTS; Boston; 7,867 sq.m.; 5,148,578; one of the original 13 colonies; Feb. 6, 1788; 6th. Royal charter.

MICHIGAN; Lansing; 57,019 sq.m.; 7,823,194; Jan. 11, 1805; Jan. 26, 1837; 26th. Northwest Territory 1787.

MINNESOTA; St. Paul; 80,009 sq.m.; 3,413,864; Mar. 3, 1849; May 11, 1858; 32nd. Northwest Territory 1787, portion acquired by Louisiana Purchase 1803.

MISSISSIPPI; Jackson; 47,223 sq.m.; 2,178,141; Apr. 7, 1798; Dec. 10, 1817; 20th. Mississippi Territory, earlier ceded by Britain to the United States under the Treaty of Paris 1783, portion acquired from Spain 1813.

MISSOURI; Jefferson City; 69,138 sq.m.; 4,319,813; June 4, 1812; Aug. 10, 1821; 24th. Louisiana Purchase 1803.

MONTANA; Helena; 145,736 sq.m.; 674,767; May 26, 1864; Nov. 8, 1889; 41st. Louisiana Purchase 1803, portion obtained from Oregon Territory 1848.

NEBRASKA; Lincoln; 76,612 sq.m.; 1,411,330; May 30, 1854; Mar. 1, 1867; 37th. Louisiana Purchase 1803.

NEVADA; Carson City; 109,788 sq.m.; 285,278; Mar. 2, 1861; Oct. 31, 1864; 36th. Ceded by Mexico 1848.

NEW HAMPSHIRE; Concord; 9,014 sq.m.; 606,921; one of the original 13 colonies; June 21, 1788; 9th. Land grants from Council for New York 1622 and 1629, made royal province 1679.

NEW JERSEY; Trenton; 7,521 sq.m.; 6,066,782; one of the original 13 colonies; Dec. 18, 1787; 3rd. Dutch settlement 1618; royal charter 1664.

NEW MEXICO; Santa Fe; 121,510 sq.m.; 951,023; Sept. 9, 1850; Jan. 6, 1912; 47th. Ceded by Mexico 1848, portion obtained by Gadsden Purchase 1853.

NEW YORK; Albany; 47,939 sq.m.; 16,782,304; one of the original 13 colonies; July 26, 1788; 11th. Dutch settlement 1623, English control 1664.

NORTH CAROLINA; Raleigh; 49,067 sq.m.; 4,556,155; one of the original 13 colonies; Nov. 21, 1789; 12th. Royal charter 1663.

NORTH DAKOTA; Bismarck; 69,457 sq.m.; 632,446; Mar. 2, 1861; Nov. 2, 1889; 39th. Louisiana Purchase 1803, portion acquired by treaty with Britain 1818.

OHIO; Columbus; 40,972 sq.m.; 9,706,397; no territorial status; Mar. 1, 1803; 17th. Northwest Territory 1787.

OKLAHOMA; Oklahoma City; 68,887 sq.m.; 2,328,284; May 2, 1890; Nov. 16, 1907; 46th. Louisiana Purchase 1803.

OREGON; Salem; 96,248 sq.m.; 1,768,687; Aug. 14, 1848; Feb. 14, 1859; 33rd. Treaty with Britain 1846.

PENNSYLVANIA; Harrisburg; 45,007 sq.m.; 11,319,366; one of the original 13 colonies; Dec. 12, 1787; 2nd. Royal grant to William Penn 1681.

RHODE ISLAND; Providence; 1,058 sq.m.; 859,488; one of the original 13 colonies; May 29, 1790; 13th. Royal charter 1663.

SOUTH CAROLINA; Columbia; 30,272 sq.m.; 2,382,594; one of the original 13 colonies; May 23, 1788; 8th. Royal charter 1663.

SOUTH DAKOTA; Pierre; 76,378 sq.m.; 680,514; Mar. 2, 1861; Nov. 2, 1889; 40th. Louisiana Purchase 1803.

TENNESSEE; Nashville; 41,762 sq.m.; 3,567,089; no territorial status; June 1, 1796; 16th. Part of North Carolina until admitted as a state.

TEXAS; Austin; 262,840 sq.m.; 9,579,677; no territorial status; Dec. 29, 1845; 28th. Republic of Texas 1845.

UTAH; Salt Lake City; 82,339 sq.m.; 890,627; Sept. 9, 1850; Jan. 4, 1896; 45th. Ceded by Mexico 1848.

VERMONT; Montpelier; 9,276 sq.m.; 389,881; no territorial status; Mar. 4, 1791; 14th. From lands of New Hampshire and New York.

VIRGINIA; Richmond; 39,838 sq.m.; 3,966,949; one of the original 13 colonies; June 26, 1788; 10th. Royal charter 1609.

WASHINGTON; Olympia; 66,709 sq.m.; 2,853,214; Mar. 2, 1853; Nov. 11, 1889; 42nd. Oregon Territory 1848.

WEST VIRGINIA; Charleston; 24,079 sq.m.; 1,860,421; no territorial status; June 20, 1863; 35th. Part of Virginia until admitted as a state.

WISCONSIN; Madison; 54,705 sq.m.; 3,951,777; Apr. 20, 1836; May 29, 1848; 30th. Northwest Territory 1787.

WYOMING; Cheyenne; 97,411 sq.m.; 330,066; July 25, 1868; July 10, 1890; 44th. Louisiana Purchase, portions ceded by Mexico 1848 and obtained from the Oregon Territory 1848.

DISTRICT OF COLUMBIA; 69 sq.m.; 763,956. Ceded by Maryland and Virginia. Seat of federal government since 1800. City of Washington incorporated in 1802.

COMMONWEALTH OF PUERTO RICO; San Juan; 3,421 sq.m.; 2,349,544; no territorial status; July 25, 1952. Ceded by Spain 1898, became a self-governing commonwealth 1950.

M*

TERRITORY OF GUAM; Agana; 209 sq.m.; 67,044, Aug. 1, 1950. Ceded by Spain 1898.

VIRGIN ISLANDS; Charlotte Amalie; 132 sq.m.; 31,904. Purchased from Denmark 1917.

In 1967 the United States administered the Canal Zone and Panama Canal, minor Caribbean Islands, American Samoa, Wake and Midway islands, the Ryukyu Islands, Canton and Enderbury islands (jointly with Britain), and the Caroline, Marianas and Marshall islands under United Nations trusteeship.

Index

Abolitionists, 258
Acheson, Dean, 119, 129, 188
Adams, John, 45, 276
Adams, John Q., 105
Adenauer, Konrad, 20, 315
Advanced Research Projects Agency, 159
Africa, prejudice in, 298
Air Force, 147, 163
  Berlin airlift by, 177–78
  communications systems in, 175
Alabama, 142, 223, 227, 301
  Negro revolution in, 222
Alaska, 218, 219
American Bar Association (ABA), on
    Supreme Court, 90–91, 313
American Civil Liberties Union, 96
American Commonwealth, The
    (Bryce), xii, xiii, 105, 255
American Dilemma, 323
American Dilemma, An (Myrdal),
    215
American Legion, 105
American Medical Association, cost
    of lobbying to, 315
Americanism
  fear of liberals in, 267
  roots of, 266
  traits of, 246, 264–65
    ultranationalism, 296–97
Americans
  aspirations of, 127
  attitudes of
    class-consciousness, 282
    dissenting opinion, 86
    equality, 91
    entitled to prejudice, 309
    federal-state relations, 233–34

Americans (*Cont.*)
  attitudes of (*Cont.*)
    fetish of youth, ix
    foreign opinions, 275
    isolationism, 131
    the left, 267
    melting pot, xiii, 291
    Negroes and whites, 302–5
    peace-loving people, 147, 148
    political allegiances, 262
    politics, 17, 21, 223–24
    rising expectations, xiv–xv
    toward their country, 311
    to Union, xiii
    untrammeled individualism, 92
    Western Europe, 209
  central planning and, 239
  character of early, x
  innocence of, 245
  origins of, 265, 288–89
  price of bigness to, 323–24
  problems of federalism and, 323
  as prosperous poor, 265
  as urban dwellers, 261
  way of life of, 295–96
  See also Anglo-Americans; Catho-
    lics; Ethnic groups; Immi-
    grants; Indians, American;
    Jews; Minorities; Negroes;
    White Anglo-Saxon Protestants
American Way of Life, glorification
    of, 295–96
Anderson, Dillon, 188
Anglo-Americans
  defined, 290
  minority, 297
  Senate dominated by, 294
  traditions of, preserved, 295

347

Anti-Mason Party, 277
Appeals, Courts of, jurisdiction of, 81
Appropriations Committee (House), 50, 51
Appropriations Committee (Senate), 60
Aristotle, 310
Arizona, 283
Arkansas, 301
Armed forces, 177–81
  American and British, compared, 181
  civilian control of, 125, 152–54, 172–73, 185–86
  deployment and strength of, 151
  distrust of politicians by, 181
  foreign policy and, 124–25
  intervention of, during Cold War, 147–48
  as instrument of national security, 187
  Korea and, 135, 183
  lobbies in Congress of, 185
  loyalty to Constitution of, 181
  in nuclear age, 164
  President as Commander in Chief of, 153, 173–75
  relation to big business, 184, 185
  right-wing extremism in, 186
  Root's reforms and, 182
  status of superpower and, 138
  tested in Vietnam, 201–2
  See also Air Force; Army; Marine Corps; Military-industrial complex; Military strategy; Navy; Strategic Air Command
Armed Services Committee (House), 50, 160, 185
Army
  communications systems of, 175
  compared to German, 180
  General Staff of, 182
  size of, 151, 152
  used to quell domestic unrest, 152
Articles of Confederation, 38
Asia, 104
  foreign policy for (1951–60), 135–36
  See also China; Japan; Laos; Thailand; Vietnam War
Atomic Energy Commission, 159, 316
Australia, 135

Australia–New Zealand–U.S. Treaty (1951), 129

Baker, Bobby, 316
Baker v. *Carr* (1960), 98
Baldwin, Stanley, 144
Ball, George, European unity and, 319–20
Baltimore *Sun*, 321
Banking and Currency Committee (House), 41
Baptists, 291
Barzun, Jacques, 265
Battle of Britain, 131
Beard, Charles, on inequality, 80
Belgium, xi, 293
Berlin (Germany), 110
  airlift to, 177
  Communist threat and, 135
  crisis in (1961), 168
Berlin Wall, 162
Bill of Rights, xii
  as curb on government, 101
  as defense of immigrants, 296
  extension of, 93, 95
Bill of Rights (British), 226
Bismarck, Otto von, 181
Black, Hugo, 76, 83
Black Muslims, 308
Black Power, 308–9
Borah, William, 61
Boston (Mass.), 292
Bourbons (conservative Democrats), Negro disfranchisement and, 299–300
Bowron, Fletcher, 253
Brennan, William J., Jr., 73, 90, 98
Bricker Amendment, 68, 214
Bright, John, 3, 5
Britain, 11, 77, 294, 323
  Battle of, 131
  compared to United States
    administration, 20–21
    age of political system, ix–x, 255
    armed forces, 181
    church attendance in, 291
    civil liberties, 96
    Foreign Office and State Department, 106
    power of the people, 78, 270, 318
    prejudice, 298
    representatives, 282–83

Britain (*Cont.*)
  compared to United States (*Cont.*)
    society, 293
    urbanization, 244
  as democratic republic, 12, 20–21, 28, 62
  entry in EEC by, xi, 41, 320
  Galbraith's view of, 320
  immigrants to, 305–6
  Indian government modeled on government of, 44–45
  Malayan uprising and, 180, 197
  Monarchy of, compared to Presidency, 5–16
  in nuclear age, 137–38, 179–80
  parties in, 72, 267, 276, 314
  respect for political institutions in, 4
  talent exported from, 297
  Trade Expansion Act and, 320
  See also Parliament; Prime Ministry
Brooke, Edward, 261, 302
Brown, Claude, 303–4
Brown v. *Board of Education* (1954), 19, 74, 87–90
Bryan, William Jennings, 256
Bryce, Lord, xiii, 77, 244
  on Americans, 1
  background of, xii
  on Constitution, x, 79
  on growth of cities, 243
  on Massachusetts charter, 227
  on power structure, 221–22
  on Speaker of the House, 59
  on two-party system, 255, 270
  on Presidents, 281
  on Republicans, 259
  on representatives, 310
  on Secretary of State, 105
  on study of American system, 1
Buchanan, James, 11
Budapest (Hungary), 147, 148
Budget, Bureau of, function of, 22–24, 67
Bull Moose Convention, 264
Bundestag, 37
Burke, Edward, 40
Burns, James MacGregor, on political parties, 268
Business
  adjustment to change by, 26[?]
  economic advisers and, 24–25

Business (*Cont.*)
  government aid to, 24
  interests of, represented in Congress, 17, 61, 313
  lobbying by, 315–17
  local interests and, 42–43
  politics and, 12, 313
  Senate and, 61
  See also Military-industrial complex
Butler, Lord, 306
Byrd, Harry, 301

Cabinet, 9, 28–33
  authority of, 8
  British and American, compared, 28–29, 318
  power of secretaries in, 29
  power of the people over, 65, 317–19
  Senate and, 320
  See also members of the Cabinet, for example: Defense, Secretary of
Calhoun, John C., xi, 57, 234
California, xii, 42, 218, 271, 274
Canada, 293
Cannon, Clarence, 60
Cannon, Joseph G., 58
Capitol, desription of, 36, 59
Cardozo, Benjamin, 85
Carmichael, Stokely, 308
Caribbean, intervention in, 149
Catholicism, Roman, 265
  melting pot and, 291
Census, Bureau of the, xiii, 259, 288
Center for the Study of Democratic Institutions, 231
Central Intelligence Agency (CIA), 22, 26, 122, 151
  creation of, 155
  overthrow of governments and, 126
  Presidency and, 31–33
  responsibilities of, 125
  Vietnam War and, 201
Central Treaty Organization (CENTO), 129
Chamberlain, Neville, 144
Chicago (Ill.), 247, 248, 293
  South Side of, 301
China, ix, 298
  American military strategy and, 172, 200

China (*Cont.*)
    intervention in Korean War of, 183
    Monroe Doctrine applied to, 209
    Open Door policy toward, 134–35, 166
    recognition of, 211–12
    as threat to peace, 139
Christian Nationalist Crusade, 212
Churchill, Winston, xi, 66, 179, 291
CIA, *see* Central Intelligence Agency
Cities, 243–54
    decay of, 236
    political machines and, 246–49
    states' relations with, 235–36, 245
    systems of government in, 249–50
    See also specific cities
Civil Rights Acts (1964–65), 58, 221, 302
Civil rights and liberties, 9, 74, 220
    British and American, compared, 96
    Congressional committees and, 57–58
    lobbying and, 316
    Negroes and, *see* Negroes—civil rights and
    Senate and, 61
    Supreme Court and, 18–19, 92
        school desegregation, 86–90
Civil Rights Commission, 302
Civil War, xi, xiii, 7, 301
    Democrats and, 256
    extremism and, 265
    as first modern war, ix, 179
    nullification and, 217
    Republicans and, 258, 260
    Supreme Court and, 79
    Union and, 45
Clark, Tom, 85
Clausewitz, Karl von, 142, 172
Clay, Henry, 258
    on drift to presidential power, 11
Clemenceau, Georges, 163
Cold War
    eclipse of military absolutism during, 186
    growth of military due to, 154
    military intervention during, 147–48
Collins, Leroy, 231–32
Common Market, *see* European Economic Community

Communism
    effects on United States of, 210
        military responses 148–49
    extension of Monroe Doctrine to, 209–10
    threats of, 135, 180, 197
Component Field Organization (CFO), as new name for embassy, 115, 117
Confederacy, Southern, xi
Confederation, xi
Congo, 147
Congress, xii, 3, 27, 36–72
    accountable to the people, 37, 312
    agriculture and, 240, 263
    committees of, *see* Congressional committees; *specific committees*
    Constitution and, 36–37, 60, 78–79
    as institution
        age of, 59, 61
        basis for democratic government, 44
    delegate system in, 39–42, 46
    effects of consensus on, 71
    elections to, 37
    federalism and, 45
    fiscal role of, 66–67
        CIA budget, 31
    foreign policy and, 7
    interests represented in, 68, 294
        business, 17, 61, 313
        local, 42–43
    general welfare and, 313–15
    national security, influence on, 204–5
    Negro rights in, 300, 303, 307
    party funds and, 273
    power of, 4, 36–37
        period of supremacy, 11–12, 14, 19
    Presidency and, *see* Presidency—Congress and
    press and, 43–44, 322
    proceedings in
        absence of debate, 43–44
        alliance of conservatives, 4, 310
        compromise process, 314–15
        legislative achievements, 59, 66
        lobbying and, 315–17
    reapportionment and, 97–99

Congress (*Cont.*)
  Republicans and, 262
  suspicion of simple majority rule in, 71
  Supreme Court and, 74–75
    legislation, 4, 68, 99–100
  See also House of Representatives; Senate
Congressional committees
  advantages of, 49
  autonomy of, 50–51, 56
  blurring of party lines in, 48
  chairmen of
    conservatism, 48, 52, 57
    efforts to curtail power, 58
    power, 53–55, 71
    Presidency and, 55–56
    as professional politicians, 46
    origins, 57
    racial segregation, 57–58
  Constitution and, 46
  list of, 47–48; *see also specific committees*
  maneuverings in, 53–54
  minorities and, 57
  passage of bills and, 49, 51–52
  power of, 45, 48
  seniority system, 52
  traditionalism in, 46
  Whigs' admiration for, 49
Congressional Quarterly, 50
Congressional Record, 44, 209
Congressmen
  accommodation and, 314
  background of, 282–83
  Bryce on, 310
  compared to Senators, 61
  constituents and, 64
  defended, 43
  as delegates, historical basis for, 39–42
  Ombudsmen and, 64
  requirement for becoming, 310
  staffs of, 43, 64–65
  three-dimensional politics and, 68
Connecticut, 218, 219, 276, 303
Consensus
  anti-Communism and, 210
  approval for, 310
  compared to British party discipline, 72

Consensus (*Cont.*)
  effects on Congress of, 71
  radical right and, 212
  as means of national unity, 71
  need for, 323
  Presidency and, 70–71
Conservative Party (British), 306
Conservatives, Congressional alliance of, 4, 310
Constitution, 5, 7, 143, 217
  amendments to, xii; *see also specific amendments*
  Congress and
    Congressional committees, 46
    legislative powers, 36–37, 60
    restrictions, 78–79
  definition of, 86
  drafted, x
  electoral system and, 99, 276
  equality and, 91–92
    civil rights, 203
    discrimination, 299
    open housing, 308–9
  federal government and, 4, 39
    balance of powers, 14–17
    Cabinet, 28
    state-federal power, 221, 222
  federalism and, 323
  founders and, 12–13
  fundamental changes in, xii
  immigrants and, 290, 296
  as landmark, 100
  law and, 78–79
  loyalty of Armed Forces to, 181
  misreading of, 69–70
  preamble to, 10, 311–12
  Presidency and
    mandate, 14–17
    power, 83, 153
    requirements for office, 281
    Twenty-second Amendment, 15, 16
  states and
    basis for, 236–38
    doctrine of pre-emption, 94
    rights, 95
  Supreme Court and, *see* Supreme Court—Constitution and
  text of, 325–41
Constitutional Convention, 227
Constitutions, state, 219, 225–28

Containment, policy of, 167
Continental Congress, 38, 154
Controlled Response, Doctrine of, 171, 173, 176
Conventions, national, 277–80
Corrupt Practices Act (1925), 273
Corwin, Edward, 206
Cuba
    invasion of (1961), 120, 126, 144, 147, 193
    missile crisis (1962), 136, 148, 186, 194
    Platt Amendment and, 150

Declaration of Independence, 38, 66, 98, 148
    American beliefs expressed in, 127
    English political thought and, x
Defense, Department of, 29, 107, 147–214
    agencies controlled by, 155–56; see also specific agencies
    budget of, 151, 161, 184, 323
    civilian work force of, 151
    communications systems in, 173–74
    creation of, 155
    foreign policy and, 122, 162–63
    physical assets of, 151–52
    role of theoreticians in, 166
    technology in, 158–60
    think factories and, 165; see also Hudson Institute; RAND Corporation
    See also Armed Forces; International Security Affairs; Joint Chiefs of Staff
Defense, Secretary of, 29, 43
    conduct of Vietnam War and, 162, 196, 319
    control of armed forces by, 152, 176
    formulation of military strategy by, 163–64
    McNamara as, 124–25
    as member of NSC, 163, 189, 195
    office of, 155–58
Defense Intelligence Agency, 163, 174
Defense Research and Engineering, Director of, 158–59
De Gaulle, Charles, xi, 20, 315, 320
Delaware, 218

Democracy, 9–11
    Constitution and, 39
    disagreement in, 86
    Locke and, 101
    power of civil service in, 318
    renewing process in, 73
    suspicion of, 97–98
Democratic National Convention (1964), 279
Democratic Party, 275, 283, 310
    absorption of populism by, 267
    age of, as party, ix
    compromise in, 258
    conventions in, 278–79
    elections and, 276–77
    election costs to (1964), 274
    electoral system and, 271
    emergence of, 256–57
    ethnic groups and, 289, 293–94
    Negro disfranchisement and, 299–300
    political machines and, 246–47
    reform movement in, 249, 250
    as regional party, 45
    and Republican, compared, 257, 259, 263–64
    shades of opinion and, 267–68
    social legislation and, 260–62
    in the South, 300
    support for, 263
    as war party, 262
De Tocqueville, Alexis, xii
Dewey, Admiral George, 36
Dillon, Douglas, 36
Diplomacy
    approach to, 107
    China and, 211–12
    computers in, 115, 117
    efficiency of, 115
    impact on armed forces of, 187
    See also State, Department of
District Courts, jurisdiction of, 81
District of Columbia, 279
Dixiecrats, 261, 276
Dominican Republic, 174
    intervention in, 18, 147, 150
Douglas, William, 83, 86, 100
Douglas-Home, Sir Alec, 20
Dred Scott case (1857), 18, 79
Dulles, John Foster, 132, 135, 265
    power of, as Secretary of State, 120
Dunmeyer, Arthur, 303

Economic Advisers, Council of, 22, 24–25
Economic Opportunity, Office of, 22, 239
  resistance to programs of, 25
Eden, Sir Anthony, Suez crisis and, 180
Eighteenth Amendment (1919), xii
Eighth Amendment, 94
Eisenhower, Dwight D., 114, 258, 281
  approach to government of, 30
  civil rights and, 19
  federal-state relations under, 238
  Massive Retaliation strategy developed under, 164
  as modern constitutional monarch, 21, 26
  1956 election costs to, 274
  NSC under, 123, 190–93
  power of Secretary of State under, 120
  Presidential nomination of, 279
  recognition of China and, 211
  Republicans under, 262
  warning on military-industrial complex by, 152, 184, 315–16
Elections
  American, compared to European, 270
  Congressional, 37
  effects of civil rights on, 270, 301, 302
  effects of reapportionment on, 97–99, 230
  precincts for, 271
  See also Primary elections
Electoral system
  conventions in, 277–78
  Electoral College in, 276–77
  primaries in, 271–73
  reapportionment as change in, 97–99, 230
  structure of, 271
  unconstitutionality of, 99
  See also Elections; Primary elections
Emergency Planning, Office of, 22
Employment Act (1946), 24
England, see Britain
Enlightenment, Age of, x, 10
Einstein, Albert, 62
Episcopalians, 291

Escobedo v. Illinois (1964), 94
Establishment, 111–15, 176
  academia and, 112
  British, profile of men in, 111
  influence of, 114, 115, 169–70
  old vs. new, 166–67
  origins of, 111
  superpower status and, 112
Ethiopia, prejudice in, 298
Ethnic groups, 290–302
  American Way of Life and, 295–97
  assimilation and, 290–92
  politics and
    importance, 285–86, 288–90, 293–94
    magic of, 307
    reversal of, 301
  as source of class differences, 292–93
  See also Immigrants; Minorities; specific ethnic groups
European Economic Community, 25, 129
  Ball and, 320
  Britain's entry in, xi, 41, 320
  as confederacy, xi
  tariff wall and, xi
Executive, see Presidency
Executive Agreements, 205, 207
Executive Order 8248 (1939), 22–23

Fair Deal, 17
Fascism, law under, 86
Federal Bureau of Investigation (FBI), Presidency and, 31–32, 33
Federal government
  aid to business by, 24
  Bill of Rights as curb on, 101
  Constitution as basis for, 4, 39
  development of, 8–9, 22–23
  executive branch of, see Presidency
  judiciary branch of, see Supreme Court
  legislative branch of, see Congress
  states and, see States—federal government and
Federalism, 324
  Congress and, 45
  Constitution and, 4, 76
  courts and, 82

Federalism (*Cont.*)
  function of, 288–89
  legislative process in, 99–100
  problems of, 322–23
  reflected in two-party system, 268
  Senate representation and, 198
  shift in power in, 11
  states in, 93
  system of, 14, 15, 277
Federalist papers, 231
Federalists, 256, 257, 276
Fifteenth Amendment (1870), xii
Finland, 293
First Amendment, 78
Fifth Amendment, 79–80, 94
Fisher, Lord, ix
Florida, 219, 231
Fong, Hiram L., 294
Food for Peace, 116
Ford Foundation, 112
Foreign Intelligence Advisory Board,
    CIA and, 33
Foreign Office (British), compared to
    State Department, 106
Foreign policy
  in Asia (1951–60), 135–36; *see also*
    China
  changes in
    domestic problems, 213
    Second World War and, 129, 145
    Soviet imperialism, 130
    superpower status and, 105, 109,
      136–39
  Congress and, 7
  Defense Department in, 162–63
  doctrines of, 132; *see also* Monroe
    Doctrine
  ethnic groups and, 294
  expansionism as, 134
  geopolitics and, 130–35, 137
  goals of, 121
  introduction of computers in, 116–
    17
  isolationism and, *see* Isolationism
  Marshall Plan as, 132
  military establishment and, 124–25
  National Policy Papers and, 116
  NSC and, 126
  nature of
    complexity, 115, 117, 128–29,
      315
    compromise, 109

Foreign policy (*Cont.*)
  nature of (*Cont.*)
    double standards, 127–28
    legalistic approach, 139–41
  neutrality as, 129
  in nuclear age, *see* Nuclear age
  praised, 139, 143, 145–56
  responsibility for making, 117–18
  role of Republicans in, 263–64
  Senate and, 205–6
  task forces in, 110
  *See also foreign policy under spe-
    cific Presidents*
Formosa Treaty (1954), 129
Fortas, Abe, 76
Foreign Affairs Committee (House),
    50
Foreign Relations Committee (Sen-
    ate), 38, 50
  prestige of chairman, 112, 207
Forrestal, James, 167
Fort Bragg (N.C.), 152
Fourteenth Amendment (1868), xii,
    79–80, 91, 93, 95
France, ix, 7, 9, 270
  nuclear-test-ban treaty and, 137
  Quai d'Orsay compared to State
    Department, 106–7
Frankfurter, Felix, 73, 97
Freeman, Orville, 232
Free-Soilers, 258
Fulbright, J. William, 207–8, 301
  advice disregarded, 38, 207
  exposure of right-wing radicals by,
    136
  influence on public opinion of, 212
Fundamental Orders, 219, 225

Galbraith, John Kenneth, 320
Gallup Poll, 294
Galveston (Tex.), city government in,
    249
Game theory, 203–4
Gardner, John, 323
Garland, Hamlin, 246
Garner, John, on Vice Presidency, 30
Garvey, Marcus, 308
General Assembly of the States, 95–
    96
General Staff Act (1903), 182
Georgia, 218, 227

Germany, ix, 172, 180; *see also* West Germany
Gibbons v. *Ogden* (1824), 94
Gideon v. *Wainright* (1963), 94
Goldberg, Arthur, 92
Goldwater, Barry, 136, 199, 212, 264, 276
  conservatism of, 10
  election campaign of, as prototype, 283–86
  ethnic politics and, 285–86, 294
  extremism and, 264–66
  lack of greatness of, 282
  as leader of Republican Party, 257
  primaries and, 272
  states' rights and, 236
Goltz, Baron Colmar von der, 179
Gorges, Sir Ferdinando, 226
Governors' Conference (1957), 238
Government
  American, defined, 21
  Congress as basis for democratic, 44
  Locke on, 101
  See also Federal government
Government of India Act (1935), 137, 306
Government Operations Committee (House), 41
Government Operations Committee (Senate), 41, 64, 65
Government Organization Manual, 29, 159
Grand Army of the Republic, 260
Grant, Ulysses S., 21, 181, 258
Gray v. *Sanders* (1961), 98
Great Society, 59, 143, 201
  administration of, 322–23
  as slogan, 17
  states' revenue and, 228
  weakness of, 262
Grodzins, Morton, 234
Groves, General Leslie, 185
Guam, 219
Guatemala, 147
Gulf of Tonkin (1964), 173

Hamilton, Alexander, xi, 36, 37, 277
  civilian control of the military and, 153
  isolationism and, 129
  theory of government of, 65
Harding, Warren G., 199, 278

Harlan, John M., 99
Harris Poll, 294
Harrison, William H., 257
Hay, John, China policy of, 105
Hawaii, flag of, 219
Hayden, Carl, 60
Health, Education, and Welfare, Secretary of, 323
Hechler, Ken, 316
Helvering v. *Davis* (1937), 237
Henry, Patrick, 3, 5, 56
Hiroshima, 147, 164
Hitch, Charles, 185
Hoar, George Frisbie, 259, 260
Holland, xi
Holmes, Oliver Wendell, 86
Hooker, Thomas, 286
Hoover, Herbert, 19, 21
Hoover, J. Edgar, 32
House, Colonel Edward M., 21
Housing and Urban Development, Department of, 239
House of Commons, 59, 255
  accountability of, 322
  individual freedom and, 44, 62–63
  members of, 62–63, 283
  scope of power of, 62–63
House of Lords, 60, 62
House of Representatives, 11, 279, 302
  caution of founders over, 10
  Defense Department and, 160
  election results and, 277
  list of committees of, 47–48; *see also specific committees*
  lobbying and, 317
  modeled on Commons, 59
  pluralistic society and, 294
  power of committees in, 46
  power struggle with Senate, 60
  scope of power of, 37
  size of, 49
  Speaker of, *see* Speaker of the House
Houston Space Center, 115
Hudson Institute, 165–66, 203
Hull, Cordell, 120
Humphrey, Hubert, 64
  1964 elections and, 284
  primaries and, 274
Huntington, Samuel P., 180

Idaho, 61
ICBM, *see* Intercontinental Ballistic Missile
Immigrants, 244–48, 287
  assimilation of, 289–90
  Bill of Rights as defense of, 296
  to Britain, 305–6
  cities and, 244–45, 252
  Constitution and, 290, 296
  Know-Nothings opposed to, 265
  Negroes and, 245, 305, 309
  political machines and, 246–48
  Presidency and, 294
  Republican Party and, 261
  U.S. as nation of, 260
  WASPs as, 259–60
  See also Ethnic groups; Minorities
Immigration Act (1966), 297
Imperialism
  American, 147, 148
  Soviet, 129–30, 135
India, ix, xi, 240, 298
  Act of 1935 and, 137, 306
  British colonialism in, 306
  government of, modeled on British, 44–45
Indians, American, 299, 309
  genocide of, 265
  wars with, 148
Industry, *see* Business
Intercontinental Ballistic Missile (ICBM), 137, 154, 175
Intergovernmental Relations, Commission on, 237–38, 241
International Association of Police Chiefs, 230
International Development, Agency for, 108, 110
International Security Affairs, Bureau for, 125, 161–62
Interstate Commerce Act (1887), 234
Israel, recognition of, 131
Iran, 147
Isolationism
  as continentalism, xiii, 41
  as foreign policy, 129
  historical outgrowth of, 130–31
  opposition to, 135
  F. D. Roosevelt and, 131

Jackson, Andrew, 153, 256
  1828 campaign of, 277

Jackson, Andrew (*Cont.*)
  greatness of, 10–11
  spoils system and, 42
  states' rights and, 234
  Supreme Court and, 75
Jackson, Henry, 192
Jackson, Robert, on civil liberties, 96
Japan, 129, 135
Jefferson, Thomas, 5, 86, 246, 276
  Declaration of Independence and, 66, 127
  as first Democratic President, 256
  greatness of, xi, 57
  on law, 83, 84
  Republicans and, 258
  on rural population, 246
  as Secretary of State, 105, 108
Jews, xiii
  anti-Semitism and, 301
  assimilation of, 291
  class tension for, 293
  community of, 288
  Palestinian policy and, 294
  segregation of, 292–93
  Supreme Court and, 295
Jim Crow, 305
John Birch Society, 212, 267
Johnson, Andrew, 19
  impeachment of, 11–12
Johnson, Lyndon B., 31, 113, 144, 148
  as Commander in Chief, 175–76
  disarmament and, 200, 212
  Dominican Republic and, 150
  Fortas appointed by, 76
  Fulbright's advice disregarded by, 207
  Great Society of, 59, 143, 201
  Gulf of Tonkin and, 173
  handling of criticism by, 55
  R. Kennedy and, 6
  1964 elections and, 56, 284
  NSC and, 123–24, 199–200
  Policy Planning Council and, 110
  relationship to Cabinet of, 30
  style of, 282
  Vietnam War and, 42, 200–2, 214
  See also Great Society
Joint Chiefs of Staff, 120, 144, 174
  as advisers, 155, 159, 164
  civilian authority and, 157
  loyalty of, 176
  organization of, 155, 156

Judiciary system, 80–82; *see also* Supreme Court
Justice, Department of, 29
  FBI and, 32

Kallen, Horace, 292, 295, 309
Kahn, Herman, as nuclear war theoretician, 165, 169, 170, 179
Kellogg Pact, 140
Kennan, George, 140
  policy of containment of, 167
Kennedy, John F., 26, 112, 148, 164
  Ball and, 319–20
  on basic goal of United States, 128
  Congressional committees and, 43, 52, 56, 58
  control of foreign-aid agencies and, 116
  defines national interest, 168
  election campaign, as prototype, 283–86
  ethnic politics and, 294
  foreign policy and
    Berlin crisis (1961), 168
    Cuban invasion, 144
    ratification of nuclear-test-ban treaty, 212
    recognition of China, 212
    Vietnam War, 194, 196, 201
  Fulbright's advice disregarded by, 207
  on inequities in United States, 311
  legend of, 6
  McNamara and, 124, 319
  NSC and, 122, 192, 194–95
  Negro revolution and, 18
  nuclear war and, 167, 193
  political career of, 30
  political organization and, 248, 270
  primary elections and, 272, 274
  relationship to Cabinet, 30
  relationship to the military, 125
  State Department under, 113, 120
  style of, 282
  transfer of power and, 26–27
Kennedy, Joseph, Sr., 292
Kennedy, Robert, 6, 192, 310
Key, V. O., Jr., 301n
Key West Agreement, 156, 157
Keynes, John Maynard, influence of, 24
Khrushchev, Nikita, 196, 210

King, Martin Luther, 308
Kirwan, Mike, 53
Kissinger, Henry, 169, 170
Know-Nothings, 258, 265–66
Korea, 135, 147, 148, 239
  armed forces and, 183
  limited nature of war in, 183
  Supreme Court and, 83
  United Nations and, 141
Korea Treaty (1953), 129
Ku Klux Klan, 265, 266, 290

Labour Party (British), 267
La Follette, Robert, 61, 258
La Guardia, Fiorello, 247
Languages spoken in the United States, xiii
Lansing, Robert, 119
Laos, 135, 147
Laski, Harold, 17
Latin America
  dependent status of, 145
  Monroe Doctrine and, 149–50, 210
  See also specific Latin-American countries
Law
  Brennan on, 73, 90
  British and American, compared, 77–78
  Bryce on, 79
  under Communism and Fascism, 86
  definition of, 86
League of Nations, 129, 141, 183
  nonparticipation of U.S. in 206
Leahy, Admiral William D., 120
Lebanon, 1957 intervention in, 147, 193
Left, absence of, 267
Legislation
  Congress and, 16–17
  Constitution and, 4
  Presidency and, 16–17
  Supreme Court and, 92
Legislative powers, *see* Congress
Legislative Reorganization Act, 46
Lend-Lease Act (1941), 119, 131
Liberty Lobby, 212
Library of Congress, 79
Lincoln, Abraham, 7, 66, 258, 261, 295
  Cabinet and, 29
  civilian control of military and, 154

Lincoln, Abraham (*Cont.*)
  federal patronage and, 42
  nomination of (1860), 278
  Union saved by, 11
Lippmann, Walter, 107
Lobbying, 315–17
Locke, John, ideas of, 101
Lodge, Henry, in 1964 primaries, 285
London, friendliness of, 293
Long, Huey, 301
Los Angeles (Calif.), 250–54, 293
  New York and, 250, 252
  riots in (1965), 251, 253–54
Louisiana, 227, 301
Louisiana Territory, 218
Luce, Admiral Stephen B., 181
Lutherans, 291

McAdoo, William, 278
MacArthur, General Douglas, 181
  dismissal of, 183–84
McCarthy, Joseph, 199, 211
McCarthyism
  as recurring phenomenon, 211, 265
  as result of anti-Communism, 210, 266
McCone Commission, 253
McIlvaine (delegate), 301
McKeldin, Theodore Roosevelt, 262
McKinley, William, 264
McKissick, Floyd, 308
McNamara, Robert S., 29–30, 164, 319
  aggressive leadership of, 157
  communications systems and, 174
  civilian authority and, 124–25, 157
  Congressional committees and, 50
  RAND Corporation and, 165
  on targets in nuclear war, 171
  on war, 147, 150
Madison, James, 86, 105
  on power, 231
  states and, 217, 234
Magna Carta (1215), 8, 77, 226
  equality and, 79–80, 91
Mahan, Admiral A. T., ix, 181
Malaya, uprising in (1948), 180, 197
Malloy v. *Hogan* (1964), 94
Manhattan District Project, 185
Manifest Destiny, xiii, 130
  as euphemism for colonialism, 181

Manpower Development and Training
  Act, 40
Mapp v. *Ohio* (1961), 94
Marine Corps, 151, 178
Marshall, General George C., 113, 135
Marshall, John, 75, 312
  extension of federal power and, 76, 79, 80
Marshall Plan, 115, 132
Massachusetts, xi, 42, 218, 226–27, 310
  Negro minority in, 302
Massachusetts Crime Commission, 229–30
Massachusetts v. *Mellon* (1923), 237
Massive Retaliation, 164, 167
Mather, Cotton, x, 265
Medicare, 145, 243
Melting pot, xiii, 290–91
Mencken, H. L., 266
Metternich, Clemens von, 111, 115, 117
Mexican War, 148
Michigan, motto of, 219
Military Establishment, *see* Air Force;
  Armed Forces; Army; Defense, Department of; Joint
  Chiefs of Staff; Marine Corps;
  Navy; Strategic Air Command
Military-industrial complex, Eisenhower's warning against, 152, 184, 315–16
Military strategy
  alternatives to nuclear war in, 169–72
  dominates the world, 172
  formulation of, 163–64
  Massive Retaliation as, 164, 167
  Monroe Doctrine and, 150
  policy of containment as, 167
  See also Nuclear war; War
Mill, John Stuart, 49
Miller, Clement W., 55
Minnesota, 64, 232, 272
Minorities
  Congressional committees and, 57
  defenselessness of, 222–23
  hostility to, 92
  party affiliation of, 263
  racialism and, 298
  See also Ethnic groups; Immigrants

Mississippi, xi, 142
Missouri, nickname of, 219
Missouri Compromise, 79
Missouri v. *Holland*, 206
Moltke, Helmuth Graf von, 179
Monarchy, British medieval, compared to Presidency, 5–16
Monroe, James, 105, 209
Monroe Doctrine, 107, 137
  Communism and, 209–10
  extended to the world, 149
  intervention in Latin America and, 149–50, 210
  NATO and, 133
  origin of, 149–50
  policy of containment and, 167
  reinterpretation of, 150
Montfort, Simon de, x, 37
Morse, Wayne, 53, 54
Moynihan Report, on Negro poor, 303
Myrdal, Gunnar, 215

Nagasaki, 147, 164
National Aeronautics and Space Council, 22, 117, 158
National Defense Act, 152
National Military Command System (NMCS), 173–74
National Policy Papers, 116, 190
National Security Act (1947), 122, 155, 157, 188
National Security Council (NSC), 9, 22, 25, 30, 31, 117, 158, 161, 188–213
  compared to *Oberkommando der Werhmacht,* 199
  creation of, 155
  departmental secretaries and, 195
  Eisenhower and, 191–92
  function of, 122, 188
  influence on foreign policy of, 126
  Johnson and, 199–200
  Kennedy and, 122, 192, 194–95
  organization of, 122–24, 126, 189, 194, 195
  Presidency and, 122–23, 193
  State Department and, 199
  Truman and, 123, 190
  Vietnam and, 200, 202
NATO, *see* North Atlantic Treaty Organization

Navy, 178, 181
Negroes, 93, 298–309, 311
  break-up of family among, 303–4
  in cities, 251–54
  civil rights and
    Congress, 300, 303, 307
    elections, 270, 301, 302
    legislation, 57–58
    political exclusion, 234, 298–300
    racial prejudice, 92, 265, 301, 303
    segregation, 293
    slavery, 298–99
    white support, 303
  immigrants and, 245, 305, 309
  leaders of, 308
  migration of, 236, 301–2, 305–6
  New Left and, 268
  at 1964 Democratic Convention, 279, 286
  party affiliation of, 263
  place in society of, 289, 323
  population growth and, 298
  proportion in population of, xiii, 288
  prospects for, 307–8
  as Republicans (1901), 301
  white Americans and, 302–5
Negro Revolution, xiv, xv
  in Alabama, 222
  Black Power in, 308–9
  civil rights legislation gained by, 57–58
  J. F. Kennedy and, 18
  1954 Supreme Court decision and, 87–90
  states' rights and, 231
Nehru, Jawaharlal, 13
Neustadt, Richard, 27
New Deal, 17, 143, 248
  as historic turning point, xiii–xiv
  Supreme Court and, 18
  unconstitutionality of, 237
New Freedom, 17
New Frontier, 17, 192, 248, 270
New Hampshire, 218, 229, 273, 274
New Jersey, 218
New Left, 91, 268
New York City, ix, 247, 278, 293, 304
  compared to Los Angeles, 250, 252
  Puerto Ricans in, 288–89
  racial troubles in, 253
New York State, 6, 218, 271, 310

New York Times, 43, 321
New Zealand, 135
Nicholson, Sir Harold, 140
Niebuhr, Reinhold, 291
Nineteenth Amendment (1920), xii
North Atlantic Council, 158
North Atlantic Treaty, 132, 133, 207
North Atlantic Treaty Organization (NATO), 135
North Carolina, 218
Northwest Territory, 218
NSC, *see* National Security Council
Nuclear age
  armed forces in, 164, 172–73
  Britain in, 137–38, 179–80
  effects on foreign policy, 105, 121, 136
  responsibility of President in, 176–77
    control of nuclear weapons, 121, 137, 142, 173
  See also Nuclear war
Nuclear-test-ban treaty, 137, 186, 212
Nuclear war
  alternative to, 169–72
  McNamara on targets in, 171
  national interest and, 169, 177
  rationalization of, 147–49, 169
  theoreticians of, 165–67

Oberkommando der Wehrmacht (OKW), 199
Oklahoma, anthem of, 219
Olney, Richard, 150
Open Door notes, 134–35
Otis, James, 86

Pacific Islands, Trust Territory of, 219
Paine, Thomas, 13, 86
Pakistan, 306
Palmer raids, 211
Parliament (British)
  candidacy for, 276
  law and, 77–78
  press and, 322
  See also House of Commons; House of Lords
Parties, *see* Political parties
Pastore, John O., 294
Patterson, William, 153
Peace Corps, 108, 110, 116

Pearl Harbor, 131, 152
Peaceful coexistence, 210
Pennsylvania, 218, 245
Pennsylvania v. *Nelson* (1956), 95
Perry, Commodore Matthew C., 265
Philadelphia (Pa.), 10, 12
Platt Amendment (1901), 150
Plessy v. *Ferguson* (1896), 87–89, 92
Polaris (missile), 159, 175, 193
Political parties, 255–87
  absence of left in, 267
  amorphousness of, 262
  in Britain, 72, 267, 276, 314
  Bryce's view of, 255, 270
  divisions within, 99, 268–69
  emergence of, 255–56
  financial contributions to, 270, 273
  half-parties among, 257
  minorities and, 263
  nominations of candidates of, 286–87
  organization of, 270
  people's participation in, 271, 314
  Presidential v. Congressional wings of, 268–70, 284–87
  Presidency and, *see* Presidency—political parties and
  roots of, 265–66
  triple revolution and, 263
  welfare state and, 264
Political machines, 246–49, 314
Polls, 209, 310
Populism, 256, 267, 299, 301
Port Huron statement, 91
Postmaster General, 8
Philippines Treaty (1951), 129
Plunkitt, George Washington, 247
Policy Planning Council, 108, 110, 140
  National Policy Papers developed by, 116, 190
Port of New York Authority, 235
Polk, William, 203
Power, balance of, in Europe, 130–31
Presbyterians, 291
Presidency, 3–35, 312
  Bryce's view on candidates for, 281
  Congress and, 5, 9, xv, 322
    committee chairmen, 55–56
    fiscal role, 67
    subordination, 15–17, 37–38, 66

Presidency (*Cont.*)
  consensus politics of, *see* Consensus
  Constitution and, *see* Constitution
    —Presidency and
  corruption and, 233
  democratic processes in, 9–11
  Electoral College and, 276–77
  image of, 33–35
  immigrants and, 294
  as institution, 23–33
  King's Men in
    intimates, 8–9
    instruments, 19–22
    as synthesists, 35
    weakness, 26–29
  medieval monarchy compared to,
    5–16, 55, 324
  national interest and, 68–69
  the people and
    mystical connection, 5
    power, 317–19
    represented, 7, 17–19, 66
  political parties and
    conventions, 277–78, 280
    impact, 268
    leadership, 45
    machine, 248
    nomination, 286–87
    primaries, 270, 274–75
    reapportionment, 99
  polls and, 209
  press and, 30, 33–34
  Prime Ministry compared to, 15,
    16, 20–21, 318
  Supreme Court and, 18–19, 74–76,
    80
    attempt to circumscribe power,
      82–84
  tenure of, 15–16
  Vice Presidency and, 30–31
President
  administration appointed by, 37
  as Commander in Chief, 133, 153,
    173–75
  as leader of the Free World, 121
  as member of NSC, 189
  in nuclear age
    control of nuclear weapons, 121,
      137, 142, 173
    extent of responsibilities, 176–77
  requirements for becoming, 273,
    281–82

President (*Cont.*)
  responsibility for national security,
    188
  F. D. Roosevelt as first modern, 12
  as own Secretary of State, 119,
    120–21, 144–45
President's Club for Johnson Commit-
    tee, 270
Press
  Congress and, 43–44, 322
  limitations of, 322
  Presidency and, 30, 33–34, 321–22
  public interest and, 321
  role of, 28, 33–34
Primary elections, 271–76
  consequences of, 278, 282
  as democratic method, 272
  in the South, 300
  staff men in, 275
Prime Ministry, 283
  compared with Presidency, 15, 16,
    20–21, 318
Privy Council, 82
Progressive Party (Roosevelt's), 258,
    264
Protestants, melting pot and, 291
Puerto Rico, 279
  representation in Congress of, 219
Puerto Ricans, 288–89, 309

Radical right
  distortion of public opinion by, 212
  Republican Party and, 264–66
  See also Americanism; Christian
    Nationalist Crusade; Conserva-
    tives; John Birch Society; Lib-
    erty Lobby; McCarthyism
RAND Corporation, 165–66, 185, 203
Randolph, A. Philip, 307
Rayburn, Sam, 58
Reconstruction, 45, 265, 299–302
Reconstruction Act (1867), 75
Reorganization Act (1946), 50
Reorganization Plan No. 6 (1953),
    156
Republican National Committee, 271,
    285
Republican National Convention
    (1952), 279
Republican National Convention
    (1964), 265, 279

Republican Party, 284
  conventions and, 278–79
  Democratic Party compared to, 257, 259, 263–64
  electoral system and, 271
  election costs to, 274
  emergence of, 258
  Goldwater and, 272, 284–85
  immigrants and, 261
  period of dominance by, 258–59
  posture of, 275
  prospects of, 261–62
  as regional party, 45
  Republicans and, 256, 310
    Congress and, 262
    conservative, 95, 261, 320
    interests represented by, 258
    Negroes as (1901), 301
    role of, in foreign policy, 263–64
    in the South, 299, 307
  right wing and, 264–66
  shades of opinion in, 264, 267
  slavery and, 258
  source of strength of, 260, 263
  Whigs compared to, 257
Research and Development Board, 155
Reuss, Henry, 40, 41
Revolution
  of rising expectations, xiv–xv, 311
  technological, see Technological revolution
  triple, xiv–xv, 71, 98, 233, 234–35
    Americanism opposed to, 266
    political parties and, 263
    problems in, 101
    states' rights, 222, 231, 234–35
  See also Negro Revolution
Rhode Island, xi, 218
Ribicoff, Abraham, 303
Rio Treaty (1947), 129, 133, 208
Roberts, Owen, Jr., 73
Robinson v. California (1962), 94
Rockefeller, Nelson, 114, 261, 272
  political effects of divorce of, 281
Rockefeller Foundation, 112
Rogers, Will, 177
Roosevelt, Franklin Delano, 16, 30, 83, 144, 248, 278, 289
  civilian control of military and, 154
  as first modern President, 12
  historical prestige of, 143

Roosevelt, Franklin Delano (Cont.)
  isolationism and, 131
  legislation and, 16–17
  Monroe Doctrine and, 150
  New Deal of, as turning point, xiii–xiv
  rise of impersonal government under, 8–9, 22–23
  Soviet sphere of influence and, 130
  State Department weakened under, 119–20
  style of, 282
  Supreme Court and, 74
  veto and, 15
Roosevelt, Theodore, 12, 16, 31, 117
  alliance with liberals of, 111
  as forerunner of modern Presidents, 264
  jingoism of, 258
  public welfare and, xiv, 17
Root, Elihu, 17, 182
Rostow, Walt, 297
Rules Committee (House), 51–52, 54
Rush-Bagot Agreement (1817), 205
Rusk, Dean, 113, 122, 128
Russia, see Soviet Union
Rutledge, John, 85

SAC (Strategic Air Command), 173
Santo Domingo, see Dominican Republic
Scammon, Richard, 259
Schlieffen Plan, 172
Science, 297
Schlesinger, Arthur, Jr., on Kennedy, 120, 144, 194
Schumpeter, Joseph, 65
Science and Technology, Office of, 22
Scott, Sir Walter, 57
Second World War, 120, 124, 182
  foreign policy and, 129, 145
  State Department and, 107, 119
  Truman's view on cause of, 183
Senate, 11, 61, 302
  Anglo-American dominance of, 294
  Cabinet officers and, 320
  compared to House of Lords, 60
  filibuster in, 61
  foreign policy and, 205–6
  list of committees of, 47–48; see also specific committees
  lobbying and, 316–17

Senate (*Cont.*)
national security and, 205
Negroes and, 300, 303
power struggle with House, 60
ratification of treaties by, 205–8
revenue and, 60
scope of power of, 37
size of, 60
states' representation in, 218
Vice President as President of, 60
Senators
background of, 282–83
compared to Congressmen, 61
liberalism of, 61
period of office of, 60
Senior Interdepartmental Group
(SIG), 199–200
Seward, William H., 278
Shays, Daniel, 13
Sherman, General William T., 179
Sherman, Roger, 38
Sherman Antitrust Act (1890), 234
SIG (Senior Interdepartmental
Group), 199–200
Sino-Soviet Bloc, 139
Sixteenth Amendment (1913), xii
Sixth Amendment, 94
Slavery, 298–99
effects of, 301
Smith Act, 95
Smith, Adam, 210
Smith, Alfred, 278
Smith, Howard, 58
Social Democrats (German), 267
Social system
use of legalities in, 79–80
foundation of, 79
South Carolina, 218, 227, 300
Southeast Asia Treaty, 129, 134
South Vietnam, *see* Vietnam war
Soviet Union, 7, 151, 164, 290
Berlin crisis (1961) and, 168
China and, 139
Cold War and, 147-48
deterrent force of, 193
imperialism of, 129–30, 135
missile crisis and, 148
Monroe Doctrine applied to, 209
as nuclear power, 136
sphere of influence of, 130
search for peaceful accommodations with, 186

Soviet Union (*Cont.*)
as superpower, 135–38
Vietnam War and, 138
Spain, 293
Speaker of the House, 39, 58, 59, 118
Special Forces, 151
Spoils system, 42, 256
Sputnik, 193
Stamp Act (1765), 142
State, Department of, 29, 105
agencies of, 108–9
annual appropriation for, 108
CIA and, 125
control over NSC, 199
Defense Department and, 122
description of, 105, 107
diplomacy of, *see* Diplomacy
foreign aid and, 110–11, 116
foreign policy and, *see* Foreign Policy
Kennedy and, 120
mass media and, 106
"open door" policy of, 105–7
relation to Establishment men, 113–14
Second World War and, 107, 119
staff of, 108–10
Supreme Court and, 93
weakened under F. D. Roosevelt, 119–20
State, Secretary of, 117–22
erosion of power of, 124, 126
importance of office of, 105, 117–18
Jefferson as, 105, 108
as member of NSC, 189, 199
national interest and, 110
national security system and, 196
President as own, 119, 120–21, 144–45
problems of, 109, 125, 315
State courts, jurisdiction of, 81–82, 94, 95, 219–20
State Governments, Council of, 235
State of the Union Message, 7, 128, 322–23
States, xii, 217–43
cities' relations with, 235–36, 245
constitutions for, 219, 225–28
dictatorship in, 232
early power of, 10–11

States (*Cont.*)
federal government and, 98, 220–25, 228, 233–34, 238–43
aid programs, 225, 238–39; 242–43
agriculture, 239–40
internal organization of, 219, 230
interstate cooperation, 235
legislatures, 229, 230, 314
list of, and territories, 343–46; *see also specific states and territories*
Madison on, 217, 234
original thirteen, 218
reasons for creation of, 218
revenue of, 219, 228–29
rural decay in, 236
sovereignty of, 44, 217–18
spoliation of land in, 230
states' rights and, 231–33
Supreme Court and, *see* Supreme Court—states and
triple revolution and, 222, 231, 234–35
Steuben, Baron von, 179
Stevens, Thaddeus, 12
Stevenson, Adlai, 103, 217, 281, 284, 290
Strategic Air Command (SAC), 173
Strategic Retaliatory Force, 174
Strike Emergency Action File, 174
Students for a Democratic Society, 91
Suez Canal crisis (1956), 148, 180, 197
Supreme Court, 73–101
American Bar Association's view of, 90–91, 313
attacked, 95–96
civil rights and, 18–19, 92
school desegregation, 86–90
Congress and, 74–75
legislation, 4, 68, 99–100
Constitution and
effect of reasoning on, 86
jurisdiction, 74–75, 81–82
reinterpretation, 73–74, 76, 80
cycles of interpretation in, 79, 97
decision-making in, 84–86
equality and, 91, 92
federal-state relationship and, 93, 236–39
Jews and, 295
Negroes and, 302

Supreme Court (*Cont.*)
as political institution, 74, 99–100
Presidency and, 18–19, 74–76, 80
attempt to circumscribe power, 82–84
role of, 312, 313
states and
doctrine of pre-emption, 94–95
effect on, 93–95
reapportionment, 97–99, 230
triple revolution and, 74, 80
Truman and, 83
Sweden, xi
Symington, Stuart, 284

Taft, William, xiv, 12, 264
Taft-Hoover Doctrine, 132
Tammany Hall, 246–47
Task force, 110
Taylor, General Maxwell, 204
Technological revolution, xiv, 159
agriculture and, 239
effect on foreign policy of, 116–17
Los Angeles and, 254
national security and, 214
Tennessee Valley Authority, 59
Tenth Amendment, 95, 220
Territories, list of, 345–46
Texas, 217, 232
Thailand, 135
Think factories, 165, 203; *see also* Hudson Institute; RAND Corporation
Thirteenth Amendment (1865), xii, 299
Thomas, Elbert, 205
Tillman, Pitchfork Ben, 300
Trade Expansion Act, 319–20
Treasury Department, 317
Truman, Harry S., 26, 31, 83, 283
on cause of Second World War, 183
civilian control and, 184
on decision-making, 28
doctrine enunciated by (1947), 132
Inaugural Address, 143
Korea and, 183
NSC and, 123, 190
recognition of China and, 211
recognition of Israel and, 131
style of, 282
Turner, Frederick Jackson, 228
Twelfth Amendment (1804), 276

Twentieth Amendment (1933), 15
Twenty-first Amendment (1933), xii
Twenty-second Amendment (1951), 15, 16
Twenty-fourth Amendment (1964), xii
Tyler, John, 257

U-2 aircraft, 172
Un-American Activities Committee (House), 45, 57
United Kingdom, see Britain
United Nations, 128
  charter of, 129
  Korea and, 141
  peace-keeping operations of, 141–42
United States, ix–xv
  brain drain by, 297
  Britain compared to, see Britain
  demography of, xii–xiii, 260, 298
  European destiny and, xi, 132, 137–38, 145
  European view of, 311
  failure of, 311–12
  as free country, 314
  historical periods in, x, xi, xiii–xiv
  League of Nations and, 206
  material success and, 307
  membership in United Nations of, 129
  political antiquity of, ix–x, 255
  paradoxes in, 324
  as pluralistic society, 289, 291–95
    classes, 292–93
    complexity, 293
    future, 296
    political collectivism, 65
    problem of governing, 315
    provincialism, 293
    religious sects in, 291
  as superpower, 105, 109, 136–39
  unity in, 6
  See also Americans; Federal government
United States Information Agency (USIA), 110, 116
Upton, General Emery, 180

Van Buren, Martin, 105
Versailles, Treaty of, 206
Vice President, 15, 29
  importance of, 9, 30–31

Vice President (Cont.)
  as member of NSC, 189
  as President of the Senate, 60
Vienna meeting (1961), 196
Vietnam War, 135, 147
  armed forces in, 180, 201–2
  balance of power and, 138
  bombing during, 148
  Congress and, 42, 44
  Defense Secretary and, 162, 196, 319
  development of, 196, 201–4
  Johnson and, 214
  Kennedy and, 194, 196, 201
  as large-scale war, 200
  NSC and, 200
Vinson, Fred M., 85
Virgin Islands, 219, 279
Virginia, 58, 218, 301
Voice of America, 110

Walker, General Edwin, 186
Wallace, George, 301
War
  as extension of politics, 142
  limited, defined, 202
  NcNamara on, 147, 150
  nuclear, see Nuclear war
War, Department of, 148, 182
War of 1812, 148, 265
Warren, Earl, 76, 80
  call to impeach, 95
  on school desegregation, 87–90
  on representation, 98–99
Washington, George, xi, 16, 57, 78, 175, 180, 276
  as commander of revolutionary army, 153
  isolationism and, 128
  party politics opposed by, 255
  the people and, 69, 125, 295
Washington, D.C., xv, 36, 306
  class-consciousness in, 293
  Negroes in, 254
  police in, 291
  press in, 321–22
Washington Post, 321
Waskow, Arthur, 170
WASP, see White Anglo-Saxon Protestants
Wattenberg, Ben, 259
Ways and Means Committee (House), 317

Wealth of Nations (Smith), 210
Weapons System Evaluation Group, 159
Webster, Daniel, 61, 258
Wehrmacht, 180
Weizmann, Chaim, 301
Welfare state, 231, 234, 264
Wesberry v. *Sanders*, 99
West Germany, 47, 250, 297, 306
  Adenauer and, 20, 315
  Fachministers in, 29
  nuclear weapons and, 137
  recovery of, 20
  Social Democrats in, 267
  voters' participation in, 270
West Point (U.S. military academy), 178
West Virginia, 316
Whig Party (Amecrican), 256–58
White, Byron, 76
White, General Thomas, 185
White Anglo-Saxon Protestants (WASP), 244, 259–60, 286, 287, 290
  class-consciousness among, 292
  decline of, 260
  extremism of, 265
  as ideal type, 295
  influence of, 294

White House, 6–8, 22, 36, 73, 302
  inaccessibility of, 7
White House office, *see* Presidency— King's Men in
Wilkins, Roy, 308
Willkie, Wendell, 278
Wilson, Harold, 12, 20
Wilson, Woodrow, xii, 29, 148, 206
  alliance with liberals of, 111
  by-passing of State Department by, 119
  civilian control of military and, 154
  on committee chairmen, 54–55
  declaration of war and, 127
  extension of President's power under, xiv, 16
Wisconsin, 61, 267
Wood, General Leonard, 179
Woodring, Harry H., 152
World Bank, 128
World Court, 128
World War II, *see* Second World War
Wyoming, 218

Yalta, 130
Yalu River, 183

Zangwill, Israel, on melting pot, 288–90